IRELAND

BED & BREAKFAST

1997

Edited by Tim Stilwell

Distributed in Great Britain & the Commonwealth by Bailey Distribution Ltd, Learoyd Road, New Romney, Kent, TN28 8XU (Tel: 01797 366905) and in the U.S.A. by Seven Hills Distributors, 49 Central Avenue, Cincinatti, Ohio, OH45202, (Tel: (513) 3813881).
Available from all good bookshops.

ISBN 0-9521909-8-2

Published by Stilwell Publishing Ltd,
59 Charlotte Road, Shoreditch, London, EC2A 3QT.
Tel: 0171 739 7179.

Editor: Tim Stilwell
Design and Maps : Nigel Simpson

Front Cover: Bushymead Country House, Ballynahinch,County Down is listed on page 21 of this directory.

Special thanks as ever go to my wife, Rosemarie McGoldrick (artist, lecturer and arbiter of good taste); to Nigel Simpson and Dean Conway (ready volunteers for sampling fried breakfasts); to Fred Lam Cham Kee for all his grid references and to Wynne and Ruth, who sorted everything out.

Typeset & Printed in Great Britain by the Guernsey Press Company Ltd, Guernsey, Channel Islands.

Contents

Introduction

This directory is really very straightforward. It sets out simply to list as many B&Bs in as many places in Ireland as possible, so that wherever you go, you know there is one nearby.

A few years ago my wife and I visited Ireland and decided to use B&Bs for accommodation on our trip. Like most visitors, our knowledge of Ireland's geography was reasonable but not brilliant. We had the Tourist Board's accommodation lists, but found it hard to match the listings to our road atlas - indeed, some places were impossible to find on any map, while others were miles away from the heading they were listed under. In the end, we just stayed in the big towns, missing out on the choice offered by the hundreds of B&Bs dotted all over the countryside.

We had had similar experiences in the UK as well. In 1993, I decided to set up a company devoted to publishing information about good, low-cost accommodation right across Britain, illustrated with proper maps and arranged in a way that everyone could understand without having to peer down narrow columns or interpret obscure symbols. The third edition of the British book appears this year. This year, too, we finally have turned our attention to Ireland.

This is therefore a book to save the reader time and money: it suits anyone who wishes to plan a trip in Ireland, who appreciates good value and who is open to ideas. The directory is quite deliberately not a guidebook. Its aim is that of any directory in any field: to be comprehensive, to offer the widest choice. By this definition, Stilwell's Directory outstrips any guidebook - we publish by far and away the largest number of B&Bs listed anywhere outside the Tourist Board's lists. What we don't do is make up the reader's mind for them. There are plenty of other B&B books that push their particular premises as 'exclusive' or 'special'. We think that a simple glance over the salient details on any page and the reader will be his or her own guide.

We have two kinds of reader in mind. The first knows exactly where to go but not where to stay. The nearest B&B is the best solution; a quick look at the right county map gives the answer. The other reader is not so sure where to go. As they browse the pages, the short descriptions provide good ideas. All information here has been supplied by the B&B owners themselves. All are bona fide B&Bs; all are on the books of the local tourist office. We should make it clear that inclusion in these pages does not imply personal recommendation. We have not visited them all individually; all we have done is write to them. The directory lists over 1,500 entries in over 650 locations throughout Northern Ireland and the Republic. The vast majority were included because they offered B&B for under £25 per person per night (in fact the average double rate per person per night in this book is £16.00 - punt or sterling).

Owners were canvassed in the summer of 1996 and responded by the end of October. They were asked to provide their lowest rates per person per night for 1997. The rates are thus forecasts and are in any case always subject to seasonal fluctuation in demand. Some information may, of course, be out of date already. Grades may go up or down, or be removed altogether. The telephone company may alter exchange numbers. Proprietors may decide to sell up and move out of the business altogether. This is why the directory has to be a yearbook; in general, though, the information published here will be accurate, pertinent and useful for many a year. The pink highlight boxes are advertisements - the B&B has paid for some extra wordage and for their entry to stand out from the page a little more.

The main aim has been to provide details that are concise and easy to understand. The only symbols used are some conventional tourist symbols. There are some abbreviations, but it should be clear what they stand for without having to refer to the keys on the first and last pages. The grades are perhaps more difficult - each inspecting organisation has its own classification system with its own definition of merit. Once again, though, the reader will soon pick out the exceptional establishments - many have high grades from each organisation. The general rule is that more facilities mean higher prices. Do not be misled into thinking that an ungraded establishment is inferior. Many B&B owners are locally registered but never apply for grades or do not wish to pay for one. They thrive on business from guests who return again and again because the hospitality is excellent. My advice is: ring around. A simple telephone call and some judicious questions will give you an impression of your host very effectively. The largest collection of B&Bs in Northern Ireland and the Republic is now laid out before you - the greatest choice available in one book. We think that your tastes and preferences will do the rest.

We have deliberately arranged the book by administrative county in alphabetical order, listing all those in Northern Ireland first, followed by all those in the Republic. Another feature of the book is that we insist on using the proper postal address. Many entries thus carry a county name different from the one they are listed under or a 'post town' that is some miles from the village. These oddities arise from the postal service's distribution system. They should not, under any circumstances, be used as a directional guide. In one case, the hamlet of Downies in Donegal is some 40 miles from its quoted 'post town' - not a journey to make in error. Used on a letter though, it does speed the mail up. If you need directions to a B&B (especially if you are travelling at night), the best solution is to telephone the owner and ask the way.

The county maps are intended to act as a general reference. They present only the locations of each entry in the directory. For a more accurate idea of the location of a B&B, use the five-figure National Grid Reference published under each location's name. Used in tandem with an Ordnance Survey map or any atlas that uses the Irish National Grid, these numbers provide first-class route-planning references. The pubs and restaurants that appear beneath each location heading are included on the recommendation of B&Bs themselves. The tankard and the knife and fork symbols show that they are local establishments where one can get a decent evening meal at a reasonable price.

Throughout the book you will find boxes offering peremptory advice to readers. These may seem of little consequence; some may even annoy. We are sorry for intruding upon your sensibilities like this but the boxes actually neaten the page. Those that request courtesy and care for the customs of your hosts need no apology, however. Opening your home to strangers, albeit for payment, requires a leap of faith for most people; B&B owners are no exceptions. We simply ask everyone to observe the usual house rules. In this way, other guests will continue to meet with a welcome when they, too, pass through.

The Editor,
Stoke Newington, November 1996.

Key to Entries

- Children welcome (from age shown in brackets, if specified)
- Off-street car parking (number of places shown in brackets)
- No smoking
- Television (either in every room or in a TV lounge)
- Pets accepted (by prior arrangement)
- Evening meal available (by prior arrangement)
- Special diets catered for (by prior arrangement - please check with owner to see if your particular requirements are catered for)
- Central heating throughout
- Suitable for disabled people (please check with owner to see what level of disability is provided for)
- Christmas breaks a speciality
- Coffee/Tea making facilities

The location heading - every hamlet, village, town and city mentioned in this directory is represented on the local county map at the head of each section.

Use the National Grid reference with Ordnance Survey of Ireland and Ordnance Survey of Northern Ireland maps and atlases. The letter refers to a 100 kilometre grid square. The first two numbers refer to a North/South grid line and the last two numbers refer to an East/West grid line. The grid reference indicates their intersection point.

Ballydream

National Grid Ref: L0050.

These are the names of nearby pubs and restaurants that serve food in the evening, as suggested by local B&Bs

Lenahan's, MacAuley's

***Tir Na N'Og**, Fairymount Road, Ballydream, Nonesuch, County Ware.*
C19th converted schoolhouse, lovely garden.
Grades: BF Approv.
Tel: **0606 51248.** Mrs O'Brien.
Rates fr: *IR£14.00*-**£16.00**.
Open: All Year
Beds: 1F 1D 1T
Baths: 1 Ensuite 2 Shared
(4) (2)

The figure in *italics* is the lowest 1996 double or twin rate per person per night. The figure in **bold** is the lowest 1996 single rate. Some establishments do not accept single bookings.

Bedrooms
F = Family
D = Double
T = Twin
S = Single

Bord Fáilte (the Irish Tourist Board) and the Northern Ireland Tourist Board (**BF** and **NITB**) have different accommodation approval systems. All Hotels are graded by 1 to 5 Stars (**St**). Guest houses in the Republic are also graded by Stars (1 to 4), while those in Northern Ireland are graded either A or B. Both Tourist Boards inspect B&B accommodation annually - such premises are entitled to show that they have been approved (**Approv**). Further details of Bord Fáilte's classifications can be had from Dublin (01 8747733); the Northern Ireland Tourist Board's classifications are available from Belfast (01232 231221). The Automobile Association (**AA**) employs two grading systems: the one for hotels uses 1 to 5 Stars (**St**) in ascending order of merit; there is also a B&B rating that uses the letter **Q** (for quality) on a scale of 1 to 4; the highest have 4 Qs and a Selected award (**Select or Prem Select**). For more details, telephone the AA in the UK on 01256 20123. The Royal Automobile Club (**RAC**) also uses a Star (**St**) system for large hotels; small hotels and B&Bs obtain the ratings 'Acclaimed' (**Acclaim**) or 'Highly Acclaimed' (**High Acclaim**). For more details, telephone the RAC in the UK on 0181-686 0088.

NORTHERN IRELAND

1 County Antrim
2 County Armagh
3 County Down
4 County Fermanagh
5 County Londonderry
6 County Tyrone

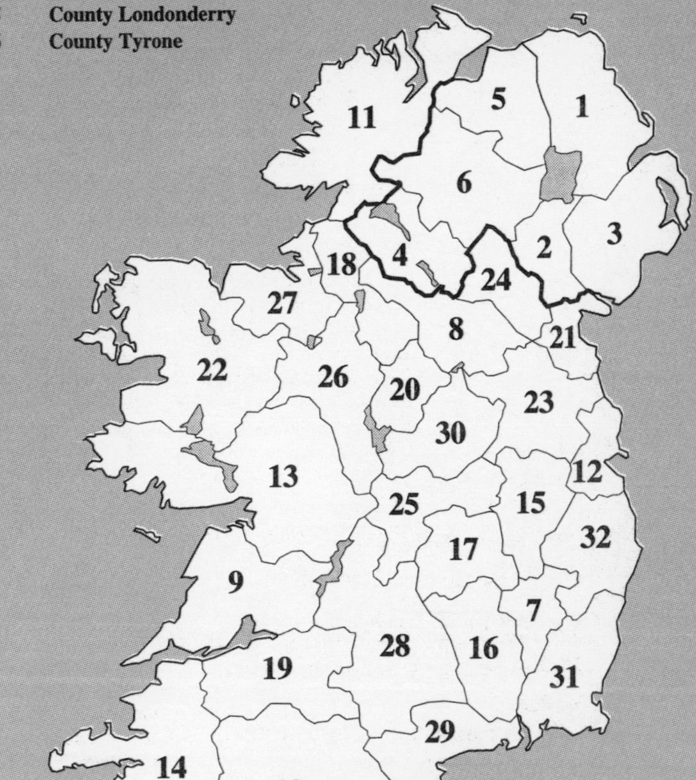

REPUBLIC OF IRELAND

7 County Carlow
8 County Cavan
9 County Clare
10 County Cork
11 County Donegal
12 County Dublin
13 County Galway
14 County Kerry
15 County Kildare
16 County Kilkenny
17 County Laois
18 County Leitrim
19 County Limerick
20 County Longford
21 County Louth
22 County Mayo
23 County Meath
24 County Monaghan
25 County Offaly
26 County Roscommon
27 County Sligo
28 County Tipperary
29 County Waterford
30 County Westmeath
31 County Wexford
32 County Wicklow

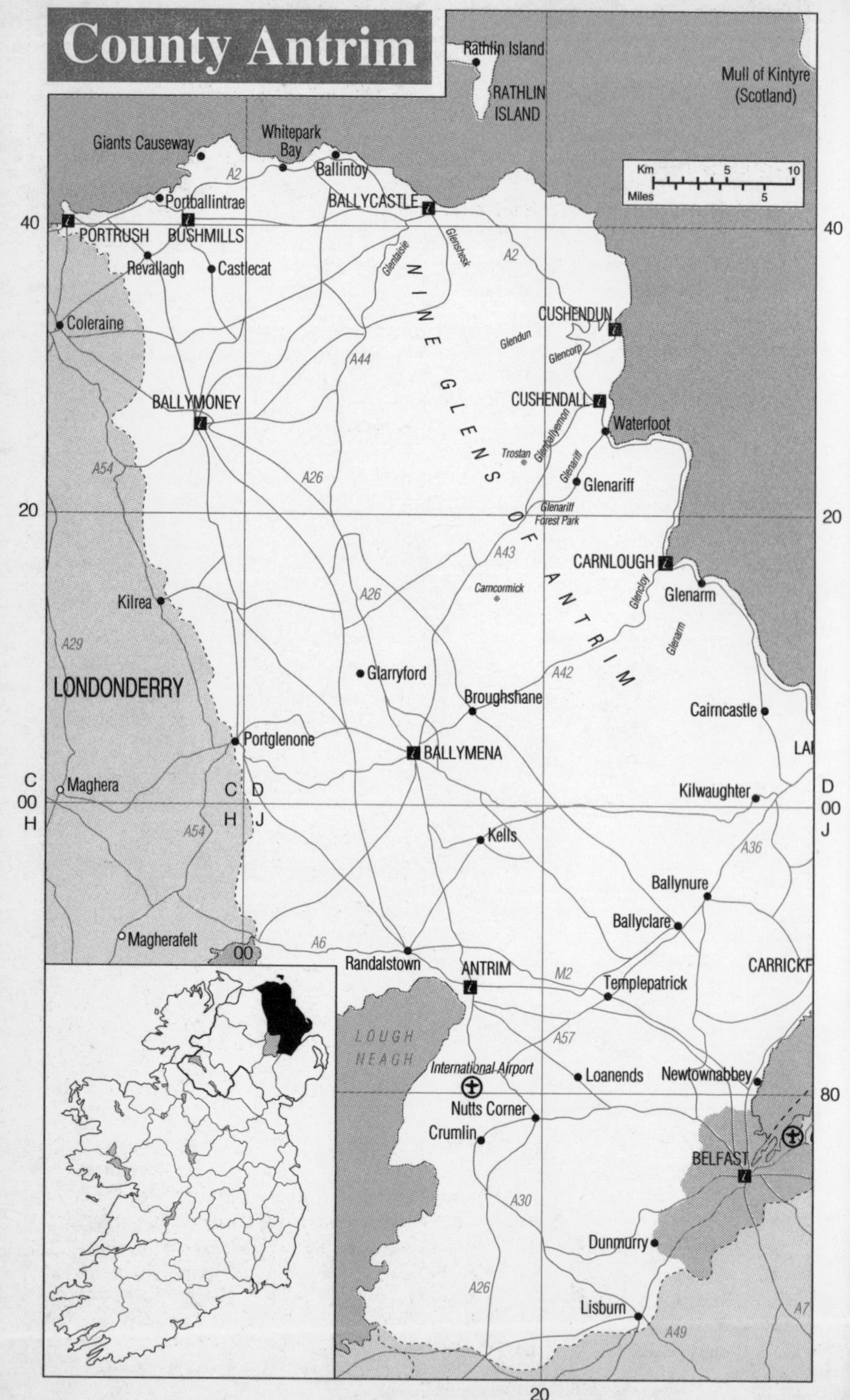

County Antrim
Rathlin Island
RATHLIN ISLAND
Mull of Kintyre (Scotland)
Km 5 10
Miles 5
Giants Causeway
Whitepark Bay
Ballintoy
Portballintrae
BALLYCASTLE
PORTRUSH
BUSHMILLS
Revallagh
Castlecat
Glentaisie
Glenshesk
A2
NINE GLENS OF ANTRIM
Coleraine
CUSHENDUN
Glendun
Glencorp
A44
BALLYMONEY
CUSHENDALL
Waterfoot
Trostan
Glenballyemon
Glenariff
Glenariff Forest Park
A54
A26
A43
CARNLOUGH
Glencloy
Glenarm
Carncormick
Kilrea
A29
LONDONDERRY
Glarryford
A42
Broughshane
Cairncastle
Portglenone
BALLYMENA
Maghera
Kilwaughter
Kells
A36
Ballynure
Ballyclare
Magherafelt
A6
Randalstown
ANTRIM
M2
Templepatrick
CARRICKF
LOUGH NEAGH
A57
International Airport
Loanends
Newtownabbey
Nutts Corner
Crumlin
BELFAST
A30
Dunmurry
Lisburn
A49
A7
40
20
00
80
C D H J

AIRPORTS

Belfast International Airport (Aldergrove) - 01849 422888.
Belfast City Airport - 01232 457745

AIR SERVICES & AIRLINES

From Belfast (International) to: ***Heathrow, Manchester, Birmingham, Glasgow.***

British Airways Express (for Logan Air). In Northern Ireland & the UK, tel. (local rate) 0345 222111. From the Republic, tel. (freefone) 1800 626747.

Belfast (International) to: ***Heathrow,*** *East Midlands.* **British Midlands** - 0345 554554.

Belfast (International) to: ***London (Stansted).*** **Air Belfast** - 0345 464748

From Belfast (City) to: ***Aberdeen, Birmingham, Blackpool, Bristol, Cardiff, East Midlands, Edinburgh, Exeter, Gatwick, Glasgow, Guernsey, Isle of Man, Bradford, Liverpool, Luton, Manchester, Southampton, Stansted.***

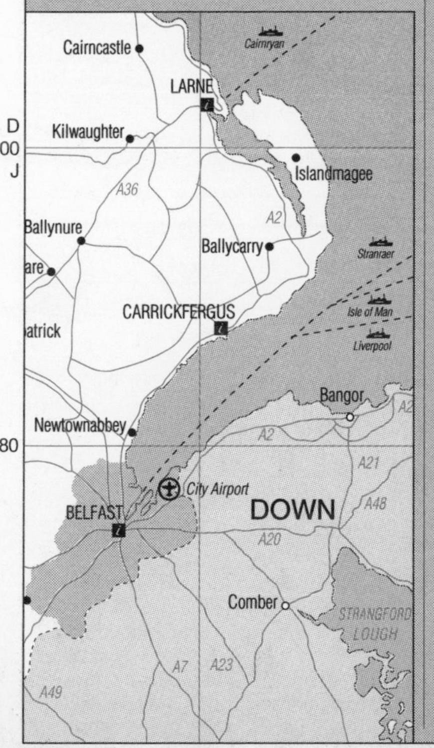

Jersey European - 01232 457200.
British Airways Express (for Manx Airlines) - in Northern Ireland & the UK, tel. (local rate) 0345 222111.
From the Republic, tel. (freefone) 1800 626747.

Gill Airways (Newcastle & Prestwick) - 01232 459777.

RAIL

The principal railway lines are: ***Belfast*** *to* ***Londonderry*** *and* ***Belfast*** *to* ***Dublin.***
For more information tel. **Northern Ireland Rail** - 01232 899411.

FERRIES

Belfast to: ***Stranraer,*** *Dumfries & Galloway (3 hrs) - and $1^{1}/_{4}$ hrs (high speed).*
Stena Sealink - 0990 204204.

Larne to: ***Cairnryan,*** *nr Stranraer, Dumfries & Galloway ($2^{1}/_{4}$ hrs) -*
P&O European Ferries - 0990 980777.

Belfast to: ***Stranraer,*** *Dumfries & Galloway ($1^{1}/_{2}$ hrs) -*
SeaCat - 0345 523523 or 01232 313543.

Belfast to: ***Liverpool*** *(11 hrs) -*
Norse Irish Ferries - 01232 779090.

TOURIST INFORMATION OFFICES

The Steeple, **Antrim**, BT41 1BJ, 018494-63113

7 Mary Street, **Ballycastle**, BT54 6QH, 01265-762024

St Annes Court, 59 North Street, **Belfast**, BT1 1NB, 01232-246609

16, Harbour Rd. **Carnlough,** BT44 OEU, 01574 885236

19 North Street, **Carrickfergus**, BT38 7DL, 01960-351121

Giants Causeway, 44 Causeway Road, **Bushmills**, BT57 8SU, 01265-731855

Carnfunnock Country Park, Coast Road, **Larne**, BT40 2LF, 01574-270541

Town Hall, Mark Street, **Portrush**, BT56 8BT, (Easter to Oct), 01265-823333

Antrim

National Grid Ref: J1587

Ramble Inn, Ella Mae's, Dunadry Inn

The Stables, *96 Milltown Road, Antrim, Co Antrim, BT41 2JJ.*
Modern family-run motel-type accommodation.
Open: All Year
Grades: NITB Approv
01849 466943
Mr McDonald
Rates fr: *£17.50*-**£20.00.**
Beds: 11T
Baths: 11 Ensuite
(100)

Maranatha, *69 Oldstone Road, Antrim, Co Antrim, BT41 4SL.*
Comfortable country home situated five minutes from Belfast International Airport.
Open: All Year (not Xmas)
Grades: NITB Approv
01849 463150
Mr & Mrs Steele
Rates fr: *£12.50*-**£15.00.**
Beds: 1D 2T
Baths: 1 Shared
(10)

Springhill, *37 Thornhill Road, Antrim, Co Antrim, BT41 2LH.*
Secluded accommodation off motorway. Convenient for scenic touring, also airport.
Open: All Year (not Xmas)
01849 469117
Mrs McKeown
Rates fr: *£15.00*-**£15.00.**
Beds: 1F 1D 1T 1S
Baths: 1 Ensuite 1 Private 1 Shared
(12)

High season, bank holidays and special events mean low availability *anywhere.*

Ballintoy

National Grid Ref: D0444

Fullerton Arms Hotel, *22 Main Street, Ballintoy, Ballycastle, Co Antrim, BT54 6LX.*
Licensed guesthouse and restaurant, public bar.
Open: All Year
Grades: NITB Grade B
012657 69613
Mrs McCaughan
Rates fr: *£18.00*-**£22.00.**
Beds: 1F 4D 1S
Baths: 6 Ensuite
(10)

Ballycarry

National Grid Ref: J4494

Craigs Farm, *90 Hillhead Road, Ballycarry, Carrickfergus, Co Antrim, BT38 9JF.*
Modernised farmhouse. Centrally heated. Rural setting. Comfortable friendly atmosphere.
Open: All Year (not Xmas)
01960 353769
Mrs Craig
Rates fr: *£15.00*-**£15.00.**
Beds: 1F 1D 1T
Baths: 2 Ensuite 1 Shared
(5)

Ballycastle

National Grid Ref: D1241

Kimark, Strand, Marine Hotel, McCarroll's Bar, Wysners

Colliers Hall, *50 Cushendall Road, Ballycastle, Co Antrim, BT54 6QR.*
Open: Easter to Oct
Grades: NITB Grade B
012657 62531
Mrs McCarry
Rates fr: *£17.50.*
Beds: 2D 1T
Baths: 2 Ensuite 1 Shared
(2) (6)
C18th house on working farm, on A2 beside golf course. Located in an area of archaeological/historic interest, near beaches, pony trekking, fishing and country walks, 2 miles from Ballycastle.

Fragrens, *34 Quay Road, Ballycastle, Co Antrim, BT54 6BH.*
Modernised C17th private house.
Open: All Year (not Xmas)
Grades: NITB Approv
012657 62168 Mrs McCook
Rates fr: *£14.00*-**£17.00**.
Beds: 5F 2D 1T
Baths: 5 Ensuite 2 Private 1 Shared
(4)

Torr Brae, *77 Torr road, Ballycastle, Co Antrim, BT54 6RQ.*
Modern comfortable farmhouse overlooking Mull of Kintyre and Torr Head. Spectacular sea view.
Open: All Year
012657 69625
Mrs McHenry
Rates fr: *£15.00*-**£18.00**.
Beds: 1F 1t 1S
Baths: 3 Ensuite

Ardmara, *34 Whitepark Road, Ballycastle, Co Antrim, BT54 6LL.*
Charming villa on North Coast road (One mile from Ballycastle).
Open: Easter to Sep
012657 69533
Mr & Mrs Herron
Rates fr: *£16.00*-**£19.00**.
Beds: 1D 2T
Baths: 1 Ensuite 1 Private 1 Shared
(4)

Gortconney Farmhouse, *52 Whitepark Road, Ballycastle, Co Antrim, BT54 6LP.*
Modern comfortable farmhouse.
Open: Easter to
Grades: NITB Approv
012657 62283 Mrs Smyth
Rates fr: *£16.00*-**£20.00**.
Beds: 2D 1T
Baths: 2 Shared
(2) (4)

Glenhaven, *10 Beechwood Avenue, Ballycastle, Co Antrim, BT54 6BL.*
Family-run B&B close to all amenities. Warm welcome.
Open: All Year (not Xmas)
Grades: NITB Approv
012657 63612 Mr Gormley
Rates fr: *£15.00*-**£18.00**.
Beds: 2D 1T
Baths: 1 Ensuite 1 Shared
(3)

Ballyclare

National Grid Ref: J2990

Tildarg House, *50 Collin Road, Ballyclare, Co Antrim, BT39 9JS.*
Comfortable C17th farmhouse in convenient location. Approved accomodation. Spacious B&B.
Open: All Year
01960 322367
Mrs Thompson
Rates fr: *£17.50*-**£20.00**.
Beds: 1F 1D 1T
Baths: 1 Ensuite 2 Shared
(1) (4)

Ballymena

National Grid Ref: D1003

The Grouse Inn

Wilmaur, *83 Galgorm Road, Ballymena, Co Antrim, BT42 1AA.*
Victorian residence, convenient to town. Hospitality tray and television in bedrooms.
Open: All Year
01266 41878
Mrs Caves
Rates fr: *£16.50*-**£20.00**.
Beds: 1F 2D 1T
Baths: 1 Ensuite 2 Shared
(5)

Beeches, *46 Lisnafillan Road, Gracehill, Ballymena, Co Antrim, BT42 1JA.*
C18th country house with view of Slemish. Three miles from Ballymena.
Open: All Year
01266 871660
Mrs Douglas
Rates fr: *£15.00*-**£18.00**.
Beds: 1F
Baths: 1 Private

Pay B&Bs by cash or cheque. Be prepared to pay up front for one night stays.

All rates are subject to alteration at the owners' discretion.

Ballymoney

National Grid Ref: C9425

Parklight, Gossoon's Wine Bar, Anglers Rest

Athdara, *25 Portrush Road, Ballymoney, Co Antrim, BT53 6BK.*
Superior townhouse accommodation situated close to town centre.
Open: All Year
Grades: NITB Approv
012656 65149
Mrs Bustard
Rates fr: *£17.00*-**£19.00.**
Beds: 1F 3D
Baths: 3 Private

Sandelwood, *98 Knock Road, Ballymoney, Co Antrim, BT53 6NQ.*
Attractive, comfortable farmhouse convenient to Giant's Causeway - North Coast.
Open: Mar to Oct
Grades: NITB Approv
012656 62621
Mrs Brown
Rates fr: *£13.50*-**£13.50.**
Beds: 1F 2D
Baths: 1 Private 1 Shared

Ballynure

National Grid Ref: J3193

Rockbank, *40 Belfast Road, Ballynure, Ballyclare, Co Antrim, BT39 9TZ.*
Comfortable farmhouse in quiet rural setting 12 miles from Belfast.
Open: All Year
01960 352261
Mrs Park
Rates fr: *£18.00*-**£18.00.**
Beds: 1F 1T 1D
Baths: 2 Ensuite 1 Shared
(5) (4)

Belfast

National Grid Ref: J3374

Errigle Inn, Pavilion Bar, Bengal Brasserie, Eglantine Inn, Malone Lodge Hotel

Lismore Lodge, *410 Ormeau Road, Belfast, BT7 3HY.*
Open: All Year (not Xmas)
Grades: NITB Grade A
01232 641205 Mr & Mrs Devlin
Rates fr: *£ 21.00*-**£ 27.00.**
Beds: 1D 5T
Baths: 5 Ensuite 4 Private 1 Shared
(2) (6)
Situated in quiet residential area of South Belfast with personal supervision by proprietors. Very comfortable home with full heating, TV, tea/coffee and fire certificate. Many walks nearby.

Marine House, *30 Eglantine Avenue, Belfast, BT9 6DX.*
Large villa with gardens front and back. Off street parking.
Open: All Year
01232 662828 / 381922
Mrs Corrigan
Rates fr: *£18.00*-**£18.00.**
Beds: 1F 2D 4T 4S
Baths: 3 Ensuite
(4)

Camera Guest House, *44 Wellington Park, Belfast, BT9 6DP.*
Impressive Edwardian residence centrally located on a quiet tree-lined avenue.
Open: All Year (not Xmas)
Grades: NITB Grade A, AA 2 Q
01232 660026 Fax no: 01232 667856
Mr Drumm
Rates fr: *£24.00*-**£30.00.**
Beds: 2F 2D 3T 2S
Baths: 8 Ensuite 1 Private

Roseleigh House, *19 Rosetta Park, Belfast, BT6 0DL.*
Deluxe accommodation in a recently renovated Victorian home.
Open: All Year
01232 644414 Mr & Mrs McKay
Rates fr: *£22.50*-**£33.00.**
Beds: 1F 3D 3T
Baths: 7 Ensuite
(0) (6)

Parador Hotel, *473 Ormeau Road, Belfast, BT7 3GR.*
Small comfortable family-run hotel. Weekly rates on request.
Open: All Year (not Xmas)
01232 491883 (also fax no)
Mr Torney
Rates fr: *£20.00*-**£25.00**.
Beds: 2D 4T 3S
(12)

Somerton Guest House, *22 Lansdowne Road, Belfast, BT15 4DB.*
Belfast's scenic Northern Hills house this convenient and cheerful villa.
Open: All Year
Grades: NITB Grade A
01232 370717
Mr & Mrs Scannell & Sharkey
Rates fr: *£17.50*-**£19.00**.
Beds: 2F 3D 2S
Baths: 2 Shared
(6) (4)

Windermere House, *60 Wellington Park, Belfast, BT9 6DP.*
Victorian house, convenient to the city centre, theatres, university and motorways.
Open: All Year (not Xmas)
Grades: NITB Grade A
01232 662693 / 665165 Misses Murray
Rates fr: *£19.00*-**£19.00**.
Beds: 1F 1D 3T 4S
Baths: 2 Ensuite 2 Shared

Bienvenue, *8 Sans Souci Park, Malone Road, Belfast, BT9 5BZ.*
Excellent Victorian house with private car park. Very central location.
Open: All Year (not Xmas)
01232 681731 Mrs Henderson
Rates fr: *£24.00*-**£38.00**.
Beds: 5D 1T
Baths: 5 Ensuite 1 Private
(6)

Pay B&Bs by cash or cheque. Be prepared to pay up front for one night stays.

Bowdens, *17 Sandford Avenue, Cypress Avenue, Belfast, BT5 5NW.*
Warm family-run town house in quiet cul-de-sac.
Open: All Year
Grades: NITB Approv
01232 652213 Mrs Bowden
Rates fr: *£15.00*-**£15.00**.
Beds: 1T 2S
Baths: 1 Shared
(2)

Broughshane

National Grid Ref: D1506

Quarrytown Lodge, *15 Quarrytown Road, Broughshane, Ballymena, Co Antrim, BT43 7LB.*
Luxurious accommodation in award-winning country house with panoramic views.
Open: All Year
01266 862027 Mrs Drennan
Rates fr: *£20.00*-**£25.00**.
Beds: 1F 1D 2T
Baths: 4 Ensuite
(6)

Bushmills

National Grid Ref: C9440

Distillers Arms

Ardeevin, *145 Main Street, Bushmills, Co Antrim, BT57 8QE.*
Comfortable family-run house convenient to Giant's Causeway and Bushmills Distillery.
Open: All Year
Grades: NITB Approv
012657 31661 Mrs Montgomery
Rates fr: *£ 15.00*-**£15.00**.
Beds: 2D 1T
Baths: 2 Ensuite 1 Private

Knocklayde View, *90 Causeway Road, Bushmills, Co Antrim, BT57 8SX.*
Country house with lovely view of countryside and so near the beauty of the Giant's Causeway.
Open: All Year
012657 32099 Mrs Wylie
Rates fr: *£13.00*-**£15.00**.
Beds: 2D

Cairncastle

National Grid Ref: D3307

Mattie's

Meeting House, *120 Brustinbrae Road, Cairncastle, Larne, Co Antrim, BT40 2RL.*
Modern comfortable home situated 1 mile inland from famous Antrim coast.
Open: Jan to Nov
01574 583252 Mrs Moore
Rates fr: *£16.00*-**£17.00.**
Beds: 1D 2T
Baths: 3 Ensuite
(4) (5)

Carnlough

National Grid Ref: D2817

Bridge Inn (McAuleys), *2 Bridge Street, Carnlough, Ballymena, Co Antrim, BT44 0ET.*
Traditional, family-run pub.
Open: All Year
Grades: NITB Grade B
01574 885669 Mr Davidson
Rates fr: *£16.00*-**£16.00.**
Beds: 1F 3D 1T
(1) (2)

Carrickfergus

National Grid Ref: J4187

North Gate Bar

Seaview, *33 Larne Road, Carrickfergus, Co Antrim, BT38 7EE.*
Delightful bungalow with sea view. Close to beach and amenities.
Open: Apr to Nov
Grades: NITB Approv
01960 363170 Mr Sutherland
Rates fr: *£15.00*-**£15.00.**
Beds: 1D 1T 1S
Baths: 3 Ensuite
(2) (2)

Marina House, *49 Irish Quarter South, Carrickfergus, Co Antrim, BT38 8BL.*
Recently refurbished and extended to the highest standard with ensuites.
Open: All Year **Grades:** NITB Approv
01960 364055 Mr & Mrs Mulholland
Rates fr: *£18.00*-**£18.00.**
Beds: 5F 2T 7S
Baths: 6 Ensuite 1 Private 2 Shared

Castlecat

National Grid Ref: C9517

Auberge de Seneirl, *28 Ballyclogh Road, Seneirl, Castlecat, Bushmills, Co Antrim, BT57 8UZ.*
Converted country school.
Open: All Year (not Xmas)
012657 41536 Mr & Mrs Defres
Rates fr: *£21.50*-**£21.50.**
Beds: 5D **Baths:** 5 Ensuite
(12)

Crumlin

National Grid Ref: J1576

Crossroads Country House, *1 Largy Road, Crumlin, Belfast, BT29 4AH.*
Victorian country house in mature grounds, day nursery in grounds.
Open: All Year
01849 452491 Mr Lorimer
Rates fr: *£15.00*-**£15.00.**
Beds: 1F 2D **Baths:** 2 Shared
(16)

Cushendall

National Grid Ref: D2427

Thornlea Hotel, Harry's

Moyle View, Coast Road, *2 Ardmoyle Park, Cushendall, Ballymena, Co Antrim, BT44 0QL.*
Open: All Year **Grades:** NITB Approv
012667 71580 Mrs Gaffney
Rates fr: *£13.00*-**£15.00.**
Beds: 2D 1T **Baths:** 1 Ensuite 2 Shared
(5)
Modern bungalow with landscaped gardens. Situated 'Heart of Glens'. Under 5 minutes walk from centre village, beach, boat club, golf course, activity centre. Ideal location for touring whole North Antrim coast. Good home cooking and warm welcome awaits you always.

Riverside, *14 Mill Street, Cushendall, Ballymena, Co Antrim, BT44 0RR.*
Ideal base for touring Glens of Antrim. Situated village centre.
Open: All Year (not Xmas)
Grades: NITB Approv
012667 71655 (also fax no)
Mr & Mrs McKeegan
Rates fr: *£15.00*-**£17.00**.
Beds: 1F 1D 1T
Baths: 2 Shared
(3)

Trosben Villa, *8 Coast Road, Cushendall, Ballymena, Co Antrim, BT44 0RU.*
Open: All Year
012667 71130
Mrs Rowan
Rates fr: *£17.50*-**£20.00**.
Beds: 3F 4D
Baths: 7 Ensuite

Thornlea Hotel, *6 Coast Road, Cushendall, Ballymena, Co Antrim, BT44 0RU.*
Family-run hotel, good food, central location, over 55's discounts.
Open: All Year
Grades: NITB 1 St, AA 2 St, RAC 2 St
012667 71223 (also fax no)
Mrs Crampton
Rates fr: *£27.50*-**£35.00**.
Beds: 1F 7D 5T
Baths: 11 Ensuite 2 Shared
(12)

Cullentra House, *16 Cloghs Road, Cushendall, Ballymena, Co Antrim, BT44 0SP.*
Modern country home. Breathtaking views. Award-winning guest house.
Open: All Year (not Xmas)
Grades: NITB Approv
012667 71762
Mrs McAuley
Rates fr: *£14.00*-**£20.00**.
Beds: 1F 1D 1T
Baths: 2 Ensuite 1 Shared
(4) (6)

The lowest **single** *rate is shown in* **bold.**

The lowest *double* rate per person is shown in *italics*.

The Burn, *63 Ballyeamon Road, Cushendall, Ballymena, Co Antrim, BT44 0SN.*
Ideally situated for that free country feeling - usual modern conveniences.
Open: All Year
012667 71733 / 01266 46111
Mrs McAuley
Rates fr: *£14.00*-**£14.00**.
Beds: 1F 1D 1S
Baths: 1 Ensuite 2 Shared
(4)

Glendale, *46 Coast Road, Cushendall, Ballymena, Co Antrim, BT44 0RX.*
Open: All Year **Grades:** NITB Approv
012667 71495 Mrs O'Neill
Rates fr: *£16.00*-**£16.00**.
Beds: 5F 1D
Baths: 5 Ensuite 1 Private
(10)

Cushendun

National Grid Ref: D2533

The Burns, *116 Torr Road, Cushendun, Ballycastle, Co Antrim, BT44 0PY.*
Large old comfortable picturesque farmhouse.
Open: All Year **Grades:** NITB 3 St
012657 62709 Mrs McKendry
Rates fr: *£15.00*-**£15.00**.
Beds: 1F 2D 1T
Baths: 1 Ensuite 1 Shared
(12)

Dunmurry

National Grid Ref: J2968

Balmoral Hotel, *Blacks Road, Dunmurry, Belfast, BT17 0ND.*
Comfortable modern hotel.
Open: All Year (not Xmas)
Grades: NITB 2 St, AA 2 St, RAC 2 St
01232 301234 Mr Ward
Rates fr: *£27.50*-**£40.00**.
Beds: 19D 25T
Baths: 44 Private

Glarryford

National Grid Ref: D2221

The Firs, *86 Duneoin Road, Glarryford, Ballymena, Co Antrim, BT44 9HH.*
Modern country bungalow convenient to many historical sites.
Open: All Year (not Xmas)
01266 685410
Miss Carson
Rates fr: *£12.00*-**£12.00.**
Beds: 2D
Baths: 1 Shared
(5) (4)

Glenariff

National Grid Ref:

Mariners Bar

4 Lurig View, *Glenariff, Ballymena, Co Antrim, BT44 0RD.*
Friendly family bungalow, sea views.
Open: All Year
012667 71618
Mrs Ward
Rates fr: *£13.00*-**£15.00.**
Beds: 2F 1D
Baths: 1 Shared
(1)

Dieskirt Farm, *104 Glen Road, Glenariff, Ballymena, Co Antrim, BT44 0RG.*
Enjoy the tranquillity of this working 2,000-acre hill farm.
Open: Easter to Xmas
Grades: NITB Approv
012667 71308 / 58769 / 71796
Fax no: 012667 71308
Mrs McHenry
Rates fr: *£13.00*-**£17.00.**
Beds: 1F 2D 1T
Baths: 2 Shared
(10)

Glenarm

National Grid Ref: D3215

Lynden's

10 Altmore Street, *Glenarm, Ballymena, Co Antrim, BT44 0AR.*
Comfortable guest house in first of Nine Glens of Antrim.
Open: All Year
01574 841307 Mrs Morrow
Rates fr: *£14.00*-**£14.00.**
Beds: 2F 3D
Baths: 1 Shared
(10)

Portree, *419 Coast Road, Glenarm, Ballymena, Co Antrim, BT44 0BB.*
Refurbished cottage with scenic views and private beach. Coal fire in TV lounge.
Open: All Year
01574 841503 Mrs Mairs
Rates fr: *£17.50*-**£20.00.**
Beds: 1D 1T
Baths: 1 Ensuite
(5)

Islandmagee

National Grid Ref: J4699

Hill Bay Inn

Hill View, *30 Middle Road, Islandmagee, Larne, Co Antrim, BT40 3SL.*
Modern comfortable country bungalow. Near sea. TV, tea and coffee facilities in all rooms.
Open: All Year (not Xmas)
Grades: NITB Approv
01960 372581 Mrs Reid
Rates fr: *£15.00*-**£18.00.**
Beds: 1F 1D 1T
Baths: 1 Ensuite 1 Shared
(6)

Kells

National Grid Ref: J1496

Springmount, *31 Ballygowan Road, Kells, Ballymena, Co Antrim, BT42 3PD.*
Friendly farmhouse in quiet location, ideal touring centre. Ballymena 12 kms.
Open: All Year
01266 891275 Mrs Bell
Rates fr: *£15.00*-**£15.00**.
Beds: 3D
Baths: 1 Shared

Kilwaughter

National Grid Ref: D3500

Kilwaughter House Hotel, *61 Shanes Hill Road, Kilwaughter, Larne, Co Antrim, BT40 2TQ.*
Peaceful family-run hotel, lovely grounds.
Open: All Year
01574 272591 Mr Dobbin
Rates fr: *£20.00*-**£20.00**.
Beds: 6D 2T 2S
Baths: 2 Ensuite
(300)

Larne

National Grid Ref: D4002

The Baile, Curran Court Hotel, Meeting House, Checkers, Dan Campbell's

Derrin House, *2 Prince's Gardens, Larne, Co Antrim, BT40 1RQ.*
Open: All Year (not Xmas)
Grades: NITB Grade A, AA 3 Q, RAC Acclaim
01574 273269 / 273762
Mrs Mills
Rates fr: *£15.00*-**£18.00**.
Beds: 2F 4D 1T
Baths: 4 Ensuite 1 Shared
(3)
Beautifully appointed Grade A guest house, family-run since 1964, full fire certificate. Private car park. All rooms have colour TV, tea/coffee facilities and electric blankets. Most are ensuite. Friendly, welcoming atmosphere, 'Highly Commended' in 1994 Galtee Breakfast Awards.

Inverbann, *7 Glenarm Road, Larne, Co Antrim, BT40 1BN.*
Attractive family property on the Antrim coast road (A2), minutes from ferries and Glens of Antrim.
Open: All Year
01574 272524 Mrs Scott
Rates fr: *£15.00*-**£17.50**.
Beds: 1F 1D 1T
Baths: 3 Ensuite
(3)

Manor Guest House, *23 Olderfleet Road, Larne, Co Antrim, BT40 1AS.*
Restored mid-Victorian house situated two minutes walk from Larne ferries and train station.
Grades: NITB Grade B
01574 273305 Miss Graham
Rates fr: *£15.00*-**£16.00**.
Beds: 2F 3D 2T 1S
Baths: 8 Ensuite
(8)

Lynden, *65 Glenarm Road, Larne, Co Antrim, BT40 1DX.*
A warm and friendly welcome with a high standard of decor throughout.
Open: All Year **Grades:** NITB Approv
01574 272626 Mrs Rennie
Rates fr: *£14.00*-**£16.00**.
Beds: 1D 1T **Baths:** 1 Shared
(2)

Lisburn

National Grid Ref: J2664

Down Royal Inn, Tidy Doffer

Strathearn House, *19 Antrim Road, Lisburn, Co Antrim, BT28 3ED.*
Comfortable family run town house, 10 minutes walk from town centre.
Open: All Year
01846 601661 Mr & Mrs McKeown
Rates fr: *£25.00*-**£20.00**.
Beds: 1F 1D 1T
Baths: 2 Ensuite 1 Private
(All) (8)

Bringing children with you? Always ask for any special rates.

The Paddock, *36a Clontara Park, Belsize Road, Lisburn, Co Antrim, BT27 4LB.*
Family home in quiet road. Close to M1 and Lisburn.
Open: All Year (not Xmas)
Grades: NITB Approv
01846 601507 Mrs Gillespie
Rates fr: *£15.00*-**£15.00**.
Beds: 1D 1T 1S
Baths: 1 Shared
(4)

Loanends

National Grid Ref: J2281

Fiddlers Inn

Mount Pleasant, *12a Carmavy Road, Loanends, Crumlin, Belfast, BT29 4TF.*
Modern bungalow with central heating - five minutes drive from airport.
Open: All Year (not Xmas)
01849 452346
Mrs Kennedy
Rates fr: *£15.00*-**£16.00**.
Beds: 2F
Baths: 1 Ensuite 1 Shared

Newtownabbey

National Grid Ref: J3480

Bellevue Arms

Perpetua House, *57 Collinbridge Park, Newtownabbey, Co Antrim, BT36 7SY.*
Open: All Year
Grades: NITB Approv
01232 833041
Mrs Robinson
Rates fr: *£18.00*-**£19.00**.
Beds: 2T 2S
Baths: 1 Ensuite 1 Private 2 Shared
(10)

Iona, *161 Antrim Road, Newtownabbey, Belfast, BT36 7QR.*
5 minutes from Cave Hill Mountain.
Open: All Year (not Xmas)
01232 842256
Mrs Kelly
Rates fr: *£16.00*-**£18.00**.
Beds: 1F 1D 2S
Baths: 2 Shared

Nutts Corner

National Grid Ref: J1977

Keef Halla, *20 Tully Road, Nutts Corner, Crumlin, Belfast, BT29 4AH.*
Open: All Year **Grades:** NITB Approv
01232 825491 (also fax no)
Mr & Mrs Kelly
Rates fr: *£18.00*-**£25.00**.
Beds: 3F 2D 1T
Baths: 6 Ensuite
(12)
Keef Halla offers luxury ensuite accommodation, adjacent to Belfast International Airport. Collection service available. All bedrooms have direct dial telephone, TV, tea/coffee and refreshments. Ideal base for touring N. Ireland. Convenient to Antrim Belfast, Dundrod and Nutts Corner.

Portballintrae

National Grid Ref: C9241

Keeve Na, *62 Ballaghmore Road, Portballintrae, Bushmills, Co Antrim, BT57 8RL.*
Modern, detached house.
Open: All Year (not Xmas)
012657 32184 Mrs Wilkinson
Rates fr: *£15.00*-**£16.00**.
Beds: 1F 1D 1S
Baths: 3 Shared
(3)

Portglenone

National Grid Ref: C9703

Wild Duck Inn

Bannside Farmhouse, *268 Gortgole Road, Portglenone, Ballymena, Co Antrim, BT44 8AT.*
Peaceful farmhouse near River Bann - forest park and picnic area nearby.
Open: All Year
01266 821262 Misses Lowry
Rates fr: *£13.50*-**£13.50**.
Beds: 1D 1T 1S **Baths:** 1 Shared
(2) (5)

The lowest **single** *rate is shown in* **bold.**

Sprucebank, *41 Ballymacombs Road, Portglenone, Ballymena, Co Antrim, BT44 8NR.*
Inviting C18th farmhouse traditionally furnished. Relaxing atmosphere. B&B at its best
Open: Mar to Oct
Grades: NITB Approv
01266 822150 / 821422 Fax no: 01266 821422 Mrs Sibbett
Rates fr: *£15.50*-**£17.50.**
Beds: 1F 2D 1T
Baths: 1 Ensuite 1 Shared
(6)

Portrush

National Grid Ref: C8540

Ramore Wine Bar, Harbour Inn

Maddybenny Farm House, *Atlantic Road, Portrush, Co Antrim, BT52 2PT.*
Open: All Year (not Xmas)
Grades: NITB Approv
01265 823394
(also fax no) Mrs White
Rates fr: *£22.50*-**£25.00.**
Beds: 2F 1T 1S **Baths:** 4 Ensuite
Award-winning B&B and 4 Star self catering cottages (6) sleep 6 or 8 persons. Own BHS approved riding centre, convenient to 7 golf courses, University, Blue Flag beaches (strands) and Causeway coast. Off A29 2 Km from Portrush.

Brookside House, *46 Mark Street, Portrush, Co Antrim, BT56 8BU.*
Comfortable family managed. Central position. Guest house.
Open: All Year
01265 824498 (also fax no) Mrs Fox
Rates fr: *£13.00*-**£15.00.**
Beds: 4F 4D 5T 2S
Baths: 2 Ensuite 2 Shared

Clarmont, *10 Lansdowne Crescent, Portrush, Co Antrim, BT56 8AY.*
Large Victorian seaview guesthouse.
Open: Jan to Nov
01265 822397 Mr & Mrs Duggan
Rates fr: *£18.00*-**£18.00.**
Beds: 5F 8D 3T 1S
Baths: 8 Ensuite

Glencroft Guest House, *95 Coleraine Road, Portrush, Co Antrim, BT56 8HN.*
Open: All Year (not Xmas)
Grades: NITB Grade B
01265 822902
Mr & Mrs Henderson
Rates fr: *£16.50*-**£20.00.**
Beds: 2F 1D 2T
Baths: 2 Ensuite 1 Shared
(10)
Large private house, secluded garden. Ground floor ensuite room. Giants Causeway twenty minutes drive. Start the day with our four course Glencroft special breakfast. Choose our traditional 'Ulster Fry' or tempting fruit platter as a 'healthy option'. Extensive menu, all home cooked.

Casa A La Mar Guest House, *21 Kerr Street, Portrush, Co Antrim, BT56 8DG.*
Small family-run guesthouse, in town centre, overlooking sea.
Open: All Year (not Xmas)
Grades: NITB Grade B
01265 822617
(also fax no) Mrs Larner
Rates fr: *£14.00*-**£14.00.**
Beds: 2F 2D 3S
Baths: 2 Ensuite 2 Shared

Causeway House, *26 Kerr Street, Portrush, Co Antrim, BT56 8DG.*
Wonderful beachside location. Minutes from stations, entertainment, shops. Warm welcome.
Open: All Year (not Xmas)
Grades: NITB Approv
01265 824847
Mr & Mrs Devenney
Rates fr: *£12.50*-**£15.00.**
Beds: 2F 2D 2T
Baths: 2 Ensuite 2 Shared
(2)

Loguestown Farmhouse, *58 Loguestown Road, Portrush, Co Antrim, BT56 8PD.*
Modern rural farmhouse. Excellent base for all Causeway Coast amenities.
Open: All Year (not Xmas)
01265 822742
Mrs Adams
Rates fr: *£14.00*-**£16.00.**
Beds: 1F 5D 1T 1S
Baths: 1 Ensuite 2 Shared
(8)

Randalstown

National Grid Ref: J0890

Lurgan West Lodge, *15a Old Staffordstown Road, Randalstown, Antrim, Co Antrim, BT41 3LD.*
Modern comfortable house within the town boundary.
Open: All Year
01849 479691 Mrs McLaughlin
Rates fr: *£12.50*-**£15.00**.
Beds: 1F 1D 2T 1S
Baths: 2 Ensuite 1 Shared
(8)

Rathlin Island

National Grid Ref: D1351

Rathlin Guest House, *The Quay, Rathlin Island, Co Antrim, BT54 6RT.*
A small family-run business on Northern Ireland's only inhabited island.
Open: Easter to Sept
Grades: NITB Grade B
012657 63917 Mr & Mrs McCurdy
Rates fr: *£15.00*-**£15.00**.
Beds: 2F 1D 1S
Baths: 1 Shared

Revallagh

National Grid Ref: C9136

Bohill Hotel

198 Ballybogey Road, *Revallagh, Bushmills, Co Antrim, BT57 8UH.*
Modern family farmhouse. 3 miles from Bushmills.
Open: Easter to Sept
012657 31793 Mrs Rankin
Rates fr: *£14.00*-**£14.00**.
Beds: 1D 1T **Baths:** 1 Shared
(2)

Templepatrick

National Grid Ref: J2486

Templeton Hotel, *882 Antrim Road, Templepatrick, Ballyclare, Co Antrim, BT39 0AH.*
Modern rural hotel, 20 minutes from city centre and 10 from International Airport.
Open: All Year
01849 432984 Mrs Kerr
Rates fr: *£30.00*-**£50.00**.
Beds: 11D 12T 1S
Baths: 24 Ensuite
(200)

Waterfoot

National Grid Ref: D2424

The Bay, *204 Garron Road, Waterfoot, Ballymena, Co Antrim, BT44 0RB.*
Open: Easter to Oct
012667 71858
Mrs Colligan
Rates fr: *£13.00*-**£14.00**.
Beds: 1F 1D 1T
Baths: 1 Shared
(1) (6)

Whitepark Bay

National Grid Ref: D0243

Whitepark House, *150 Whitepark Road, Whitepark Bay, Ballintoy, Ballycastle, Co Antrim, BT54 6NH.*
C18th house, spacious rooms, log fire.
Open: All Year (not Xmas)
012657 31482
Mr & Mrs Isles
Rates fr: *£20.00*-**£26.00**.
Beds: 2D 1T
Baths: 1 Shared
(8)

County Armagh

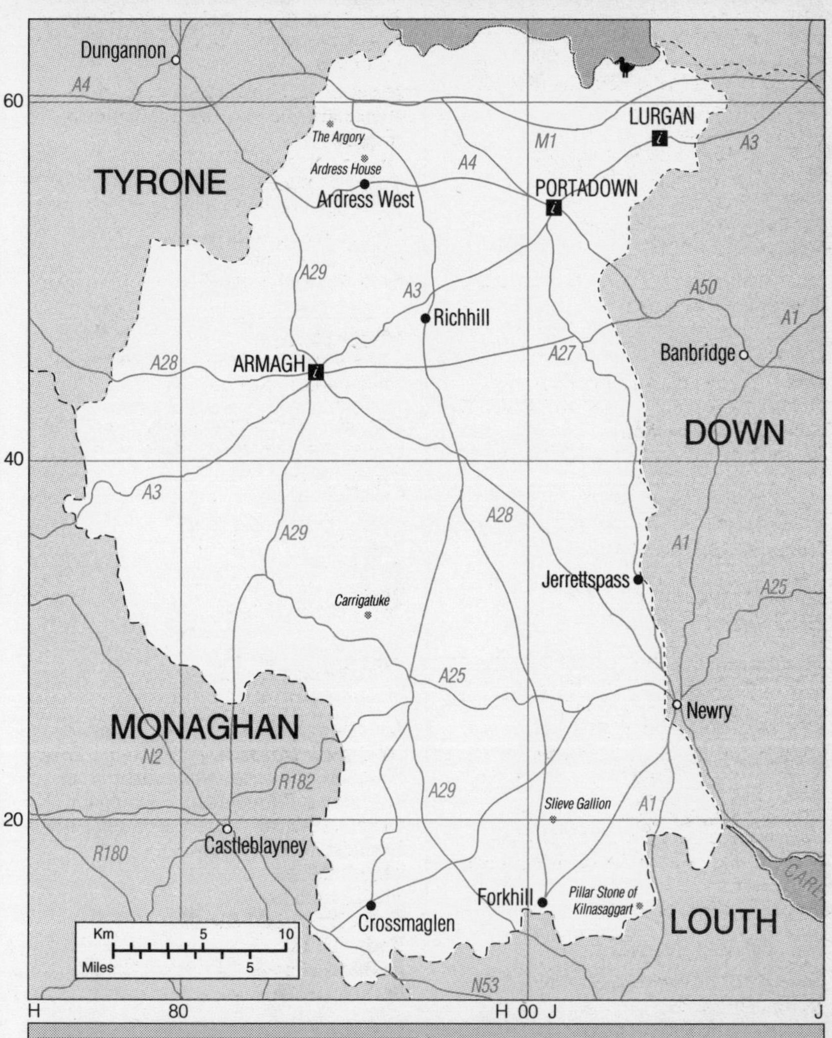

RAIL

In Co Armagh, the main Belfast to Dublin line passes through ***Lurgan***, ***Portadown*** and on towards ***Newry***.
Tel. **Northern Ireland Rail** - 01232 899411 for timetable information.

BUS

The main bus links are: ***Armagh** to **Belfast*** (twice an hour) and ***Armagh** to **Dublin*** (once daily).

Tel. **Ulsterbuses** for these and other destinations - 01232 333000.

TOURIST INFORMATION OFFICES

40 English Street, **Armagh**, BT61 7BA, 01861-521800

Town Hall, 6 Union Street, **Lurgan**, BT66 8DY, 01762-323757

Town Hall, **Portadown**, 01762-353260

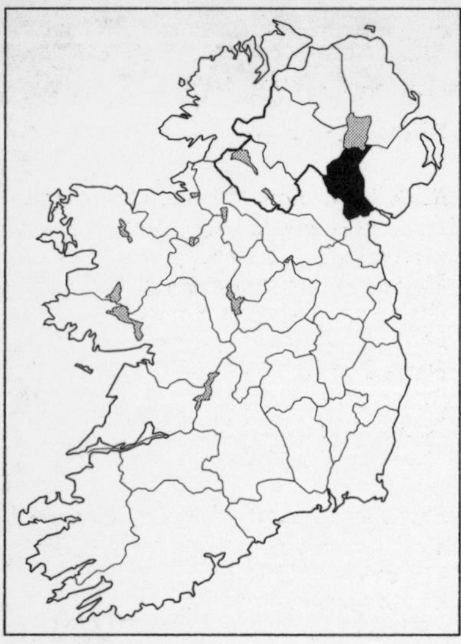

Ardress West

National Grid Ref: H9055

125 Summerisland Road, *Ardress West, Portadown, Craigavon, Co Armagh, BT62 1SJ.*
Modern home in lovely rural countryside in the Apple County of Armagh.
Open: All Year
01762 851437 Mrs Neville
Rates fr: *£12.50*-**£12.50**.
Beds: 1D 1T
Baths: 1 Shared

Armagh

National Grid Ref: H8745

Dean's Hill, *College Hill, Armagh, BT61 9DF.*
Open: All Year
01861 524923 Mrs Armstrong
Rates fr: *£22.00*-**£16.00**.
Beds: 1D 1T 1S
Baths: 2 Ensuite 1 Shared
This comfortable Georgian country home is set in wooded grounds with farm and includes a cosy guests' library/sitting room with open fire, tennis court and croquet lawn. 10 minutes' walk to historic Armagh City with its museums, cathedrals and restaurants.

Desart, *99 Cathedral Road, Armagh, BT61 8AE.*
Private house in mature grounds within walking distance of city.
Open: All Year (not Xmas)
01861 522387
Mrs McRoberts
Rates fr: *£15.00*-**£17.50**.
Beds: 3T

Crossmaglen

National Grid Ref: H9015

Murtagh's Pub

Likane Farmhouse, *10 Corliss Road, Crossmaglen, Newry, Co Armagh, BT35 9AY.*
Restored country house. Panoramic views. Close to many amenities.
Open: All Year (not Xmas)
01693 868348
Mr & Mrs Forde
Rates fr: *£16.00*-**£12.00**.
Beds: 1D 1S
Baths: 1 Ensuite 1 Shared
(4)

Forkhill

National Grid Ref: J0115

Lakeview, *34 Church Road, Forkhill, Newry, Co Down, BT35 9SX.*
Spacious bungalow with magnificent views, in rural mountain countryside.
Open: All Year
Grades: NITB Approv
01693 888382
Mrs O Neill
Rates fr: *£14.00*-**£15.00**.
Beds: 2F 1D
Baths: 1 Ensuite 1 Private 1 Shared
(5)

Irish Grid References are for villages, towns and cities - *not* for individual houses.

Jerrettspass

National Grid Ref: J0534

Brass Monkey

Deerpark, *177 Tandragee Road, Jerrettspass, Drumbanagher, Newry, Co Down, BT35 6LP.*
C17th stone built farmhouse in beautiful countryside.
Open: All Year (not Xmas)
01693 821409
Mrs Thompson
Rates fr: *£15.00*-**£15.00**.
Beds: 1F 1D 1S
Baths: 1 Ensuite 2 Private

Lurgan

National Grid Ref: J0758

Ashburn Hotel, *81 William Street, Lurgan, Craigavon, Co Armagh, BT66 6JB.*
Family-owned comfortable hotel close to town centre.
Open: All Year (not Xmas)
Grades: NITB 1 St
01762 325711
Mr McConaght
Rates fr: *£25.00*-**£30.00**.
Beds: 3F 4D 4T 1S
Baths: 12 Ensuite
(30)

The lowest *double* rate per person is shown in *italics*.

Portadown

National Grid Ref: J0053

Parkview Bar

Redbrick Country House, *Corbrackey Lane, Portadown, Craigavon, Co Armagh, BT62 1PQ.*
Modern luxury house. Rural setting.
Open: All Year (not Xmas)
01762 335268 Mrs Stephenson
Rates fr: *£16.00*-**£16.00**.
Beds: 4D 3T
Baths: 4 Ensuite 2 Shared
(4) (10)

Bannview Squash Club, *60 Portmore Street, Portadown, Craigavon, Co Armagh, BT62 3NF.*
Luxury ensuite bedroom accommodation.
Open: All Year (not Xmas)
01762 336666 Mr Black
Rates fr: *£19.00*-**£24.00**.
Beds: 10T
Baths: 10 Ensuite
(17)

Richhill

National Grid Ref: H9447

Ballinahinch House, *47 Ballygroobany Road, Richhill, Armagh, BT61 9NA.*
Early Victorian farmhouse with large garden. On a working farm.
Open: Easter to Oct
01762 870081 (also fax no)
Mrs Kee
Rates fr: *£15.00*-**£16.00**.
Beds: 1F 1D 1T
Baths: 2 Private
(20)

County Down

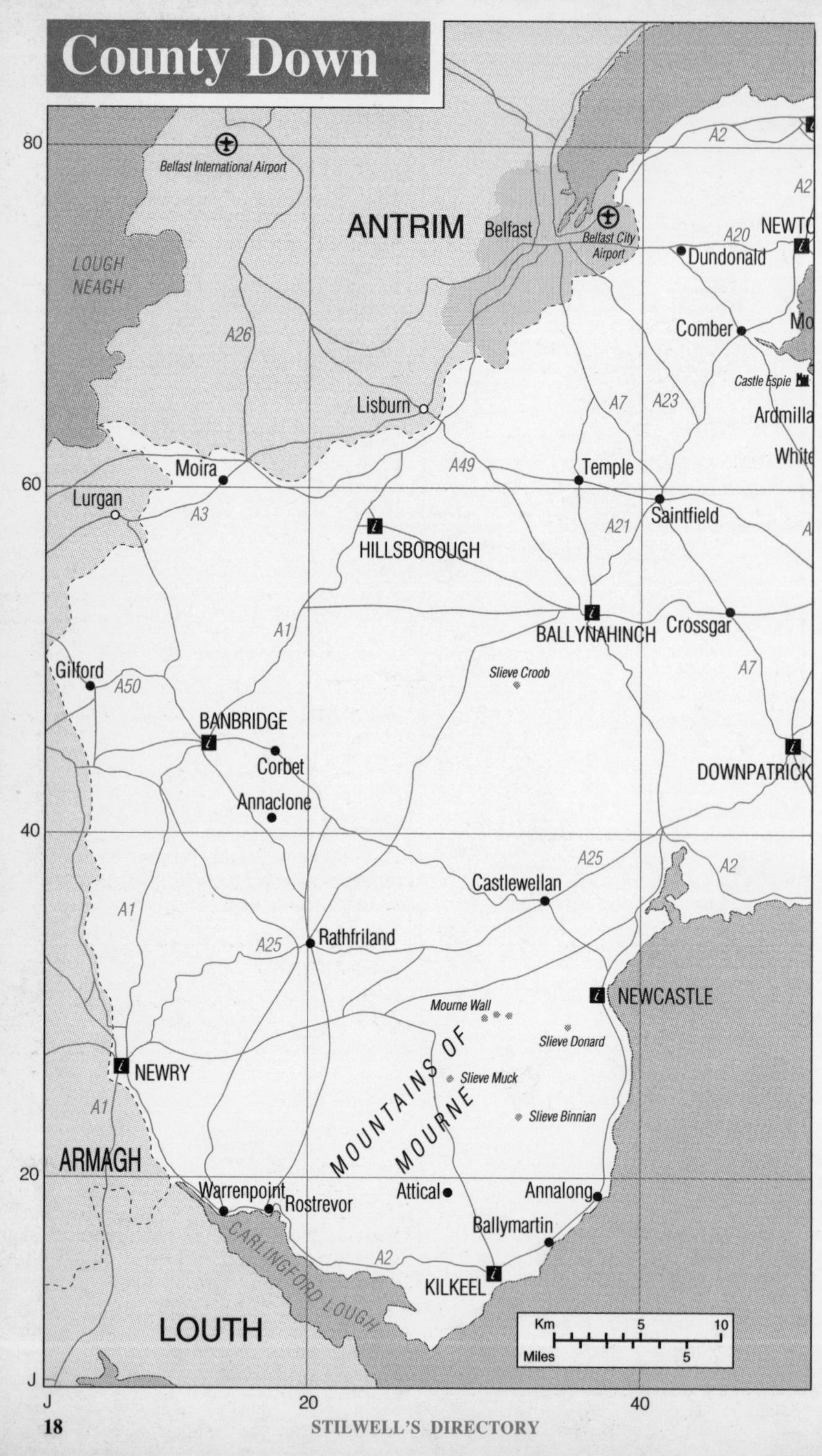

Belfast International Airport
LOUGH NEAGH
ANTRIM
Belfast
Belfast City Airport
NEWTC
Dundonald
Comber
Castle Espie
Ardmilla
White
Lisburn
Moira
Lurgan
Temple
Saintfield
HILLSBOROUGH
BALLYNAHINCH
Crossgar
Slieve Croob
Gilford
BANBRIDGE
Corbet
Annaclone
DOWNPATRICK
Castlewellan
Rathfriland
NEWCASTLE
Mourne Wall
Slieve Donard
Slieve Muck
Slieve Binnian
MOUNTAINS OF MOURNE
NEWRY
ARMAGH
Warrenpoint
Rostrevor
Attical
Annalong
Ballymartin
KILKEEL
CARLINGFORD LOUGH
LOUTH
A2
A20
A26
A7
A23
A49
A3
A21
A1
A50
A25
Km 5 10
Miles 5
80
60
40
20
J
20
40

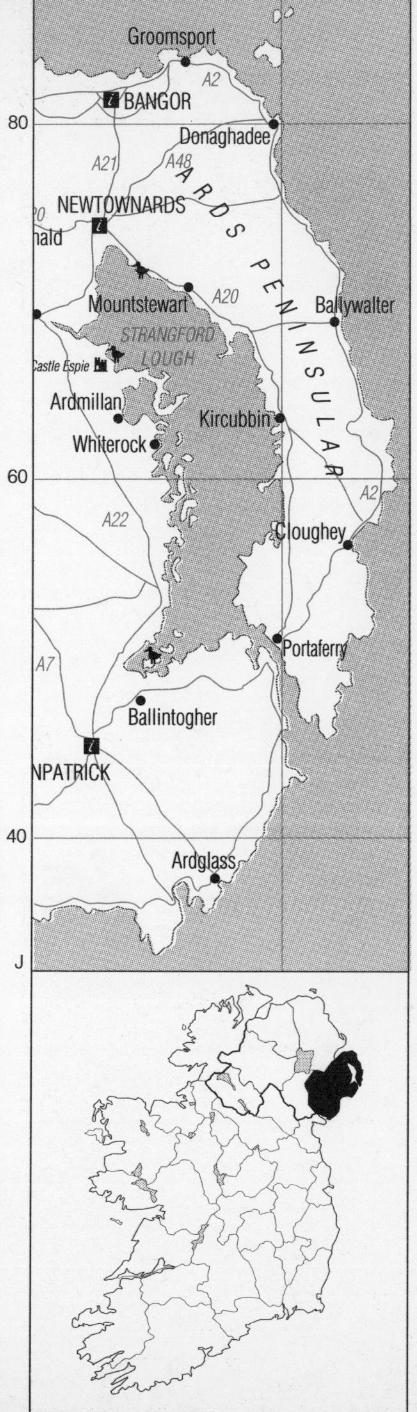

RAIL

The major rail service in County Down linked to the national network is the ***Bangor*** *to* ***Belfast*** commuter line running along the southern coast of **Belfast Lough**.
Tel. **Northern Ireland Rail** on 01232 899411 for timetable information.

BUS

There are good bus links to ***Belfast*** from all major towns in County Down.
Tel. **Ulsterbuses** (01232 333000).

TOURIST INFORMATION OFFICES

55 Windmill Street, **Ballynahinch**, BT24 8HB, 01238-561950

Downshire Leisure Centre, Downshire Road, **Banbridge**, BT32 3JY, 01820-23322

34 Quay Street, **Bangor**, BT20 5ED, 01247-270069

Market Square, **Hillsborough**, Co Antrim BT28 1AG, 01846-663377

Recreation Hall, Mourne Esplanade, **Kilkeel**, Newry, BT34 4DB, 01693-764666

The Newcastle Centre, Central Promenade, **Newcastle**, BT33 0AA, (Easter to Oct), 01396-722222

Tourist Office,Townhall **Newry**, BT35 6HR, 01693-68877

31 Regent Street, **Newtownards**, BT23 4AD, 01247-826846

Annaclone

National Grid Ref: J1841

Meadowview, *26a Monteith Road, Annaclone, Banbridge, Co Down, BT32 5LS.*
Modern, chalet bungalow in the heart of the Brontë homeland.
Open: All Year (not Xmas)
018206 62954 Mr & Mrs McAvoy
Rates fr: *£12.00*-**£15.00.**
Beds: 2F **Baths:** 1 Shared
(All) (3)

Moor Lodge, *20 Ballynafern Road, Annaclone, Banbridge, Co Down, BT32 5AE.*
Family-run modern farmhouse in Brontë countryside. Home cooking a speciality.
Open: All Year (not Xmas)
018206 71516 Mr & Mrs McClory
Rates fr: *£17.00*-**£22.00**.
Beds: 1F 2D 1T
Baths: 1 Shared
(8)

Annalong

National Grid Ref: J3719

Kilmorey Arms Hotel, Halfway House, Harbour Bar

The Sycamores, *52 Majors Hill, Annalong, Newry, Co Down, BT34 4QR.*
Traditional farmhouse accommodation with panoramic view of Mourne Mountains.
Open: All Year **Grades:** NITB Approv
013967 68279 Mrs McKee
Rates fr: *£17.00*-**£20.00**.
Beds: 1F 1D 1T
Baths: 3 Ensuite
(6)

Kamara B & B, *106A Kilkeel Road, Annalong, Newry, Co Down, BT34 4TJ.*
Modern comfortable bungalow with both mountain and sea views.
Open: All Year
013967 68072 Mrs Gordon
Rates fr: *£14.00*-**£14.00**.
Beds: 1F 1D
Baths: 1 Private
(0) (5)

Fair Haven, *16 Moneydarragh Road, Annalong, Newry, Co Down, BT34 4TY.*
Modern bungalow in Mourne. Breath-taking scenery. Hill-walking nearby.
Open: All Year (not Xmas)
013967 68153 Mrs Jardine
Rates fr: *£15.00*-**£16.00**.
Beds: 1F 1D 1T
Baths: 2 Ensuite 1 Shared

The lowest **single** *rate is shown in* **bold.**

Irish Grid References are for villages, towns and cities - *not* for individual houses.

Ardglass

National Grid Ref: J5637

Strand Farm, *231 Ardglass Road, Ardglass, Downpatrick, Co Down, BT30 7UL.*
Modernised old farmhouse (working farm).
Open: Mar to Oct
01396 841446
Mrs Donnan
Rates fr: *£14.00*-**£15.00**.
Beds: 1F 1D 1T
Baths: 1 Ensuite 1 Shared
(10)

Ardmillan

National Grid Ref: J5062

Barnageeha, *90 Ardmillan Road, Ardmillan, Killinchy, Newtownards, Co Down, BT23 6QN.*
Internationally important bird site, superb scenery. Award-winning food.
Open: All Year
Grades: NITB Approv
01238 541011
Mr & Mrs Crawford
Rates fr: *£22.50*-**£25.00**.
Beds: 3T 1S
Baths: 3 Ensuite
(30)

Attical

National Grid Ref: J2819

Hillview, *18 Bog Road, Attical, Newry, Co Down, BT34 4HT.*
Working farm in Mourne mountains.
Open: All Year (not Xmas)
016937 64269
Mrs Trainor
Rates fr: *£12.50*-**£18.00**.
Beds: 1F 1D 1T 1S
Baths: 1 Ensuite 1 Private 1 Shared

Ballintogher

National Grid Ref: J5147

Cuan Bar

***Hillcrest,** 157 Strangford Road, Ballintogher, Downpatrick, Co Down, BT30 7JZ.*
Family-run farmhouse in the heart of Down. Overlooking Strangford Lough.
Open: All Year (not Xmas)
Grades: NITB Approv
01396 612583
Mrs Fitzsimons
Rates fr: *£14.00*-**£16.00**.
Beds: 2D 1T
Baths: 1 Ensuite 1 Shared
(6)

Ballymartin

National Grid Ref: J3416

***Wyncrest,** 30 Main Road , Ballymartin, Kilkeel, Newry, Co Down, BT34 4NU.*
All-Ireland winner of the Galtee Best Breakfast.
Open: Easter to Oct
Grades: NITB Grade A
016937 63012 / 65988
Fax no: 016937 63012
Mrs Adair
Rates fr: *£19.50*-**£24.50**.
Beds: 3D 2T 1S
Baths: 4 Ensuite 1 Shared
(6)

Ballynahinch

National Grid Ref: J3652

Millbrook Lodge Hotel

***Bushymead Country House,** 86 Drumaness Road, Ballynahinch, Co Down, BT24 8LT.*
Large classical-style country house in the heart of County Down on main A24 Route.
Open: All Year
Grades: NITB Approv
01238 561171
Mrs Murphy
Rates fr: *£15.00*-**£13.00**.
Beds: 2F 3D 3T 2S
Baths: 7 Ensuite 3 Shared
(30)

***Cornerhouse,** 182 Dunmore Road, Ballynahinch, Co Down, BT24 8QQ.*
Modern farmhouse in beautiful country-side, tropical butterfly-house, 9 miles Newcastle Forest Parks.
Open: Jun to Sep
01238 562670
Mrs Rogan
Rates fr: *£15.00*-**£15.00**.
Beds: 1F 1D
(4)

Ballywalter

National Grid Ref: J6268

***Greenlea,** 48 Dunover Road, Ballywalter, Newtownards, Co Down, BT22 2LE.*
Modern comfortable farmhouse with beautiful views over the Irish Sea to Scotland.
Open: All Year (not Xmas)
Grades: NITB Approv
012477 58218
Mrs McIvor
Rates fr: *£14.00*-**£16.00**.
Beds: 1F 1D 2T 1S
Baths: 3 Shared
(12)

Banbridge

National Grid Ref: J1245

***Springhill,** 132 Ballygowan Road, Banbridge, Co Down, BT32 3QX.*
Central, all amenities, ensuite, TV. Welcoming atmosphere, parties negotiable.
Open: All Year
018206 23882
Mrs Shanks
Rates fr: *£16.00*-**£17.00**.
Baths: 2 Ensuite
(10)

Phoning Northern Ireland from outside the Republic? Dial 08 before the full area code.

Bangor

National Grid Ref: J5081

Jamaica Inn, Jenny Watts, Sands Hotel, The Steamer, Donegan's, Crawfordsburn Inn, Royal Marine

Highfield Country House, *531 Belfast Road, Bangor, Co Down, BT19 1UN.*
Open: All Year
Grades: NITB Approv
01247 853693 Mrs Finlay
Rates fr: *£18.00*-**£18.00**.
Beds: 2T 1S
Baths: 1 Ensuite 1 Shared
P TV
Modern bungalow set in wooded countryside with beautiful view over Belfast Lough, convenient to Crawfordsburn village and Helens Bay. Belfast 10 miles, Bangor three miles. Belfast City Airport 15 minutes drive. Folk Museum five minutes drive. No evening meals.

Glendale House, *77 Southwell Road, Bangor, Co Down, BT20 3AE.*
Family-run guest house close to all amenities and marina.
Open: All Year
01247 468613
Mrs Blachford
Rates fr: *£14.00*-**£14.00**.
Beds: 1F 1D 1T
Baths: 1 Shared
TV V

Seacrest, *98 Seacliff Road, Bangor, Co Down, BT20 5EZ.*
Family run guesthouse overlooking Belfast Lough. Five minutes from town centre.
Open: All Year (not Xmas)
01247 461935 Mrs Marsden
Rates fr: *£14.00*-**£16.00**.
Beds: 1F 1D 2T
P (2) TV V

Bramble Lodge, *1 Bryansburn Road, Bangor, Co Down, BT20 3RY.*
Town location three minutes marina, two minutes train/coach terminals.
Open: All Year (not Xmas)
01247 457924 Mrs Hanna
Rates fr: *£18.00*-**£20.00**.
Beds: 1D 2T
Baths: 3 Ensuite
(3) P (3) TV V

Asda-Kern Bed & Breakfast, *18 Prospect Road, Bangor, Co Down, BT20 5DA.*
Warm welcome. Centrally heated, CTV, tea/coffee, electric blanket, hair-dryers in bedrooms.
Open: Easter to Oct
Grades: NITB Approv
01247 461309 Mrs Graham
Rates fr: *£13.25*-**£14.00**.
Beds: 1F 1D 1T
Baths: 1 Shared
(4) P (2) TV

Castlewellan

National Grid Ref: J3435

Chestnut Inn

Chestnut Inn, *28 Lower Square, Castlewellan, Bangor, BT31 9DW.*
Old established licensed inn in pleasant rural setting.
Open: All Year
Grades: NITB Grade B
013967 78247 / 78344
Mr & Mrs King
Rates fr: *£19.00*-**£21.00**.
Beds: 2F 5T
Baths: 7 Ensuite
P (10) TV V

Treetops, *39 Circular Road, Castlewellan, Co Down, BT31 9ED.*
Attractive modern bungalow in spacious gardens with ample parking facilities.
Open: All Year
013967 78132 Mrs King
Rates fr: *£13.00*-**£17.00**.
Beds: 1F 1D 3T
Baths: 1 Ensuite 1 Shared
P TV V

Cloughey

National Grid Ref: J6356

Coastal Lodge Hotel, *204 Main Road, Cloughey, Newtownards, Co Down, BT22 1JA.*
Traditional hotel situated in a quiet rural village on the coast.
Open: All Year (not Xmas)
012477 72100 Miss McVeigh
Rates fr: *£25.00*-**£35.00**.
Beds: 1F 3D 4T 1S
Baths: 9 Ensuite
P (20) TV V

Comber

National Grid Ref: J4568

TT Lounge

Flax Mill House, *117 Glen Road, Comber, Newtownards, Co Down, BT23 5QT.*
Open: All Year
Grades: NITB Approv
01247 873253
Mrs McEntee
Rates fr: *£16.00*-**£17.00**.
Beds: 1F 1D 1S
Baths: 2 Private
(10)

Corbet

National Grid Ref: J1644

Anglers Rest, Harry's Bar, Downshire Arms

Heathmar, *37 Corbet Road, Corbet, Banbridge, Co Down, BT32 3SH.*
Comfortable beds, good food, friendly hospitality, convenient to all attractions.
Open: All Year
018206 22348
Mrs Fleming
Rates fr: *£13.00*-**£15.00**.
Beds: 2F 1T
Baths: 2 Ensuite 1 Private
(12)

Crossgar

National Grid Ref: J4552

Villager

Hillhouse, *53 Killyleagh Road, Crossgar, Downpatrick, Co Down, BT30 9EE.*
Secluded Georgian guest house (Listed). Spacious accommodation. Belfast 14 miles.
Open: All Year (not Xmas)
Grades: NITB Approv
01396 830792
Mrs Davison
Rates fr: *£17.50*-**£20.00**.
Beds: 3F 1D 1T
Baths: 4 Ensuite 1 Private
(12) (20)

Donaghadee

National Grid Ref: J5979

Moat Inn, The Stables

Waterside Shanaghan, *154 Warren Road, Donaghadee, Co Down, BT21 0PN.*
Modern coastal bungalow convenient to many National Trust properties.
Open: All Year (not Xmas)
Grades: NITB Approv
01247 888167 Mrs Beattie
Rates fr: *£15.00*-**£15.00**.
Beds: 1F 1D 1T 1S
Baths: 1 Ensuite 3 Private
(8)

The Deans, *52 Northfield Road, Donaghadee, Co Down, BT21 0BD.*
Modern comfortable villa in beautiful seaside location. Three minutes walk to town centre.
Open: All Year
01247 882204 Mrs Wilson
Rates fr: *£15.00*-**£18.00**.
Beds: 1F 1D 1T 1S
Baths: 1 Ensuite 1 Shared
(4)

Dundonald

National Grid Ref: J4273

TT Lounge, Russells Cellars

The Cottage, *377 Comber Road, Dundonald, Belfast, BT16 0XB.*
Lovingly restored 200-year-old cottage with oak beams.
Open: All Year **Grades:** NITB Approv
01247 878189 Mrs Muldoon
Rates fr: *£17.00*-**£18.00**.
Beds: 2D
Baths: 1 Shared
(6)

Pay B&Bs by cash or cheque. Be prepared to pay up front for one night stays.

Gilford

National Grid Ref: J0648

Halls Mill Inn

Mount Pleasant, *38 Banbridge Road, Gilford, Craigavon, Co Armagh, BT63 6DJ.*
Approved country house in beautiful countryside central for touring Northern Ireland.
Open: All Year
Grades: NITB Approv
01762 831522
Mrs Buller
Rates fr: *£12.50*-**£14.00**.
Beds: 1F 2D 1T 1S
Baths: 2 Shared
(10)

Groomsport

National Grid Ref: J5483

The Stables

Islet Hill, *21 Bangor Road, Groomsport, Bangor, Co Down, BT19 6JF.*
Traditional Ulster farmhouse in arable fields with lovely sea views.
Open: All Year
Grades: NITB Approv
01247 464435
Mr Mayne
Rates fr: *£17.50*-**£17.50**.
Beds: 2F
Baths: 1 1 Private
(5)

Hillsborough

National Grid Ref: J2458

The Hillside, The Plough

Cashel-Eanen, *26 Comber Road, Hillsborough, Co Down, BT26 6LN.*
Modern comfortable country house. One mile historical village, five minutes M1/A1.
Open: All Year (not Xmas)
01846 682380 (also fax no)
Mrs Shannon
Rates fr: *£17.50*-**£20.00**.
Beds: 1D 1T 1S
Baths: 1 Ensuite 1 Private

Kilkeel

National Grid Ref: J3014

Kilmorey Arms Hotel, Cranfield House Hotel

Morne Abbey, *16 Greencastle Road, Kilkeel, Newry, Co Down, BT34 4DE.*
Country house on mixed farm. A warm welcome assured. **Open:** Easter to Oct
Grades: NITB Grade B
016937 62426 Mrs Shannon
Rates fr: *£17.00*-**£17.00**.
Beds: 1F 2D 2T
Baths: 3 Ensuite 2 Shared
(10)

Kilmorey Arms Hotel, *41 Greencastle Street, Kilkeel, Newry, Co Down, BT34 4BH.*
Long established hotel in centre of Kilkeel. Good food and accommodation.
Open: All Year **Grades:** NITB 2 St
016937 62220 / 62801 Mrs McMurray
Rates fr: *£22.50*-**£28.00**.
Baths: 27 Ensuite
(30)

Iona, *161 Newcastle Road, Kilkeel, Newry, Co Down, BT34 4NN.*
Comfortable Georgian farmhouse in the heart of the Mournes.
Open: All Year (not Xmas)
Grades: NITB Approv
016937 62586 Mr & Mrs Fitzpatrick
Rates fr: *£16.00*-**£20.00**.
Beds: 1F 1D 2S **Baths:** 2 Shared
(6)

Kircubbin

National Grid Ref: J6062

Wild Fowler, Grey Abbey

Lough View, *31 Rowreagh Road, Kircubbin, Newtownards, Co Down, BT22 1AS.*
Overlooking Strangford Lough. Near Kirkstown racecourse, golf club, Lough Cowey fishing.
Open: All Year **Grades:** NITB Approv
012477 38324 Mrs McCullough
Rates fr: *£15.00*-**£15.00**.
Beds: 1D 1T 1S
Baths: 2 Ensuite 2 Private 1 Shared

Moira

National Grid Ref: J1460

Ballycanal Manor, *2 Glenavy Road, Moira, Craigavon, Co Down, BT67 0LT.*
Grade A guesthouse. Family-run. Five minutes walk from Moira railway station. **Open:** All Year
01846 611923 Mrs Brown
Rates fr: *£22.50*-**£27.00**.
Beds: 5D
(20)

Mountstewart

National Grid Ref: J5569

Ballycastle House, *20 Mountstewart Road, Mountstewart, Newtownards, Co Down, BT22 2AL.*
200-year-old farmhouse modernised with every convenience and luxury.
Grades: NITB Approv
012477 88357 Mrs Deering
Rates fr: *£18.00*-**£21.00**.
Beds: 3D
Baths: 3 Ensuite
(1) (4)

Newcastle

National Grid Ref: J3731

Mariner Hotel, Percy French's, Burrendale Hotel, The Pavilion, McClennons

Grasmere, *16 Marguerite Park, Newcastle, Co Down, BT33 0PE.*
Modern bungalow in quiet residential area - beautiful surroundings and mountain views.
Open: All Year (not Xmas)
013967 26801 Mrs McCormick
Rates fr: *£15.00*-**£18.00**.
Beds: 1F 1D 1S
Baths: 1 Private 1 Shared
(2)

Beverley, *72 Tollymore Road, Newcastle, Co Down, BT33 0JN.*
Other self catering cottages available.
Open: All Year
013967 22018 Mrs McNeilly
Rates fr: *£17.50*-**£20.00**.
Beds: 1D
Baths: 1 Ensuite
(1)

Beach House, *22 Downs Road, Newcastle, Co Down, BT33 0AG.*
Victorian seaside guesthouse.
Open: All Year
013967 22345
Mrs Macauley
Rates fr: *£17.50*-**£22.50**.
Beds: 1F 1D 1T
Baths: 1 Shared
(2)

Homeleigh, *7 Slievemoyne Park, Newcastle, Co Down, BT33 0JD.*
Central heating, electric blankets.
Open: All Year (not Xmas)
013967 22305
Mrs McBride
Rates fr: *£13.00*-**£14.00**.
Beds: 1F 1D 1S
Baths: 1 Shared
(4) (2)

Castlebridge House, *2 Central Promenade, Newcastle, Co Down, BT33 0AB.*
Open: All Year (not Xmas)
Grades: NITB Approv
013967 23209
Mrs Lynch
Rates fr: *£14.00*-**£14.00**.
Beds: 2F 2D 1S
Baths: 1 Shared

Harbour House, *4 South Promenade, Kilkeel Road, Newcastle, Co Down, BT33 0EX.*
Family-run small inn at the foot of Slieve Donard Mountain.
Open: All Year
Grades: NITB Grade B
013967 23445 / 23535
Mr & Mrs Connolly
Rates fr: *£17.00*-**£25.00**.
Beds: 1F 3D
Baths: 4 Ensuite
(1)

Phoning Northern Ireland from the Republic? Dial 08 before the full area code.

Newry

National Grid Ref: J0826

Brass Monkey

Marymount, *Windsor Avenue, Newry, Co Down, BT34 1EG.*
Modern bungalow set in beautiful gardens. Walking distance of town centre.
Open: All Year (not Xmas)
Grades: NITB Approv
01693 61099
Mr & Mrs O'Hare
Rates fr: *£16.00*-**£16.00.**
Beds: 1D 2T
Baths: 1 Ensuite 1 Shared

Newtownards

National Grid Ref: J4874

Strangford Arms Hotel, Ballyharry Road House, Wildfowler Inn

Drumcree House, *18a Ballyblack Road East, Ballyreagh, Newtownards, Co Down, BT22 2AB.*
Modern country house, beautiful gardens. Convenient to many tourist attractions.
Open: All Year (not Xmas)
01247 862198
Mrs Forde
Rates fr: *£15.00*-**£17.50.**
Beds: 2D 1T
Baths: 1 Ensuite 1 Private 1 Shared

Ard Cuan, *3 Manse Road, Newtownards, Co Down, BT23 4TP.*
Victorian home in 1-acre garden.
Open: All Year (not Xmas)
Grades: NITB Approv
01247 811302
Mrs Kerr
Rates fr: *£15.00*-**£15.00.**
Beds: 1D 1T
Baths: 1 Shared

17 Ballyrogan Road, *Newtownards, Co Down, BT23 4ST.*
Open: All Year
01247 811693 Mrs McKibbin
Rates fr: *£17.50*-**£17.50.**
Beds: 1T 1S
(6)

Edenvale, *130 Portaferry Road, Newtownards, Co Down, BT22 2AJ.*
Beautifully restored Georgian farmhouse.
Open: All Year (not Xmas)
Grades: NITB Approv
01247 814881 Mrs Whyte
Rates fr: *£20.00*-**£25.00.**
Beds: 1F 1D 1T
Baths: 3 Ensuite
(6)

Portaferry

National Grid Ref: J5950

Portaferry Hotel, Scots Man, Cuan Inn

22 The Square, *Portaferry, Co Down, BT22 1LW.*
Centre of village. Convenient to all amenities.
Open: All Year (not Xmas)
01247 728412
Mrs Adair
Rates fr: *£13.00*-**£14.00.**
Beds: 1F 1D 1S
Baths: 1 Ensuite 1 Shared

Rathfriland

National Grid Ref: J1933

Rathglen Villa, *7 Hilltown Road, Rathfriland, Newry, Co Down, BT34 5NA.*
Country house. Panoramic views of the Mourne Mountains.
Open: Easter to Oct
Grades: NITB Grade A
018206 38090
Mrs Magine
Rates fr: *£15.00*-**£16.00.**
Beds: 1F 1D 2T
Baths: 1 Ensuite 1 Shared
(10)

Irish Grid References are for villages, towns and cities - *not* for individual houses.

Rostrevor

National Grid Ref: J1718

Top of the Town

Fir Trees, *16 Killowen Old Road, Rostrevor, Newry, Co Down, BT34 3AD.*
Modern bungalow overlooking Carlingford Lough. Private parking. Warm welcome.
Open: All Year **Grades:** NITB Approv
016937 38602 Mr & Mrs Donnan
Rates fr: *£15.00*-**£19.00**.
Beds: 2D 1T
Baths: 1 Ensuite 1 Shared
(4)

Forestbrook House, *11 Forestbrook Road, Rostrevor, Newry, Co Down, BT34 3BT.*
Listed C18th house in Fairy Glen.
Open: All Year
016937 38105 Mrs Henshaw
Rates fr: *£15.00*-**£16.00**.
Beds: 1F 2D 1T
Baths: 2 Private
(8)

Saintfield

National Grid Ref: J4059

The Hill, *Peartree Road, Saintfield, Ballynahinch, Co Down, BT24 7JY.*
Country farmhouse central to golfing, fishing and beautiful Mourne Mountains.
Open: All Year
01238 511330 Mrs Rice
Rates fr: *£12.50*-**£14.00**.
Beds: 1F 1D 1T
Baths: 1 Shared
(10)

Always telephone to get directions to the B&B - you will save time!

Temple

National Grid Ref: J3660

Laurel House, *99 Carryduff Road, Temple, Lisburn, Co Antrim, BT27 6YL.*
Comfortable farmhouse on main Belfast to Newcastle road, food recommended.
Open: All Year **Grades:** NITB Grade B
01846 638422 Mr Stephens
Rates fr: *£17.50*-**£25.00**.
Beds: 3F 1D 3T
Baths: 2 Shared
(3) (50)

Warrenpoint

National Grid Ref: J1418

Carlingford Bay Hotel

Lough View, *10 Osborne Promenade, Warrenpoint, Newry, Co Down, BT34 3NQ.*
Seaside setting overlooking views of Carlingford Lough, Cooley and Mourne Mountains.
Open: All Year (not Xmas)
Grades: NITB Approv
016937 73067 Mr McCabe
Rates fr: *£15.00*-**£17.50**.
Beds: 2D 1T
Baths: 3 Ensuite
(1) (50)

Whiterock

National Grid Ref: J5261

Balloo House, Daft Eddies

Tides Reach, *107 Whiterock Road, Whiterock, Killinchy, Newtownards, Co Down, BT23 6PU.*
On shores of Strangford Lough in Area of Outstanding Natural Beauty.
Open: All Year
Grades: NITB Approv
01238 541347 Mrs Booth
Rates fr: *£19.00*-**£20.00**.
Beds: 1D 2T
Baths: 2 Ensuite 1 Private
(5)

County Fermanagh

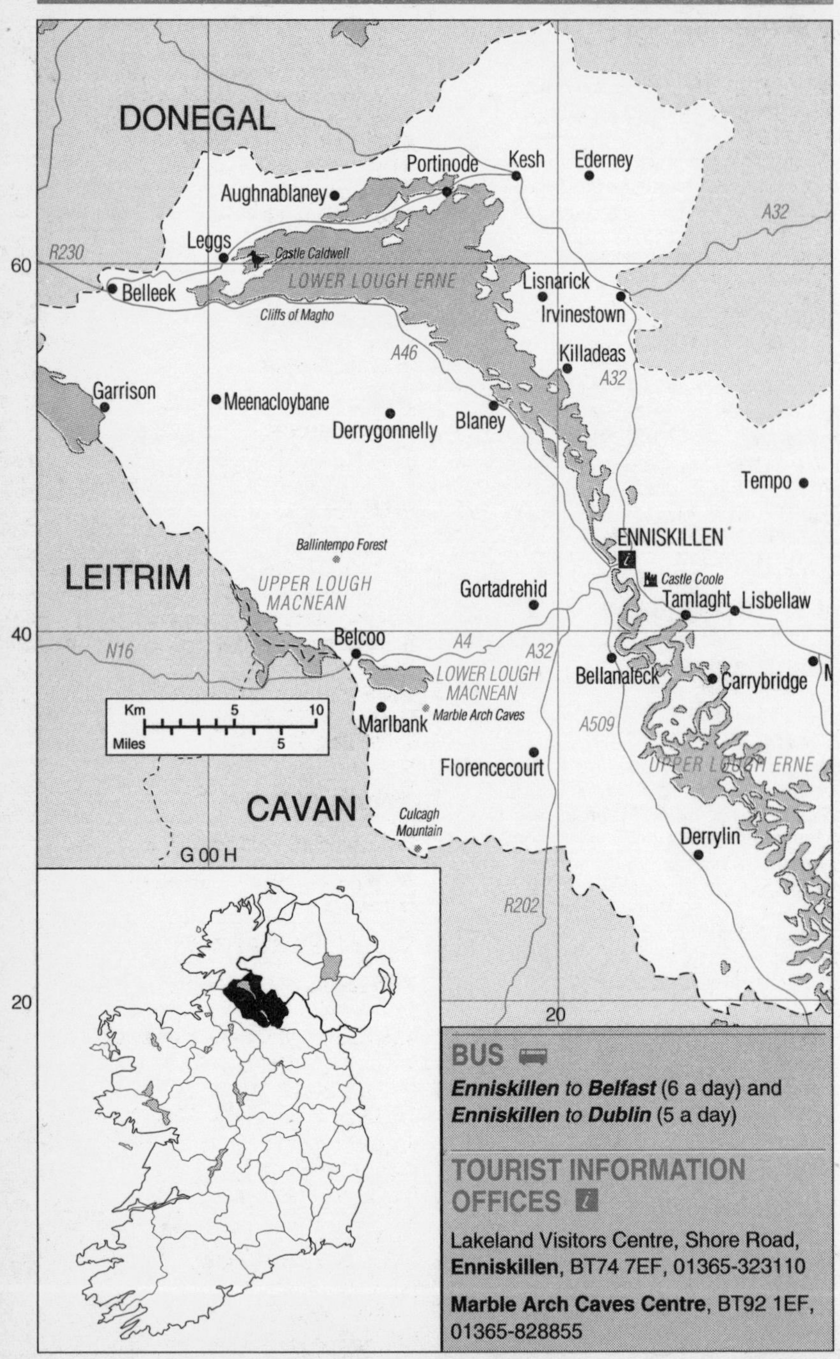

BUS

Enniskillen** to **Belfast (6 a day) and ***Enniskillen** to **Dublin*** (5 a day)

TOURIST INFORMATION OFFICES

Lakeland Visitors Centre, Shore Road, **Enniskillen**, BT74 7EF, 01365-323110

Marble Arch Caves Centre, BT92 1EF, 01365-828855

Aughnablaney

National Grid Ref: H0763

Drum Rush Lodge, Lough Erne Hotel

Manville House, *Aughnablaney, Letter, Kesh, Enniskillen, Co Fermanagh, BT93 2BF.*
Comfortable old house in beautiful setting overlooking Lough Erne, Sligo Hills.
Open: Easter to Oct
Grades: NITB Grade A
013656 31668 Mrs Graham
Rates fr: *£15.00*-**£16.00**.
Beds: 1F 2D 1T 1S **Baths:** 2 Shared
(5) (6)

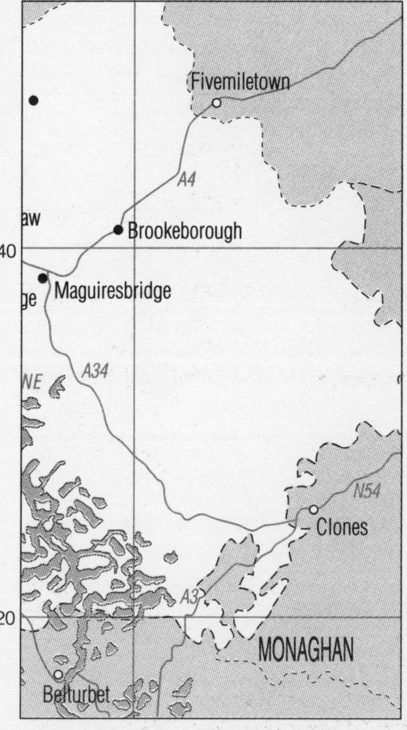

Always telephone to get directions to the B&B - you will save time!

Belcoo

National Grid Ref: H0838

Leo's Bar

Corralea Forest Lodge, *Corralea, Belcoo, Enniskillen, Co Fermanagh, BT93 5DZ.*
All rooms ensuite with patio doors.
Open: Mar to Sep
Grades: NITB Grade A
01365 386325
Mr & Mrs Catterall
Rates fr: *£18.00*-**£21.00**.
Beds: 1D 3T
Baths: 4 Ensuite
(4)

Bellanaleck

National Grid Ref: H2338

Sheeling

Hillcrest, *Bellanaleck, Enniskillen, Co Fermanagh, BT92 2BA.*
Modern bungalow situated in Bellanaleck Village five miles from Enniskillen (A509).
Open: All Year (not Xmas)
Grades: NITB Approv
01365 348392
Mrs Clements
Rates fr: *£14.00*-**£14.00**.
Beds: 1F 1D 1T
(6)

Belleek

National Grid Ref: G9459

Moohans Fiddlestone Inn

Moohans, *Fiddlestone, 15-17 Main Street, Belleek, Enniskillen, Co Fermanagh, BT93 5XX.*
Traditional Irish pub and guesthouse in the centre of Belleek, beside Belleek Pottery and River Erne.
Open: All Year
013656 58008
Mr McCann
Rates fr: *£18.00*-**£18.00**.
Beds: 1F 1D 3T
Baths: 5 Private
(1)

Blaney

National Grid Ref: H1553

Blaney Guest House, *Blaney Post Office, Blaney, Enniskillen, Co Fermanagh, BT93 7ER.*
Modern comfortable farmhouse. Lake Shore Road A46. Eight miles Enniskillen.
Open: Apr to Nov
Grades: NITB Approv
013656 41206 Mr & Mrs Robinson
Rates fr: *£15.00*-**£16.00.**
Beds: 3F 1D **Baths:** 3 Ensuite
(6)

Brookeborough

National Grid Ref: H3840

Norfolk House, *Killykeeran, Brookeborough, Enniskillen, Co Fermanagh, BT94 4AQ.*
Family-run country house in peaceful countryside. **Open:** All Year
013655 31681 Mrs Norton
Rates fr: *£14.00*-**£14.00.**
Beds: 1F 1D 1T 1S
Baths: 2 Ensuite 1 Shared

Carrybridge

National Grid Ref: H2937

Carrybridge Hotel

Carrybridge Hotel, *Carrybridge, Lisbellaw, Enniskillen, Co Fermanagh, BT94 5NG.*
Family-run hotel situated on the shores of Lough Erne.
Open: All Year (not Xmas)
01365 387148 Ms Clyde
Rates fr: *£25.00*-**£25.00.**
Beds: 1D 7T 4S **Baths:** 1 Shared

Aghnacarra House, *Carrybridge, Lisbellaw, Enniskillen, Co Fermanagh, BT94 5NF.*
Purpose-built guest house in picturesque sourroundings. Ideal base for tourists/anglers.
Open: All Year **Grades:** NITB Grade A
01365 387077 Mrs Ensor
Rates fr: *£14.00*-**£19.00.**
Beds: 2F 2D 2T
Baths: 2 Ensuite 2 Shared
(5) (10)

Wil-Mer Lodge, *Carrybridge Road, Carrybridge, Farnamullen, Enniskillen, Co Fermanagh, BT94 5EA.*
Modern accommodation in centre of lakeland.
Open: All Year (not Xmas)
01365 387045
Mrs Mulligan
Rates fr: *£13.00*-**£13.00.**
Beds: 1F 1D 1T
Baths: 2 Ensuite 2 Shared
(5)

Derrygonnelly

National Grid Ref: H1252

Meadow View, *Sandhill, Derrygonnelly, Enniskillen, Co Fermanagh, BT93 6ER.*
Modern, comfortable house. Peaceful setting.
Open: Easter to Sep
013656 41233 Mrs Wray
Rates fr: *£15.50*-**£15.50.**
Beds: 1F 2D
Baths: 2 Ensuite 1 Shared
(6)

Derrylin

National Grid Ref: H2728

Hollytree Farm, *Drumanybeg, Knockaraven PO, Derrylin, Enniskillen, Co Fermanagh, BT92 9QN.*
Comfortable working farm on the shores of Upper Lough Erne.
Open: All Year
Grades: NITB Approv
013657 48319 Mrs Whittendale
Rates fr: *£16.00*-**£16.00.**
Beds: 1F 2D **Baths:** 2 Ensuite 1 Shared

Ederney

National Grid Ref: H2264

Greenwood Lodge, *Erne Drive, Ederney, Kesh, Enniskillen, Co Fermanagh, BT93 0EF.*
Well-appointed guest house, good food, personal service. Ideal for touring.
Open: All Year (not Xmas)
Grades: NITB Grade B
013656 31366 Mrs McCord
Rates fr: *£13.00*-**£15.50.**
Beds: 4D 2T 1S
Baths: 3 Ensuite 2 Shared
(10)

Enniskillen

National Grid Ref: H2344

The Crows Nest, Mulligans, Franco's, Saddlers Restaurant

Abbeyville, *1 Willoughby Court, Portora, Enniskillen, Co Fermanagh, BT74 7EX.*
Modern B&B, convenient to National Trust properties, leisure facilities and Marble Arch Caves.
Open: All Year (not Xmas)
Grades: NITB Approv
01365 327033 Mrs McMahon
Rates fr: *£15.00*-**£20.00**.
Beds: 1F 2D 1T
Baths: 1 Ensuite 1 Shared
(12) (6)

Drumcoo House, *32 Cherryville, Cornagrade Road, Enniskillen, Co Fermanagh, BT74 4FY.*
Modern guest house in quiet suburbs of Enniskillen. Bait/tackle storage.
Open: All Year **Grades:** NITB Grade B
01365 326672 Mrs Farrell
Rates fr: *£15.00*-**£17.00**.
Beds: 2F 1D 1T 1S
Baths: 4 Ensuite 1 Shared
(8)

Belmore Court Motel, *Tempo Road, Enniskillen, Co Fermanagh, BT74 6HX.*
Modern 30 bedroom motel. Own private car park. Ideal touring centre.
Open: All Year (not Xmas)
Grades: NITB Approv
01365 326633 Fax no: 01365 326362
Mr McCartney
Rates fr: *£22.50*-**£40.00**.
Beds: 11F 13D 6T
Baths: 30 Ensuite
(30)

Mountview, *61 Irvinestown Road, Drumclay, Enniskillen, Co Fermanagh, BT74 6DN.*
House of character in large garden. Snooker room. Half mile to town.
Open: All Year (not Xmas)
Grades: NITB Grade A
01365 323147 Mrs McChesney
Rates fr: *£16.00*-**£18.00**.
Beds: 1F 2D
Baths: 2 Ensuite 1 Shared

Florencecourt

National Grid Ref: H1734

MacNean Bistro

The Crest, *Rossaa, Florencecourt, Enniskillen, Co Fermanagh, BT92 1BR.*
Modern farm bungalow overlooking Lough MacNean, four miles to Marble Arch Caves.
Open: Easter to Sep
Grades: NITB Approv
01365 348317 / 322727 Mrs Reid
Rates fr: *£14.00*-**£15.00**.
Beds: 2D 1T
Baths: 2 Ensuite 1 Shared
(4)

Gortadrehid

National Grid Ref: H1842

The Moorings

Riverside Farm, *Gortadrehid, Culkey Post Office, Enniskillen, Co Fermanagh, BT92 2FN.*
Riverside Farm is 2 miles west of Enniskillen, central for touring.
Open: All Year **Grades:** NITB Grade B
01365 322725 Mrs Fawcett
Rates fr: *£15.00*-**£16.00**.
Beds: 3F 1D 2T **Baths:** 1 Ensuite

Irvinestown

National Grid Ref: H2358

Drumshane Hotel, Mahons Hotel

Fletchers Farm, *Drumadravey, Irvinestown, Enniskillen, Co Fermanagh, BT94 1LQ.*
Farmhouse situated near country park and Fermanagh Lakes.
Open: All Year
013656 21351 Mrs Knox
Rates fr: *£14.00*-**£16.00**.
Beds: 1F 3D 1T
Baths: 4 Ensuite
(10)

The lowest **single** *rate is shown in* **bold.**

Kesh

National Grid Ref: H1863

Lough Erne Hotel, Drumshane Hotel, Drumrush Lodge, Riverside Restaurant

Ardess Craft Centre, *Ardess House, Kesh, Enniskillen, Co Fermanagh, BT93 1NX.*
Renovated Georgian rectory (1780) in secluded grounds near Lough Erne.
Open: All Year (not Xmas/New Year)
013656 31267 Mrs Pendry
Rates fr: *£11.25*-**£14.25**.
Beds: 3D 1T **Baths:** 4 Ensuite

Roscolban House, *Enniskillen Road, Kesh, Enniskillen, Co Fermanagh, BT93 1TF.*
Modern comfortable guesthouse. Quiet and conveniently situated with a friendly welcome.
Open: All Year (not Xmas)
013656 31096 Mrs Stronge
Rates fr: *£15.00*-**£17.50**.
Beds: 2F 1T
Baths: 2 Ensuite 1 Shared
(6)

Killadeas

National Grid Ref: H2054

The Waterfront, Manor House Hotel, Lough Erne Hotel

Brindley Guest House, *Tully, Killadeas, Enniskillen, Co Fermanagh, BT94 1RE.*
Brindley has fantastic views over the Lough. Ground floor rooms.
Open: All Year (not Xmas)
013656 28065 Mrs Flood
Rates fr: *£18.00*-**£21.00**.
Beds: 1F 3D 4T
Baths: 6 Ensuite 1 Shared
(14)

Always telephone to get directions to the B&B - you will save time!

The Beeches, *Killadeas, Enniskillen, Co Fermanagh, BT94 1NZ.*
Uninterrupted views over Lough Erne. Boating and fishing from grounds.
Open: All Year (not Xmas)
Grades: NITB Approv
013656 21557
Mr & Mrs Ternan
Rates fr: *£15.00*-**£18.00**.
Beds: 1F 2D
Baths: 2 Ensuite 1 Private

Rossfad House, *Killadeas, Enniskillen, Co Fermanagh, BT94 2LS.*
A Georgian country house on Lower Lough Erne. Lake views.
Open: Easter to Nov
Grades: NITB Approv
01365 388505 Mrs Williams
Rates fr: *£12.50*-**£15.00**.
Beds: 1F 1D 1T
Baths: 1 Ensuite 1 Private
(4)

Leggs

National Grid Ref: H0160

The Black Cat Cove

Dulrush House, *Leggs PO, Leggs, Enniskillen, Co Fermanagh, BT93 2AF.*
Modern comfortable farmhouse on the shores of Lough Erne.
Open: Easter to Sep
013656 58066
Mrs Gormley
Rates fr: *£14.00*-**£14.00**.
Beds: 1D 1T 1S

Lisbellaw

National Grid Ref: H3041

Glencar Bar

Clitana, *Leambreslin, Lisbellaw, Enniskillen, Co Fermanagh, BT94 5EX.*
Clitana is situated on main A4. Modern comfortable house in country area.
Open: All Year
Grades: NITB Approv
01365 387310 Mrs Beacom
Rates fr: *£13.15*-**£13.15**.
Beds: 1F 1D 1T
Baths: 2 Ensuite

Lisnarick

National Grid Ref: H1958

Drumshane Hotel

Rushindoo House, *378 Killadeas Road, Lisnarick, Co Fermanagh, BT94 1PS.*
Modern comfortable bungalow set in the heart of Fermanagh Lakeland.
Open: All Year
013656 21220 Mrs Anderson
Rates fr: *£15.00*-**£18.00**.
Beds: 1F 2D 2T
Baths: 5 Ensuite
(6)

Maguiresbridge

National Grid Ref: H3438

Killyhevlin Hotel

Derryvree House, *200 Belfast Road, Maguiresbridge, Enniskillen, Co Fermanagh, BT94.*
Comfortable farmhouse, convenient to Upper and Lower Lough Erne.
Open: All Year **Grades:** NITB Approv
01365 531251 Mr & Mrs Bothwell
Rates fr: *£12.50*-**£13.00**.
Beds: 1F 1D 1T

Meenacloybane

National Grid Ref: H0053

Heathergrove, *Meenacloybane, Garrison, Belleek, Co Fermanagh, BT93 4AT.*
Family-run farm guesthouse.
Open: All Year (not Xmas)
Grades: NITB Grade B
013656 58362 Mrs Duffy
Rates fr: *£12.50*-**£20.00**.
Beds: 3D 3T
Baths: 6 Ensuite

Portinode

National Grid Ref: H1364

Tudor Farm, *619 Boa Island Road, Portinode, Kesh, Enniskillen, Co Fermanagh, BT93 8AQ.*
Waterfront home - boat trips to Heritage sites - private jetty.
Open: Easter to Oct
Grades: NITB Approv
013656 31943 Mr McCreery
Rates fr: *£15.00*-**£18.00**.
Beds: 3F 4D 1T
Baths: 4 Ensuite 1 Private 1 Shared
(10)

Tamlaght

National Grid Ref: H2741

Mulligans

Dromard House, *Tamlaght, Enniskillen, Co Fermanagh, BT74 4HR.*
Outstanding situated B&B, lake & woodlands walks.
Open: All Year (not Xmas)
01365 387250 Mrs Weir
Rates fr: *£16.00*-**£20.00**.
Beds: 1F 2D 1T **Baths:** 4 Ensuite
(4)

Tempo

National Grid Ref: H3547

Milltown Manor Restaurant

The Forge, *43 Main Street, Tempo, Enniskillen, Co Fermanagh, BT94 3LU.*
Pleasant comfortable, family-run home. All leisure facilities minutes away. Central location. Good food.
Open: All Year **Grades:** NITB Approv
013655 41359 Mrs White
Rates fr: *£14.00*-**£14.00**.
Beds: 1F 1D 1T 1S
Baths: 3 Ensuite 1 Shared
(10)

County Londonderry

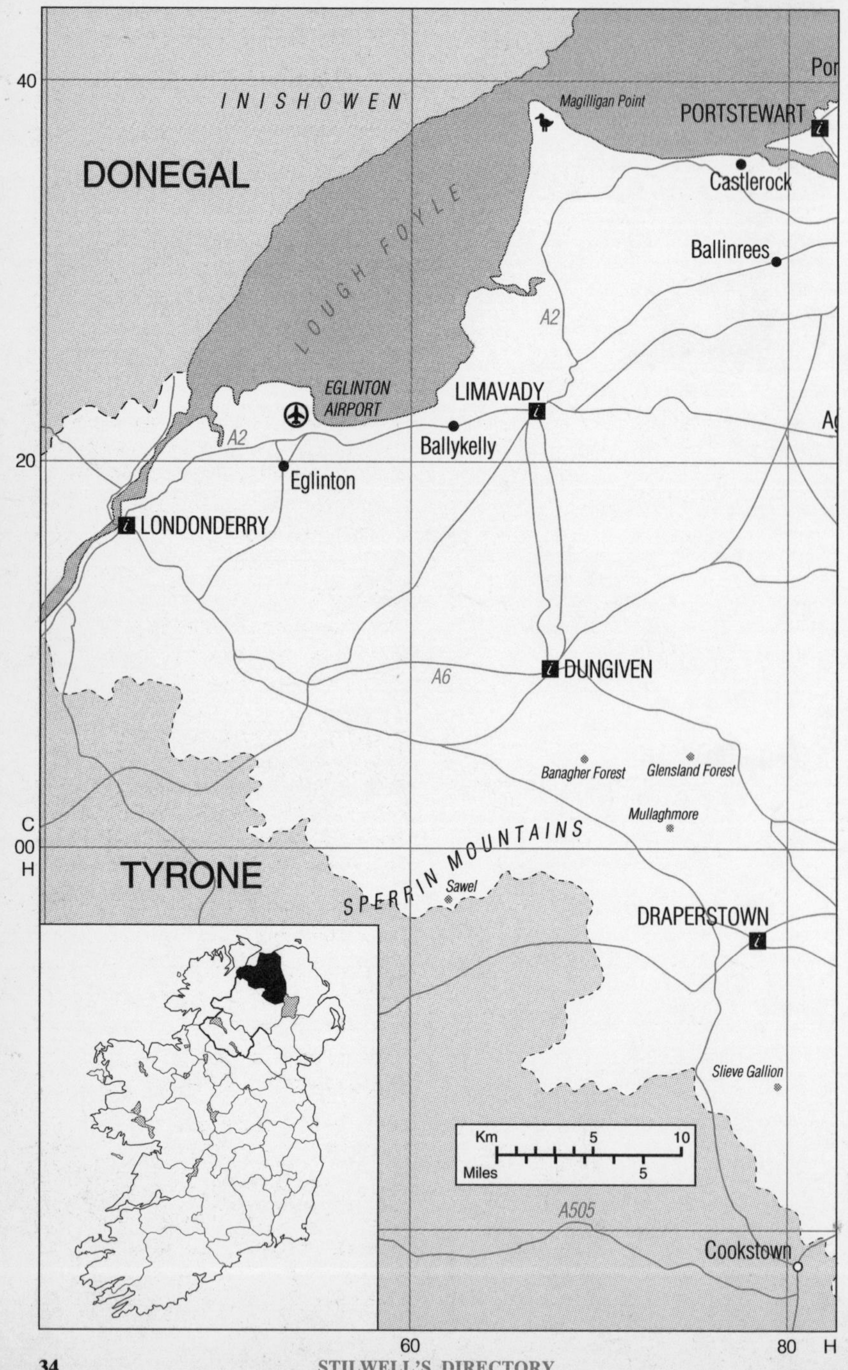

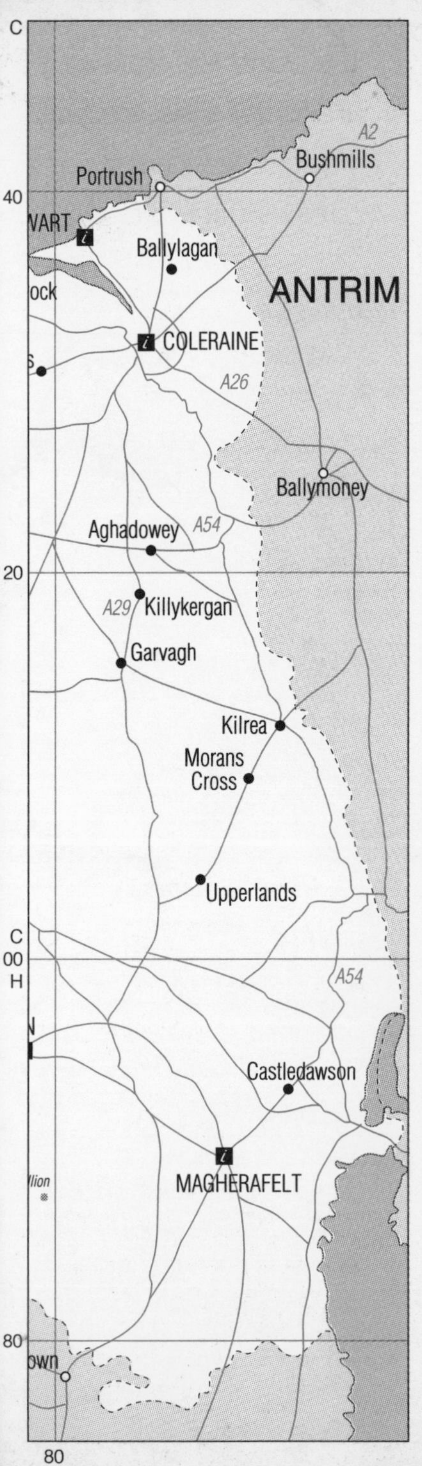

AIRPORTS

Eglinton Airport, tel. 01504 810784

AIR SERVICES & AIRLINES

Londonderry *to* ***Glasgow, Manchester***.

British Airways Express. From the Republic, tel. (freefone) 1800 626747. In Northern Ireland & the UK, tel. (local rate) 0345 222111.

Also **Jersey European** fly to many other UK mainland airports, flying from ***Londonderry*** via ***Belfast***, tel. 01232 457200

RAIL

Londonderry is at the end of the main line that leads to ***Belfast***, *via* ***Coleraine, Ballymoney, Ballymena*** *and* ***Antrim***.

Change at **Antrim** for **Belfast International Airport**.

BUS

Ulsterbuses run services from ***Londonderry*** to most large towns in Northern Ireland, tel 01504 262261.

TOURIST INFORMATION OFFICES

Benone Tourist Complex, 53 Benone Avenue, **Magilligan**, Limavady, BT49 0HA, (Easter to Oct), 01504-750555

Railway Road, **Coleraine**, (Open all year), 01265 44723

3 Chapel Road, **Dungiven**, Londonderry, BT47 4RS, (Easter to Oct), 01504-742074

Council Offices, 7 Connell Street, **Limavady**, BT49 0HA, 01504-722226

Bishop Street, **Londonderry**, BT48 6PW, 01504-267284

Council Offices, 43 Queens Avenue, **Magherafelt**, BT45 6BX, 01648-32151

Town Hall, The Crescent, **Portstewart**, BT55 7AB, (Easter to Oct), 01265-832286

Aghadowey

National Grid Ref: C2085

Greenhill House, *24 Greenhill Road, Aghadowey, Coleraine, Co Londonderry, BT51 4EU.*
Georgian country guest house recommended in international guides and recipient of awards.
Open: Mar to Oct
Grades: AA 5 Q, Prem Select
01265 868241
Fax no: 01265 868 241
Mrs Hegarty
Rates fr: *£24.00*-**£29.00**.
Beds: 2F 2D 2T
Baths: 6 Ensuite
(10)

Ballinrees

National Grid Ref: C7930

Rockmount, *241 Windyhill Road, Ballinrees, Coleraine, Co Londonderry, BT51 4JN.*
Large country house 3 miles Coleraine, 3 miles from beach, warm welcome.
Open: Easter to Sep
Grades: NITB Approv
01265 42914 Mrs Kerr
Rates fr: *£13.00*-**£13.00**.
Beds: 2D
Baths: 1 Shared

Ballykelly

National Grid Ref: C6221

Drummond Hotel, *481 Clooney Road, Ballykelly, Co Londonderry, BT49 9HP.*
Family-run hotel, excellent cuisine, friendly atmosphere, beautiful surrounding scenery.
Open: All Year
015047 22121 Mr Peoples
Rates fr: *£23.00*-**£25.00**.
Beds: 2F 13D 10T 2S
Baths: 25 Ensuite

The lowest **single** *rate is shown in* **bold.**

Irish Grid References are for villages, towns and cities - *not* for individual houses.

Ballylagan

National Grid Ref: C8736

Portrush Harbour Bar

Ballylagan House, *31 Ballylagan Road, Ballylagan, Coleraine, Co Londonderry, BT52 2PQ.*
Traditional farmhouse on working farm.
Open: All Year (not Xmas)
01265 822487 Mrs Lyons
Rates fr: *£16.00*.
Beds: 2F 3D
Baths: All Ensuite
(0) (8)

Castledawson

National Grid Ref: H9292

99 Old Town Road, *Castledawson, Magherafelt, Co Londonderry, BT45 8BZ.*
Modern bungalow in beautiful countryside convenient to towns.
Open: All Year
01648 468741
Mr & Mrs Buchanan
Rates fr: *£15.00*-**£15.00**.
Beds: 1F 2D
Baths: 1 Shared
(20)

Castlerock

National Grid Ref: C7736

Carneety House, *120 Mussenden Road, Castlerock, Coleraine, Co Londonderry, BT51 4TX.*
300-year-old farmhouse in beautiful countryside by the sea.
Open: All Year (not Xmas)
01265 848640 Mrs Henry
Rates fr: *£16.00*-**£17.00**.
Beds: 2D 1T
Baths: 1 Ensuite 1 Shared
(5) (4)

Coleraine

National Grid Ref: C8532

Bushtown House Hotel, Charly's Bistro, Salmon Leap

Coolbeg, *2e Grange Road, Coleraine, Co Londonderry, BT52 1NG.*
Open: All Year
Grades: NITB Approv
01265 44961 Mrs Chandler
Rates fr: *£18.00*-**£20.00**.
Beds: 1F 3T 1S
Baths: 3 Ensuite 2 Shared
(6)
Modern bungalow set in pleasant gardens on edge of town. TV and tea/coffee facilities. 2 ensuite bedrooms fully wheelchair accessible. Ideal for touring North Antrim coast. Royal Portrush and 4 other golf courses, fishing and riding nearby.

Cairndhu, *4 Cairn Court, Ballycairn Road, Coleraine, Co Londonderry, BT51 3BW.*
Personal attention, good food, in modern bungalow near Causeway Coast.
Open: All Year (not Xmas)
Grades: NITB Approv
01265 42854 Mr & Mrs Eyre
Rates fr: *£14.00*-**£16.00**.
Beds: 1D 1T
Baths: 1 Shared
(4)

Bellvue, *43 Greenhill Road, Blackhill, Coleraine, Co Londonderry, BT51 4EU.*
Listed building with magnificent views of North Antrim Hills.
Open: All Year
Grades: NITB Approv
01265 868797
Mrs Morrison
Rates fr: *£16.00*-**£16.00**.
Beds: 2D 1T
Baths: 1 Shared
(3) (6)

The lowest *double* rate per person is shown in *italics*.

Draperstown

National Grid Ref: H7894

Mary Dat's

Moyola View, *35 Tobermore Road, Draperstown, Magherafelt, Co Londonderry, BT45 7HJ.*
Modern comfortable house, overlooking the Moyola River and Sperrin Mountains.
Open: All Year
01648 28495
Mrs Flanagan
Rates fr: *£16.00*-**£16.00**.
Beds: 2D 1T
Baths: 1 Shared

Dungiven

National Grid Ref: C6809

Castle Inn

Bradagh, *132 Main Street, Dungiven, Londonderry, Co Londonderry, BT47 4LG.*
Detached town centre house.
Open: All Year (not Xmas)
Grades: NITB Approv
015047 41346
Mrs McMackens
Rates fr: *£13.50*-**£13.50**.
Beds: 1F 1T 1S
Baths: 2 Shared
(3)

Eglinton

National Grid Ref: C5220

Glen House Hotel, Happy Landing, Station Inn,The Villager

Greenan Farm, *25 Carmoney Road, Eglinton, Londonderry, BT47 3JJ.*
Panoramic view. Private parking. 6 miles Londonderry. Convenient Eglinton Airport.
Open: All Year (not Xmas)
Grades: NITB Approv
01504 810422
Mrs Montgomery
Rates fr: *£15.00*-**£15.00**.
Beds: 1F 1T

***Onchan,** 3 Ballygudden Road, Eglinton, Londonderry, BT47 3AD.*
Converted C17th church building in rural surroundings.
Open: All Year
01504 810377
Mrs McCauley
Rates fr: *£15.00*-**£15.00**.
Beds: 2D 1T
Baths: 1 Ensuite 1 Shared
(3) (6)

***Longfield Farm,** 132 Clooney Road, Eglinton, Londonderry, BT47 3DX.*
Comfortable, Victorian farmhouse. On A2 midway Derry - Limavady.
Open: Easter to Oct
01504 810210
Mrs Hunter
Rates fr: *£15.00*-**£17.00**.
Beds: 1F 2T
Baths: 1 Private 1 Shared
(3)

Garvagh

National Grid Ref: C8315

Imperial Hotel

***Imperial Hotel,** 38 Main Street, Garvagh, Coleraine, Co Londonderry, BT51 5AD.*
Open: All Year
012665 58218 / 58643
Mr Mullan
Rates fr: *£19.00*-**£24.00**.
Beds: 2F 5D 2T
Baths: 8 Ensuite 1 Shared
Quiet family hotel 15 miles from Causeway Coast, ideally situated base for golfing, fishing and walking holidays. Local walking club. Information available.

***Fairview,** 53 Grove Road, Garvagh, Coleraine, Co Londonderry, BT51 5NY.*
Modern comfortable farmhouse in quiet countryside. Near fishing, golfing, parachuting.
Open: All Year
012665 58240 Mr & Mrs Stewart
Rates fr: *£13.00*-**£13.00**.
Beds: 1F 1T
Baths: 1 Shared
(2) (10)

Killykergan

National Grid Ref: C8419

***Heathfield House,** 31 Drumcroon Road, Killykergan, Coleraine, Co Londonderry, BT51 4EB.*
Charming old farmhouse, large garden, ideal base Causeway Coast, Glens of Antrim.
Open: All Year
012665 58245 Mrs Torrens
Rates fr: *£16.00*-**£20.00**.
Beds: 1D 2T
Baths: 2 Ensuite 1 Private

Kilrea

National Grid Ref: C9212

***Beechmount,** 197 Drumagarner Road, Kilrea, Coleraine, Co Londonderry, BT51 5TP.*
Modern, comfortable country house, tranquil countryside, convenient to airports, ferries.
Open: All Year (not Xmas)
012665 40293 Mrs Palmer
Rates fr: *£17.50*-**£17.50**.
Beds: 2F 1S
Baths: 1 Shared
(0)

Limavady

National Grid Ref: C6722

***Whitehill,** 70 Ballyquin Road, Limavady, Co Londonderry, BT49 9EY.*
Modern farmhouse. Ideal base for touring Giants Causeway and Donegal.
Open: All Year
015047 22306 Mrs McCormick
Rates fr: *£16.00*-**£16.00**.
Beds: 1F 1D 1T
Baths: 2 Ensuite 1 Private
(2) (10)

Irish Grid References are for villages, towns and cities - *not* for individual houses.

Londonderry

National Grid Ref: C4316

Alexander Arms, Magnet Bar, Brendan's, Rafters, Schooners, Decks Bar

Groarty House, *62 Groarty Road, Londonderry, BT48 0JY.*
Open: All Year **Grades:** NITB Approv
01504 261403 Mrs Hyndman
Rates fr: *£13.50*-**£13.50**.
Beds: 1F 1D 1T
Baths: 1 Shared
Farmhouse set in the peace and tranquillity of the countryside, three miles from city centre, beautiful views overlooking town and Foyle Estuary. From Londonderry take Buncrana Road (A2), past Templemore Sports Complex, turn left after Texaco Station. Follow signs.

153 Culmore Road, *Londonderry, BT48 8JH.*
Was a farm house with lovely view Owlmore and Donegal Point.
Open: All Year
01504 352932 Mrs Wiley
Rates fr: *£11.00*-**£12.00**.
Beds: 1F 2D
Baths: 1 Shared
(6 mths) (5)

Abode, *21 Dunnwood Park, Victoria Road, Londonderry, BT47 2NN.*
Modern family country house. Good parking. Central heating. Golf nearby.
Open: All Year (not Xmas)
Grades: NITB Approv
01504 44564 Mrs Dunn
Rates fr: *£12.00*-**£12.00**.
Beds: 1F 1D 1T 1S
Baths: 3 Shared
(8)

Banks of the Faughan Motel, *69 Clooney Road, Londonderry, BT47 3PA.*
Modern motel. Ideal base for touring Derry, Donegal, North Antrim.
Open: All Year **Grades:** NITB Approv
01504 860242 (also fax no)
Mrs Gourley
Rates fr: *£16.00*-**£19.00**.
Beds: 1F 6D 4T 1S
Baths: 6 Ensuite 2 Shared

Braehead House, *22 Braehead Road, Londonderry, BT48 9XE.*
Georgian farmhouse situated on hill overlooking River Foyle and golf course. **Open:** Mar to Sep
Grades: NITB Approv
01504 263195 Mrs McKean
Rates fr: *£15.00*-**£15.00**.
Beds: 1F 1T 1S **Baths:** 1 Shared

No 10, *10 Crawford Square, Londonderry, BT48 7HR.*
Spacious, modernised Victorian house in unspoilt Victorian Square five minutes walk from city centre.
Open: All Year (not Xmas)
01504 265000 Mr & Mrs McGoldrick
Rates fr: *£15.00*-**£15.00**.
Beds: 3D 1T **Baths:** 4 Ensuite
(8)

Magherafelt

National Grid Ref: H8990

Laurel Villa, *60 Church Street, Magherafelt, Co Londonderry, BT45 6AW.*
Attractive Victorian townhouse. One hour maximum to anywhere in Northern Ireland. **Open:** All Year
01648 32238 Fax no: 01648 301459
Mrs Kielt
Rates fr: *£18.00*-**£18.00**.
Beds: 1F 1D 1T 2S
Baths: 1 Ensuite 1 Shared
(6)

Irish Grid References are for villages, towns and cities - *not* for individual houses.

Morans Cross

National Grid Ref: C9008

Beech Mount, *Killy Gullib, Morans Cross, Upperlands, Coleraine, Co Londonderry, BT51 5TP.*
Modern comfortable farmhouse in tranquil countryside convenient to airports, ferries.
Open: All Year
Grades: NITB Approv
01266 540293 Mrs Palmer
Rates fr: *£15.00*-**£15.00**.
Beds: 2F 1S
Baths: 1 Shared
(6)

Portstewart

National Grid Ref: C8137

Shannanaghs, Edgewater Hotel, Heathron Diner, Montague Arms, West Bay View Hotel, The York

Rockhaven, *17 Portrush Road, Portstewart, Co Londonderry, BT55 7DB.*
Open: All Year **Grades:** NITB Grade A
01265 833846
Mrs Mann
Rates fr: *£18.50*-**£20.00**.
Beds: 2F 2D 3T
Baths: 5 Ensuite 2 Shared
(8)
Comfortable, friendly, family home situated in quiet residential area overlooking golf course with uninterrupted views over sea to Donegal Hills. Ideal centre for golf, fishing, walking and touring North Coast area. Pleasant ten minute stroll to Port Stewart Promenade.

The lowest **single** *rate is shown in* **bold.**

The lowest *double* rate per person is shown in *italics*.

Strandeen, *63 Strand Road, Portstewart, Co Londonderry, BT55 7LU.*
Open: All Year (not Xmas)
Grades: NITB Approv
01265 833159
Mrs Caskey
Rates fr: *£20.00*-**£25.00**.
Beds: 3T **Baths:** 3 Ensuite
(5)
Enjoy peace and every comfort in a beautiful home furnished with original paintings, fresh flowers and good books. Stunning ocean views from pretty ensuite rooms. Traditional Irish breakfast overlooking the beach. Short walk to golf course or promenade. No smoking.

Oregan, *168 Station Road, Portstewart, Co Londonderry, BT55 7PU.*
Modern bungalow with luxurious accommodation.
Open: Feb to Nov
Grades: NITB Grade A
01265 832826 Mrs Anderson
Rates fr: *£18.00*-**£25.00**.
Beds: 3F 4D 2T
Baths: 8 Ensuite 1 Private
(8)

Atlantic House, *1 Atlantic Circle, Portstewart, Co Londonderry, .*
Open: June to end-Sept
Grades: ETB Approv
01265 836325 Mr Fletcher
Rates fr: *£15.00*-**£15.00**.
Beds: 3F 3D 2S
Baths: 3 Ensuite 1 Shared
(0) (10)
Town house close to the prom with sea views from all rooms, ensuite rooms available. You can even hear the waves crashing on the rocks.

Always telephone to get directions to the B&B - you will save time!

Akaroa, *75 The Promenade, Portstewart, Co Londonderry, BT55 7AF.*
Convenient to golf course. Very central for touring the Causeway Coast.
Open: All Year
Grades: NITB Approv
01265 832067 Miss McGarry
Rates fr: *£15.00*-**£15.00.**
Beds: 3T 3S
Baths: 3 Ensuite

Ard Na Tra, *9 Seaview Drive North, Portstewart, County Derry, BT55 7JY.*
Modern house with panoramic views beside golf course, beach and promenade.
Open: Mar to Oct
01265 832768 Mrs Brolly
Rates fr: *£16.00*-**£19.00.**
Beds: 1F 1D
Baths: 2 Ensuite
(2)

Chez Nous, *1 Victoria Terrace, Portstewart, Co Londonderry, BT55 7BA.*
Small B&B. Spectacular scenery, walking, golf, wonderful food all nearby.
Open: All Year
01265 832608 Mr & Mrs Nicholl
Rates fr: *£14.50*-**£14.50.**
Beds: 1F 1D 1S **Baths:** 1 Shared

Upperlands

National Grid Ref: C8704

Sperrin-View, *110a Drumbolg Road, Upperlands, Maghera, Co Londonderry, BT46 5UX.*
Modern comfortable farmhouse in tranquil countryside convenient to airports, ferries. **Open:** All Year
01266 822374 Mrs Crockett
Rates fr: *£17.00*-**£17.50.**
Beds: 2F 1S **Baths:** 1 Shared
(6)

County Tyrone

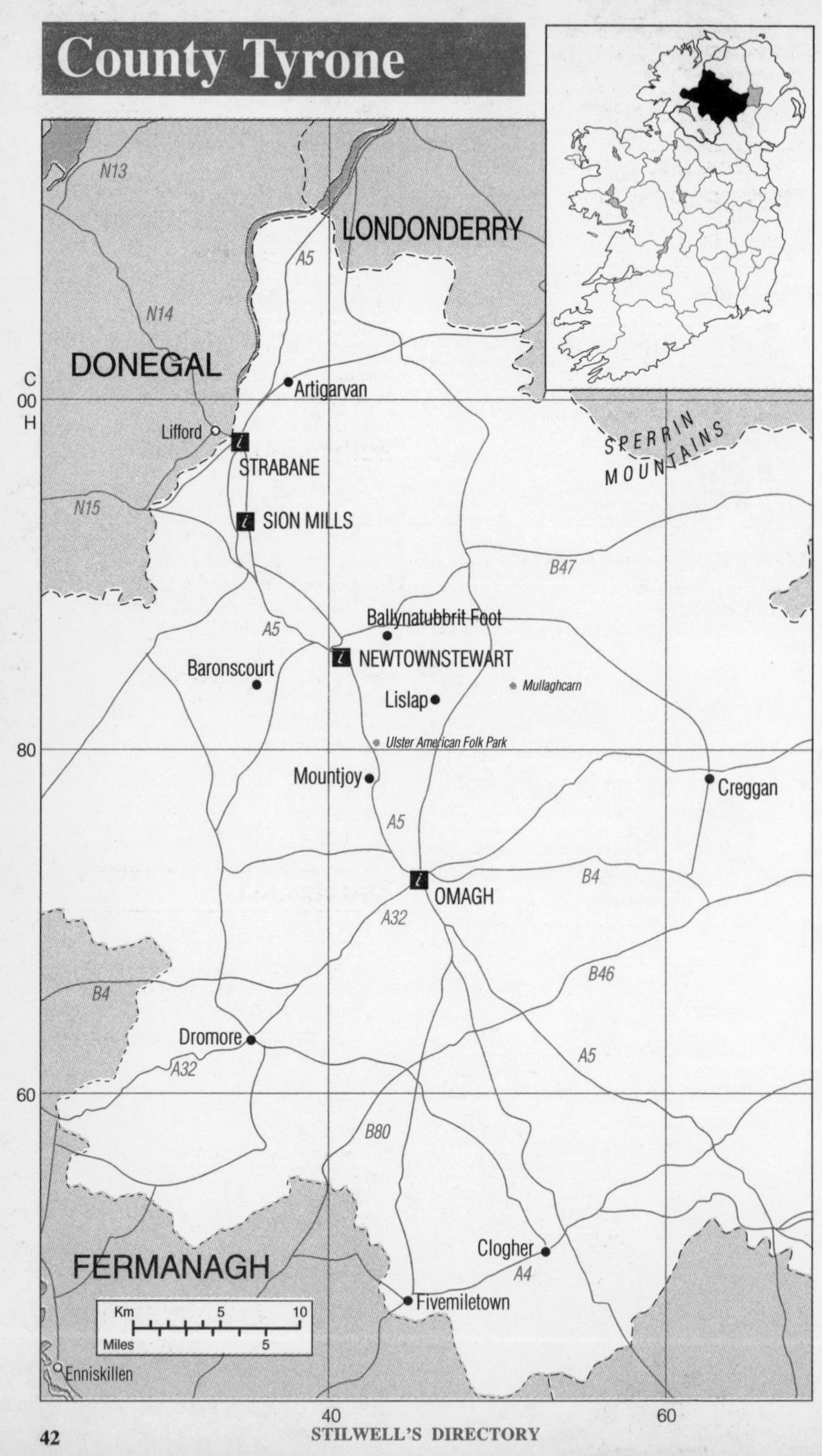

BUS

For information on buses from **Omagh**, tel **Ulsterbus** on 01662 242711

TOURIST INFORMATION OFFICES

Council Office, Burn Road, **Cookstown**, BT80 8DT, (Easter to Oct) 01648-766727

Killymabdy Tourist Information Centre Ballybawley Road, **Dungannon** BT70 1TF, 01868-767259

Main Street, **Newtownstewart**, Omagh, BT78 4BA, (Easter to Oct), 01662-661560

1 Market Street, **Omagh**, BT78 1EE, 01662-247831

Melmount Road, **Sion Mills**, Strabane, BT82 9EX, (Easter to Oct), 01662-658027

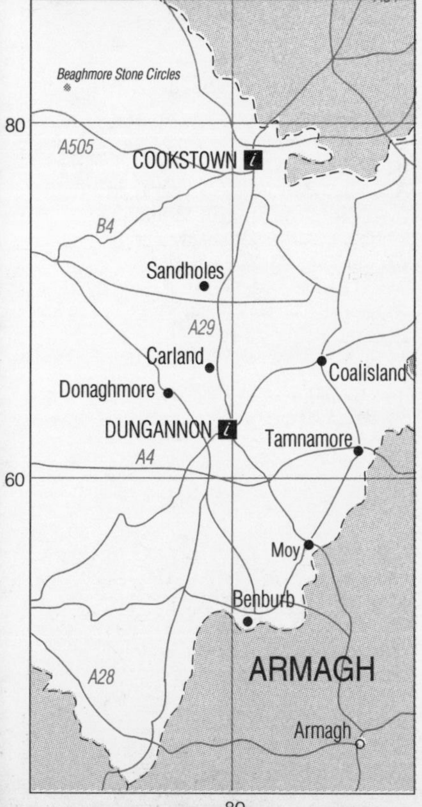

Artigarvan

National Grid Ref: C3800

Ballantines, *38 Leckpatrick Road, Artigarvan, Strabane, Co Tyrone, BT82 0HB.*
Comfortable country home. Visitors' lounge/conservatory. Panoramic views, spacious garden.
Open: All Year (not Xmas)
01504 882714
Mrs Ballentine
Rates fr: *£13.00*-**£13.00**.
Beds: 2D 1T 1S
Baths: 1 Private 1 Shared
(20)

Ballynatubbrit Foot

National Grid Ref: H4585

Mellon Country Inn

Woodbrook Farm, *21 Killymore Road, Ballynatubbrit Foot, Newtonstewart, Co Tyrone, BT78 4DT.*
Modern working farm.
Open: All Year (not Xmas)
Grades: NITB Approv
016626 61432
Mrs McFarland
Rates fr: *£12.50*-**£12.50**.
Beds: 1F 1D 1S
Baths: 1 Ensuite 1 Shared
(4) (6)

Baronscourt

National Grid Ref: H3583

Hunting Lodge Hotel, *Letterbin Road, Baronscourt, Newtownstewart, Omagh, Co Tyrone, BT78 4HR.*
Hotel in converted C19th schoolhouse.
Open: All Year
Grades: NITB 1 St
016626 61679 / 61122
Mr McKenna
Rates fr: *£25.00*-**£25.00**.
Beds: 2F 5D 7T
Baths: 14 Ensuite
(100)

The lowest **single** *rate is shown in* **bold.**

Benburb

National Grid Ref: H8152

Benburb Conference Centre, *10 Main Street, Benburb, Dungannon, Co Tyrone, BT71 7LA.*
Converted C19th stables and coachroom located in breathtaking grounds.
Open: All Year
01861 548170 Mrs Mullin
Rates fr: *£10.50*-**£12.00**.
Beds: 1F 2D 8T 17S
Baths: 4 Shared

Carland

National Grid Ref: H7866

Gables Restaurant

Creevagh Lodge, *Carland, Dungannon, Co Tyrone, BT70 3LQ.*
On hilltop overlooking typical Tyrone rolling countryside.
Open: All Year
Grades: NITB Grade A
01868 761342 / 761337
Mr & Mrs Nelson
Rates fr: *£14.50*-**£17.00**.
Beds: 3D 2T 5S
Baths: 3 Ensuite 3 Shared
(1) (20)

Clogher

National Grid Ref: H5442

Ratory, *Clogher, Co Tyrone, BT76 0UT.*
Victorian farmhouse on Fintona road. B168. One mile from village. Restful setting.
Open: All Year (not Xmas)
016625 48288 Mr & Mrs Johnston
Rates fr: *£15.00*-**£15.00**.
Beds: 1D
Baths: 1 Private
(6)

All details shown are as supplied by B&B owners in Autumn 1996.

Coalisland

National Grid Ref: H8465

McGirr's, *11 The Square, Coalisland, Dungannon, Co Tyrone, BT71 4LN.*
Modern licensed guest house combined with olde world public house.
Open: All Year **Grades:** NITB Approv
01868 747324 Mr McGirr
Rates fr: *£17.50*-**£15.00**.
Beds: 1F 5D 5S **Baths:** 11 Ensuite

Cookstown

National Grid Ref: H8177

Royal Hotel, *64 Coagh Street, Cookstown, Co Tyrone, BT80 8NG.*
Lively family-run hotel just two minutes from town centre.
Open: All Year **Grades:** NITB 1 St
016487 62224 Mrs Henry
Rates fr: *£25.00*-**£25.00**.
Beds: 3D 6T 1S **Baths:** 10 Ensuite

Creggan

National Grid Ref: H6278

Heatherlea, *222 Barony Road, Creggan, Omagh, Co Tyrone, BT79 9AQ.*
Accommodation set in a rural area in the foothills of the Sperrin Mountains. Halfway between Omagh and Cookstown. **Open:** All Year
016627 61555 Mr & Mrs Donaghy
Rates fr: *£12.50*-**£12.50**.
Beds: 1D 1T

Donaghmore

National Grid Ref: H7664

Top Bar Restaurant

Clanmor, *6 Church View, Donaghmore, Dungannon, Co Tyrone, BT70 3EY.*
Modern comfortable country house. Convenient to all the village amenities.
Open: All Year (not Xmas)
Grades: NITB Approv
01868 761410 Mr & Mrs Grimes
Rates fr: *£15.00*-**£16.00**.
Beds: 2D 1T **Baths:** 2 Shared
(6)

Dromore

National Grid Ref: H3462

Oakland House, *19 Holme Road, Dromore, Omagh, Co Tyrone, BT78 3BX.*
Split level bungalow situated main A4 Road from Omagh to Donegal.
Open: Easter to Oct
Grades: NITB Approv
01662 898305 Mrs Mills
Rates fr: *£12.50*-**£12.50**.
Beds: 1F 2D **Baths:** 1 Shared
(5)

Dungannon

National Grid Ref: H8761

Viscount Restaurant

Cohannon Inn Autolodge, *212 Ballynakelly Road, Cohannon, Tamnamore, Dungannon, Co Tyrone, BT71 6HJ.*
Quality and service at a convenient location, outstanding value.
Open: All Year **Grades:** NITB 2 St
01868 724488 Miss Bradley
Rates fr: *£19.95*-**£31.95**.
Beds: 20F 12D 18T **Baths:** 50 Ensuite

The Town House, *32 Northland Row, Dungannon, Co Tyrone, BT71 6AP.*
Large Victorian town house, short walk to all amenities.
Open: All Year **Grades:** NITB Approv
01868 723975 Mr & Mrs Cochrane
Rates fr: *£13.00*-**£14.00**.
Beds: 1F 1D 1T 3S
Baths: 2 Shared
(6)

Fivemiletown

National Grid Ref: H4448

Valley Hotel, Four Ways Hotel

Four Ways Hotel, *41-45 High Street, Fivemiletown, Co Tyrone, BT75 0LE.*
Excellent modern town centre hotel.
Open: All Year
013655 21260 Mr Armstrong
Rates fr: *£22.00*-**£25.00**.
Beds: 1F 7D 2T
(20)

Valley Villa, *92 Colebrook Road, Corcreevy, Fivemiletown, Co Tyrone, BT75 0SA.*
Collection and drop-off near Ulster Way. **Open:** All Year (not Xmas)
013655 21553 Mrs Malone
Rates fr: *£15.00*-**£15.00**.
Beds: 2D 1S **Baths:** 2 Ensuite
(5)

Lislap

National Grid Ref: H4782

Hillcrest Farm, *Lislap, Gortin Glen, Omagh, Co Tyrone, BT79 7UE.*
Comfortable farmhouse on working dairy farm. **Open:** All Year (not Xmas)
Grades: NITB Approv
016626 48284 Mrs McFarland
Rates fr: *£12.00*-**£13.00**.
Beds: 1F 1D **Baths:** 2 Shared
(6)

Mountjoy

National Grid Ref: H4277

Mellon Country Inn

Killynure, *95 Castletown Road, Mountjoy, Omagh, Co Tyrone, BT78 5RG.*
Two storey dwelling, comfortable, with great view from each window.
Open: All Year **Grades:** NITB Approv
016626 61482 Mrs Sterritt
Rates fr: *£12.50*-**£14.00**.
Beds: 1D 1S **Baths:** 2 Private

Moy

National Grid Ref: H8555

Stables Inn, Tomney's

Muleany House, *86 Gorestown Road, Moy, Dungannon, Co Tyrone, BT71 7EX.*
Family-run guest house just outside picturesque village. Home from home atmosphere.
Open: All Year (not Xmas)
Grades: NITB Grade A
01868 784183 Mr & Mrs Mullen
Rates fr: *£17.00*-**£20.00**.
Beds: 3F 3D 3T **Baths:** 9 Ensuite
(10)

Charlemont House, *4 The Square, Moy, Dungannon, Co Tyrone, BT71 7SG.*
Large Georgian residence. Situated in the Moy square beside all amenities.
Open: All Year
01868 784755 / 784 895
Fax no: 01868 784895
Mrs McNeice
Rates fr: *£12.50*-**£15.00**.
Beds: 3F 2D 1T 1S

Newtownstewart

National Grid Ref: H4085

Melcon Inn

Angler's Rest, *12 Killymore Road, Newtownstewart, Omagh, Co Tyrone, BT78 4DT.*
Modern comfortable bungalow in beautiful countryside beside Ulster Way. Salmon fishing. **Open:** All Year
016626 61167 / 61543
Mr & Mrs Campbell
Rates fr: *£14.00*-**£14.00**.
Beds: 1D 1T 1S **Baths:** 2 Private
(6) (5)

Sion Mills

National Grid Ref: H3493

Mellons Pub, Fir Trees Hotel

Bide-a-Wee, *181 Melmount Road, Sion Mills, Strabane, Co Tyrone, BT82 9LA.*
Friendly, comfortable Tudor house. Tennis court, swimming pool, mature gardens.
Open: All Year (not Xmas)
Grades: NITB Approv
016626 59571 Ms Fletcher
Rates fr: *£15.00*-**£15.00**.
Beds: 1F 1D 1T 1S
Baths: 2 Shared

Pay B&Bs by cash or cheque. Be prepared to pay up front for one night stays.

Irish Grid References are for villages, towns and cities - *not* for individual houses.

Strabane

National Grid Ref: H3497

Mill House Restaurant

Bowling Green House, *6 Bowling Green, Strabane, Co Tyrone, BT82 8AS.*
Open: All Year (not Xmas)
Grades: NITB Approv
01504 884787 Mr & Mrs Casey
Rates fr: *£13.00*-**£13.00**.
Beds: 1F 2D **Baths:** 1 Shared
(1) (30)
Spacious period residence centrally situated Strabane. TV, tea facilities. Central heating in all rooms. Car parking adjacent to house, evening meals arranged.

Mulvin Lodge, *117 Mulvin Road, Strabane, Co Tyrone, BT82 9JR.*
Farmhouse accommodation in quiet, relaxing surroundings with good home cooking.
Open: All Year
016626 58269 Mrs Smith
Rates fr: *£14.00*-**£14.00**.
Beds: 2D
Baths: 1 Private
(8)

Tamnamore

National Grid Ref: H8761

Cohannon Inn Autolodge, *212 Ballynakelly Road, Cohannon, Tamnamore, Dungannon, Co Tyrone, BT71 6HJ.*
Quality and service at a convenient location, outstanding value.
Open: All Year **Grades:** NITB 2 St
01868 724488 Miss Bradley
Rates fr: *£19.95*-**£31.95**.
Beds: 20F 12D 18T
Baths: 50 Ensuite

County Carlow

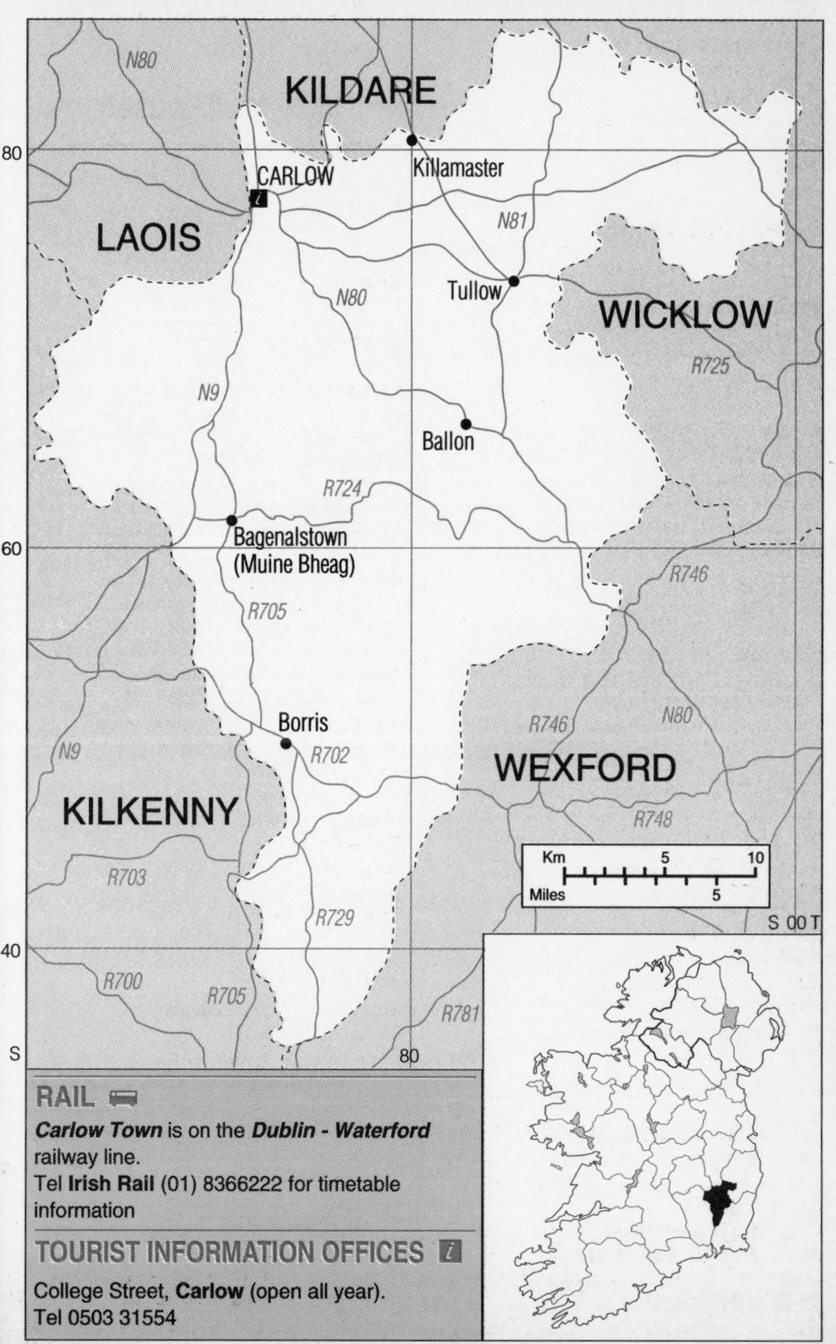

RAIL

Carlow Town is on the ***Dublin - Waterford*** railway line.
Tel **Irish Rail** (01) 8366222 for timetable information

TOURIST INFORMATION OFFICES

College Street, **Carlow** (open all year).
Tel 0503 31554

Bagenalstown (Muine Bheag)

National Grid Ref: S7162

St Martins, *6 Royal Oak Road, Bagenalstown (Muine Bheag), Co Carlow.*
Town house in quiet suburb.
Open: All Year
0503 21186 Mr Taylor
Rates fr: *IR£15.00*-**IR£17.00.**
Beds: 2D 2T
Baths: 1 Ensuite 1 Shared
(2) (1)

Lorum Old Rectory, *Bagenalstown (Muine Bheag), Co Carlow.*
Mid C19th rectory with a great reputation for hospitality and food.
Open: All Year (not Xmas)
Grades: BF Approv
0503 75282 Fax no: 0503 75455
Mrs Smith
Rates fr: *IR£25.00*-**IR£30.00.**
Beds: 1F 4D **Baths:** 5 Ensuite
(10)

Ballon

National Grid Ref: S8366

Sherwood Park House, *Kilbride, Ballon, Tullow, Carlow.*
Our early Georgian home is on a 100-acre mixed farm set in rolling parklands.
Open: All Year
Grades: AA 4 Q, Select
0503 59117 Mrs Owens
Rates fr: *IR£23.00*-**IR£28.00.**
Beds: 2F 1D 1T **Baths:** 4 Ensuite

Borris

National Grid Ref: S7350

Yreen Drake, O'Connors

Breen's, *Main Street, Borris, Co Carlow.*
Near Borris Castle, the residence of the MacMurrough family and Mount Leinster.
Open: All Year
0503 73231 Mrs Breen
Rates fr: *IR£13.50*-**IR£13.50.**
Beds: 1F 1D 1T 1S **Baths:** 1 Shared

Carlow

National Grid Ref: S7277

Reedys, The Little Owl, Pasta Paradise, Lane Court Hotel

Barrowville Town House, *Kilkenny Road, Carlow.*
Open: All Year
Grades: BF 3 St, AA 4 Q, RAC High Acclaim
0503 43324 Fax no: 0503 41953
Mr Dempsey
Rates fr: *IR£19.00*-**IR£20.00.**
Beds: 2F 2D 2T 1S
Baths: 7 Ensuite
(12) (12)
Regency townhouse in own grounds. Antique furnishings. Buffet and full Irish breakfast. Located on N9 beside N80. 3 minutes walk to town-centre, pubs and restaurants. Ideal for touring South-East, Midlands, Kilkenny, Glendalough. Ferries 1.5 hours. Credit cards accepted. German spoken!

Shalom, *Kilkenny Road, Carlow.*
All rooms TV. Warm welcome. Old world atmosphere. Family-run.
Open: All Year **Grades:** BF Approv
0503 31886 Mrs Kavanagh
Rates fr: *IR£16.00*-**IR£17.00.**
Beds: 5F 1D 2T 1S
Baths: 5 Ensuite 1 Shared

Westlow, *Green Lane, Dublin Road, Carlow.*
Modern comfortable family-run townhouse in Carlow town.
Open: All Year (not Xmas)
0503 43964 Mrs Farrell
Rates fr: *IR£15.00*-**IR£15.00.**
Beds: 2D 2T
Baths: 2 Ensuite 2 Shared
(6)

Phoning from outside the Republic?

Dial 00353 and omit the initial '0' of the area code.

Dolmen House, *Brownshill, Carlow.*
Rural panoramic setting, adjacent to world famous Brownshill Dolmen. Tea/coffee on arrival. Golf close by.
Open: Jul to Sep
Grades: BF Approv
0503 42444 Mrs Caesar
Rates fr: *IR£12.50*-**IR£13.50**.
Beds: 3D 1T 1S
(10)

Killamaster

National Grid Ref: S8080

Killamaster House, *Killamaster, Carlow.*
Luxury farm bungalow. Tea and scones on arrival. Tea-making facilities in bedrooms.
Open: Mar to Sep
0503 63654 (also fax no)
Mr & Mrs Walsh
Rates fr: *IR£15.00*-**IR£15.00**.
Beds: 3D 1T
Baths: All Ensuite

Tullow

National Grid Ref: S8573

Sherwood Park House, *Kilbride, Ballon, Tullow, Carlow.*
Timeless elegance, warm welcome awaits you at Sherwood.
Open: All Year
Grades: AA 4 Q
0503 59117
Fax no: 0503 59355
Mrs Owens
Rates fr: *IR£23.00*-**IR£28.00**.
Beds: 2F 1D 1T
Baths: 4 Ensuite

Laburnum Lodge, *Bundody Road, Tullow, Carlow.*
Elegant Georgian house. In large garden, walking distance town. Hairdryers.
Open: All Year
0503 51718 Mrs Byrne
Rates fr: *IR£16.00*-**IR£20.00**.
Beds: 2F 2D 2T
Baths: 6 Ensuite
(8)

County Cavan

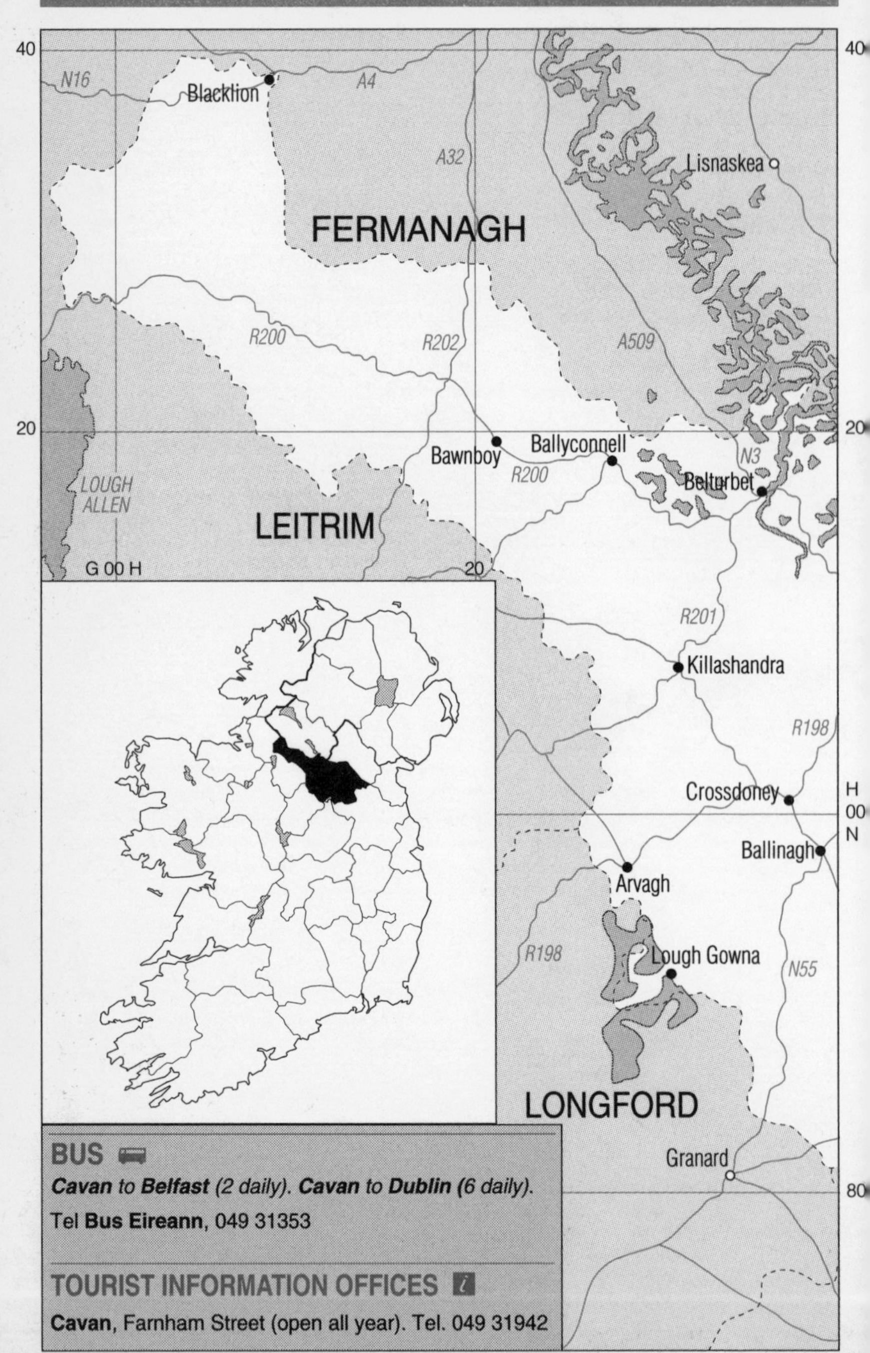

BUS

***Cavan** to **Belfast** (2 daily). **Cavan** to **Dublin** (6 daily).*

Tel **Bus Eireann**, 049 31353

TOURIST INFORMATION OFFICES

Cavan, Farnham Street (open all year). Tel. 049 31942

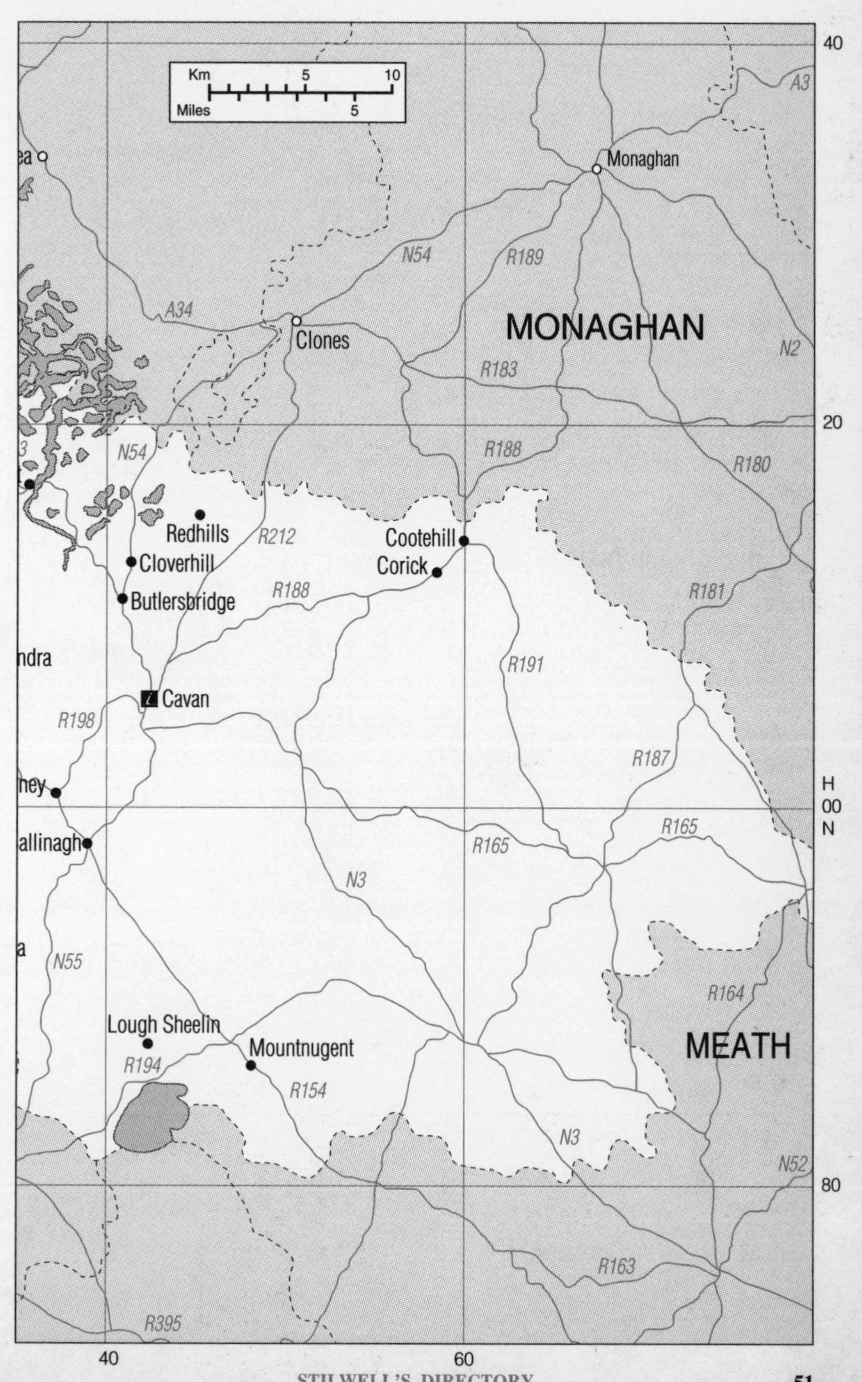
Km
5
10
Miles
5
Monaghan
N54
R189
A34
Clones
MONAGHAN
N2
R183
R188
R180
N54
Redhills
R212
Cootehill
Cloverhill
Corick
Butlersbridge
R188
R181
R191
Cavan
R198
R187
R165
R165
N3
N55
R164
Lough Sheelin
Mountnugent
MEATH
R194
R154
N3
N52
R163
R395
40
20
H
00
N
80
40
60

Arvagh

National Grid Ref: N2797

Farrangarve, *Arvagh, Cavan.*
Newly built, modern, very attractive, comfortable farmhouse in heart of Lakeland.
Open: Easter to Oct
Grades: BF Approv
049 35357 Mrs Barry
Rates fr: *IR£13.00*-**IR£13.00**.
Beds: 1D 2T 2S
Baths: 1 Ensuite 3 Shared

Ballinagh

National Grid Ref: N3998

Bavaria House, *Garrymore, Ballinagh, Cavan.*
Unique C19th Georgian house, beautiful garden, ideal touring base.
Open: Apr to Oct
Grades: BF Approv
049 37452 Mrs Kiebler
Rates fr: *IR£14.50*-**IR£19.50**.
Beds: 1D 2T
Baths: 1 Ensuite 1 Shared
(8) (5)

Ballyconnell

National Grid Ref: H2718

Anglers Rest, Bay Leaf

Anglers Rest, *Ballyconnell, Belturbet, Co Cavan.*
Super little inn, good food, we know all the best fishing spots.
Open: All Year
049 26391 Mr McGoldrick
Rates fr: *IR£15.00*-**IR£18.00**.
Beds: 7D
Baths: 7 Ensuite
(20)

Mount View, *Greaghrehen, Ballyconnell, Belturbet, Co Cavan.*
Modern two storey country home in the heart of the Lakelands.
Open: All Year
Grades: BF Approv
049 26456 Mrs Kelly
Rates fr: *IR£16.00*-**IR£18.00**.
Beds: 1F 1D 1T
Baths: 1 Ensuite 1 Shared
(5)

Woodford Lodge, *Ballyconnell, Belturbet, Co Cavan.*
Beautiful house in landscaped gardens with Japanese Koi ponds, beside the Woodford River.
Open: All Year
Grades: BF Approv
049 26198
Mrs Priest
Rates fr: *IR£17.50*-**IR£20.00**.
Beds: 2F 1T
Baths: 3 Ensuite
(1) (16)

Bawnboy

National Grid Ref: H2119

Cosgraves

The Keepers' Arms, *Bawnboy, Ballyconnell, Belturbet, Co Cavan.*
The charm of a restored coaching-house, situated in scenic, tranquil surroundings.
Open: All Year
049 23318
Mrs McKiernan
Rates fr: *IR£14.00*-**IR£18.00**.
Beds: 3D 1T
Baths: 2 Ensuite 2 Shared
(10)

Belturbet

National Grid Ref: H3617

Erne View House, *9 Bridge Street, Belturbet, Co Cavan.*
Town house.
Open: All Year (not Xmas)
Grades: BF Approv
049 22289
Mrs McGreevey
Rates fr: *IR£13.50*-**IR£16.00**.
Beds: 4 F
Baths: 2 Ensuite 2 Shared
(5)

Irish Grid References are for villages, towns and cities - *not* for individual houses.

Kilduff House, *Kilduff, Belturbet, Co Cavan.*
Large modern house overlooking Drumlin countryside 3 km from town.
Open: Apr to Nov
Grades: BF Approv
049 22452
Mrs Braiden
Rates fr: *IR£14.50*-**IR£14.50.**
Beds: 3T
Baths: 2 Shared
(12) (6)

Hilltop Farm, *Belturbet, Co Cavan.*
Modern comfortable farmhouse. Warm friendly atmosphere. Home cooking and baking.
Open: All Year (not Xmas)
049 22114
Mrs Dunne
Rates fr: *IR£13.00*-**IR£18.00.**
Beds: 6F 2D 2T
Baths: 8 Ensuite 2 Shared
(12)

Blacklion

National Grid Ref: H0838

Lough MacNean House, *Blacklion, Co Cavan.*
Georgian town house refurbished to modern standards retaining its elegant ambience. Award-winning restaurant 'Egon Ronay's'.
Open: All Year (not Xmas)
Grades: BF Approv
072 53022
Fax no: 072 53404
Rates fr: *IR£20.00*-**IR£22.00.**
Beds: 2F 6D 2T
Baths: 10 Ensuite
(8)

Butlersbridge

National Grid Ref: H4110

Ford House, *Deredis, Butlersbridge, Cavan.*
Modern farmhouse in scenic area over-looking River Annalee; angler's paradise.
Open: May to Nov
049 31427 Mrs Mundy
Rates fr: *IR£14.00*-**IR£16.00.**
Beds: 1F 2D 2T 1S
Baths: 2 Ensuite 1 Private
(8)

Cavan

National Grid Ref: H4205

Old Priory Restaurant

Oakdene, *29 Cathedral Road, Cavan.*
Semi-detached town house set in picturesque gardens.
Open: All Year (not Xmas)
Grades: BF Approv
049 31698
Mrs Gaffney
Rates fr: *IR£14.50*-**IR£19.00.**
Beds: 1F 2D 1T 1S
Baths: 1 Ensuite 1 Shared

Cloverhill

National Grid Ref: H4114

Fortview House, *Drumbran, Cloverhill, Belturbet, Co Cavan.*
Excellent home cooking, farm walks, first-class fishing, free supper, home from home.
Open: Easter to Oct
049 38185 Mrs Smith
Rates fr: *IR£13.00*-**IR£13.00.**
Beds: 3F 1D 2T
Baths: 1 Private 2 Shared

Cootehill

National Grid Ref: H6014

White Horse Hotel, Riverside House

Riverside House, *Cootehill, Co Cavan.*
Victorian house set among mature trees overlooking river. Four ensuite.
Open: All Year (not Xmas)
049 52150
Fax no: 049 52100
Mrs Smith
Rates fr: *IR£15.00*-**IR£20.00.**
Beds: 2F 2D 2T
Baths: 4 Ensuite 3 Shared
(8)

The lowest **single** *rate is shown in* **bold.**

The lowest *double* rate per person is shown in *italics*.

Knockvilla, *Station Road, Cootehill, Co Cavan.*
Semi-detached house, gardens front and back. Five minutes walk to town.
Open: All Year (not Xmas)
Grades: BF Approv
049 52203 Mrs Coyel
Rates fr: *IR£13.50*-**IR£15.00**.
Beds: 1F 2D 1T 1S
Baths: 1 Ensuite 1 Shared
(4)

Corick

National Grid Ref: H5712

Drum Moir House, *Corick, Cootehill, Co Cavan.*
Modern comfortable home in beautiful countryside. Visit mushroom farm.
Open: Easter to Oct
Grades: BF Approv
049 53044 Mrs McPhillips
Rates fr: *IR£14.00*-**IR£14.00**.
Beds: 1F 2D 1T 2S
Baths: 2 Ensuite 2 Shared
(10)

Crossdoney

National Grid Ref: H3701

Casey's

Lisnamandra, *Crossdoney, Cavan.*
C17th award-winning farmhouse, famous for its breakfast menu.
Open: Easter to Oct
049 37196 Fax no: 049 37111
Mr & Mrs Neill
Rates fr: *IR£14.50*-**IR£14.50**.
Beds: 4F 1D 1S
Baths: 4 Ensuite 1 Private 3 Shared
(12)

All rates are subject to alteration at the owners' discretion.

Killashandra

National Grid Ref: H3107

Clooneen House, *Clooneen, Killashandra, Cavan.*
Friendly home. Killashandra 2 km. Fishing, golf, horse-riding nearby. Dublin 2 hours.
Open: Easter to Oct
049 34342 (also fax no)
Mrs O'Reilly
Rates fr: *IR£13.00*-**IR£18.00**.
Beds: 2F 1D 1T
Baths: 2 Ensuite 2 Shared

Snakiel House, *Snakiel, Killashandra, Cavan.*
Modern, comfortable house in scenic area, overlooking lake.
Open: All Year (not Xmas)
049 34392
Mrs McGearty
Rates fr: *IR£15.00*-**IR£16.50**.
Beds: 1F 2T
Baths: 3 Ensuite

Drumbo House, *Killashandra, Cavan.*
Modern farmhouse, set in traditional rural scenic countryside.
Open: All Year (not Xmas)
Grades: BF Approv
049 34356
Mr & Mrs Burns
Rates fr: *IR£IR12.50*-**IR£IR12.50**.
Beds: 1F 2D 1T
Baths: 2 Ensuite 3 Shared
(8)

Lough Gowna

National Grid Ref: H3092

Lake View House, *Cornamuckla, Lough Gowna, Cavan.*
Modern bungalow overlooking lakes and river, in beautiful countryside.
Open: All Year
043 83233
Mrs Smith
Rates fr: *IR£13.00*-**IR£14.00**.
Beds: 1D 2T 1S
Baths: 2 Shared
(3)

High season, bank holidays and special events mean low availability *anywhere.*

Lough Sheelin

National Grid Ref: N4287

Crover House Hotel

Leggetts' Guest House, *Sheelin Pier, Kilnahard, Ballyheelan, Lough Sheelin, Kilnaleck, Kells, Co Meath.*
Newly refurbished rooms, all ensuite. Picturesque setting overlooking Lough Sheelin. **Open:** Easter to Oct
Grades: BF Approv
049 36741 / 36373 Ms Leggetts
Rates fr: *IR£13.50*-**IR£15.00**.
Beds: 1F 1D 4S **Baths:** 6 Ensuite

On the border? Look at the neighbouring county, too

Mountnugent

National Grid Ref: N4886

Ross House

Ross Castle, *Mountnugent, Kells, Co Meath.*
Open: Easter to Nov
049 40218 / 40237 Mrs Liebe-Harkort
Rates fr: *IR£18.00*-**IR£23.00**.
Beds: 3F 1D 1S
Baths: 3 Ensuite 2 Shared
(12)
Find exclusive retreat in C16th castle. The trace of ancient history combined with modern comfort. In four double rooms ensuite. Magnificent view over Lough Sheelin. Scenic background of Orvin and Sabrina's love story. Boats, tennis, horse-riding. Sauna and jacuzzi in neighbouring Ross House.

Redhills

National Grid Ref: H4416

Hillside, *Shannon Wood, Redhills, Cavan,*
Hillside ensures you comfort. Friendly, fishing, golfing and horse-riding locally.
Open: Apr to Nov **Grades:** BF Approv
047 55125 Mrs Smith
Rates fr: *IR£15.00*-**IR£18.00**.
Beds: 1F 1D 1T 1S
Baths: 1 Ensuite 2 Shared

County Clare

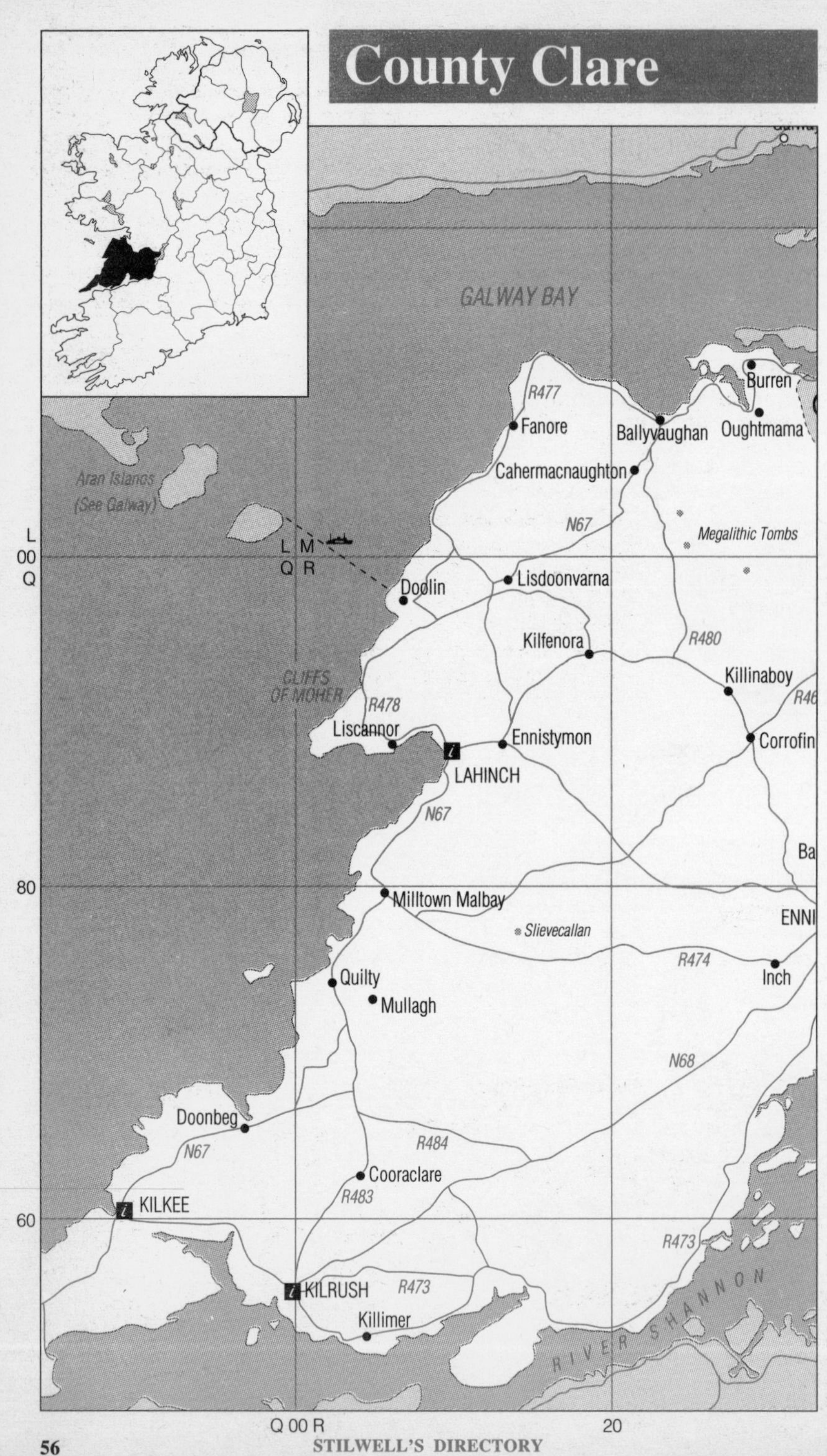

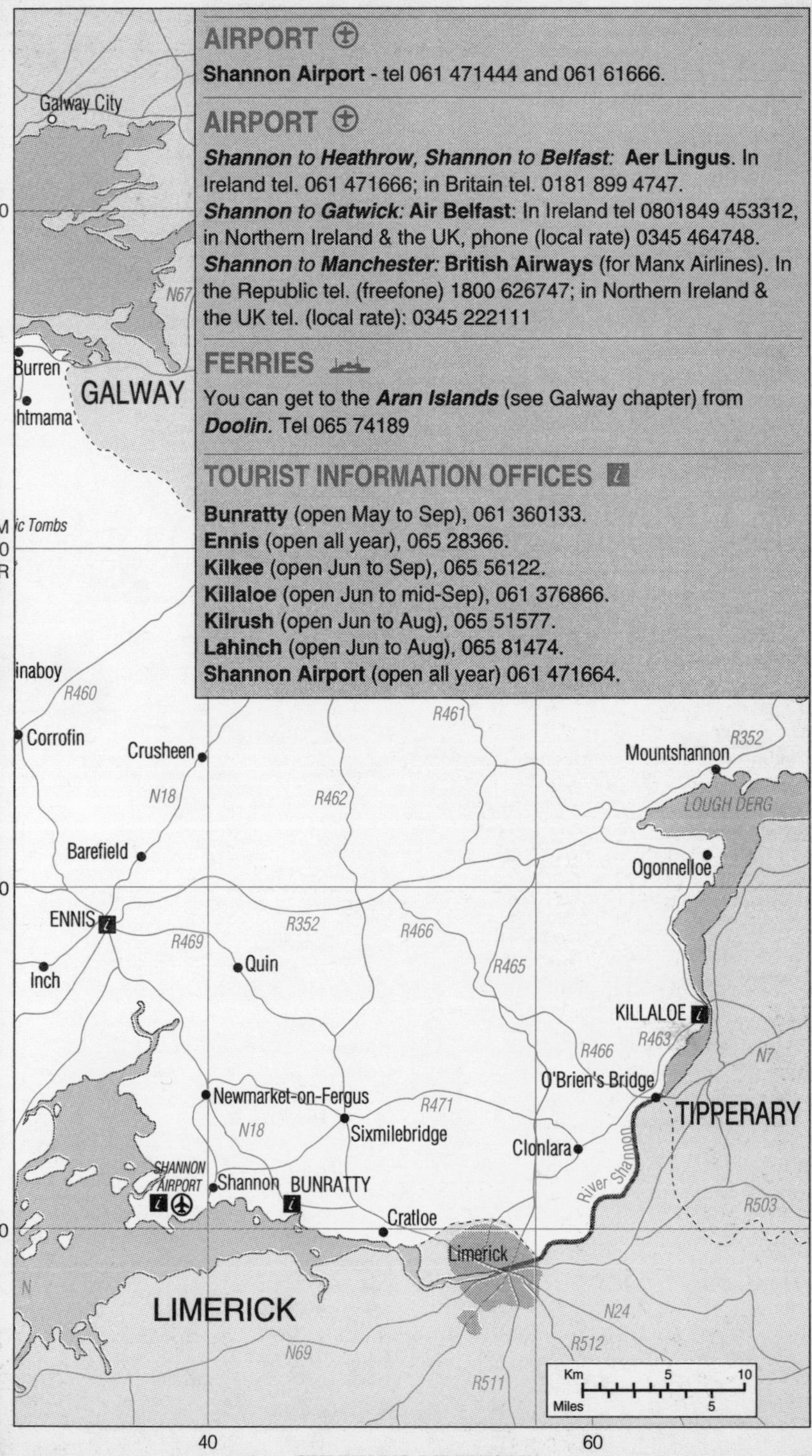

AIRPORT

Shannon Airport - tel 061 471444 and 061 61666.

AIRPORT

***Shannon** to **Heathrow**, **Shannon** to **Belfast**:* **Aer Lingus**. In Ireland tel. 061 471666; in Britain tel. 0181 899 4747.
***Shannon** to **Gatwick**:* **Air Belfast**: In Ireland tel 0801849 453312, in Northern Ireland & the UK, phone (local rate) 0345 464748.
***Shannon** to **Manchester**:* **British Airways** (for Manx Airlines). In the Republic tel. (freefone) 1800 626747; in Northern Ireland & the UK tel. (local rate): 0345 222111

FERRIES

You can get to the ***Aran Islands*** (see Galway chapter) from ***Doolin***. Tel 065 74189

TOURIST INFORMATION OFFICES

Bunratty (open May to Sep), 061 360133.
Ennis (open all year), 065 28366.
Kilkee (open Jun to Sep), 065 56122.
Killaloe (open Jun to mid-Sep), 061 376866.
Kilrush (open Jun to Aug), 065 51577.
Lahinch (open Jun to Aug), 065 81474.
Shannon Airport (open all year) 061 471664.

Ballyvaughan

National Grid Ref: M2308

Monks Bar

***Rockhaven,** Cahermacnaughton, Ballyvaughan, Galway.*
Open: Apr to Sep
Grades: BF Approv
065 74454 Mrs McDonagh
Rates fr: *IR£15.00*-**IR£18.00**.
Beds: 1F 1D 1T
Baths: 2 Ensuite 1 Private
Modern comfortable farmhouse in the Burren. Signposted 1 km off N67, 7 km south of Ballyvaughan, 7 km north of Lisdoonvarna. Home baking. Warm welcome. Peat fires. Tea/coffee on arrival.

***Rusheen Lodge,** Knocknagrough, Ballyvaughan, Galway.*
This modern guest house boasts RAC awards for Best Guest House. Also gardens.
Open: Feb to Oct
Grades: BF 4 St, AA 4 Q, RAC High Acclaim
065 77092
Fax no: 065 77152 Ms McGann
Rates fr: *IR£20.00*-**IR£25.00**.
Beds: 3D 3T
Baths: 6 Ensuite
(2) (8)

***Oceanville,** Coast Road, Ballyvaughan, Galway.*
Open: Easter to Oct
Grades: BF Approv
065 77051 Mrs Martyn
Rates fr: *IR£16.00*.
Beds: 2D 3T
Baths: 5 Ensuite
(6)
Modern accommodation with panoramic views of Galway Bay and the Burren. Within walking distance of bars and restaurants on the seafront.

Barefield

National Grid Ref: R3683

***Carraig Mhure,** Barefield, Ennis, Co Clare.*
Warm welcome always, spring water, turf fires, in beautiful countryside.
Open: All Year (not Xmas)
Grades: BF Approv, AA 3 Q
065 27106 Mrs Morris
Rates fr: *IR£12.00*-**IR£15.00**.
Beds: 1F 2D 1T 1S
Baths: 4 Ensuite 1 Private
(6)

***Ashleigh,** Cregard, Barefield, Ennis, Co Clare.*
Modern B&B 5 km from Ennis. Close to cliffs, banquets, golf and fishing.
Open: Easter to Nov
065 27187
Mrs Meaney
Rates fr: *IR£16.00*-**IR£21.00**.
Beds: 3F 2D
Baths: 5 Ensuite
(10)

Bunratty

National Grid Ref: R4561

Durty Nelly's, Jibber McGees, Bunratty Castle Hotel

***Rockfield House,** Hill Road, Bunratty, Ennis, Co Clare.*
Bungalow overlooking River Shannon beside castle and Durty Nelly's.
Open: All Year (not Xmas)
Grades: BF Approv
061 364391 (also fax no)
Mrs Garry
Rates fr: *IR£16.00*-**IR£25.00**.
Beds: 1F 2D 3T
Baths: 6 Ensuite
(10)

***Innisfree,** Bunratty East, Bunratty, Ennis, Co Clare.*
Comfortable, friendly, ground floor rooms, magnificent view close to castle.
Open: All Year (not Xmas)
061 369773
Mrs McCarthy
Rates fr: *IR£15.00*-**IR£18.00**.
Beds: 1F 1D 3T
Baths: 4 Ensuite 1 Shared
(6)

Bunratty Woods House, *Bunratty, Ennis, Co Clare.*
Two minutes from Bunratty Castle and Folk Park.
Open: All Year
Grades: BF Approv
061 369689
Mrs O'Donovan
Rates fr: *IR£16.50* -**IR£25.00** .
Beds: 3F 2D 1T
Baths: 6 Ensuite
(12) (20)

Burren

National Grid Ref: M2812

Linnanes, Monks Bar, Partners, White Thorn

Burren Grove, Dooneen, *Burren, Galway.*
Open: Jun to Sep
Grades: BF Approv
065 78081
Mr & Mrs Shannon
Rates fr: *IR£15.00*-**IR£20.00**.
Beds: 1F 2D
Baths: 3 Ensuite
Modern bungalow situated on hilltop with view of sea. Situated on N67 between Kinvara and Ballyvaughan. Ideal for touring the Burren. Mature orchard to front.

Burren Oaks, *Oughtmama, Bellharbour, Burren, Galway, Co Clare,*
Modern farmhouse located between Ballyvaughan and Kinvara .
Open: Apr to Sep
Grades: BF Approv
065 78043
Mr & Mrs Flaherty
Rates fr: *IR£16.00*-**IR£21.00**.
Beds: 1F 3T
Baths: 4 Ensuite
(8)

Phoning from outside the Republic?
Dial 00353 and omit the initial '0' of the area code.

The lowest *double* rate per person is shown in *italics*.

Cahermacnaughton

National Grid Ref: M2304

Rockhaven, *Cahermacnaughton, Ballyvaughan, Galway.*
Open: Apr to Sep
Grades: BF Approv
065 74454
Mrs McDonagh
Rates fr: *IR£15.00*-**IR£18.00.**
Beds: 1F 1D 1T
Baths: 2 Ensuite 1 Private
Modern comfortable farmhouse in the Burren. Signposted 1 km off N67, 7 km south of Ballyvaughan, 7 km north of Lisdoonvarna. Home baking. Warm welcome. Peat fires. Tea/coffee on arrival.

Clonlara

National Grid Ref: R6263

Shemond House, *Killaloe Road, Clonlara, Limerick.*
Modern dormer bungalow, five minutes Limerick City, 25 minutes Shannon Airport.
Open: Mar to Oct
Grades: BF Approv
061 343767 Mrs Devine
Rates fr: *IR£16.00*-**IR£21.00**.
Beds: 2F 2D 2T 1S
Baths: 5 Ensuite 1 Shared
(8)

Cooraclare

National Grid Ref: R0462

Tubridy House, *Cooraclare, Kilrush, Co Clare.*
On tourist route between Kerry/Galway, Tennis court, fishing tackle shed, private carpark. Home cooking.
Open: Easter to Dec
Grades: AA 3 St
065 59246 / 59033 Ms Tubridy
Rates fr: *IR£15.00*-**IR£22.00**.
Beds: 6F 3T **Baths:** 9 Ensuite
(50)

Corrofin

National Grid Ref: R2888

Riverside House, *The Bridge, Corrofin, Ennis, Co Clare.*
Modern family bungalow, close to The Burren. Traditional entertainment locally.
Open: Easter to Oct
Grades: BF Approv
065 37795
Mrs Mc Mahon
Rates fr: *IR£15.50*-**IR£19.00**.
Beds: 1F 1D 1T
Baths: 1 Ensuite 1 Shared
(5)

Cratloe

National Grid Ref: R4860

Durty Nelly's

Rossloe, *Cratloe Cross, Cratloe, Near Bunratty, Ennis, Co Clare.*
Modern rambler bungalow overlooking River Shannon near Bunratty Castle.
Open: Easter to End Sept
061 387205
Mrs Callaghan
Rates fr: *IR£15.50*-**IR£20.00**.
Beds: 1F 1D 1T
Baths: 3 Ensuite
(4) (5)

Crusheen

National Grid Ref: R3988

Lahardan House, *Crusheen, Ennis, Co Clare.*
Open: All Year
Grades: AA Listed, RAC Acclaim
065 27128
Fax no: 065 27319
Mr & Mrs Griffey
Rates fr: *IR£18.00*-**IR£21.00**.
Beds: 2F 3D 3T
Baths: 8 Ensuite
Family residence in peaceful countryside. Ample room to relax and dine. All rooms ensuite, direct dial telephones, TVs, hairdryers, central heating. Fishing, shooting, golf, pitch and putt available in the area. Pony trekking arranged.

The lowest **single** *rate is shown in* **bold.**

Doolin

National Grid Ref: R0897

McGanns, McDermotts, O'Connors

Daly's, *Doolin, Ennis, Co Clare.*
Open: All Year **Grades:** BF Approv
065 74242 Fax no: 065 74668
Mrs Daly
Rates fr: *IR£17.00*-**IR£20.00**.
Beds: 4F **Baths:** 4 Ensuite
(7)
Adjacent to O'Connor's pub, world famous for traditional Irish music, song, dance and now serving superb food specialising in local produce. Nearby ferry to the historic Aran Islands. Ideal base for walking, cycling, touring, golfing, fishing, pony-trekking, swimming.

St Martins, *Glasha, Doolin, Ennis, Co Clare.*
Attractive bungalow situated in quiet scenic countryside location.
Open: Apr to Oct
Grades: BF Approv
065 74306 Mrs McMahon
Rates fr: *IR£16.00*-**IR£19.00**.
Beds: 2D 1T
Baths: 2 Ensuite 1 Private 1 Shared
(1)

Island View, *Cliffs of Moher Road, Doolin, Ennis, Co Clare.*
Open: Mar to Nov
Grades: BF Approv
065 74346 (also fax no)
Mr & Mrs Sims
Rates fr: *IR£14.00*-**IR£14.00**.
Beds: 2F 2D
Baths: 3 Ensuite 1 Private
(6)
Modern warm bungalow on elevated site. Extensive breakfast menu. Home baking a speciality. Recommended by La Guide du Routard, Lonely Planet Guide, Philadelphia Inquirer. Tea and scones on arrival. Transport to local traditional music pubs. Orthopaedic beds. Credit cards accepted.

Riverdale Farm House, *Gortaclob, Doolin, Ennis, Co Clare.*
Comfortable fourth generation family home. Suitable base for touring.
Open: Mar to Nov
065 74257 Mrs Fitzgerald
Rates fr: *IR£14.00*-**IR£19.00.**
Beds: 3D 1T
Baths: 2 Ensuite 3 Shared
(4)

Churchfield, *Doolin, Ennis, Co Clare.*
Modern two storey house in village with views of sea and cliffs.
Open: All Year (not Xmas)
Grades: BF Approv
065 74209 Mrs Fitzgerald
Rates fr: *IR£14.00*-**IR£20.00.**
Beds: 2F 2D 2T
Baths: 5 Ensuite 1 Shared
(15)

Killilagh House, *Roadford, Doolin, Ennis, Co Clare.*
Converted from award-winning restaurant to comfortable guest house in Doolin.
Open: Feb to Nov
065 74392
Rates fr: *IR£16.00*-**IR£27.00.**
Beds: 3F 2D 3T
Baths: 8 Ensuite
(12)

St Catherines, *Doolin, Ennis, Co Clare,*
Family-run farmhouse. Scenic location. Ideal base for touring the Burren.
Open: Mar to Nov
Grades: BF Approv
065 74103 Mrs Canavan
Rates fr: *IR£16.00*-**IR£19.00.**
Beds: 3D 1T
Baths: 4 Ensuite
(6)

Westfield House, *Carnane, Doolin, Ennis, Co Clare.*
Modern, spacious, comfortable bungalow in a quiet location 2 km from Doolin Village. Sea view. Orthopaedic beds. Excellent food.
Open: Easter to Oct
Grades: BF Approv
065 74192 Mr Roche
Rates fr: *IR£16.00*-**IR£20.00.**
Beds: 2D 2T
Baths: 4 Ensuite
(20)

Doonbeg

National Grid Ref: Q9766

An Tintean, Morrisseys Bar, Bridge Tavern, Igoe Inn

Aran, *Kilkee Road, Doonbeg, Kilrush, Co Clare.*
Country home with panoramic views of sea and countryside, electric blankets. Fishing, swimming, Irish music.
Open: Easter to Oct
Grades: BF Approv
065 55014 Mrs Walsh
Rates fr: *IR£13.50*-**IR£19.00.**
Beds: 1F 1D 1T
Baths: 1 Shared
(4)

An Tintean, *Doonbeg, Kilrush, Co Clare.*
Traditional guest house in centre of seaside village. All rooms ensuite.
Open: All Year **Grades:** BF Approv
065 55036
Fax no: 065 55344
Ms Killeen
Rates fr: *IR£15.00*-**IR£15.00.**
Beds: 3F 3D
Baths: 6 Ensuite
(5)

Ennis

National Grid Ref: R3377

Brannigan's, Roslevan Arms, The Clare Hills, May Kearneys, West County Inn, La Fontana, Howleys, Brogans, Brandons, Knoxs

Clare Hills, *Lahinch Road, Ennis, Co Clare.*
Open: All Year (not Xmas)
Grades: BF 2 St
065 28311 Fax no: 065 28381
Mr Lucey
Rates fr: *IR£15.00*-**IR£18.00.**
Beds: 1F 4D 2T
Baths: 7 Ensuite
(10)
Overlooking the medieval town of Ennis this purpose built guest house is ideally located for touring Co Clare, including the Cliffs of Moher, the Burren and the Shannon Lakelands. All rooms have TV, phone, hairdryer and ensuite facilities.

***Moyville**, Lahinch Road, Ennis, Co Clare.*
Open: Easter to Nov
Grades: BF Approv
065 28278
Mrs Finucane
Rates fr: *IR£15.00*-**IR£20.00**.
Beds: 1F 2D 1T
Baths: 4 Ensuite
(5) (5)
Modern comfortable home on N85 to Burren, Cliffs of Moher. Ideally situated for golfing, fishing and sightseeing and within walking distance of Ennis town centre. TV lounge. Electric blankets and hairdryer in rooms. Traditional Irish music available locally.

***Glenomra House,** Limerick Road, Ennis, Co Clare.*
Newly purpose built to highest standard. Within walking distance of town (200 m).
Open: All Year (not Xmas)
065 20531
Mrs Earlie
Rates fr: *IR£16.00*-**IR£20.00**.
Beds: 2F 5D 1T
Baths: 8 Ensuite
(16)

***St Patricks,** Corebeg, Ennis, Co Clare.*
Open: All Year
065 40122 (also fax no)
Mr & Mrs Grogan
Rates fr: *IR£14.00*-**IR£19.00**.
Beds: 1D 2T
Baths: 2 Ensuite 1 Shared
(3)
Comfortable home in quiet scenic area. Ideal location for Knappogue, Cragganowen, Bunratty, Burren, Cliffs of Moher, golfing, fishing, traditional music.

***Camelot,** Kilrush Road, Ennis, Co Clare.*
Hospitable home. Walking distance of town. Base for touring Co Clare.
Open: Easter to Oct
Grades: BF Approv
065 24093 Mrs Kilcawley
Rates fr: *IR£14.00*-**IR£18.00**.
Beds: 2F 1D 2T
Baths: 3 Ensuite
(7)

***Ardlann**, 6 Fernhill, Galway Road, Ennis, Co Clare.*
Georgian style house in quiet cul-de-sac. 2 minutes town centre.
Open: All Year (not Xmas)
Grades: BF Approv
065 40173
Mrs Lynch
Rates fr: *IR£15.00*-**IR£20.00**.
Beds: 1D 2T
Baths: 1 Ensuite 1 Shared
(4)

***Magowna House Hotel,** Inch, Ennis, Co Clare.*
Open: All Year (not Xmas)
Grades: AA 2 St
065 39009
Fax no: 065 39258
Mr Murphy
Rates fr: *IR£23.00*-**IR£29.00**.
Beds: 3F 5D 2T
Baths: 10 Ensuite
(35)
Delightfully located family-run country house hotel on 12 acres. Close to major tourist attractions of Shannon region and Shannon airport. Excellent golf, fishing and quiet scenic walks. Friendly, hospitable atmosphere. A place to relax, unwind and enjoy.

***Oakley, 10 Woodlawn,** Lahinch Road, Ennis, Co Clare.*
Spacious home, quiet location. Touring centre Burren, etc. Shannon Airport 20 minutes.
Open: May to Oct
065 29267
Mrs Normoyle
Rates fr: *IR£14.00*-**IR£19.50**.
Beds: 2F 2D 1T
Baths: 2 Ensuite 2 Shared
(7) (7)

***Ashleigh,** Cregard, Barefield, Ennis, Co Clare.*
Modern B&B 5 km from Ennis. Close to cliffs, banquets, golf and fishing.
Open: Easter to Nov
065 27187
Fax no: 065 27331
Mrs Meaney
Rates fr: *IR£16.00*-**IR£21.00**.
Beds: 3F 2D
Baths: 5 Ensuite
(10)

Massabiele, *Off Quinn Road, Ennis, Co Clare.*
Beautiful family home, peaceful rural area, all weather tennis court.
Open: Easter to October
065 29363
Mrs O'Loughlin
Rates fr: *IR£16.00*-**IR£19.00**.
Beds: 2F 2D 1T
Baths: 4 Ensuite 1 Shared
(0)

Carbery House, *Kilrush Road, Ennis, Co Clare.*
Route 68. All comforts of home. Convenient to airport and attractions.
Open: Easter to Oct
Grades: BF Approv
065 24046 Mrs Roberts
Rates fr: *IR£16.00*-**IR£20.00**.
Beds: 2D 2T 1S
Baths: 3 Ensuite 1 Private 1 Shared
(6)

Ennistymon

National Grid Ref: R1388

O'Looneys, Archway Bar, Falls Hotel, Linnanes

Station House, *Ennis Road, Ennistymon, Ennis, Co Clare.*
Open: All Year (not Xmas)
Grades: BF Approv
065 71149
Fax no: 065 71709
Mrs Cahill
Rates fr: *IR£16.00*-**IR£21.00**.
Beds: 4 F 1D 1T
Baths: 6 Ensuite
Modern family B&B ideal for touring Burren, Cliffs of Moher, Arran Islands, golf, fishing, pony trekking locally. TV, hairdryers, tea, coffee, direct dial telephones in all bedroom.

Hilbrook Farm, *Lahinch Road, Ennistymon, Ennis, Co Clare.*
Spacious modern farmhouse on elevated site with lovely views.
Grades: BF Approv
065 71164 Mrs Houlihan
Rates fr: *IR£16.00*-**IR£18.00**.
Beds: 1F 2D 1T
Baths: 4 Ensuite
(2) (8)

Grovemount House, *Lahinch Road, Ennistymon, Ennis, Co Clare.*
Open: Apr to Oct
Grades: BF 3 St, AA 4 Q, RAC High Acclaim
065 71431
Fax no: 065 71823
Mrs. Linnore
Rates fr: *IR£16.50*-**IR£25.00**.
Beds: 1F 7D
Baths: 8 Ensuite
Grovemount House is a modern family-run guesthouse situated on the outskirts of Ennistymon and just 1 .5 miles from Lahinch Golf Course and Leisure Centre. We offer easy access to the world famous Cliffs of Moher and the vast Burren region.

Fanore

National Grid Ref: M1307

Admirals Rest, Monks

Rocky View Farmhouse, *Fanore, Ballyvaghan, Galway.*
Open: Mar to Nov
Grades: BF Approv
065 76103
Mrs Linnane
Rates fr: *IR£15.00*-**IR£18.00**.
Beds: 1F 1D 3T 1S
Baths: 6 Ensuite
(10) (8)
Farmhouse situated in the heart of Burren, Ireland's largest Karst region famous for its flora and fauna. Peaceful and quiet area, beautiful view of Aran Islands and Galway Bay. Ideal base for walkers and all nature lovers.

Admirals Resaurantt, *Coast Road, Fanore, Co Clare.*
Open: Easter to Oct
065 76105 Fax no: 065 76161
Mr MacNamara
Rates fr: *IR£16.00*-**IR£21.00**.
Beds: 9F 5D 4T
Baths: 9 Ensuite
(5)
Admiral's restaurant and accommadation is a renowned haven for nature lovers wishing to explore the splendour of the Burren Wilderness where the last of Europe's stone-age race live. Galway Bay, Connemara and the Aran Islands are directly in front.

Inch

National Grid Ref: R2975

Magowna House Hotel, *Inch, Ennis, Co Clare.*
Open: All Year (not Xmas)
Grades: AA 2 St
065 39009 Fax: 065 39258 Mr Murphy
Rates fr: *IR£23.00*-**IR£29.00**.
Beds: 3F 5D 2T **Baths:** 10 Ensuite
(35)
Delightfully located family-run country house hotel on 12 acres. Close to major tourist attractions of Shannon region and Shannon airport. Excellent golf, fishing and quiet scenic walks. Friendly, hospitable atmosphere. A place to relax, unwind and enjoy.

Kilfenora

National Grid Ref: R1894

Kilearaagh House, *Kilfenora, Ennis, Co Clare.*
In the heart of the Burren. All rooms ensuite. Country place 400 yards from oldest village in the West of Ireland.
Open: Apr to Sep **Grades:** BF Approv
065 88042 Mrs Clancy
Rates fr: *IR£17.00*-**IR£20.00**.
Beds: 5F 1D 1T 1S
Baths: 5 Ensuite 1 Private 1 Shared

Burren Farmhouse, *Ballybreen, Kilfenora, Ennis, Co Clare.*
Charming old-style farmhouse in a unique flowery location.
Open: All Year (not Xmas)
065 71363 Mr & Mrs Doorty
Rates fr: *IR£14.00*-**IR£17.00**.
Beds: 3D **Baths:** 2 Shared
(3)

Kilkee

National Grid Ref: Q8860

Atlantic Hotel, *Kilkee, Kilrush, Co Clare,*
Modern, comfortable, on beach besides harbour; golf-course, scuba. Restaurant, bar, entertainment.
Open: May to Sep
Grades: BF Approv
065 56388 / 56435
Rates fr: *IR£16.00*-**IR£24.00**.
Beds: 48D **Baths:** 48 Ensuite
(60)

Killaloe

National Grid Ref: R7073

Goosers Pub, Lakeside Hotel

Rathmore House, *Ballina, Killaloe, Limerick.*
Modern family home, near Lough Dere, ideal touring base.
Open: May to Sep
Grades: BF Approv
061 379296
Mrs Byrnes
Rates fr: *IR£14.50*-**IR£18.00**.
Beds: 4F 2D
Baths: 4 Ensuite 2 Shared
(1) (8)

Weldons Farmhouse, *Boher, Killaloe, Limerick.*
Modern comfortable farmhouse in scenic countryside, ideal base for anglers.
Open: Easter to Nov
Grades: BF Approv
061 379202
Mrs Weldon
Rates fr: *IR£15.00*-**IR£16.00**.
Beds: 1F 2D 2T 1S
Baths: 2 Ensuite 2 Private 2 Shared
(6)

Killimer

National Grid Ref: R0453

Fortfield Farm, *Killimer, Kilrush, Co Clare.*
Modern spacious Mansard residence, with panoramic view.
Open: Mar to Oct
Grades: BF Approv
065 51457
Mr & Mrs Cunningham
Rates fr: *IR£14.00*-**IR£19.00**.
Beds: 2F 2D 1T
Baths: 3 Ensuite

Woodland Farm, *Drumdigus, Killimer, Kilrush, Co Clare.*
Modern, spacious bungalow. Home-made brown bread served each morning.
Open: Apr to Sep
065 53033 Mrs Kelly
Rates fr: *IR£13.50*-**IR£15.00**.
Beds: 2F 1D
Baths: 2 Ensuite 1 Shared

Kilnaboy

National Grid Ref: R2792

Bofey Quinns

Cottage View, *Kilnaboy, Corrofin, Ennis, Co Clare.*
Spacious bungalow, ideal base for touring The Burren. Warm, welcome.
Open: Easter to Oct **Grades:** BF Approv
065 37662 Mrs Fogarty
Rates fr: *IR£15.00*-**IR£18.00**.
Beds: 1F 2D 1T 1S **Baths:** 3 Ensuite
(6)

Fergus View, *Kilnaboy, Corrofin, Ennis, Co Clare.*
Fourth generation family home, situated in the Burren area.
Open: Easter to 1st Oct
Grades: AA 3 Q
065 37606 Fax no: 065 37192
Mr & Mrs Kelleher
Rates fr: *IR£15.50*-**IR£21.50**.
Beds: 4F 2D **Baths:** 5 Ensuite 1 Shared
(6)

Kilrush

National Grid Ref: Q9955

Tubridys, Morrisseys, Kelly's

Fortfield Farm, *Killimer, Kilrush, Co Clare.* **Open:** March to Ocotber
Grades: BF Approv
065 51457 Mr & Mrs Cunningham
Rates fr: *IR£14.00*-**IR£19.00**.
Beds: 2F 2D 1T **Baths:** 3 Ensuite
Modern spacious mansard residence, with deer and llamas etc. Located 1km off Killimer Ferry-Kilrush N67 road (signposted). Visitor farm. 1 mile from Killimer Car Ferry. Convenient to Shannon Airport.

Knockerra House, *Knockerra, Kilrush, Co Clare.*
Family-run country manor situated on extensive private grounds in peaceful tranquil setting.
Open: Easter to Sep
065 51054 Mrs Troy
Rates fr: *IR£15.00*-**IR£17.00**.
Beds: 1F 3D
Baths: 3 Ensuite 3 Shared
(5)

Shannon View, *Moyne, Kilrush, Co Clare.*
Open: Easter to Sep
065 51240
Mr & Mrs O'Brien
Rates fr: *IR£12.00*-**IR£16.00**.
Beds: 2F 2D 1T
Baths: 4 Ensuite 1 Private
Country bungalow. Short walk through farm to Shannon Estuary and Beach on N67. 5 minutes from Killimer/Tarbert ferry. 2 km from Kilrush with its golf course and marina fishing. Ideal for touring Cliffs of Moher or Ring of Kerry.

Old Parochial House, *Cooraclare, Kilrush, Co Clare.*
Unforgettable hospitality, comfort in our family home (c.1872) on R483, village 1km.
Open: Easter to Oct
065 59059 Fax no: 065 51006
Mr & Mrs O'Neill
Rates fr: *IR£14.00*-**IR£16.00**.
Beds: 1F 2D 1T
Baths: 2 Ensuite 2 Shared

Jemes, *Aylevarroo, Kilrush, Co Clare.*
Modern bungalow on Shannon Estuary offering panoramic views of Kerry & Clare.
Open: May to Sep
Grades: BF Approv
065 51822 Mrs Nolan
Rates fr: *IR£14.00*-**IR£16.00**.
Beds: 1F 2D 1T
Baths: 2 Ensuite 1 Private 1 Shared

Lahinch

National Grid Ref: R0988

Kennys Pub, Shamrock Inn, O'Looneys

Veranda View, *School Road, Attycristora, Lahinch, Ennis, Co Clare.*
Friendly home in tranquil surroundings. Breathtaking sea and land views.
Open: May to Sep
065 71521
Mr & Mrs Reynolds
Rates fr: *IR£14.00*-**IR£19.00**.
Beds: 1F 1D 1T
Baths: 1 Ensuite 2 Shared
(3)

Corcomroe, *Station Road, Lahinch, Ennis, Co Clare.*
Town-house in Lehinch, convenient local amenities. Central-heating, TV in rooms.
Open: May to Sep
Grades: BF Approv
065 81363
Mrs McGlennon
Rates fr: *IR£14.95*.
Beds: 3T **Baths:** 3 Ensuite
(3)

Liscannor

National Grid Ref: R0688

Anchor Inn, Captains Deck

Harbour Sunset, *Cliffs of Moher Road, Rannagh, Liscannor, Ennis, Co Clare.*
Open: Apr to Nov
065 81039 (also fax no)
Mrs O'Gorman
Rates fr: *IR£14.00*-**IR£19.00**.
Beds: 1F 2D 1T
Baths: 3 Ensuite 1 Private
(0) (6)
Charming old-style farmhouse in a setting of green fields ovelooking golf-course and beach set on an 86-acre dairy farm. Family play Irish music around open peat fire. Farm museum. *On parle Français*. Hair-dryers. Home-baking.

Sea Haven, *Rockmount, Liscannor, Ennis, Co Clare.*
Spacious home beside Cliffs of Moher. Guide book recommended. Sea views.
Open: All Year (not Xmas)
Grades: BF Approv
065 81385
Fax no: 065 81417
Mr & Mrs Blake
Rates fr: *IR£16.00*-**IR£20.00**.
Beds: 2F 2D 2T
Baths: 6 Ensuite 1 Private
(6)

Right on the border?

Look at the neighbouring

county, too

Lisdoonvarna

National Grid Ref: R1398

Royal Spa Hotel, Roadside Tavern, Kincora House, Irish Arms

Benrue Farmhouse, *Lisdoonvarna, Ennis, Co Clare.*
Open: Easter to Oct
Grades: BF Approv
065 74059
Fax no: 065 74273
Mr & Mrs Casey
Rates fr: *IR£14.00*-**IR£19.00**.
Beds: 2F 2D 2T
Baths: 4 Ensuite 2 Private
Modern comfortable farmhouse in the Burren Region where a warm welcome awaits you. Excellent home cooking with emphasis on seafood. Extensive breakfast menu. Located 6 km from Lisdoonvarna & 12 km from Ballyvaughan off N67 road. Tea/coffee & scones served on arrival. Guests may bring own wine.

Woodview, *Coast Road, Lisdoonvarna, Ennis, Co Clare.*
Warm welcoming cottage on lovely countryside near Cliffs of Moher.
Open: Easter to Oct
065 74387
Mrs O'Halloran
Rates fr: *IR£13.00*-**IR£17.00**.
Beds: 1D 2T
Baths: 3 Ensuite 1 Private
(10) (8)

Deise, *Bog Road, Lisdoonvarna, Ennis, Co Clare.*
Open: Easter to Oct
Grades: BF Approv
065 74360 (also fax no)
Mrs MacNamara
Rates fr: *IR£15.00*-**IR£21.00**.
Beds: 2F 1T 1S
Baths: 4 Ensuite
(6)
Relax in The Burren, the unique limestone region of Eire, in Lisdoonvarna, famous for its Spa Well and 'matchmaking season'. Visit the Cliffs of Moher, golf in Lahinch and hear Irish music in Doolin. Enjoy the good food, drink and company here.

Fermona, *Bog Road, Lisdoonvarna, Ennis, Co Clare.*
Walking distance to pubs, restaurants and spa wells. On main road to Doolin and Cliffs. **Open:** Easter to Oct
065 74243 Mrs Fitzpatrick
Rates fr: *IR£8.00*-**IR£21.00.**
Beds: 4D 1T **Baths:** 5 Ensuite
(8)

Sunville, *off Doolin Road, Lisdoonvarna, Ennis, Co Clare.*
Open: All Year
065 74065 (also fax no) Mrs Petty
Rates fr: *IR£16.00*-**IR£20.00.**
Beds: 1F 2D 2T **Baths:** 5 Ensuite
Situated in peaceful surroundings, off N67. All rooms ensuite, tea/coffee-making facilities, electric blankets. Ideal for walking or touring The Burren. Near Cliffs of Moher, Doolin ferry to Aran Islands. Lahinch Golf Club 9 miles. Access/Visa.

O'Neill's Town Home, *St Brendans Road, Lisdoonvarna, Ennis, Co Clare.*
Modernised period townhouse, welcoming atmosphere, renowned cooking, in town centre **Open:** May to Oct
065 74208 Fax no: 065 74435
Mrs O'Neill
Rates fr: *IR£17.00*-**IR£22.00.**
Beds: 1D 3T 4S
Baths: 8 Ensuite 1 Shared
(6)

Ore A Tava, *Lisdoonvarna, Ennis, Co Clare.*
Modern bungalow. All rooms with TV, telephone, hairdryers. In quiet area.
Open: Easter to Oct
Grades: BF Approv, AA 3 Q
065 74086 Fax no: 065 74547 Mrs Stack
Rates fr: *IR£16.00*-**IR£21.00.**
Beds: 4D 2T **Baths:** 6 Ensuite
(6)

Ravine Hotel, *Lisdoonvarna, Ennis, Co Clare.*
Elegant old world residence, own grounds, town centre, excellent base for touring. **Open:** All Year (not Xmas)
Grades: BF Approv, AA 1 St
065 74043 Rates fr: *IR£15.00*-**IR£15.00**
Beds: 1F 4D 5T 1S
Baths: 8 Ensuite 2 Shared
(10)

Burren Breeze, *The Wood Cross, Lisdoonvarna, Ennis, Co Clare.*
Near Doolin, Cliffs of Moher, Aran Islands ferry, 'The Burren Way' walking route and Ailwee Cave.
Open: All Year
Grades: BF Approv
065 74263 Mrs O'Loughlin
Rates fr: *IR£13.50*-**IR£22.00.**
Beds: 2F 2D 2T
Baths: 6 Ensuite

Milltown Malbay

National Grid Ref: R0579

Leagard House, *Mulagh Road, Milltown Malbay, Ennis, Co Clare.*
Open: Easter to Oct
Grades: BF Approv
065 84324
Mrs Hannon
Rates fr: *IR£14.00*-**IR£19.00.**
Beds: 2F 2D 2T
Baths: 3 Ensuite 2 Shared
House in quiet surroundings. Ideal touring centre for Cliffs of Moher, The Burren and Aran Islands. One hour from Shannon Airport, 0.5 hours from Shannon Car Ferry. Golf, beaches, fishing locally. Traditional music nightly in local pubs.

Mountshannon

National Grid Ref: R7186

Derg Lodge, *Mountshannon, Limerick.*
Excellent, friendly accommodation - check it out for yourself.
Open: All Year
061 927180 (also fax no)
Mrs Waterstone
Rates fr: *IR£14.00*-**IR£19.00.**
Beds: 1F 2D 1T
Baths: 2 Shared
(5)

Many rates vary according to season - the lowest are shown here.

Mullagh

National Grid Ref: R0573

Quilty Tavern

Westacres Farmhouse, *Clonadrum, Mullagh, Quilty, Ennis, Co Clare.*
Open: All Year (not Xmas)
Grades: BF Approv
065 87358 Mrs Torpey
Rates fr: *IR£14.00*-**IR£18.00**.
Beds: 3D
Baths: 3 Ensuite
(2) (6)
Luxury farmhouse on N67 Coast Road, ideally situated between Killimer, car ferry (Kerry) and Cliffs of Moher. Panoramic views of surrounding countryside and coastline, home baking and warm welcome awaits. Tea/coffee making facilities.

Fionnuaire, *Mullagh, Quilty, Ennis, Co Clare.*
Friendly farmhouse on working dairy farm in beautiful countryside. Happy holidays.
Open: Apr to Oct
Grades: BF Approv
065 87179 Mr & Mrs Donnellan
Rates fr: *IR£14.00*-**IR£18.00**.
Beds: 1F 1T 1S
Baths: 1 Ensuite
(10)

Newmarket-on-Fergus

National Grid Ref: R3968

Hunters Lodge, Tradaree Arms, Weavers Inn

Ardkeen, *Monument Cross, Newmarket-on-Fergus, Ennis, Co Clare.*
Open: All Year (not Xmas)
Grades: BF Approv
061 368160 Mrs O'Shea
Rates fr: *IR£13.00*-**IR£16.00**.
Beds: 1F 1D 1T 1S
Baths: 2 Shared
10 minutes Shannon Airport, 4 golf courses within 15 minutes. Tee times arranged. Front and back flower gardens. Back overlooks stud farm and rambling fields. Front you see the River Fergus in the distance. Lawns front and back. Quiet, warm and friendly home.

Golf View, *Latoon Cross, Newmarket-on-Fergus, Ennis, Co Clare.*
Modern, comfortable new home overlooking golf course and River Fergus.
Open: All Year
061 368095
Fax no: 065 28624 Mrs Hogan
Rates fr: *IR£16.00*.
Beds: 4F 2D 1T **Baths:** 4 Ensuite

Tara Green Country Home, *Ballycally, Newmarket-on-Fergus, Ennis, Co Clare,*
Shannon Airport three miles. Modern, friendly, in rural setting. Traditional music nearby.
Open: All Year
Grades: BF Approv
061 472989 Ms O'Brien
Rates fr: *IR£15.00*-**IR£20.00**.
Beds: 2F 1D 2T
Baths: 4 Ensuite 1 Private
(1) (6)

O'Brien's Bridge

National Grid Ref: R6667

The Shannon Cottage, *O'Brien's Bridge, Killaloe, Limerick.*
200-year-old cottage with river views from all bedrooms.
Open: Feb to Nov
061 377118
Fax no: 061 377966 Mrs Hyland
Rates fr: *IR£14.00*-**IR£16.00**.
Beds: 1F 1D 2T
Baths: 3 Ensuite 1 Shared
(6)

Inishlosky, *O'Brien's Bridge, Killaloe, Limerick.*
Modern family comfy home on banks of River Shannon - bliss!
Open: All Year (not Xmas)
Grades: BF Approv
061 37740 Mrs Aherne
Rates fr: *IR£15.00*-**IR£15.00**.
Beds: 3T
Baths: 1 Ensuite 2 Shared

The lowest **single** *rate is shown in* **bold.**

Ogonnelloe

National Grid Ref: R6982

Lantern Guest House, *Ogonnelloe, Scarriff, Limerick.*
Comfortable house with fully licensed restaurant overlooking lake and mountains. **Open:** Feb to Oct
Grades: BF 3 St, AA 3 Q, RAC Acclaim
061 923034 Fax no: 061 923139 Mr Hogan
Rates fr: *IR£19.00*-**IR£21.00**.
Beds: 2F 2D 2T
Baths: 6 Ensuite
(5) (20)

Oughtmama

National Grid Ref: M2808

Burren Oaks, *Oughtmama, Bellharbour, Burren, Galway, Co Clare,*
Modern farmhouse in The Burren located between Ballyvaughan and Kinvara.
Open: Apr to Sep **Grades:** BF Approv
065 78043 Mr & Mrs Flaherty
Rates fr: *IR£16.00*-**IR£21.00**.
Beds: 1F 3T **Baths:** 4 Ensuite
(8)

Quilty

National Grid Ref: R0274

Clonmore Lodge, *Quilty, Ennis, Co Clare,*
Farmhouse overlooking Atlantic. Pitch & putt, tennis, ponies. Families welcome. Local pub.
Open: Easter to Nov
Grades: BF Approv
065 87020 Mr & Mrs Daly
Rates fr: *IR£13.00*-**IR£16.00**.
Beds: 3F 3D 1T 2S
Baths: 9 Ensuite 1 Private
(20)

Quin

National Grid Ref: R4174

Hunters Lodge, Tradaree Arms, Weavers Inn

Ardsolus Farm, *Quin, Ennis, Co Clare,*
Spacious Agri-Tourism award-winning 300-year-old fifth-generation farmhouse on 120-acre working dairy-farm.
Open: Jan to Nov **Grades:** BF Approv
065 25601 (also fax no) Mrs Hannon
Rates fr: *IR£15.00*-**IR£19.00**.
Beds: 1F 2D 1T
Baths: 2 Ensuite 1 Shared
(6)

Shannon

National Grid Ref: R4162

Valhalla, *Uranbeg, Shannon, Co Clare,*
Modern house situated 10 minutes Bunratty/Knappogue Castles, 10 minutes Shannon Airport.
Open: All Year **Grades:** BF Approv
061 368293 Mrs Collins
Rates fr: *IR£16.00*-**IR£20.00**.
Beds: 2F 1D **Baths:** 3 Ensuite
(6)

Shannon Airport

National Grid Ref: R3861

Carrygarry House

Tara Green Country Home, *Ballycally, Newmarket-on-Fergus, Shannon Airport, Co Clare.*
Warm welcome to Irish/Polish home. rganic garden, home cooking.
Open: All Year **Grades:** BF Approv
061 472989 Ms O'Brien
Rates fr: *IR£15.00*-**IR£20.00**.
Beds: 2F 1D 2T
Baths: 4 Ensuite 1 Private
(1) (6)

Sixmilebridge

National Grid Ref: R4866

The Village Diner

Fortwilliam, *Sixmilebridge, Ennis, Co Clare.*
Lovely farmhouse set in beautiful gardens in beautiful countryside.
Open: May to Oct
Grades: BF Grade A
061 369216 Mrs O'Dea
Rates fr: *IR£16.00*-**IR£19.00**.

The lowest *double* rate per person is shown in *italics*.

County Cork

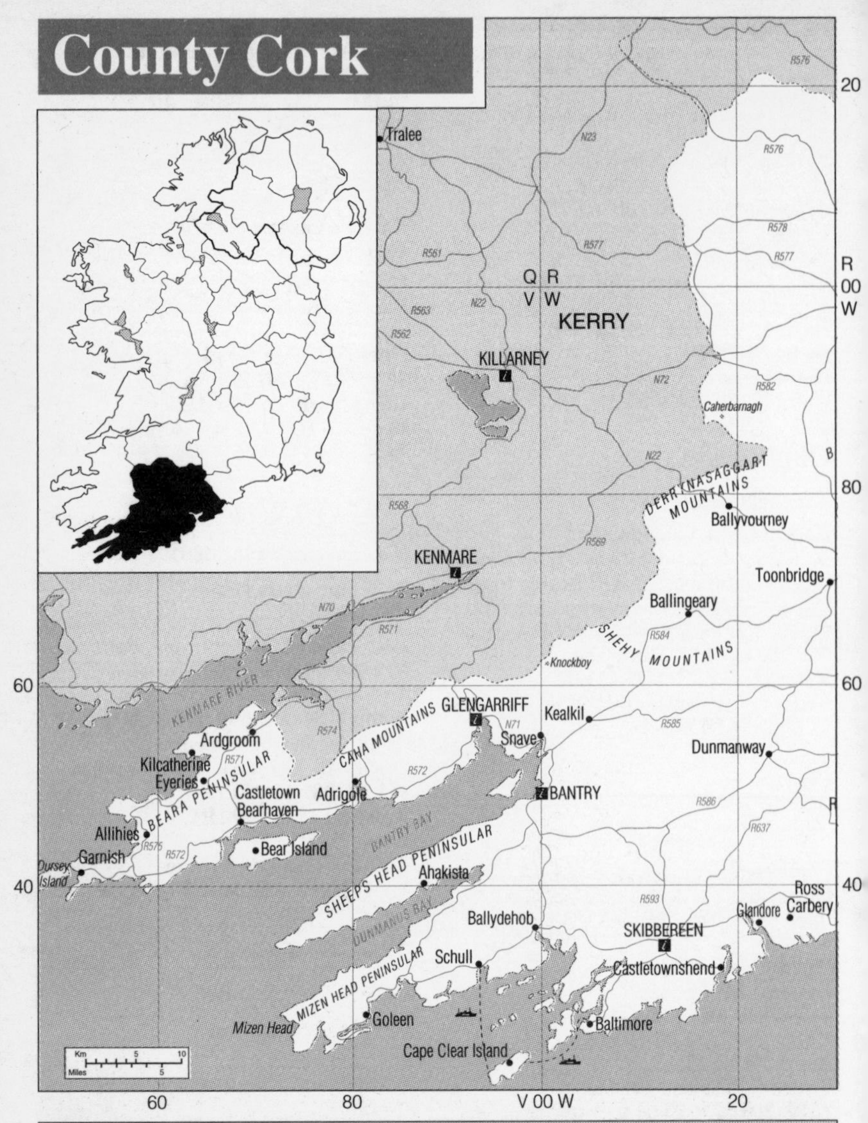

AIRPORT

Cork Airport - tel 021 313131

AIR SERVICES & AIRLINES

Cork** to: **Heathrow, Manchester, Birmingham. **Aer Lingus** - In Republic tel. 021 327155; in Northern Ireland & the UK tel. 0181 899 4747.

Cork** to **Stansted.
Ryanair. In Republic - 01 6774422. In N Ireland & the UK - 0171 435 7101.

***Cork** to **Exeter**, **Bristol**.* **Air South West** - (in UK only) 01392 446447.

RAIL

Cork City is at the end of a major line to ***Dublin*** via ***Thurles*** and ***Portlaoise***.

There is also a branch line to ***Youghal***. Phone **Irish Rail** - 021 506766.

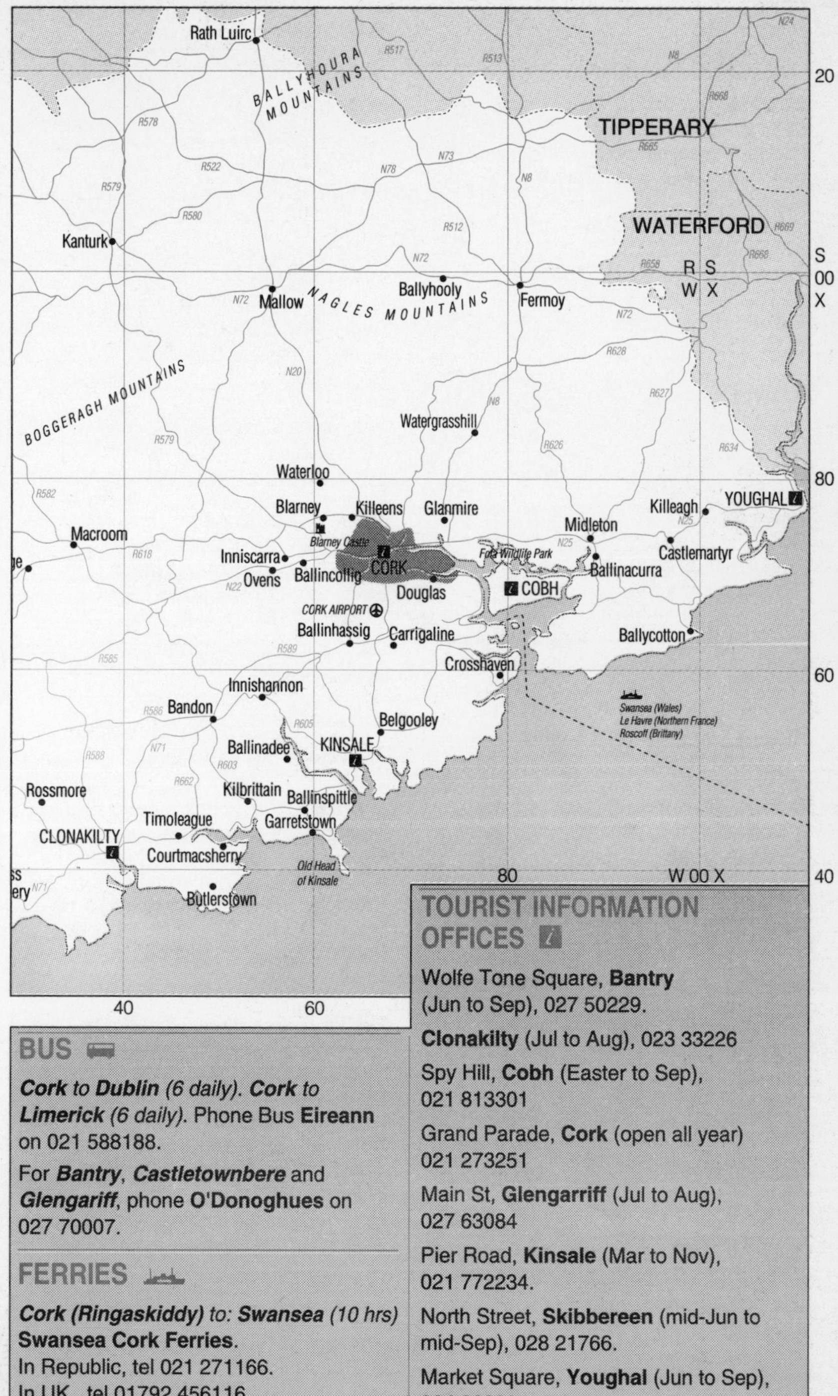

BUS

***Cork** to **Dublin** (6 daily). **Cork** to **Limerick** (6 daily).* Phone Bus **Eireann** on 021 588188.

For ***Bantry***, ***Castletownbere*** and ***Glengariff***, phone **O'Donoghues** on 027 70007.

FERRIES

***Cork (Ringaskiddy)** to: **Swansea** (10 hrs)*
Swansea Cork Ferries.
In Republic, tel 021 271166.
In UK , tel 01792 456116.

TOURIST INFORMATION OFFICES

Wolfe Tone Square, **Bantry** (Jun to Sep), 027 50229.

Clonakilty (Jul to Aug), 023 33226

Spy Hill, **Cobh** (Easter to Sep), 021 813301

Grand Parade, **Cork** (open all year) 021 273251

Main St, **Glengarriff** (Jul to Aug), 027 63084

Pier Road, **Kinsale** (Mar to Nov), 021 772234.

North Street, **Skibbereen** (mid-Jun to mid-Sep), 028 21766.

Market Square, **Youghal** (Jun to Sep), 024 92390.

Adrigole

National Grid Ref: V8050

Beachmount, *Trafrask East, Adrigole, Bantry, Co Cork.*
Farmhouse accommodation. Beach, mountain, lakes, golf. Panoramic views. Scenic walks.
Open: Easter to Oct **Grades:** BF Approv
027 60075 Mrs O'Sullivan
Rates fr: *IR£13.00*-**IR£13.00.**
Beds: 1F 1D 1T 1S
Baths: All Shared

Ocean View, *Faha East, Trafrask, Adrigole, Bantry, Co Cork.*
Open: Easter to Oct
Grades: BF Approv **027 60069**
Mrs O'Sullivan
Rates fr: *IR£14.50*-**IR£16.00.**
Beds: 1F 1D 1T 2S **Baths:** 2 Shared
(5)
Modern comfortable farmhouse in scenic surroundings overlooking beautiful Bantry Bay. Along the Ring of Beara and located 1 km from the New Beara Way walking route. Ideal centre for touring the Beara Peninsula and Ring of Kerry. Golfing, fishing, swimming locally.

Bayview Farmhouse, *Faha, Adrigole, Bantry, Co Cork.*
Working farmhouse outside Adrigole.
Open: May to Sep
027 60026 Mrs O'Sullivan
Rates fr: *IR£14.00*-**IR£19.00.**
Beds: 4D 1T **Baths:** 1 Shared

Ahakista

National Grid Ref: V8740

Jim's Place

Hillcrest House, *Ahakista, Durrus, Bantry, Co Cork.*
Traditional farm guest house on 'Sheeps Head' Peninsula.
Open: Easter to Oct
Grades: BF Approv
027 67045 Mrs Hegarty
Rates fr: *IR£15.00*-**IR£20.00.**
Beds: 2F 1D 1T
Baths: 3 Ensuite 1 Shared
(4) (6)

Allihies

National Grid Ref: V5845

O'Neill's

Sea View Guest House, *Allihies, Bantry, Co Cork.*
Family-run guest house on the Beara Way.
Open: All Year **Grades:** BF Approv
027 73004 Mrs O'Sullivan
Rates fr: *IR£16.00*-**IR£20.00.**
Beds: 5D 5T
Baths: 6 Ensuite 1 Shared

Sea Haven Lodge, *Allihies, Bantry, Co Cork.*
Modern, comfortable house, overlooking Ballydonegan Bay.
Open: All Year
027 73225 Mr & Mrs Irwin
Rates fr: *IR£15.00*-**IR£18.00.**
Beds: 2F 4D 1T **Baths:** 2 Shared

Ardgroom

National Grid Ref: V6955

Holly Bar, Village Inn

O'Brien's, *Ardgroom, Bantry, Co Cork,*
Modern, comfortable family-run house.
Open: All Year
027 74019 Mrs O'Brien
Rates fr: *IR£13.00*-**IR£15.00.**
Beds: 2D 1T
Baths: 1 Ensuite 1 Shared

Skellig House, *Ardgroom, Bantry, Co Cork.*
Modern, comfortable, family-run house.
Open: May to Aug
027 74234 Mrs Lowney
Rates fr: *IR£12.50*-**IR£12.50.**
Beds: 2D 1T **Baths:** 1 Shared

Bringing children with you? Always ask for any special rates.

Canfie House, *Canfie, Ardgroom, Bantry, Co Cork.*
Family-run, comfortable modern bungalow on working farm. Views across Ardgroom Harbour
Open: Apr to Sep
027 74105 Mrs Leahy
Rates fr: *IR£15.00*.
Beds: 1F 1D 1T 1S
Baths: 13.00

Panorama, *Coast Road, Ardgroom, Bantry, Co Cork.*
Beautiful views over Kenmare Bay to the Kerry Mountains.
Open: All Year
027 74148
Mr & Mrs Heinz
Rates fr: *IR£12.50*-**IR£12.50**.
Beds: 1D 1T
Baths: 2 Ensuite

Ballinacurra

National Grid Ref: W8871

Lough Carrig , *Ballinacurra, Midleton, Co Cork.*
Georgian residence in beautiful grounds overlooking the sea. Private and peaceful.
Open: Feb to Dec
Grades: BF Approv
021 631952
Fax no: 021 613707
Mr & Mrs Byrne
Rates fr: *IR£16.50*-**IR£20.00**.
Beds: 2D 2T
Baths: 2 Shared
(30)

Phoning from outside the Republic?

Dial 00353 and omit the initial '0' of the area code.

Ballinadee

National Grid Ref: W5651

Glebe House, *Ballinadee, Bandon, Co Cork.*
Charming family-run Georgian rectory close to wooded banks of the Bandon Estuary and Kinsale.
Open: All Year **Grades:** AA 4 Q
021 778294 Fax no: 021 778456
Mrs Bracken
Rates fr: *IR£22.50*-**IR£30.00**.
Beds: 2F 1S **Baths:** 3 Ensuite
(30)

Ballincollig

National Grid Ref: W5971

Tatler Jack, White Horse Inn

Milestone, *Ovens, Ballincollig, Cork.*
Ideal base to explore West Cork/Killarney/Kinsale.
Open: All Year **Grades:** BF Approv
021 872562 Mrs Cronin
Rates fr: *IR£16.00*-**IR£20.00**.
Beds: 1F 1D 3T **Baths:** 5 Private
(6)

Westfield House, *West Village, Ballincollig, Cork.*
Convenient to Blarney Castle, airport, ferry. Early breakfast. Attractive garden.
Open: All Year (not Xmas)
021 871824 Mrs Cotter
Rates fr: *IR£14.00*-**IR£16.00**.
Beds: 2F 1D 1T
Baths: 3 Ensuite 1 Private
(5)

Ballingeary

National Grid Ref: W1567

Cois Na Coille, *Gurteenakilla, Ballingeary, Macroom, Co Cork.*
Modern bungalow in peaceful scenic location. Painters' and photographers' paradise.
Open: All Year (not Xmas/New Year)
Grades: BF Approv
026 47172 (also fax no)
Mr & Mrs Kelleher
Rates fr: *IR£14.00*-**IR£14.00**.
Beds: 1F 2D 1T
Baths: 1 Ensuite 1 Private 1 Shared

Ballinhassig

National Grid Ref: W6362

Speckled icons: Blanchfield House

Blanchfield House, *Rigsdale, Ballinhassig, Cork.*
Open: Easter to Nov
Grades: BF Approv, AA 2 Q
021 885167
Fax no: 021 885805
Ms Blanchfield
Rates fr: *IR£17.00*-**IR£22.00.**
Beds: 2F 2D 2T
Baths: 2 Ensuite 1 Shared
(15)
Period country home and restaurant overlooking main Cork/Bandon Road (N71). Private salmon & trout angling (Bandon river). Deep-sea angling, golf, tennis, sailing, diving, windsurfing, beaches, horse riding, pony trekking locally. Group/weekly rates - also self catering lodge.

Ballinspittle

National Grid Ref: W5846

Speckled Door, Old Head, Hurleys, Pink Elephant

Raheen House, *Kilgobbin, Ballinspittle, Kinsale, Co Cork.*
Luxury farmhouse, beautiful countryside, views of the Old Head of Kinsale.
Open: Apr to Oct
Grades: BF Approv
021 778173 (also fax no)
Mrs Sweetman
Rates fr: *IR£15.00*-**IR£20.00.**
Beds: 1F 2D 1T
Baths: 2 Ensuite 2 Shared
(20)

Please respect a B&B's wishes regarding children, animals & smoking.

Ballycotton

National Grid Ref: W9963

Fawcetts, The Pier

Spanish Point Guest House, *Ballycotton, Midleton, Co Cork.*
Open: All Year
Grades: BF 3 St
021 646177
Fax no: 021 646179
Mrs Tattan
Rates fr: *IR£18.00*-**IR£22.00.**
Beds: 2F 3D
Baths: 5 Ensuite
(20)
Gourmet restaurant & guest house set in cliff face overlooking Ballycotton Bay - panoramic views. Enjoy a relaxing stay or meal at Spanish Point Seafood Restaurant. Here you will experience an atmosphere of hospitality, complemented by local cuisine, based on local produce & fresh fish caught from our own trawler.

Gorse Hill, *Ballycotton, Midleton, Co Cork.*
Beautiful seaside scenery, service, comfort to match. Village one mile.
Open: All Year (not Xmas)
Grades: BF Approv
021 646713
Mrs Murray
Rates fr: *IR£17.00*-**IR£20.00.**
Beds: 1F 4T
Baths: 4 Ensuite 1 Shared
(10)

Ballydehob

National Grid Ref: V9835

Ballydehob Inn, Duggans Rest, Annie's Restaurant

Ballydehob Inn, *Ballydehob, Skibbereen, Co Cork.*
Open: All Year (not Xmas)
Grades: BF Approv
028 37139
Mrs Morris
Rates fr: *IR£15.00*-**IR£18.00.**
Beds: 2F 2D 1T
Baths: 3 Ensuite 2 Shared
(8) (3)

Ballyhooly

National Grid Ref: W7299

Mills Inn

The Old Vicarage, *Ballyhooly, Mallow, Co Cork.*
Old vicarage on edge of village overlooking River Blackwater.
Open: All Year (not Xmas)
025 39356
Mrs Dacres Dixon
Rates fr: *IR£17.50*-**IR£17.50**.
Beds: 2F 1T 1S
Baths: 1 Ensuite 1 Shared
(9) (5)

Ballyvourney

National Grid Ref: W1977

Mills Inn

The Mills Inn, *Ballyvourney, Macroom, Co Cork.*
One of Ireland's oldest inns, set in acres of landscaped gardens. Award-winning traditional bar/restaurant, excellent cuisine
Open: All Year
Grades: BF 4 St, AA 4 Q, RAC High Acclaim
026 45237
Fax no: 026 45454
Mr Scannell
Rates fr: *IR£25.00*-**IR£30.00**.
Beds: 2F 5T 5D
Baths: 12 Ensuite

Baltimore

National Grid Ref: W0526

Casey's Cabin

Rathmore House, *Baltimore, Skibbereen, Co Cork.*
Georgian type house overlooking harbour. Scenic area. Home cooking.
Open: All Year
028 20362
Mrs O'Driscoll
Rates fr: *IR£16.00*-**IR£18.00**.
Beds: 1F 2D 2T 1S
Baths: 6 Ensuite
(15)

Bandon

National Grid Ref: W4955

Munster Arms

St Annes, *Clonakilty Road, Bandon, Co Cork.*
Georgian house, walled gardens, conveniently located for all West Cork.
Open: All Year
Grades: BF Approv
023 44239
Mrs Buckley
Rates fr: *IR£16.00*-**IR£21.00**.
Beds: 2F 2D 1T 1S
Baths: 6 Ensuite
(8)

Bantry

National Grid Ref: W0048

The Snug, Hungry Trout, Vickery's Inn, O'Connor's Seafood Restaurant

Vickery's Inn, *New Street, Bantry, Co Cork.*
Open: All Year (not Xmas)
027 50006 (also fax no)
Ms Vickery
Rates fr: *IR£15.00*.
Beds: 2F 8D 1T 2S
Baths: 8 Ensuite 2 Shared
Originally a coaching inn established 1850, Vickery's Inn offers comfortable accommodation with full bar and restaurant facilities at reasonable prices. Traditional music and ballads in the bar during the season. Ideally situated to explore scenic West Cork. Start 'The Sheep's Head Way' from here.

Dromcloc House, *Bantry, Co Cork.*
Seaside dairy farm. Signposted 2 km west of Bantry. Fishing, tennis court.
Open: Mar to Nov
Grades: BF Approv
027 50030
Mrs Crowley
Rates fr: *IR£14.00*.
Beds: 2F 2D 2T
Baths: 4 Ensuite 2 Shared
(20)

Leyton, *23 Slip Lawn, Bantry, Co Cork,*
Modern home, quiet locality overlooking Bantry town (1 km). All amenities nearby.
Open: May to Sep
Grades: BF Approv
027 50665 Mrs Harrington
Rates fr: *IR£14.00*-**IR£18.00**.
Beds: 1F 1D 1T
Baths: 2 Ensuite 1 Shared
(2)

Bay View Lodge, *Gories, Bantry, Co Cork,*
Modern bungalow and dairy farm overlooking Bantry Bay. Farm walks.
Open: All Year **Grades:** BF Approv
027 50515 Mr & Mrs O'Shea
Rates fr: *IR£14.00*.
Beds: 1D
Baths: 2 Ensuite

Doire Liath, *Newtown, Bantry, Co Cork.*
A comfortable bungalow close to Bantry's beautiful town centre. A family welcome awaits.
Open: All Year (not Xmas)
Grades: BF Approv
027 50223 Mrs Linehan
Rates fr: *IR£16.00*-**IR£18.00**.
Beds: 2D 1T
Baths: 2 Ensuite 1 Private
(3)

Sorrento, *Gouree More, Bantry, Co Cork.*
Modern bungalow on main Bantry/Glengarriff Road overlooking Lake.
Open: Easter to Oct
027 50335 Mrs O'Sullivan
Rates fr: *IR£12.00*.
Beds: 2D 2T
Baths: 2 Ensuite 2 Shared
(10)

Dunauley, *Seskin, Bantry, Co Cork.*
Country house, comfortable accommodation; situated on side of hill overlooking Bantry Bay and Caha Mountains.
Open: May to Sep
Grades: BF Approv
027 50290 Mrs McAuley
Rates fr: *IR£16.00*-**IR£21.00**.
Beds: 1F 2D 2T
Baths: 2 Ensuite 1 Shared
(10) (5)

Bear Island

National Grid Ref: V7044

Harbour View, *Bear Island, Beara, Co Cork.*
Peaceful surroundings, unsurpassed scenic beauty. House overlooking Berehaven harbour.
Open: All Year (not Xmas)
027 75011 Mrs O'Sullivan
Rates fr: *IR£14.00*-**IR£16.00**.
Beds: 2F 3T
Baths: 2 Ensuite 1 Private 2 Shared
(12)

Belgooley

National Grid Ref: W6644

Hawthorn House, *Belgooley, Kinsale, Co Cork.*
Country home set in beautiful gardens.
Open: Easter to Oct
021 774005 Ms O'Riordan
Rates fr: *IR£16.00*-**IR£21.00**.
Beds: 2D 3T
Baths: 3 Ensuite 2 Shared

Blarney

National Grid Ref: W6175

Muskerry Arms, Blairs Inn, Castle Hotel, Ryans on the Green

Firgrove, *1 Castle Close Villas, Blarney, Cork.*
Modern comfortable home, friendly atmosphere. Adjacent bus/castle. In village.
Open: Mar to Nov **Grades:** BF Approv
021 381403 Mrs O'Brien
Rates fr: *IR£15.00*-**IR£20.00**.
Beds: 4F 2D 1T 1S
Baths: 2 Ensuite 1 Private 1 Shared
(8) (3)

Travellers Joy, *Tower, Blarney, Cork.*
Restful accommodation. Quiet location, private parking. Set in prize-winning gardens.
Open: Feb to Dec
Grades: BF Approv
021 385541 Mrs O'Shea
Rates fr: *IR£14.00*-**IR£15.00**.
Beds: 1F 1D 1T 1S
Baths: 2 Ensuite 1 Shared

Rosemount, *The Square, Blarney, Cork,*
Modern comfortable home. Private parking, minutes to castle, shops, entertainment.
Open: Easter to Nov
021 385584 Mrs Cronin
Rates fr: *IR£14.00*-**IR£18.00**.
Beds: 1F 2D 2T
Baths: 3 Ensuite 2 Shared
(8)

Kilarney House, *Station Road, Blarney, Cork.*
Purpose built luxury accommodation. Adjacent to castle, shops and entertainment.
Open: All Year
021 381841 Mrs Morgan
Rates fr: *IR£17.00*-**IR£23.00**.
Beds: 4T **Baths:** 4 Ensuite
(6)

Bohernamona, *Courtbrack, Blarney, Cork.*
Attractive farmhouse in peaceful countryside 6.5 km Blarney. Signposted on R617.
Open: May to Oct
021 385181 (also fax no)
Mrs Murray
Rates fr: *IR£15.00*-**IR£20.00**.
Beds: 1F 3D 1T
Baths: 3 Ensuite 2 Shared

Ath Dara, *Kerry Road, Tower, Blarney, Cork.*
Hospitality assured. Comfortable bungalow. Blarney 3 km. Pubs, restaurants nearby.
Open: All Year (not Xmas)
Grades: BF Approv
021 381143 (also fax no)
Mr Symons
Rates fr: *IR£14.00*-**IR£18.00**.
Beds: 2D 2T 1S
Baths: 3 Ensuite 2 Shared
(1) (6)

Yvory House, *Killowen, Blarney, Cork.*
Luxurious modern bungalow set in scenic farming location overlooking Blarney Castle.
Open: Apr to Oct
021 381128 Mrs Sisk
Rates fr: *IR£15.00*-**IR£19.00**.
Beds: 1F 2D 1T
Baths: 2 Ensuite 2 Shared
(6)

Buena Vista, *Station Road, Blarney, Cork.*
Modern, comfortable townhouse - 0.5 km from Blarney Castle. TV in all bedrooms.
Open: All Year (not Xmas)
021 385035
Mr & Mrs Callaghan
Rates fr: *IR£16.00*-**IR£22.00**.
Beds: 3F 2D
Baths: 5 Ensuite

Heather Lodge, *Kerry Road, Tower, Blarney, Cork.*
Modern dormer bungalow in peaceful scenic countryside.
Open: Mar to Dec
021 381216
Mrs Collins
Rates fr: *IR£16.00*-**IR£18.00**.
Beds: 2D 1T
Baths: 2 Ensuite 1 Private
(8)

Elmgrove House, *Shournagh Road, Blarney, Cork.*
Cottage-style house in wooded area on banks of River Shournagh.
Open: All Year (not Xmas)
Grades: BF Approv
021 385136
Mr & Mrs Lyons
Rates fr: *IR£13.50*-**IR£13.50**.
Beds: 1F 2D 1T
Baths: 4 Ensuite
(6)

Butlerstown

National Grid Ref: W4938

Sea Court, *Butlerstown, Bandon, Co Cork.*
Open: Jun to Aug
Grades: BF Approv
023 40151 Mr Elder
Rates fr: *IR£22.50*-**IR£22.50**.
Beds: 1F 3D 2T
Baths: 5 Ensuite 1 Private
(12)
Sea Court, Butlerstown. Listed Georgian country mansion on scenic Seven Heads Peninsula in West Cork, located between Kinsale and Clonakilty. Most rooms have a distant ocean view and all are furnished primarily with antiques. Fishing, swimming riding and golf available locally.

Cape Clear Island

National Grid Ref: V9521

Cluain Mara, *Cape Clear Island, Co Cork.*
Island-based superior accommodation, for bird-watching, dolphin/whale watching, lovers of nature.
Open: All Year **Grades:** BF Approv
028 39153 Mr O'Driscoll
Rates fr: *IR£15.00*-**IR£15.00**.
Beds: 1F 2D 1T 1S
Baths: 3 Ensuite 1 Shared
(4)

Carrigaline

National Grid Ref: W7261

Owenbue Bar, Rosie's Bar

Willows, *Ballea Road, Carrigaline, Cork.*
Open: All Year (not Xmas)
021 372669 Mrs O'Leary
Rates fr: *IR£16.00*-**IR£19.00**.
Beds: 4F 1D 1T
Baths: 4 Ensuite 2 Shared
Split level house. Warm welcome. Fishing, golfing, horse riding, beaches. Restaurants, airport and ferryport 3 km. Early morning breakfast.

Castlemartyr

National Grid Ref: W9674

The Stock of Barley

Sundown House, *Kilmountain, Castlemartyr, Midleton, Co Cork.*
Modern bungalow in scenic countryside. Close access to sandy beaches.
Open: Apr to Nov **Grades:** BF Approv
021 667375 Mrs Quinlan
Rates fr: *IR£14.00*-**IR£19.00**.
Beds: 4D
Baths: 2 Ensuite
(6)

Bringing children with you? Always ask for any special rates.

Castletown Berehaven

National Grid Ref: V6846

Nicky's, Old Bank House, Patrick's, Old Cottage Restaurant

Castletown House, *The Old Bank Seafood Restaurant, Castletown Berehaven, Bantry, Co Cork.*
Originally a bank. Front gardens. Seafood restaurant - local cheese a speciality. **Open:** All Year
027 70252 Fax no: 027 70054
Mr & Mrs Harrington
Rates fr: *IR£15.50*-**IR£13.50**.
Beds: 1F 1D 1T 1S **Baths:** 1 Ensuite

Realt Na Mara, *Castletown Berehaven, Bantry, Co Cork.*
Comfortable home overlooking the sea. Personal attention guaranteed.
Open: All Year **Grades:** BF Approv
027 70101 Mrs Donegan
Rates fr: *IR£16.00*-**IR£20.00**.
Beds: 1F 4D
Baths: 4 Ensuite 1 Private

Rodeen, *Castletown Berehaven, Bantry, Co Cork.*
Lovely comfortable bungalow with great views over the sea.
Open: All Year
027 70158 Mrs Gowan
Rates fr: *IR£17.00*-**IR£20.00**.
Beds: 4D 1T 1S **Baths:** 6 Ensuite

Bay View House, *West End, Castletown Berehaven, Bantry, Co Cork.*
Nice od-fashioned house in the town centre.
Open: Jun to Sep **Grades:** BF Approv
027 70099 Mrs Murphy
Rates fr: *IR£14.00*-**IR£16.00**.
Beds: 3D **Baths:** 1 Shared
(12)

Sea Breeze, *Derrymihan, Castletown Berehaven, Bantry, Co Cork.*
Fantastic views over harbour, newly decorated modern home.
Open: All Year **Grades:** BF Approv
027 70508 Mrs McGurn
Rates fr: *IR£16.00*-**IR£25.00**.
Beds: 1F 2D **Baths:** 3 Ensuite

Ballellin, *3 Camewoods, Castletown Berehaven, Bantry, Co Cork.*
Modern bungalow overlooking harbour. Paintings and antiques.
Open: Apr to Sep
Grades: BF Approv
027 70424 (also fax no)
Mrs Wrigley
Rates fr: *IR£15.00*-**IR£17.00**.
Beds: 1F 2D 1T
Baths: 3 Ensuite 1 Private
(5)

Castletownshend

National Grid Ref: W1831

Mary Ann's Bar

Woodlands, *Coast Road, Castletownshend, Skibbereen, Co Cork,*
Comfortable family-run bed &breakfast with beautiful large garden.
Open: All Year (not Xmas)
Grades: BF Approv
028 36125
Mrs O'Neill
Rates fr: *IR£15.00*-**IR£15.00**.
Beds: 2D 2T 1S
Baths: 2 Ensuite 1 Shared

Clonakilty

National Grid Ref: W3841

The Sandlighter, The Sugar, Fernhill House Hotel, Imperial Hotel

Shalom, *Ballyduvane, Clonakilty, Co Cork.*
Modern bungalow in rural setting, situated on the N71.
Open: All Year (not Xmas)
Grades: BF Approv
023 33473
Mrs Moore
Rates fr: *IR£14.00*-**IR£15.00**.
Beds: 3D
Baths: 3 Ensuite

The lowest **single** *rate is shown in* **bold.**

The lowest *double* rate per person is shown in *italics*.

Desert House, *Clonakilty, Co Cork.*
Georgian farmhouse on dairy farm overlooking Clonakilty town and Bay.
Open: All Year
Grades: BF Approv
023 33331
Mrs Jennings
Rates fr: *IR£16.00*-**IR£21.00**.
Beds: 2F 2D 1T
Baths: 4 Ensuite 1 Private
(10)

Dunmore House, *Muckross, Clonakilty, Co Cork.*
Old family home. Overlooking Atlantic Ocean. Private golf course.
Open: All Year (not Xmas)
Grades: BF 3 St
023 33352
Fax no: 023 34686
Rates fr: *IR£30.00*-**IR£35.00**.
Beds: 6F 9D
Baths: 15 Ensuite
(108)

Liscubba House, *Rossmore, Clonakilty, Co Cork.*
Old comfortable farmhouse in beautiful countryside. Home baking/cooking, fresh organic vegetables.
Open: All Year (not Xmas)
023 38679
Mrs Beechinor
Rates fr: *IR£14.00*-**IR£14.00**.
Beds: 1F 2D 1T 1S
Baths: 1 Shared
(0)

Hillside Farm, *Kilgarriffe, Clonakilty, Co Cork.*
Old style farmhouse on working farm. Brown bread demonstrations.
Open: Easter to Oct
023 33139
Mrs Helen
Rates fr: *IR£15.00*-**IR£18.00**.
Beds: 2F 1D 1T
Baths: 2 Ensuite 2 Shared
(10)

Nordav, *Western Road, Clonakilty, Co Cork.*
Modern home, award-winning gardens, two suites, room with kitchenette.
Open: All Year (not Xmas)
023 33655 Mrs McMahon
Rates fr: *IR£14.00*-**IR£20.00**.
Beds: 2F 2D 2T
Baths: 5 Ensuite 1 Private
(4)

Wytchwood, *Emmet Square, Clonakilty, Co Cork.*
Exclusive ensuite accommodation in a quiet cul-de-sac off Kennedy Gardens.
Open: Mar to Oct
023 33525 Mrs Hayes
Rates fr: *IR£16.00*-**IR£18.00**.
Beds: 1F 3D 1T 1S
Baths: 5 Ensuite 1 Private

Cobh

National Grid Ref: W8067

Marlogue Inn, Rinn Ronain Hotel, Chapters

Waterway, *East Ferry Road, Cobh, Co Cork.*
Quiet scenic island location on seafront. Frommer Guide Recommended.
Open: Apr to Sep **021 812451**
Mrs Shorten **Rates fr:** *IR£14.00*-**IR£19.00**.
Beds: 1D 2T **Baths:** 1 Ensuite 1 Shared
(3)

Tearmann, *Ballynoe, Cobh, Co Cork.*
Lovely traditional house and gardens 2 km Cobh, 25 minutes Ringaskiddy Port.
Open: Mar to Oct **Grades:** BF Approv
021 813182 Fax no: 021 814011
Mrs Maddox **Rates fr:** *IR£14.50*-**IR£18.00**.
Beds: 1F 1D 1T
Baths: 2 Ensuite 1 Private
(4)

Glebe House, *Tay Road, Cobh, Co Cork.*
Modern friendly home near Fota wildlife, Ringaskiddy ferries, golf, fishing, sailing. Cobh 2 km.
Open: Easter to Oct
021 811373 (also fax no)
Mrs & Mrs Coughlan
Rates fr: *IR£14.00*-**IR£18.00**.
Beds: 1F 1T **Baths:** 1 Ensuite 1 Shared
(6)

Robin Hill Guest Hill, *Lake Road, Rushbrooke, Cobh, Co Cork.*
Charming period house of character overlooking Cork Harbour. Licensed restaurant.
Open: All Year (not Xmas)
Grades: BF 2 St
021 811395 Mr Gould
Rates fr: *IR£14.00*-**IR£16.00**.
Beds: 4F 1D 1T 1S
Baths: 2 Ensuite 2 Shared
(10)

Cork

National Grid Ref: W6772

Crows Nest, Isaac's, Reidys Wine Vaults, Rochester Park Hotel, Barry's Bar,

Antoine House, *Western Road, Cork.*
Open: All Year
Grades: BF 2 St, AA 3 St
021 273494
Fax no: 021 273092
Mr Cross
Rates fr: *IR£16.50*-**IR£18.00**.
Beds: 5D 3T 3S
Baths: 4 Ensuite
Antoine House, located at gateway to West Cork and Kerry. For business or pleasure an ideal base from which to explore. Less than 1 mile from city centre and in close proximity to airport, train, ferry, Blarney and Fota.

White Lodge, *Airport Cross, Kinsale Road, Cork.*
Modern comfortable bungalow in beautiful rural setting, Cork City 5 km, Cork Airport 3 minutes.
Open: All Year (not Xmas)
021 961267 Ms Bayer
Rates fr: *IR£14.00*-**IR£12.00**.
Beds: 1F 2D 1T 2S
Baths: 3 Ensuite 1 Private 1 Shared
(7)

All details shown are as supplied by B&B owners in Autumn 1996

Victoria Lodge, *Victoria Cross, Cork.*
Open: All Year (not Xmas)
Grades: BF 4 St
021 542233 Fax no: 021 542572
Mr Long
Rates fr: *IR£22.00*-**IR£25.00**.
Beds: 5F 10D 10T 5S
Baths: 30 Ensuite
(35)
Cork's newest exclusive B&B - a former monastery, standing in mature gardens. Secure private car park. All bedrooms with bath, TV, direct dial telephone, central heating, tea-making facilities. Lift to each floor. Minutes from city centre.

Kent House, *47 Lower Glanmire Road, Cork.*
Modern comfortable guest house next to railway and bus station.
Open: All Year
Grades: BF Approv
021 504260 Mrs Flynn
Rates fr: *IR£11.00*-**IR£13.00**.
Beds: 2F 2D 2T
Baths: 4 Ensuite 2 Shared

Gabriel House, *Summer Hill, St Lukes, Cork.*
Open: All Year
Grades: BF 2 St
021 500333
Fax no: 021 500178
Ms King
Rates fr: *IR£15.00*-**IR£20.00**.
Cork City. Gabriel House, Summer Hill, St Lukes. Phone 021 500333. Fax 500178. B&B from 12.50 sharing. Rooms ensuite. TV, phone, hairdryer. Beautiful harbour views, gardens. Breakfast served from 5.00 a.m. Dinner served from 6.30 p.m. Wine licence. Refreshments served 24 hours. Private parking. Pets welcome. Laundry service.

Sarto, *2 Lislee Road, Rochestown Road, Cork.*
Comfortable family home in quiet residential area. Convenient for airport & ferry.
Open: All Year (not Xmas)
021 895579 Mrs Brien
Rates fr: *IR£14.00*-**IR£19.00**.
Beds: 2F 2D 2T
Baths: 4 Ensuite 2 Shared
(3)

Acorn House, *14 St Patricks Hill, Cork,*
Open: All Year (not Xmas)
Grades: BF 2 St
021 502474
Mrs West
Rates fr: *IR£17.00*-**IR£22.00**.
Beds: 4D 3T 2S
Baths: 6 Ensuite 1 Shared
Beautifully restored large city centre Georgian house - close to restaurants, pubs, theatres. Horse riding, golf. Five minutes bus/rail.

Tara House, *52 Lower Glanmire Road, Cork.*
100 year-old town house. Convenient to city and as a base for touring South West.
Open: All Year (not Xmas)
021 500294
Mrs Chambers
Rates fr: *IR£13.00*-**IR£13.00**.
Beds: 2F 2D 1T 1S
Baths: 4 Ensuite 2 Shared

St Kilda's, *Western Road, Cork.*
Open: All Year (not Xmas)
Grades: BF 3 St
021 273095
Fax no: 021 275015
Mrs Hickey
Rates fr: *IR£16.00*-**IR£18.00**.
Beds: 11F 2D 1T
Baths: 12 Ensuite 1 Shared
(12)
St Kilda's Guest House offers the highest standard of accommodation and service. Direct dial phones, hairdryers, hospitality trolley in guest lounge. Private car park. Credit cards accepted. Proprietors: Pat and Pauline Hickey.

Korlym, *Carrigaline Road, Douglas, Cork.*
House of character with spacious sun lounge. Interesting books and garden.
Open: Apr to Oct
Grades: BF Approv
021 893858
Ms Canniffe
Rates fr: *IR£14.00*-**IR£19.00**.
Beds: 2D 2T
Baths: 2 Ensuite 2 Shared
(4)

Fatima House, *Grange Road, Douglas, Cork.*
Open: All Year
Grades: BF Approv
021 362536 (also fax no)
Mrs O'Shea
Rates fr: *IR£15.00*-**IR£20.00**.
Beds: 2F 2D 1T
Baths: 4 Ensuite 1 Private 2 Shared
(5)
Modern warm comfortable home. Family-run. Off airport, Kinsale Road N27. Signposted at Little Chef. Very easily located. Convenient to Cork/Swansea Ferry Port. Pubs, restaurants, shopping malls, leisure centres, golf courses, laundry. Visa and Sterling accepted. House taxi, city bus.

Courtmacsherry

National Grid Ref: W5042

Lifeboat Inn

Travara Lodge, *Courtmacsherry, Bandon, Co Cork.*
A Georgian house sheltered by woodlands overlooking Courtmacsherry's magnificent bay.
Open: Mar to Nov
Grades: BF 2 St
023 46493 (also fax no) Ms Guy
Rates fr: *IR£18.00*-**IR£20.00**.
Beds: 3D 3T
Baths: 6 Ensuite
(6)

Woodpoint, *Courtmacsherry, Bandon, Co Cork.*
C18th farmhouse situated on coastal peninsular with 30 acres of private woodland.
Open: All Year (not Xmas)
Grades: BF Approv
023 46427 (also fax no) Mrs Gannon
Rates fr: *IR£16.00*-**IR£20.00**.
Beds: 1D 4T
Baths: 5 Ensuite
(8)

Always telephone to get directions to the B&B - you will save time!

Crosshaven

National Grid Ref: W8060

Crown Bar

Berminghams, *Camden Road, Crosshaven, Cork.*
Open: All Year
021 831181 Mr & Mrs Bermingham
Rates fr: *IR£15.00*-**IR£16.00**.
Beds: 2F 2D 2T 1S
Baths: 5 Ensuite 1 Shared
(8)
Lovely country house convenient to fishing village. Central heating. Beautiful views of Cork Harbour and yachting marinas (3). Deep Sea and shore angling. Golf and surfing. Cork Airport 9 miles. Cork-Swansea ferries 8 miles.

Douglas

National Grid Ref: W7069

Bullys, Barrys, O'Driscolls

Glanmalure, *Carrigaline Road, Douglas, Cork.*
Open: Mid Jan to mid Dec
Grades: BF Approv
021 894324 Mrs French
Rates fr: *IR£14.00*-**IR£19.00**.
Beds: 1F 2D 1T
Baths: 1 Ensuite 2 Shared
(8)
Detached modern comfortable bungalow on Route 609. Off street parking. Personal attention. Warm welcome. Early breakfasts. Walking distance shop, pubs, restaurants, churches, cinemas. Convenient airport, ferryport, sandy beach, city centre. Ideal base for touring. Golf, fishing, sailing, horseriding, etc.

Dunmanway

National Grid Ref: W2352

Parkway Hotel

Model Farm House, *Bantry Road, Dunmanway, Co Cork.*
Tudor-style, C19th house adjacent swimming pool, bus, cinema.
Open: Easter to Oct
023 45133 (also fax no) Mrs Cahalane
Rates fr: *IR£15.00*-**IR£15.00**.
Beds: 1F 2D **Baths:** 1 Private 1 Shared

Eyeries

National Grid Ref: V6450

Cussane House, *Eyeries, Bantry, Co Cork.*
Modern house with great views over Coulagh Bay to the Kerry Mountains.
Open: May to Aug
027 74178 Mrs Coghlan-Mason
Rates fr: *IR£15.00*-**IR£17.00.**
Beds: 1F 1D 1T
Baths: 1 Private 1 Shared

Shamrock, *Strand Road, Eyeries, Bantry, Co Cork.*
Working farm, overlooking the sea.
Open: Feb to Nov **Grades:** BF Approv
027 74058 Mrs O'Sullivan
Rates fr: *IR£13.00*-**IR£13.00.**
Beds: 2F 3D **Baths:** 2 Shared
(8)

Coulagh Bay House, *Eyeries, Bantry, Co Cork.*
Newly renovated house overlooking Coulagh Bay.
Open: Apr to Oct **Grades:** BF Approv
027 74013 Mrs O'Neill
Rates fr: *IR£15.00*-**IR£15.00.**
Beds: 1F 3D 2T
Baths: 6 Ensuite

Fermoy

National Grid Ref: W8198

Ardvarna, *Duntaheen Road, Fermoy, Co Cork.*
Modern comfortable bungalow in quiet area. Traditional hospitality guaranteed.
Open: Jun to Oct
025 31858 Mrs Crowley
Rates fr: *IR£14.00*-**IR£18.00.**
Beds: 1D 2T **Baths:** 2 Shared
(3)

Please respect a B&B's wishes regarding children, animals & smoking.

The lowest *double* rate per person is shown in *italics*.

Garnish

National Grid Ref: V5241

Windy Point House, *Garnish, Allihies, Bantry, Co Cork.*
Modern bungalow overlooking Dursey Island, all bedrooms with sea views.
Open: Apr to Oct
027 73017 Mr & Mrs Sheehan
Rates fr: *IR£15.00*-**IR£18.00.**
Beds: 3D 1T **Baths:** 4 Ensuite

Garretstown

National Grid Ref: W5846

Hurley's, Speckled Door

Waterfall House, *Garretstown, Kinsale, Co Cork.*
Modern house with tennis court on 8 acres, with views of the Old Head. 400 metres from Garretstown beach. Home baking.
Open: All Year
Grades: BF Approv
021 778359 Fax: no. 021 778359
Mrs Humberstone
Rates fr: *IR£17.00*-**IR£20.00.**
Beds: 1F 1D 1T 1S
Baths: 4 Ensuite
(8) (6)

Glandore

National Grid Ref: W2235

Glandore Inn

Kilfinnan Farm, *Glandore, Skibbereen, Co Cork.*
Modernised farmhouse, overlooking picturesque Glandore Harbour, quiet, peaceful surroundings, breathtaking scenery. **Open:** All Year
028 33233 Mrs Mehigan
Rates fr: *IR£14.00*-**IR£50.00.**
Beds: 1F 1D 1T
Baths: 1 Ensuite 2 Shared
(6)

Glanmire

National Grid Ref: W7275

Kilmore, *Sallybrook, Glanmire, Cork.*
Modern, comfortable family home in country, convenient to Cork City.
Open: All Year (not Xmas)
021 821388 Mrs Aimson
Rates fr: *IR£13.00*-**IR£16.00**.
Beds: 2F 2D 1T
Baths: 1 Ensuite 2 Shared

Glengarriff

National Grid Ref: V9256

Eccles Hotel, The Hungry Trout, Johnny Barrys, Casey's Hotel

Carraig Dubh House, *Droumgarriff, Glengarriff, Bantry, Co Cork.*
Open: Mar 15 to Oct
Grades: BF Approv
027 63146 Mrs Connolly
Rates fr: *IR£16.50*-**IR£20.00**.
Beds: 4D
Baths: 3 Ensuite 1 Private
(10)
Comfortable family home, set 150m off main road. Quiet and peaceful, overlooking Glengarriff Harbour and Caha Mountain Range. Only 0.5 km from golf club. Close to lake and sea for fishing. A perfect area for walking and water activities. Vouchers accepted

Ardnagashel Lodge, *Glengarriff, Bantry, Co Cork.*
Modern comfortable home in quiet sylvan setting. Central for touring.
Open: Apr to Oct **Grades:** BF Approv
027 51687 Mrs Ronayne
Rates fr: *IR£17.00*-**IR£30.00**.
Beds: 1D 2T
Baths: 3 Ensuite

High season, bank holidays and special events mean low availability *anywhere.*

Phoning from outside the Republic?

Dial 00353 and omit the initial '0' of the area code.

Carraig Liath, *Rossnasunsogue, Glengarriff, Bantry, Co Cork.*
Modern spacious bungalow, overlooking bay and Garnish Island.
Open: May to Oct
027 63327
Ms O'Mahony
Rates fr: *IR£15.00*-**IR£20.00**.
Beds: 2D 1T
Baths: 3 Ensuite
(0) (10)

Cois Coille, *Glengarriff, Bantry, Co Cork.*
Modern, comfortable home in quiet wooded area. Views over harbour.
Open: Apr to Oct
Grades: BF Approv
027 63202 Mrs Barry-Murphy
Rates fr: *IR£17.00*-**IR£22.00**.
Beds: 2F 2D 2T
Baths: 6 Ensuite

The Heights, *Carrigrour, Glengarriff, Bantry, Co Cork.*
Family-run farmhouse B&B, on a hill, 550 ft up above the harbour. We'll collect you!
Open: Mar to Oct **Grades:** BF Approv
027 63088 Mrs Harrington
Rates fr: *IR£17.00*-**IR£21.00**.
Beds: 1F 2D 1T

Magannagan Farm, *Derryconnery, Glengarriff, Bantry, Co Cork.*
Working farm with great views to Sugar Loaf Mountain.
Open: Apr to Oct
Grades: BF Approv
027 63361 Mrs O'Shea
Rates fr: *IR£16.00*-**IR£21.00**.
Beds: 3D
Baths: 2 Ensuite 1 Private

Goleen

National Grid Ref: V8128

The Heron's Cove, *Goleen Harbour, Goleen, Skibbereen, Co Cork.*
Comfortable rooms, good food and a seaside terrace!
Open: All Year (not Xmas)
028 35225 Mrs Hill
Rates fr: *IR£15.50*-**IR£18.50.**
Beds: 3D 2T
Baths: 5 Ensuite
(10)

Inniscarra

National Grid Ref: W5771

Blair's Inn

Chiriqui, *Canons Cross, Inniscarra, Cork.*
Comfortable restful home with mature grounds. Cork - Killarney scenic route.
Open: May to Oct **Grades:** BF Approv
021 871061 Mr & Mrs Roche
Rates fr: *IR£17.00*-**IR£25.00.**
Beds: 2D 2T **Baths:** 4 Ensuite
(4)

Knocklawn Wood, *Curraleigh, Inniscarra, Blarney, Cork.*
Picturesque, peaceful, electric blankets. Hot muffins on arrival. Fishing. Lee Valley. Near Blarney. R618.
Open: All Year **Grades:** BF Approv
021 870284 (also fax no)
Mrs O'Donovan
Rates fr: *IR£15.00*-**IR£18.00.**
Beds: 1F 1D 2T
Baths: 3 Ensuite 1 Shared
(6)

Innishannon

National Grid Ref: W5457

Ballymountain House, *Innishannon, Cork.*
Georgian style period country residence on working farm.
Open: All Year (not Xmas)
Grades: BF Approv, RAC Listed
021 775366 (also fax no)
Mrs Cummins
Rates fr: *IR£14.50*-**IR£18.00.**
Beds: 2F 3D 1T
Baths: 3 Ensuite 2 Shared

Kanturk

National Grid Ref: R3803

The Vintage Bar

Rosnalee Lodge, *Kilarney Road, Kanturk, Mallow, Co Cork.*
Comfortable welcoming family home situated on Killarney Road (N72).
Open: All Year **Grades:** BF Approv
029 56033 Mrs Kelleher
Rates fr: *IR£13.00*-**IR£15.00.**
Beds: 1F 2D 1T
Baths: 1 Ensuite 2 Shared

Kealkil

National Grid Ref: W0456

Graceland, *Kealkil, Bantry, Co Cork.*
Ideally located for touring/hiking. All amenities nearby. Wine licence.
Open: All Year **Grades:** BF Approv
027 66055 Fax no: 027 51749
Mrs Brennan
Rates fr: *IR£14.00*-**IR£19.00.**
Beds: 1F 1D 2T
Baths: 3 Ensuite 1 Private
(4)

Kilbrittain

National Grid Ref: W5247

Pink Elephant, Casino House

Seafield Farmhouse, *Glaunavaud, Kilbrittain, Bandon, Co Cork.*
Elevated farmhouse overlooking beach. Breathtaking views of sea and country-side.
Open: Easter to Nov
Grades: BF Approv
02349818 Ms Fielding
Rates fr: *IR£15.00*-**IR£18.00.**
Beds: 2F 3D
Baths: 4 Ensuite 1 Private
(4)

The lowest *double* rate per person is shown in *italics*.

Kilcatherine

National Grid Ref: V6353

Glor na Mara, *Kilcatherine, Eyeries, Bantry, Co Cork.*
Modern bungalow overlooking Coulagh Bay. **Open:** May to Oct
027 74012 Mrs Crowley
Rates fr: *IR£12.00*-**IR£12.00.**
Beds: 2D 1T
Baths: 2 Ensuite 1 Private

Killeagh

National Grid Ref: X1077

Tattans Bar, The Old Thatch

Ballymakeigh, *Killeagh, Youghal, Co Cork.*
National award-winning creeper-clad 300 year old farmhouse. Superb food
Open: Feb to Nov
Grades: AA 4 Q
024 95184 Mrs Browne
Rates fr: *IR£22.00*-**IR£27.00.**
Beds: 5F 2D
Baths: 7 Ensuite

Bromley, *Killeagh, Youghal, Co Cork.*
Modern home near Fota Wildlife Park.
Open: Mar to Oct **Grades:** BF Approv
024 95235 Mrs Fogarty
Rates fr: *IR£16.00*-**IR£19.00.**
Beds: 1F 1D 2T **Baths:** 4 Ensuite

Tattans, *Killeagh, Youghal.*
C18th pub and guest house in scenic village near seaside on N25.
Open: Mar to Oct
Grades: BF Approv, AA 3 St
024 95173 Mrs Tattan
Rates fr: *IR£17.00*-**IR£20.00.**
Beds: 2F 2D 2T
Baths: 5 Ensuite 1 Shared
(1) (8)

All details shown are as supplied by B&B owners in Autumn 1996

High season, bank holidays and special events mean low availability *anywhere.*

Killeens

National Grid Ref: W6475

Sunset Ridge Hotel, *Killeens, Blarney, Cork.*
Open: All Year
021 385271
Rates fr: *IR£20.00*-**IR£25.00.**
Beds: 5F 10D 10T 5S
Baths: 30 Ensuite
Family-run hotel, well known locally for its wholesome food. All rooms ensuite, satellite TV, telephone, full bar licence. Admission-free entertainment. Ample parking. Nature trail walk to Blarney Village adjacent to hotel. Friendly family, cots, baby-sitters.

Kinsale

National Grid Ref: W6450

1601 Bar, Katie's, White House, Blue Haven, Spinnaker Bar, Copper Grill, Castle Park, Shanakee, The Bulman, The Spaniard

The Gallery, *The Glen, Kinsale, Co Cork.*
Open: All Year
Grades: BF Approv
021 774558
Ms Crowley
Rates fr: *IR£20.00*-**IR£25.00.**
Beds: 4D
Baths: 4 Ensuite
(10)
The Gallery is centrally located in Ireland's gourmet capital and was awarded Best Residential Premises 1994-95. It is noted for its delightful ambience and charming decor. The Gallery is owned and run by two artists.

Lighthouse, *The Rock, Kinsale, Co Cork.*
Open: All Year
021 772734 Mrs O'Gorman
Rates fr: *IR£12.50*-**IR£40.00**.
Beds: 1F 4D 1T
Baths: 5 Ensuite
(10) (4)
Tudor style house. Antiques special feature. Four poster and canopy beds. Quiet location within walking distance of restaurants, pubs, historic sites and Marina. Panoramic harbour view from upstairs bedrooms. Breakfast menu. Recommended by world's top guides. Internationally acclaimed. Open all year.

Scellig, *Ardbrack, Kinsale, Co Cork.*
Open: All Year (not Xmas)
021 772832 Mrs Hurley
Rates fr: *IR£13.55*-**IR£20.00**.
Baths: 2 Ensuite 1 Private
(3)
Scellig House, overlooking Kinsale Harbour, is situated on the route to Summercove and Charles Fort. All rooms have superb sea-views, two with private balcony/patios. Kinsale centre is just 3 minutes drive away (or a 15 minute walk). Fromner, La Guide recommended.

Setanta, *1 Haven Hill, Summercove, Kinsale, Co Cork.*
Spacious rooms. Magnificent views of Kinsale. Personally run. Breakfast menu.
Open: Mar to Oct
021 772761 Mrs Allen
Rates fr: *IR£17.50*-**IR£20.00**.
Beds: 1D 2T **Baths:** 3 Ensuite
(3) (3)

Villa Maria, *Cork Road, Kinsale, Co Cork.*
Open: Mar to Nov **Grades:** BF Approv
021 772627 Mrs Sheehan
Rates fr: *IR£16.00*-**IR£22.00**.
Beds: 2F 3D 1T
Baths: 5 Ensuite
(3) (6)
We welcome you to stay at Villa Maria in olde worlde Kinsale, gourmet capital of Ireland. Great pub entertainment. Historic buildings. Airport 12 miles, ferryport 14 miles. Lovely walks. Conservatory for guests, also garden. We will make you very welcome. On Cork-Kinsale bus route.

Walyunga, *Sandycove, Kinsale, Co Cork.*
Open: Feb to Nov **Grades:** BF Approv
021 774126 Mrs Levis
Rates fr: *IR£16.00*-**IR£21.00**.
Beds: 2F 2D 1T
Baths: 4 Ensuite 1 Shared
(5) (5)
Bright spacious modern bungalow, unique design. Quiet location. Panoramic ocean and valley views. Landscaped garden and patio seats overlooking ocean. Sandy beaches and scenic coastal walks nearby. Bright comfortable rooms. Choice of breakfasts, warm and friendly atmosphere.

Ashling, *Bandon Road, Kinsale, Co Cork.*
Attractive modern ranch style bungalow with harbour views, parking, garden.
Open: Mar to Oct **Grades:** BF Approv
021 774127 Mrs McGlennon
Rates fr: *IR£14.00*-**IR£18.00**.
Beds: 1F 3D 1T
Baths: 4 Ensuite 1 Private
(5)

Danabel, *Sleaveen, Kinsale, Co Cork.*
Open: All Year
021 774087 Mrs Price
Rates fr: *IR£17.00*-**IR£25.00**.
Beds: 1F 2D 1T
Baths: 4 Ensuite
Modern house in quiet area. Town centre two minutes. Close to beaches, fishing, golf. Off main Cork road. Orthopaedic beds. Tea-making facilities in bedrooms. Travel Agents Vouchers accepted.

Murphys Farm House, *Kinsale, Co Cork.*
Open: March to Oct
021 772229
Fax no: 021 774176
Mrs Murphy
Rates fr: *IR£17.00*-**IR£17.00**.
Beds: 3D
Baths: 3 Ensuite
(6)
Lavishly modernised farm house. Central heating: 1 mile from seaside, Kinsale (fishing: swimming: boating), 18-hole & 9-hole golf courses nearby also horse riding near. 9 miles to Cork Airport: 16 miles to Cork harbour (Ringaskiddy), city 17 miles.

Ferny Field, *Tissasson, Whitecastle, Kinsale, Co Cork.*
Open: Apr to Oct
Grades: BF Approv
021 774539
Mr & Mrs Keohane
Rates fr: *IR£15.00*-**IR£25.00.**
Beds: 1F 4D
Baths: 3 Ensuite 2 Shared
(10)
Purpose-built dormer bungalow on two acres of landscaped gardens, overlooking the Bandon Estuary. Breakfast menu which can be enjoyed in sun lounge. TV lounge. New 18-hole golf course nearby. Private parking. Non-smoking. Gourmet capital Ireland 3 miles.

Rockville, *The Rock, Kinsale, Co Cork.* Modern, comfortable bungalow with magnificent views of Kinsale town and Harbour.
Open: All Year (not Xmas)
Grades: BF Approv
021 772791 Mrs Gray
Rates fr: *IR£16.00*-**IR£20.00.**
Beds: 1F 2D 1T
Baths: 3 Ensuite 1 Private
(4)

Compass Hill Lodge, *Compass Hill, Kinsale.*
Open: All Year (not Xmas)
Grades: BF Approv
021 774707
Fax no: 021 774788 Mr & Mrs Donohoe
Rates fr: *IR£20.00*-**IR£25.00.**
Beds: 2F 2D 1T
Baths: 5 Ensuite
(8)
Overlooking Bandon Estuary and bird sactuary. Within 10 minutes walk to town centre. All rooms have panoramic views, direct dial, television, orthopaedic beds with crisp white linen. Breakfast menu served in consevatory. Tennis court. Non-smoking. Mecca for golfers and sailors.

Jaina, *Pike Cross, Kinsale, Co Cork.* Modern luxurious bungalow, Spanish style breakfast conservatory patio, beautiful garden.
Open: All Year **Grades:** BF Approv
021 772692 Mrs Ahern
Rates fr: *IR£17.00*-**IR£22.00.**
Beds: 1F 1D 1T
Baths: 3 Ensuite
(4)

The lowest *double* rate per person is shown in *italics.*

Sea Gull House, *Cork Street, Kinsale, Co Cork.*
Open: Easter to Nov
Grades: BF Approv
021 772240
Mr & Mrs O'Neill
Rates fr: *IR£17.00*-**IR£20.00.**
Beds: 2D 2T 2S
Baths: 4 Ensuite

Family run home in Kinsale town. Next door to Desmond Castle and guided tours. Convenient to pubs, restaurants and beaches. Call to Tap Tavern Bar when in Kinsale. Family-run and music.

15 Main Street, *Kinsale, Co Cork.* Town centre historic building now a comfortable friendly family home.
Open: All Year (not Xmas)
021 774169
Mr & Mrs O'Farrell
Rates fr: *IR£14.00*-**IR£20.00.**
Beds: 1F 3D
Baths: 3 Ensuite 1 Shared

Hillside House, *Camphill, Kinsale, Co Cork.*
Open: All Year (not Xmas)
Grades: BF Approv
021 772315
Mrs Griffin
Rates fr: *IR£13.50.*
Beds: 1F 2D 3T
Baths: 6 Ensuite
(6)
Comfortable spacious home with lovely sea view. Beautifully landscaped gardens, situated on the camp site of the Battle of Kinsale. 10 mins walk from town centre. Open all year. Conservatory for guests only.

The lowest **single** *rate is shown in* **bold.**

Macroom

National Grid Ref: W3373

Abbey Hotel, Mills Inn, Auld Triangle Inn, Furys Pub, Victoria, River Inn

An Cuason, *Coolavokig, Macroom, Co Cork.*
Open: Easter to October
026 40018 Mrs Moynihan
Rates fr: *IR£14.00*-**IR£19.00**.
Beds: 1F 2D 3T
Baths: 5 Ensuite 1 Shared
Tranquil location on N22, convenient to Killarney, Blarney, Bantry, Ring of Kerry. Golf, fishing, walking. Breakfast menu, landscaped gardens, bicycle shed, downstairs accommodation. Credit cards accepted. Fresh home baking. Ideal base for touring South-West.

Firmount, *Killarney Road, Macroom, Co Cork.*
Modern two storey house, rural setting, overlooking golf course and river.
Open: All Year (not Xmas)
Grades: BF Approv
026 41186 Mrs McCarthy
Rates fr: *IR£16.00*-**IR£20.00**.
Beds: 1F 2D 1T 1S
Baths: 2 Ensuite 2 Shared
(6)

Coolcower House, *Macroom, Co Cork,*
Centrally located large country residence overlooking the River Lee. N22 Cork - Killarney.
Open: March to Nov
Grades: BF 2 St
026 41695 Fax no: 026 42119
Ms Casey
Rates fr: *IR£18.00*-**IR£20.00**.
Beds: 2F 2D 4T 2S
Baths: 10 Ensuite
(100)

Fountain House, *Cork Road, Macroom, Co Cork.*
Situated lakeside in beautiful Lee Valley. Ground floor rooms, ensuite.
Open: Easter to Nov
026 41424 Mrs Mulcahy
Rates fr: *IR£14.00*-**IR£18.00**.
Beds: 1F 2D 3T
Baths: 6 Ensuite
(12)

Mallow

National Grid Ref: W5598

Black Lamb Restaurant, Ruffles Restaurant, Kepplers Restaurant

Oaklands, *Springwood, Killarney Road, Mallow, Co Cork.*
Open: Mar to Nov
Grades: BF Approv, AA 3 Q
022 21127 (also fax no)
Mrs O'Donovan
Rates fr: *IR£28.00*-**IR£14.00**.
Beds: 1F 2D 1T
Baths: 2 Ensuite 1 Shared
(6)
AA 3 Q Recommended, luxurious detached home, set in landscaped gardens, in quiet location off Killarney Road (N72) near N20/N72 roundabout. Minutes to town and train. Orthopaedic beds, clock/radio, hairdryers. Breakfast menu. Secure private parking.

Midleton

National Grid Ref: W8874

Stock of Barley, Midleton Park, Farmgate Restaurant

Lough Carrig , *Ballinacurra, Midleton, Co Cork.*
Georgian residence in beautiful grounds overlooking the sea. Private and peaceful.
Open: Feb to Dec
Grades: BF Approv
021 631952 Fax no: 021 613707
Mr & Mrs Byrne
Rates fr: *IR£16.50*-**IR£20.00**.
Beds: 2D 2T
Baths: 2 Shared
(30)

Heathcliff, *Bailick Avenue, Castleredmond, Midleton, Co Cork.*
Select, modern home, quiet central location, breakfast menu, complimentary refreshments.
Open: All Year (not Xmas)
Grades: BF Approv
021 631901 Mrs Murphy
Rates fr: *IR£16.00*-**IR£18.00**.
Beds: 1F 1D 1T
Baths: 3 Ensuite
(1) (6)

***Sundown House,** Kilmountain, Castlemartyr, Midleton, Co Cork.*
Modern bungalow in scenic countryside. Close access to sandy beaches.
Open: Apr to Nov
Grades: BF Approv
021 667375
Mrs Quinlan
Rates fr: *IR£14.00*-**IR£19.00**.
Beds: 4D
Baths: 2 Ensuite
(6)

Ovens

National Grid Ref: W5420

Tatler Jack, White Horse

***Milestone,** Ovens, Ballincollig, Cork.*
Family-run home, highly commended. Ideal base to explore West Cork / Killarney / Kinsale.
Open: All Year
Grades: BF Approv
021 872562
Mrs Cronin
Rates fr: *IR£16.00*-**IR£20.00**.
Beds: 1F 1D 3T
Baths: 5 Private
(6)

Rath Luirc

National Grid Ref: R5323

***Marengo,** Ballyhea, Rath Luirc, (Charleville), Co Cork.*
Modern country home with beautiful mountain scenery. Hill-walking, golfing nearby.
Open: All Year
Grades: BF Approv
063 89658 Ms O'Riordan
Rates fr: *IR£14.00*-**IR£19.00**.
Beds: 2F 2T
Baths: 4 Ensuite
(4)

Irish Grid References are for villages, towns and cities - *not* for individual houses.

Ross Carbery

National Grid Ref: W2836

O'Callaghan Walshe Fish Restaurant, Carbery Arms, Country Kitchen

***Orchard,** Newtown, Ross Carbery, Co Cork.*
Modern country home on edge of seaside village. Perfect location for a quiet relaxing holiday.
Open: May to Sep **Grades:** BF Approv
023 48555 Mrs Kelly
Rates fr: *IR£15.00*-**IR£15.00**.
Beds: 2D 1T
Baths: 3 Ensuite
(3)

Rossmore

National Grid Ref: W3147

***Liscubba House,** Rossmore, Clonakilty, Co Cork.*
Old comfortable farmhouse in beautiful countryside. Home baking/cooking, fresh organic vegetables.
Open: All Year (not Xmas)
023 38679 Mrs Beechinor
Rates fr: *IR£14.00*-**IR£14.00**.
Beds: 1F 2D 1T 1S
Baths: 1 Shared
(0)

Schull

National Grid Ref: V9231

Blue Courtyard Bar Restaurant, La Coquille, Black Sheep Inn

***Corthna Lodge,** Corthna, Schull, Skibbereen, Co Cork.*
Open: Apr to Oct
Grades: BF 3 St
028 28517 Mr & Mrs Strickner
Rates fr: *IR£18.00*-**IR£25.00**.
Beds: 1F 3D 2T
Baths: 6 Ensuite 6 Private
(10)
Corthna Lodge country house is set overlooking the fishing village of Schull. It is surrounded by mountains and overlooking the sea. You can enjoy our patio area and gardens. The house is well furnished, tastefully decorated and quiet.

Old Bank House, *Schull, Skibbereen, Co Cork.*
Open: Easter to Sep **Grades:** AA 3 Q
028 28306 Mrs Donovan
Rates fr: *IR£16.00.*
Beds: 2F 1D 1T
Baths: 3 Ensuite 1 Private
(4)
Spacious, comfortable, turn-of-the-century family home. Adjacent to all amenities. Ideal location for relaxing holiday.

White Castle Cottage, *Ardintenant, Schull, Skibbereen, Co Cork.*
Detached cottage in colourful, sheltered garden. Quiet rural/coastal setting.
Open: All Year (not Xmas)
Grades: BF Approv
028 28528 Mrs Holt
Rates fr: *IR£13.00*-**IR£16.00**.
Beds: 1D 1T
Baths: 1 Shared
(4)

East End Hotel, *Main Street, Schull, Skibbereen, Co Cork.*
Family-run hotel overlooking Schull's magnificent harbour within walking distance of cosmopolitan village.
Open: All Year (not Xmas)
Grades: BF 2 St
028 28101 Ms Roche
Rates fr: *IR£17.00*-**IR£17.00**.
Beds: 3F 6D 7T 2S
Baths: 14 Ensuite 2 Shared

Skibbereen

National Grid Ref: W1233

Foleys Bar, Windmill Tavern

Sunnyside, *42 Mardyke Street, Skibbereen, Co Cork.*
Open: All Year
Grades: BF Approv
028 21365 Mrs Gill
Rates fr: *IR£15.00*-**IR£20.00**.
Beds: 1F 2D 2T 1S
Baths: 4 Ensuite 2 Shared
(5) (4)
Highly recommended, comfortable, spacious, very peaceful location in Skibbereen Town. Complimentary tea/coffee. Home baking. Bicycle storage. Wet clothes dried. Travel Agents Vouchers accepted. Close to pubs and restaurants. Signposted on R595.

Whispering Trees, *Baltimore Road, Skibbereen, Co Cork.*
Modern comfortable detached house on own grounds off Baltimore Road.
Open: Feb to Oct
Grades: BF Approv, AA 3 Q
028 21376
Mrs O'Sullivan
Rates fr: *IR£16.00*-**IR£20.00**.
Beds: 1F 3D 1T 1S
Baths: 5 Ensuite 1 Private
(10)

Illenside, *18 Bridge Street, Skibbereen, Co Cork.*
Large Victorian private house in the middle of the town.
Open: All Year (not Xmas)
Grades: BF 1 St
028 21605
Mr Collins
Rates fr: *IR£14.00*-**IR£14.00**.
Beds: 1F 2D 1T 2S
Baths: 2 Shared

Woodview, *off Baltimore Road, Skibbereen, Co Cork.*
Modern home, quiet location. Close to town centre.
Open: All Year
028 21740
Mrs O'Cinneide
Rates fr: *IR£16.00*-**IR£18.00**.
Beds: 1F 1D 1T
Baths: 2 Ensuite 1 Shared
(6)

Laughtons Little Acre, *Cork Road, Skibbereen, Co Cork.*
Ideally situated within walking distance of Skibbereen.
Open: All Year
Grades: BF Approv
028 22528
Mr & Mrs Laughton
Rates fr: *IR£12.00*-**IR£12.00**.
Beds: 2F 1D 2T
Baths: 5 Ensuite
(6)

All details shown are as supplied by B&B owners in Autumn 1996.

Snave

National Grid Ref: V9954

Odvane Falls Hotel, Bantry Bay Hotel, The Snug

Leaca House, *Snave, Ballylickey, Bantry, Co Cork.*
Open: Easter to Oct
Grades: BF Approv
027 51792 Mullins
Rates fr: *IR£16.00*-**IR£14.00**.
Beds: 2D 1S
Baths: 2 Ensuite 1 Shared
(6)
Spacious modern bungalow on the main Bantry/Glengarriff Road, N71. Its peaceful, tranquil rural setting is enhanced by panoramic views of Bantry Bay and miles of scenic countryside. Ideal base to stay when touring the South-West Coast.

Timoleague

National Grid Ref: W4743

Harbour Heights, *Timoleague, Bandon, Co Cork.*
Open: All Year (not Xmas)
Grades: BF Approv
023 46232
Mr & Mrs O'Donovan
Rates fr: *IR£16.00*-**IR£16.00**.
Beds: 1F 2D 1T
Baths: 3 Ensuite 1 Shared
(8)
Welcome to Harbour Heights. Family run. Spacious bungalow overlooking Courtmacsherry Bay. TV lounge and conservatory. Breakfast menu. Close to fishing, golf, watersports and coastal walks. Hospitality tray on arrival. Ideal base for touring West Cork. Kinsale 20 Km.

Pay B&Bs by cash or cheque. Be prepared to pay up front for one night stays.

Right on the border? Look at the neighbouring county, too

Toonbridge

National Grid Ref: W2970

The Auld Triangle

Kellehers Farmhouse, *Toonbridge, Macroom, Co Cork.*
Award winning exclusive modern farmhouse situated in beautiful woodland countryside. **Open:** Apr to Oct
026 41572 Mrs Kelleher
Rates fr: *IR£14.00*-**IR£14.00**.
Beds: 1F 3D 1T 1S
Baths: 1 Ensuite 1 Private 2 Shared
(15)

Watergrasshill

National Grid Ref: W7684

Father Prout Restaurant, The Watercress Diner

Ashgrove, *Watergrasshill, Cork.*
Modern house located in village and convenient to Cork City.
Open: All Year (not Xmas)
Grades: BF Approv
021 889220 Mrs Cronin
Rates fr: *IR£12.00*-**IR£14.00**.
Beds: 1F 1D 2T
Baths: 1 Ensuite 2 Shared

Waterloo

National Grid Ref: W6078

Christy Hotel Bar

Waterloo Inn, *Waterloo, Blarney, Cork.*
Country pub and B&B 1.5 miles from Blarney Stone in beautiful countryside.
Open: Easter to Nov
Grades: BF Approv
021 385113 Ms Doran
Rates fr: *IR£15.00*-**IR£18.00**.
Beds: 1F 2D 1T 1S
Baths: 3 Ensuite 2 Private
(15)

Youghal

National Grid Ref: X1077

Ahernes, Devonshire Hotel, Walter Raleigh Hotel, Earl of Orrery

Ballymakeigh, *Killeagh, Youghal, Co Cork.*
Open: Feb to Nov **Grades:** AA 4 Q
024 95184 Mrs Browne
Rates fr: *IR£25.00*-**IR£27.00.**
Beds: 5F 2D **Baths:** 7 Ensuite
National award-winning creeper-clad 300-year-old farmhouse. Delightful ambience, superb food, fine wines, seafood Galtee. Breakfast of the Year. 1 mile off N25, signposted Killeagh at Old Thatch. Brillant golf courses, Trabolgan holiday centre, Blue Flag beaches. Fota Wildlife Park nearby.

Devonshire Arms, *Pearse Square, Youghal, Co Cork.*
Old world antique furnished family hotel. **Open:** All Year (not Xmas)
Grades: BF 2 St, AA 2 St, RAC 2 St
024 92018 Fax no: 024 92900
Rates fr: *IR£28.00*-**IR£35.00.**
Beds: 10F 2D 8T
Baths: 10 Ensuite 10 Private
(Yes)

Avonmore House, *South Abbey, Youghal, Co Cork.*
Open: All Year (not Xmas)
Grades: BF Approv
024 92617 Mrs Gaine
Rates fr: *IR£15.00*-**IR£18.00.**
Beds: 1F 3D 1T 1S
Baths: 6 Ensuite
(10)
Beautifully renovated C18th Georgian house with all mod cons. 3 minute walk Youghal's famous clock tower and town centre. Private parking. Frommers Recommended. TV, hairdryers, tea/coffee-making facilities in rooms.

Walter Raleigh Hotel, *Youghal, Co Cork.*
Open: All Year
Grades: BF 2 St
024 92011
Fax no: 024 93560
Mr Murphy
Rates fr: *IR£23.00*-**IR£23.00.**
Baths: 26 Ensuite
A family run & owned hotel beside a Blue Flag beach, excellent beach, excellent food. All sporting facilities nearby, 10 golf courses, heritage town. Ideal touring location.

Bayview House, *Front Strand, Youghal, Co Cork.*
Beautifully restored Victorian residence 50 metres from magnificent Youghal Beach.
Open: Easter to Oct
Grades: BF Approv
024 92824
Ms Yeomans
Rates fr: *IR£16.00*-**IR£18.00.**
Beds: 1F 3D **Baths:** 4 Ensuite

Bromley, *Killeagh, Youghal, Co Cork.*
Modern home - 8 km from Youghal on N25 Rosslare - Cork Road. Two good pubs serving meals. Near Fota Wildlife Park and sandy beaches.
Open: Mar to Oct
Grades: BF Approv
024 95235 Mrs Fogarty
Rates fr: *IR£16.00*-**IR£19.00.**
Beds: 1F 1D 2T
Baths: 4 Ensuite

Always telephone to get directions to the B&B - you will save time!

County Donegal

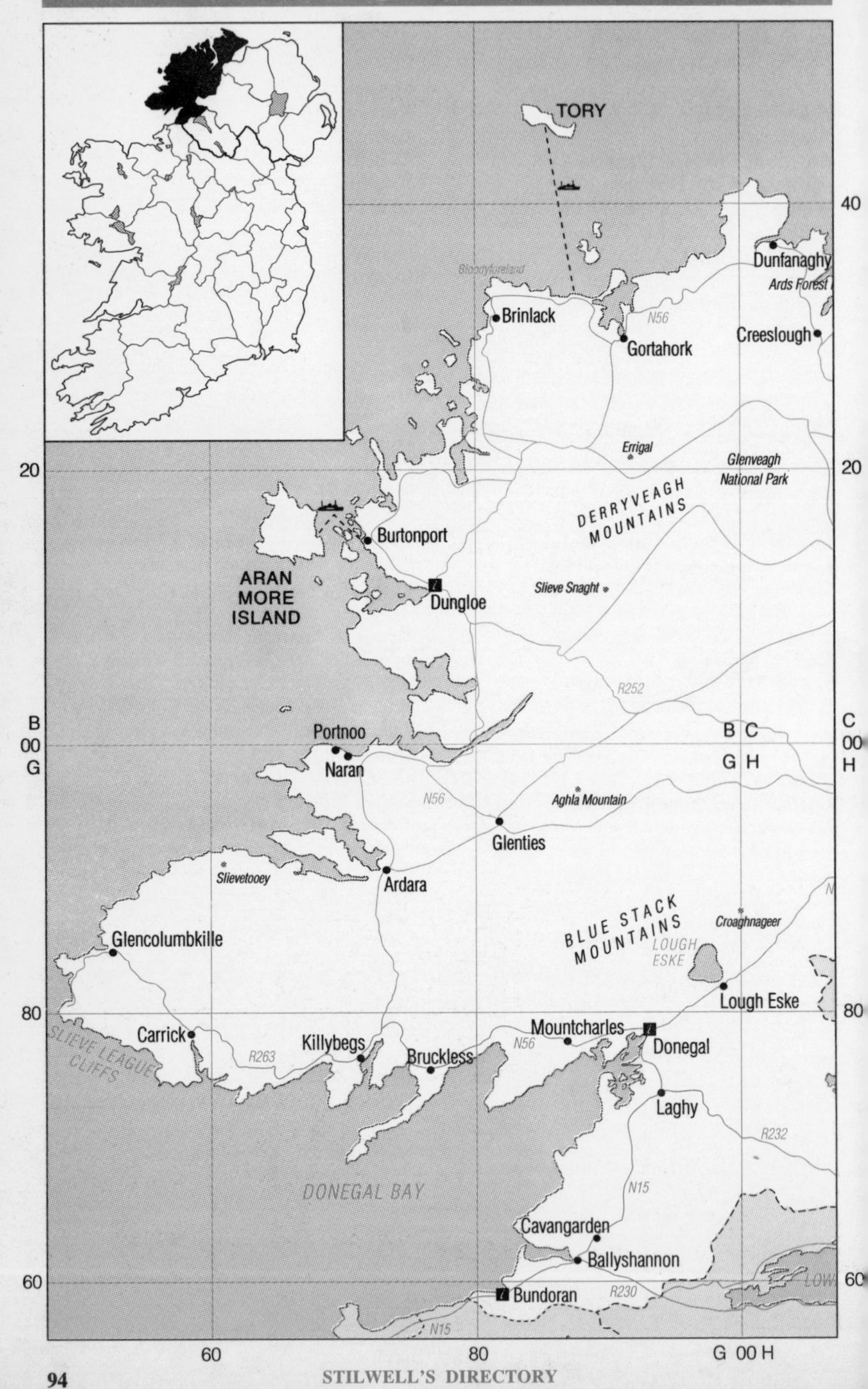

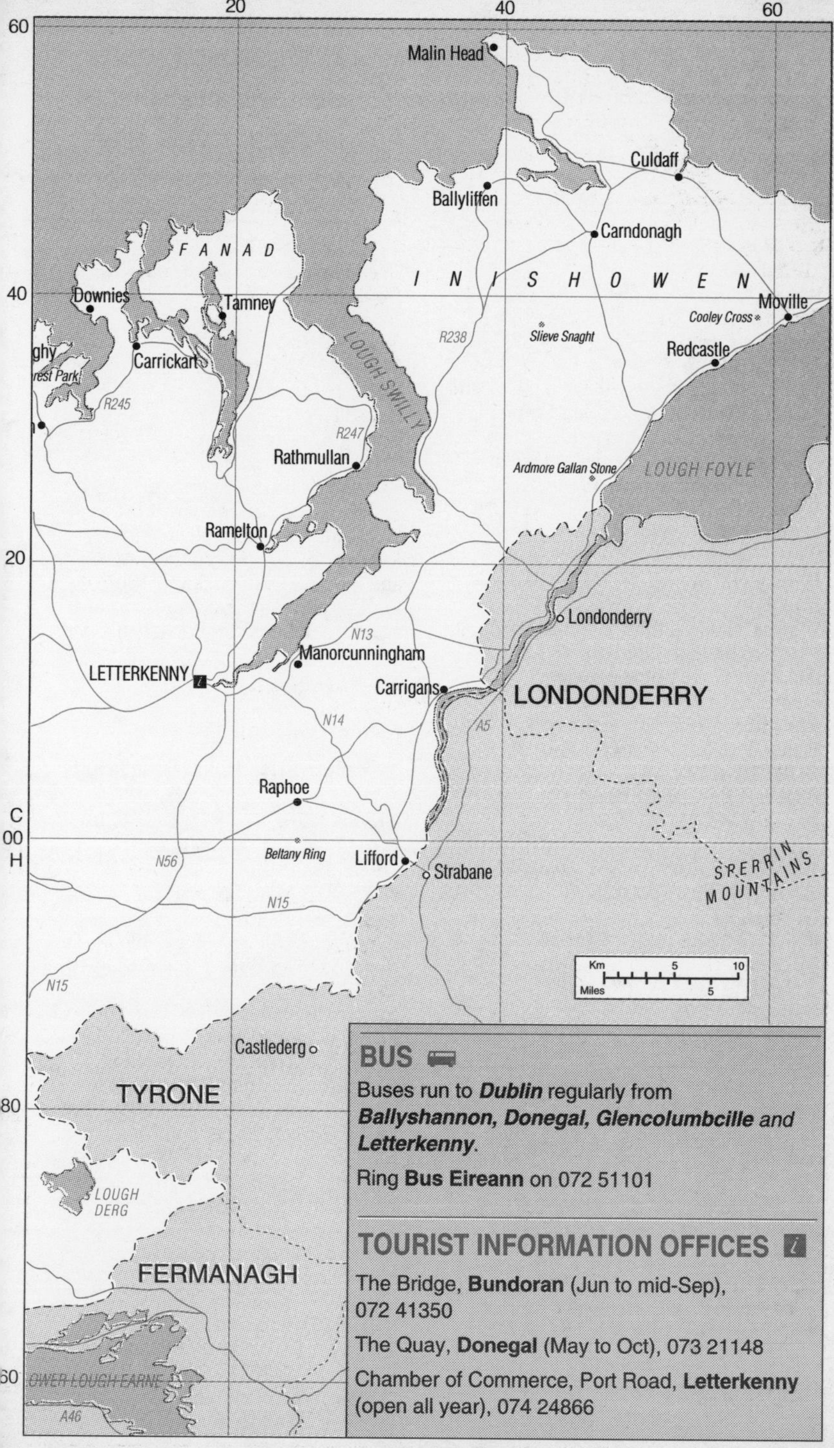

BUS

Buses run to ***Dublin*** regularly from ***Ballyshannon, Donegal, Glencolumbcille*** and ***Letterkenny***.

Ring **Bus Eireann** on 072 51101

TOURIST INFORMATION OFFICES

The Bridge, **Bundoran** (Jun to mid-Sep), 072 41350

The Quay, **Donegal** (May to Oct), 073 21148

Chamber of Commerce, Port Road, **Letterkenny** (open all year), 074 24866

Ardara

National Grid Ref: G7390

Nancy's Bar, Nesbitt Arms

***Bayview Country House,** Portnoo Road, Ardara, Donegal.*
Open: Feb to Dec
075 41145 (also fax no)
Mr & Mrs Bennett
Rates fr: *IR£16.00*-**IR£21.00**.
Beds: 2F 2D 2T 1S
Baths: 7 Ensuite
(10)
Spacious bungalow, extensive lawns and gardens overlooking sea and Owena River situated 0.5 miles from Ardara. Large parking area. Regional Galtee breakfast award winner 1994. All rooms ensuite. Tea/coffee facilities. Turf fire in lounge. Credit cards accepted.

***Homeward Bound,** Hillhead, Ardara, Donegal.*
Unusual modern family home. Elevated location, breathtaking views - mountains/sea. Great home cooking.
Open: All Year (not Xmas)
075 41246 Mr & Mrs Campbell
Rates fr: *IR£16.00*-**IR£21.00**.
Beds: 1F 4D 4T 1S
Baths: 8 Ensuite 2 Shared
(4)

***Woodhill House,** Ardara, Donegal.*
Open: All Year (not Xmas)
Grades: BF 3 St
075 41112 Fax no: 075 41516
Mr Yates
Rates fr: *IR£23.00*-**IR£18.00**.
Beds: 6D 1T 2S
Baths: 9 Ensuite
(20)
A historic coastal manor house overlooking the beautiful Donegal Highlands. The house, set in its own grounds, offers ensuite accommodation, a high quality restaurant, fully licensed bar and occasional live music. All major credit cards accepted.

The lowest *double* rate per person is shown in *italics*.

High season, bank holidays and special events mean low availability *anywhere*.

***Greenhaven,** Portnoo Road, Ardara, Donegal.*
Open: All Year (not Xmas)
Grades: BF Approv
075 41129 Mr & Mrs Molloy
Rates fr: *IR£14.50*.
Beds: 1F 3D 2T
Baths: 6 Ensuite
(6)
Located on edge of heritage town of Ardara. Ideal centre for touring Donegal's breathtaking scenic areas. Relax and enjoy excellent view of sea and mountains from dining room, lounge, patio and garden. Visa card accepted. Choice for breakfast.

Ballyliffen

National Grid Ref: C3848

Ballyliffen Hotel, Strand Hotel

***Ard na Mara,** Tornabratley, Ballyliffen, Carndonagh, Co Donegal.*
Open: Jan to Nov
077 76816 (also fax no)
Mrs Alsabti
Rates fr: *IR£15.00*-**IR£17.00**.
Beds: 1D 1T **Baths:** 1 Shared
(12) (6)
Modern spacious house. Peaceful, lovely countryside. Warm welcome, luxury bathroom, home cooking, tea/coffee anytime. Convenient to beaches, golf, scenic walks. Log fire on cool evenings. Every comfort catered for.

***Hillcrest,** Ballyliffen, Lifford, Co Donegal.*
Modern bungalow, beautiful scenery. Family run, home baking.
Open: All Year (not Xmas)
077 76151 Mrs Sweeney
Rates fr: *IR£14.50*-**IR£13.00**.
Beds: 2F 1D 1S
Baths: 2 Ensuite 1 Shared
(0)

Ballyshannon

National Grid Ref: G8761

Embers

Channel View, *The Abbey, Ballyshannon, Donegal.*
Beautiful bungalow overlooking Erne Estuary, near restored Abbey Mills. Water wheels.
Open: Easter to Sep
Grades: BF Approv
072 51713 Mrs Brennan
Rates fr: *IR£16.00*-**IR£20.00**.
Beds: 1F 2D 1T
Baths: 2 Ensuite 2 Shared
(5)

Brinlack

National Grid Ref: B8231

Foreland Heights Hotel

Ard Na Mara, *Chapel Road, Brinlack, Bloodyforeland, Letterkenny, Co Donegal.*
Modern, comfortable bungalow - with a panoramic view of Atlantic Ocean and surrounding islands.
Open: Easter to Sep
Grades: BF Approv
075 31364 Mrs Ferry
Rates fr: *IR£13.00*-**IR£15.00**.
Beds: 1F 2D 1S
Baths: 1 Ensuite 1 Shared
(1) (6)

Bruckless

National Grid Ref: G7676

Castle Murray Restaurant, Blue Haven Bar

Bruckless House, *Bruckless, Dunkineely, Donegal.*
C18th house with gardens & parkland. Connemara pony stud. Traditional farmyard.
Open: Easter to Oct
Grades: BF Approv
073 37071 Fax no: 073 37070
Mrs Evans
Rates fr: *IR£25.00*-**IR£25.00**.
Beds: 1D 1T 2S
Baths: 1 Ensuite 1 Shared
(6)

Castlereagh House, *Castlereagh, Bruckless, Donegal.*
Early C20th farmhouse situated in scenic area with panoramic views.
Open: Apr to Oct
Grades: BF Approv
073 37202
Mrs Henry
Rates fr: *IR£16.00*-**IR£21.00**.
Beds: 2D 1T
Baths: 3 Ensuite
(1) (6)

Bundoran

National Grid Ref: G8259

Marlborough House, Foxes Lair

Fitzgerald's , *Bundoran, Donegal.*
Comfortable town centre bistro bar overlooking sea, serving excellent food.
Open: All Year (not Xmas)
Grades: BF 2 St
072 41336
Mrs O'Donnell
Rates fr: *IR£15.00*-**IR£15.00**.
Beds: 2F 4D 4T 3S
Baths: 10 Ensuite 1 Private 1 Shared
(15)

Aughrus, *Tullan, Strand Road, Bundoran, Donegal.*
Modern bungalow beside the sea with ensuite rooms and parking.
Open: Easter to Sep
Grades: BF Approv
072 41556
Mrs Davey
Rates fr: *IR£16.00*-**IR£18.00**.
Beds: 1F 2D
Baths: 2 Ensuite 1 Private
(4) (4)

Bayview Guest House, *Main Street, Bundoran, Donegal.*
Georgian style guest house with uninterrupted view of Donegal Bay.
Open: All Year (not Xmas)
Grades: BF 2 St
072 41296
Fax no: 074 41147
Mr Grath
Rates fr: *IR£16.00*-**IR£23.00**.
Beds: 6F 9D 3T 1S
Baths: 18 Ensuite
(7)

Burtonport

National Grid Ref: B7115

Lobster Pot, Moorings, Teach Kilindarragh

Campbell's Pier House, *Burtonport, Letterkenny, Co Donegal.*
Comfortable period house overlooking scenic fishing harbour. Family run for over 30 years.
Open: All Year (not Xmas)
Grades: BF 2 St
075 42017 Campbell (Director)
Rates fr: *IR£14.00*-**IR£14.00**.
Beds: 3F 5D 3T 1S
Baths: 8 Ensuite 2 Shared
(10)

Carndonagh

National Grid Ref: C4645

Corncrake Restaurant

Radharc Na Coille, *Tiernaleague, Carndonagh, Lifford, Co Donegal.*
Modern house (family-run B&B), 1 km from Carndonagh town.
Open: Easter to Oct
Grades: BF Approv
077 74471 Ms Mc Cool
Rates fr: *IR£14.00*-**IR£15.00**.
Beds: 1F 2D 2T 1S
Baths: 3 Ensuite 2 Shared

Carrick

National Grid Ref: G5878

Village Restaurant (Kilcar)

Rockville, *Roxborough, Kilcar, Carrick, Donegal.*
Luxury bungalow overlooking Donegal Bay - beside Europe's highest sea-cliffs.
Open: All Year **Grades:** BF Approv
073 39107 Ms M Hughes
Rates fr: *IR£14.50*-**IR£19.50**.
Beds: 1F 2D 1T
Baths: 3 Ensuite 1 Private
(3) (6)

The lowest **single** *rate is shown in* **bold.**

Always telephone to get directions to the B&B - you will save time!

Carrickart

National Grid Ref: C1336

Sonas, *Upper Carrick, Carrickart, Letterkenny, Co Donegal.*
Modern dormer style bungalow, in beautiful quiet countryside overlooking Mulroy Bay.
Open: All Year
074 55401
Fax no: 074 55195
Mr & Mrs Gallagher
Rates fr: *IR£16.00*-**IR£21.00**.
Beds: 3D 1T
Baths: 4 Ensuite 1 Private
(1) (6)

Carrigans

National Grid Ref: C3611

Mount Royd, *Carrigans, Lifford, Co Donegal.*
Large spacious detached creeper-clad house with many home comforts.
Open: All Year
Grades: BF Approv, AA 4 Q
074 40163 Mrs Martin
Rates fr: *IR£16.00*-**IR£19.00**.
Beds: 3F 1D
Baths: 4 Ensuite

Cavangarden

National Grid Ref: G8863

Cavangarden House, *Cavangarden, Ballyshannon, Donegal.*
Spacious 1750 Georgian house on 380 acres. Private driveway, antique furniture, log fires, charming atmosphere, scenic views.
Open: Feb to Nov
072 51365
Mrs McCaffrey
Rates fr: *IR£16.00*-**IR£18.00**.
Beds: 2F 2D 2T
Baths: 6 Ensuite
(10)

Creeslough

National Grid Ref: C0530

Cora Cutters Restaurant, Red Roof

***McFadden's**, Creeslough, Letterkenny, Co Donegal.*
B&B central to lakes, forests, mountains, hills and Blue Flag beaches.
Open: Easter to Sep
Grades: BF Approv
074 38061
Mrs McFadden
Rates fr: *IR£13.00*-**IR£14.00**.
Beds: 1F 3D
Baths: 3 Ensuite 1 Shared
(10)

Culdaff

National Grid Ref: C5248

McGrory's

***Culdarff House**, Culdaff, Lifford, Co Donegal.*
300-year-old farmhouse in own wooded grounds ten minutes walk from beautiful beach.
Open: Mar to Oct
077 79103 Mrs Mills
Rates fr: *IR£15.00*-**IR£18.00**.
Beds: 2F 2D 2T
Baths: 2 Shared
(10)

Donegal

National Grid Ref: G9278

Old Castle Bar, Harbour Restaurant, Blueberry Tearooms

***Belle View**, Lurganboy, Ballyshannon Road, Donegal.*
Open: Easter to Nov
Grades: BF Approv
073 22167
Mrs Lawne
Rates fr: *IR£16.00*-**IR£18.00**
Beds: 3F 2D 2T
(6)
Nice, peaceful location off the main Donegal road. Modern accommodation in a restful touring location, overlooking Donegal bay, Blue Stack moutains. Le Guide de Routard listed. Beside craft village, golf course & nearby beaches.

***The Atlantic Hotel**, Main Street, Donegal.*
Open: All Year (not Xmas)
073 21187 Mr Browne
Rates fr: *IR£12.50*-**IR£16.00**.
Beds: 3F 8D 4T 3S
Baths: 8 Ensuite 8 Shared
(14)
Beautifully maintained family-run guest house in the centre of Donegal town, beside all bars, shops and restaurants. Plenty of local amenities. TV and tea and coffee facilities in all bedrooms. Private secure car parking. Access, Visa and Mastercard accepted.

***Maranatha**, The Glebe, Donegal.*
Modern home overlooking Donegal Bay five minutes walk to town.
Open: All Year (not Xmas)
Grades: BF Approv
073 22671 Mrs Ryle
Rates fr: *IR£15.00*-**IR£20.00**.
Beds: 2F 1D 1T
Baths: 2 Ensuite 1 Shared
(4)

***Island View House**, Ballyshannon Road, Donegal,*
Large Georgian two storey. Private house overlooking Donegal Bay.
Open: All Year
Grades: BF Approv
073 22411 Mrs Dowds
Rates fr: *IR£16.50*-**IR£25.00**.
Beds: 2F 1D 1T
(6 mnths) (4)

***The Waters Edge**, The Glebe, Donegal,*
Spectacular home with gardens rolling down to Donegal Bay.
Open: All Year (not Xmas)
Grades: BF Approv
073 21523 Mrs McGowan
Rates fr: *IR£15.00*-**IR£25.00**.
Beds: 2D 1T 1F
Baths: 4 Ensuite
(6)

High season, bank holidays and special events mean low availability *anywhere.*

Glebe, *Ballyshannon Road, Donegal.*
Dormer bungalow beside, overlooking Donegal Bay. Five minutes walk from town.
Open: Easter to Oct
073 21223 Mrs Murray
Rates fr: *IR£16.00*-**IR£20.00**.
Beds: 1F 2D 2T
Baths: 3 Ensuite 2 Private
(4)

Windermere, *Quay Street, Donegal.*
Townhouse accommodation in the centre of Donegal town.
Open: All Year (not Xmas)
073 21323
Mr Ryle
Rates fr: *IR£13.00*-**IR£14.00**.
Beds: 2F 6D 2T
Baths: 2 Ensuite 3 Shared
(1)

Downies

National Grid Ref: C0938

North Star Pub, Weavers

An Crossog, *Downies, Letterkenny, Co Donegal.*
Open: Easter to Oct
Grades: BF Approv, RAC Listed
074 55498
Mrs Herraghty
Rates fr: *IR£14.00*-**IR£20.00**.
Beds: 2D 2T
Baths: 3 Ensuite 1 Private
Gracious country home overlooking the Atlantic. 500 metres off Atlantic Drive Scenic Route. 30 km from Letterkenny on R245 Road. Sandy beaches, golf, horseriding nearby. Recommended by American and European guide books for good food and hospitality. Breakfast/dinner menus.

High season, bank holidays and special events mean low availability *anywhere.*

Dunfanaghy

National Grid Ref: C0137

Arnold's Bistro

Rosman House, *Figart, Dunfanaghy, Letterkenny, Co Donegal.*
Open: All Year
Grades: BF Approv
074 36273
Mrs McHugh
Rates fr: *IR£16.00*-**IR£21.00**.
Beds: 3F 2D 1T
Baths: 6 Ensuite
(8)
Rosman House is on an elevated site with spectacular views of Horn Head, Muckish Mountain, and Sheephaven Bay. '300 Best B&Bs' recommended. All rooms with radio, TV, electric blankets, tea/coffee making facilities, hairdryers. Convenient to beach, golf, riding, fishing and Glenveagh.

Dungloe

National Grid Ref: B7711

Sweeny's Hotel, Michael O'Donnell Bar, Doherty's Restaurant, Riverside Bistro

Park House, *Carnmore, Dungloe, Donegal.*
Located in a prime fishing area. Group discounts in the off season.
Open: All Year
075 21351
Mrs O'Donnell
Rates fr: *IR£16.00*-**IR£18.00**.
Beds: 3F 4D 4T 2S
Baths: 9 Ensuite 1 Private 3 Shared
(All) (15)

Chalet, *Marameelan, Meenacross, Dungloe, Donegal.*
Modern seafront bungalow, sandy beach, scenic walks, fishing, golf, horse-riding.
Open: Jun to Sep
Grades: BF Approv
07521068 Mrs Boyle
Rates fr: *IR£14.00*-**IR£15.00**.
Beds: 1F 2D
Baths: 1 Ensuite

Innisheen, *Quay Road, Dungloe, Donegal.*
Family home overlooking Dungloe Bay. Nice relaxed atmosphere, home baking.
Open: May to Oct **Grades:** BF Approv
075 22062 Mrs Gallagher
Rates fr: *IR£13.00*-**IR£13.00**.
Beds: 1D 1T 1S **Baths:** 1 Shared

Roinnis, *Mill Road, Dungloe, Donegal.*
Spacious modern bungalow, seaside. Ideal touring centre for North-West Donegal.
Open: Apr to Oct **Grades:** BF Approv
075 21094 Mrs McCole
Rates fr: *IR£14.00*-**IR£18.00**.
Beds: 2F 2D
Baths: 2 Ensuite 1 Shared

Glencolumbkille

National Grid Ref: G5384

Glencolumbkille Hotel

Brackendale, *Cashel, Glencolumbkille, Donegal.*
Modern bungalow, in a valley which is a walker's paradise
Open: All Year
073 30038 Mrs Cunningham
Rates fr: *IR£14.00*-**IR£17.00**.
Beds: 2D 1F 1S
Baths: 2 Ensuite 1 Shared
(5)

Scrigmor House, *Lower Dooey, Glencolumbkille, Donegal.*
Modern bungalow. Views over sea. In heart of Donegal Mountains.
Open: Jun to Sep **Grades:** BF Approv
073 30174 Mrs Doherty
Rates fr: *IR£13.00*-**IR£15.00**.
Beds: 1F 2D 1T 1S
Baths: 1 Ensuite 2 Shared
(6)

Ros Mor, *Malinmore, Glencolumbkille, Donegal.*
Modern two storey house overlooking the Atlantic Ocean, magnificent views.
Open: Easter to Sep
073 30083 Mrs O'Gara
Rates fr: *IR£14.00*-**IR£16.00**.
Beds: 1F 2D
Baths: 3 Ensuite 1 Private

Glenties

National Grid Ref: G8194

Highland's Hotel

Avalon, *Glen Road, Glenties, Donegal.*
Open: Feb to Nov
075 51292 Ms Boyle
Rates fr: *IR£14.00*-**IR£19.00**.
Beds: 1F 2D 1T
Baths: 3 Ensuite 1 Private
Beautifully situated bungalow in scenic surrounds of the Bluestack Mountains. Ideal touring base. Glenties - 1995 winners of Ireland's Tidiest Town. Setting for Brian Friel's award winning play 'Dancing at Lughnasa' and also the home of the navvy poet, Patrick McGill.

Oakdale Farmhouse, *Derries, N56 Route, Glenties, Donegal.*
Comfortable farmhouse set in picturesque countryside, ideal for touring Donegal.
Open: Easter to Oct
Grades: BF Approv
075 51262 Mrs O'Donnell
Rates fr: *IR£16.00*-**IR£21.00**.
Beds: 2D 2T
Baths: 3 Ensuite 1 Shared

Gortahork

National Grid Ref: B9130

An Shorlan Hotel, *Gortahork, Letterkenny, Co Donegal.*
Golf, horse-riding, surfing, hill-walking, cycling, motorcycle club, 4x4 Discovery Club.
Open: Easter to Oct
Grades: BF 1 St
074 35259 / 65189
Mr & Mrs Bonner
Rates fr: *IR£10.00*-**IR£16.00**.
Beds: 2F 5D 3T 1S
Baths: 11 Ensuite 1 Private 1 Shared
(10) (50)

The lowest *double* rate per person is shown in *italics*.

Killybegs

National Grid Ref: G7176

Pier Bar, Pat McGinleys

Lismolin Country Home, *Fintra Road, Killybegs, Donegal.*
Modern spacious family home in quiet scenic location. Turf fires.
Open: All Year (not Xmas)
Grades: BF Approv
073 31035
Mrs Cahill
Rates fr: *IR£16.00*-**IR£19.50**.
Beds: 3F 1D 1T
Baths: 5 Ensuite
(5)

Lough Head House, *Killybegs, Donegal.*
Modern bungalow overlooking Killybegs Harbour.
Open: Easter to Oct
073 31088
Mrs McKeever
Rates fr: *IR£14.50*-**IR£20.00**.
Beds: 1D 2T
Baths: 2 Ensuite 1 Shared

Laghy

National Grid Ref: G9474

Moorland Country Guesthouse, *Ballinakillew Mountain, Laghy, Donegal.*
Newly-built guesthouse with family character, situated in wild high moor/hill landscape
Open: All Year
Grades: BF 3 St
073 34319
Rates fr: *IR£15.00*-**IR£20.00**.
Beds: 4D 4T
Baths: 8 Ensuite
(20)

Always telephone to get directions to the B&B - you will save time!

Letterkenny

National Grid Ref: C1711

Silver Tassie, Clanree Hotel

Whitepark, *Ballyraine, Letterkenny, Co Donegal.*
Spacious home, garden patio area with sun-lounge. Ideal touring base.
Open: All Year (not Xmas)
Grades: BF Approv
074 24067 Mr & Mrs O'Donnell
Rates fr: *IR£16.00*-**IR£20.00**.
Beds: 4F 2D
Baths: 6 Ensuite
(8)

Hillcrest House, *Sligo Road, Lurgybrack, Letterkenny, Co Donegal.*
Modern home on N56 to Sligo overlooking town and river.
Open: All Year (not Xmas)
Grades: BF Approv, AA 3 Q, RAC 2 St, Acclaim
074 22300 / 25137
Fax no: 074 25137
Mrs Maguire
Rates fr: *IR£15.00*-**IR£20.00**.
Beds: 2F 2D 2T
Baths: 5 Ensuite 1 Private
(12)

Radharc Na Gluis, *Carnamuggagh, Kilmacrennan Road, Letterkenny, Co Donegal.*
Frommer Recommended, spacious house overlooking town on N56 to Dunfanaghy.
Open: All Year (not Xmas)
Grades: BF Approv
074 25139 / 22090 Mrs Bradley
Rates fr: *IR£16.00*-**IR£21.00**.
Beds: 5F 1D
Baths: 6 Ensuite
(1) (8)

Bella Vista, *Derry Road, Dromore, Letterkenny, Co Donegal.*
Secluded quiet residence overlooking Lough Swilly. Frommer Recommended 1995.
Open: Easter to Oct
074 22529 Mrs Lee
Rates fr: *IR£14.00*-**IR£15.00**.
Beds: 1F 2D 1T
Baths: 3 Ensuite 1 Shared

Glencairn Houe, *Ramelton Road, Letterkenny, Co Donegal.*
Panoramic view from patio. Near Mount Errigal Hotel. Comfortable accommodation.
Open: All Year **Grades:** BF Approv
074 24393 / 25242 Mrs McCleary
Rates fr: *IR£16.00*-**IR£20.00.**
Beds: 4D 2T
Baths: 5 Ensuite 1 Private

Lifford

National Grid Ref: H3398

Martha's Vineyard, Fir Trees Hotel, McCauley's

Haw Lodge, *The Haw, Lifford, Co Donegal.*
Open: Mar to Nov
Grades: BF Approv, RAC Listed
074 41397/41985 Fax: 074 41985
Mrs Patterson
Rates fr: *IR£14.00*-**IR£16.00.**
Beds: 1F 2D 1T
Baths: 2 Ensuite 1 Private 1 Shared
(8)
A warm welcome awaits you at this charming old farmhouse where guests return year after year. Situated on N15 Road to Donegal town. Excellent touring centre or overnight stop. Golf, fishing, horse riding, greyhound racing and good restaurants locally. Livestock farm. Access/Visa accepted.

Hall Greene, *Porthall, Lifford, Co Donegal.*
Friendly family-run C17th farmhouse, central for touring.
Open: All Year (not Xmas)
074 41318 Mr & Mrs McKean
Rates fr: *IR£14.00*-**IR£19.00.**
Beds: 2F 1D 1T
Baths: 2 Ensuite 2 Shared

Rossborough House, *Lifford, Co Donegal.*
Detached period house sited in town yet in country.
Open: All Year (not Xmas)
074 41132 Mrs Quigley
Rates fr: *IR£15.00*-**IR£15.00.**
Beds: 2F 2T 4D 2S
Baths: All Ensuite
(1)

Lough Eske

National Grid Ref: G9882

McGroarty's, The Diamond

Eske View, *Lough Eske, Barnesmore, Donegal.*
Open: Easter to Sep
Grades: BF Approv
073 22087 Mrs Pearson
Rates fr: *IR£15.00*-**IR£20.00.**
Beds: 2D 1T **Baths:** 3 Ensuite
(7) (6)
Luxurious accommodation. Ensuite bedrooms. Bedrooms and lounge have spectacular views of Lough Eske and the Blue Stack Mountains. Large mature gardens. Ideal touring base. Peaceful and quiet with panoramic view of surrounding countryside. Personal service by proprietors.

Malin Head

National Grid Ref: C3958

Barraicin, *Malin Head, Inishowen, Co Donegal.*
Modern comfortable bungalow, near Ireland's most northerly point. Peaceful scenic surroundings.
Open: Easter to Oct
Grades: BF Approv
077 70184 (also fax no) Mrs Doyle
Rates fr: *IR£14.00*-**IR£17.00 .**
Beds: 1F 1D 1T
Baths: 1 Ensuite 1 Shared
(3)

Manorcunningham

National Grid Ref: C2411

Silver Tassie, Readars Bar, Clanree Hotel

Isle View House, *Manorcunningham, Letterkenny, Co Donegal.*
Dormer bungalow, panoramic view of Lough Swilly, central for touring. Colour TV, tea-making facilities and hair-dryers in rooms.
Open: All Year (not Xmas)
074 57367 / 57303 Mrs Duggan
Rates fr: *IR£13.00*-**IR£15.00.**
Beds: 1F 2D 1T
Baths: 2 Ensuite 2 Shared

Mountcharles

National Grid Ref: G8677

Seamount, Meehans Bar

Coast Road Guest House, *Main Street, Mountcharles, Donegal.*
Open: All Year (not Xmas)
Grades: BF 1 St
073 35018
Rates fr: *IR£14.00*-**IR£15.00.**
Beds: 1F 2D 1T 1S
Baths: 2 Ensuite 1 Shared
(1)
Coast road guest house, Mountcharles, Co. Donegal. Open all year (not Xmas). Rates from IR£14.00, 2 Ensuite, 2 Double, 1 Single. Ideal centre for touring Donegal. 18 hole golf course nearby, fishing, beach and scenic walks. Personal attention.

Moville

National Grid Ref: C6138

Kealy's

Gulladuff House, *Malin House, Moville, Inishowen, Letterkenny, Co Donegal.*
1788 house in private wooded grounds - Ireland's oldest bridge. Fishing.
Open: All Year
077 82378 Fax no: 01504 372187
Ms Canavan
Rates fr: *IR£13.00*-**IR£15.00.**
Beds: 1F 1D 1T
Baths: 1 Ensuite 1 Shared
(1)

Naran

National Grid Ref: G7098

Naran Inn

Thalassa Country Home, *Naran, Portnoo, Donegal.*
Modern family home. Overlooking ocean. Golf course. Magnificent coastal region.
Open: Feb to Nov
075 45151 Mrs Friel
Rates fr: *IR£15.00*-**IR£16.00.**
Beds: 3F 1D
Baths: 4 Ensuite
(4)

Phoning from outside the Republic?

Dial 00353 and omit the initial '0' of the area code.

Portnoo

National Grid Ref: G6999

Lake House Hotel, *Clooney, Portnoo, Donegal.*
Home away from home but we look after you well.
Open: Mar to Nov **075 45123**
Rates fr: *IR£12.00*-**IR£16.00.**
Beds: 4F 4D 4T 2S
Baths: 6 Ensuite 1 Shared
(20)

Ramelton

National Grid Ref: C2221

Mirabeau Steak House, Bridge Bar

Ardeen, *Ramelton, Letterkenny, Co Donegal.*
Old country home overlooking river. Convenient to beaches, national park.
Open: Easter to Oct
074 51243 Mrs Campbell
Rates fr: *IR£17.00*-**IR£18.50.**
Beds: 1F 2D 1T 1S
Baths: 2 Ensuite 3 Private 2 Shared
(10)

Crammond, *Market Square, Ramelton, Letterkenny, Co Donegal.*
Comfortable C18th house in centre of village. Central for touring Donegal.
Open: Easter to Oct
Grades: BF Approv
074 51055 Mrs Corry
Rates fr: *IR£14.00*-**IR£18.50.**
Beds: 2F 1D 1T **Baths:** 2 Shared
(6)

The lowest **single** *rate is shown in* **bold.**

Raphoe

National Grid Ref: C2503

Central Hotel

Strabane Road, *Raphoe, Lifford, Co Donegal.*
Modern bungalow three minutes walk from Raphoe town, ideal base for touring, Giants Causeway. Tea facilities, TV in all rooms. Home baking.
Open: Easter to Nov
074 45410 Mrs Chambers
Rates fr: *IR£14.00.*
Beds: 2F 1T
Baths: 2 Ensuite
(2) (4)

Rathmullan

National Grid Ref: C2927

Carriglough House, *Saltpans, Rathmullan, Letterkenny, Co Donegal.*
Farmhouse in tranquil setting, by secluded lake, woods and hill.
Open: Mar to Nov **Grades:** BF Approv
074 58197 Mrs Hodgson
Rates fr: *IR£14.00*-**IR£14.00.**
Beds: 1F 1T 1S
Baths: 2 Shared
(3)

Redcastle

National Grid Ref: C3555

Redcastle Hotel, Loyle Hotel, McNamons Hotel, Rosatos Bar

Fernbank, *Redcastle P O, Redcastle, Lifford, Co Donegal.*
My house is situated overlooking beautiful Lough Foyle, Inishowen.
Open: Easter to Dec
Grades: BF Approv
077 83032 Mrs McLaughlin
Rates fr: *IR£16.00*-**IR£16.00.**
Beds: 1F 3D
Baths: 2 Ensuite 1 Private 2 Shared

Tamney

National Grid Ref: C1938

Avalon, *Tamney, Fanad Peninsular, Letterkenny, Co Donegal.*
Traditional farmhouse in scenic countryside. Warm welcome assured. Good food. **Open:** Easter to Oct
074 59031 Mrs Borland
Rates fr: *IR£14.00*-**IR£18.00.**
Beds: 1F 1D 1T 1S
Baths: 1 Ensuite 1 Shared
(10)

County Dublin

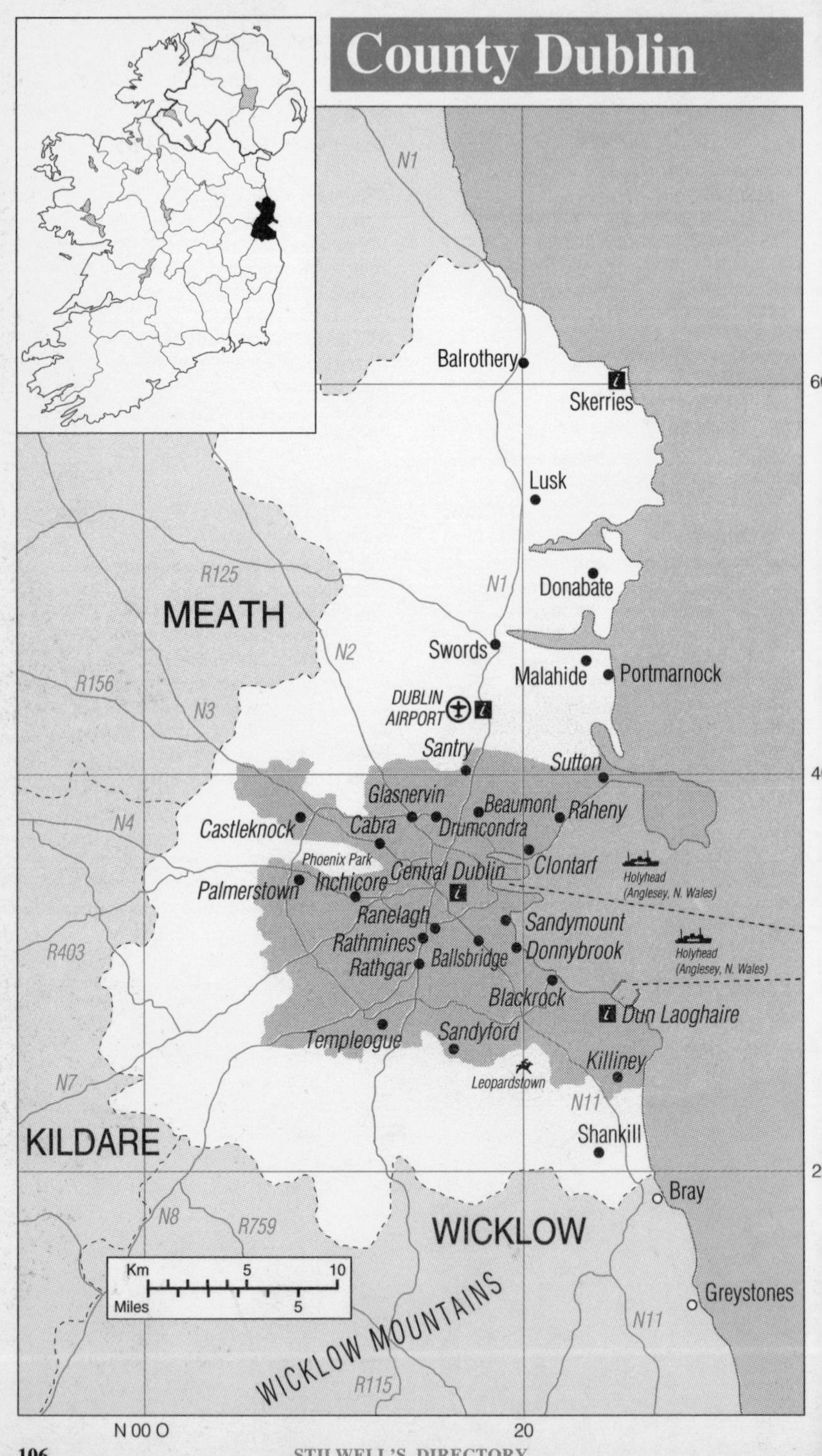

AIRPORTS

Dublin Airport - 01 8445900

AIR SERVICES & AIRLINES

***Dublin** to **Birmingham, Bradford, Bristol, East Midlands, Edinburgh,Glasgow, Heathrow, Manchester, Newcastle**.*

Aer Lingus - in Republic, tel. 01 8370011 - in UK tel. 0181 899 4747.

***Dublin** to **Birmingham, Glasgow (Prestwick), Liverpool, London (Gatwick), London (Luton), London (Stansted), Manchester**.*

Ryanair - In Republic, tel 01 6774422 - in UK, tel 0171 435 7101.

RAIL

***Dublin** (Connolly)* serves the North, Northwest and East Coast with lines to ***Belfast, Londonderry, Sligo, Wexford** and **Rosslare**.*

Dublin** (Heuston)* serves the West, South and South West with lines to ***Galway, Westport (Mayo), Limerick, Cork, Tralee** and **Waterford.

For timetable details phone **Irish Rail**: 01 8366222

FERRIES

***Dun Laoghaire** to **Holyhead** (Car Ferry 3½ hrs, High Speed Sea 99 mins, Catamaran 1¾ hrs) -*
Stena Sealink - tel in Republic 01 2808844 - in UK 01233 647047/615455)

***Dublin** to **Holyhead** (3½ hrs) -*
Irish Ferries - in Republic, tel 01 6610511 - in UK tel 0151 227 3131.

BUS

There are bus services to all major towns in the Republic and Northern Ireland.

Tel **Bus Eireann** on 01 8366111

TOURIST INFORMATION OFFICES

Dublin Airport (open all year), tel 01 8376387

14 Upper O'Connell Street, **Dublin** 1 (open all year), tel. 01 8747733

The Port, **Dun Laoghaire** (open all year), tel. 01 2806984

Skerries, 01 8490888

Balrothery

National Grid Ref: O2061

Balrothery Inn

***6 Knightswood,** Balrothery, Balbriggan, Co Dublin.*
Open: May 16 to Oct 5
Grades: BF Approv
01 8411621 Mrs Clarke
Rates fr: *IR£16.50*-**IR£25.00**.
Beds: 2D 1T
Baths: 1 Ensuite 2 Shared
(3)
Modern comfortable detached residence in quiet rural setting. Convenient to airport, golf courses, seaside and hostelry. Situated off N1.

The lowest *double* rate per person is shown in *italics*.

The lowest **single** *rate is shown in* **bold.**

Donabate

National Grid Ref: O2250

Beaverton Golf Club

***Tir Na Nog,** Beaverstown, Donabate, Co Dublin.*
Modern farmhouse, seaview, ponies, sheep on farm, 15 minutes drive to airport.
Open: All Year (not Xmas)
01 8436864
Mrs Heneghan
Rates fr: *IR£15.00*-**IR£20.00**.
Beds: 2F 2T
Baths: 3 Ensuite 1 Shared
(1) (8)

Dublin — Ballsbridge

National Grid Ref: O1831

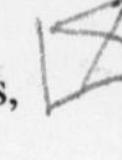

Jury's Hotel, Kitty O'Shea's, Bellamy's

***Darren House,** 7 Pembroke Road, Ballsbridge, Dublin 4.*
Beautiful Georgian residence. Top of Baggot Street.
Open: All Year (not Xmas)
Grades: BF Approv
01 6606126
Fax no: 01 6607979
Mr Liston
Rates fr: *IR£25.00*-**IR£38.00**.
Beds: 2F 2T
Baths: 4 Ensuite
(1) (3)

Dublin — Beaumont

National Grid Ref: O1738

Beaumont House

***St Rita's Guest House,** 11 Coolatree Close, Beaumont, Dublin 9.*
Situated off main Airport road. 5 mins from Airport. Open all year.
Open: All Year
Grades: BF Approv
01 8360760
Mrs McLoughlin
Rates fr: *IR£15.00*-**IR£18.50**.
Beds: 4F 2D 2T
Baths: 2 Ensuite

Dublin — Blackrock

National Grid Ref: O2228

O'Rourke's, Coopers Restaurant, The Brasserie

***Idone House,** Newtown Avenue, Blackrock, Co Dublin.*
Lovely Georgian home with sea view and village atmosphere.
Open: All Year
Grades: BF Approv
01 2882330
Mrs Potter
Rates fr: *IR£23.00*-**IR£32.00**.
Beds: 1F 1D 2T 2S
Baths: 6 Ensuite
(4)

Dublin — Cabra

National Grid Ref: O1237

Halfway House, Turnstile, Hole in the Wall

***Wyoming,** 173 Navan Road, Cabra, Dublin 7.*
Comfortable town house on main road three miles from Dublin.
Open: All Year (not Xmas)
Grades: BF Approv
01 8380154 Mrs Dexter
Rates fr: *IR£18.00*-**IR£25.00**.
Beds: 2D 1S
Baths: 2 Ensuite 1 Shared
(3)

Dublin — Castleknock

National Grid Ref: O0837

Half Way House Restaurant, Scotts Restaurant

***Deerpark House,** Castleknock Road, Phoenix Park Gates, Castleknock, Dublin 15.*
Large detached old world house completely restored to high standard.
Open: All Year **Grades:** BF Approv
01 8207466 Mrs McKay
Rates fr: *IR£17.50*-**IR£20.00**.
Beds: 2F 3D 2T
Baths: 6 Ensuite 1 Private
(9)

Dublin — Central Dublin

National Grid Ref: O1634

Old Stand, Big Tree

***Kellys Hotel,** 36 South Great George's Street, Central Dublin, Dublin 2.*
Open: All Year (not Xmas)
Grades: BF 1 St
01 6779277 Fax no: 01 6713216
Mr Lynam
Rates fr: *IR£24.00*-**IR£34.00**.
Beds: 2F 6D 10T 6S **Baths:** 16 Ensuite
(12)
Kelly's is one of the few remaining family run hotels in the centre of Dublin. Unbeatable value in the centre of Dublin. Within walking distance of all amenites. Public car parks beside hotel, recommended by International Tour Guides.

High season, bank holidays and special events mean low availability *anywhere.*

***Marian,** 21 Upper Gardiner Street, Central Dublin, Dublin 1.*
Open: All Year **Grades:** BF 1 St
01 8744129 McElroy
Rates fr: *IR£15.00*-**IR£15.00.**
Beds: 1F 2D 2T 1S
Baths: 4 Shared
(3) P (6) TV V
The Marian is a family-run guest house. Situated in part of Georgian Dublin just five minutes walk from city centre and all shopping areas, cinemas, theatres and museums. Our house is tastefully decorated, centrally heated, all usual amenities.

***Clifden House,** 32 Gardiner Place, Central Dublin, Dublin 1.*
City centre, refurbished Georgian home, on airport bus route. Family run.
Open: All Year (not Xmas)
Grades: BF 3 St, AA 3 Q, RAC Listed
01 8746364 Fax no: 01 8746122
Mr Lalor
Rates fr: *IR£20.00*-**IR£25.00.**
Beds: 3F 1D 4T 2S **Baths:** 10 Ensuite
P (12) TV V

Dublin — Clontarf

National Grid Ref: O2036

Holly Brook Hotel, Clontarf Castle, Yacht Pub, Les Amis, Dolly Mount House

***Hollybrook Park House,** 10 Hollybrook Park, Clontarf, Dublin 3.*
Charming period house, secluded grounds. Convenient city, airport, ferry and beach.
Open: March to Oct
Grades: BF Approv
01 8339656 Mrs Shouldice
Rates fr: *IR£20.00*-**IR£26.00.**
Beds: 1F 1D 1T
Baths: 2 Ensuite 1 Shared
(3) P (3) TV

***Aishling Hous[e]** Clontarf, Dubli[n]*
Beautiful home ... city/port/airport. ... menu.
Open: All Year (...
Grades: BF Appr...
01 8338400 Fax n...
Mrs Mooney
Rates fr: *IR£20.00*...
Beds: 3F 3D
Baths: 6 Ensuite
P TV V

***Villa,** 150 Howth Road, Clontarf, Dublin 3.*
Ensuite rooms with TV, tea-making, private parking, excellent public transport.
Open: All Year (not Xmas)
01 8332377 Mrs Betson
Rates fr: *IR£18.00*-**IR£22.00.**
Beds: 2F 1D 1T 1S
Baths: 4 Ensuite 2 Private 2 Shared
(1) P (6) TV V

***Springvale,** 69 Kincora Drive(off Kincora Grove), Clontarf, Dublin 3.*
Modern house, quiet residential area. 15 minutes airport, ferry, city centre.
Open: All Year (not Xmas)
Grades: BF Approv
01 8333413 Mrs Kavanagh
Rates fr: *IR£16.50*-**IR£20.00.**
Beds: 1F 2D 1T
Baths: 2 Shared
(10) P (4) TV V

***Currow,** 144 Kincora Road, Clontarf, Dublin 3.*
Corner house in prime residential area in north east suburbs of Dublin City.
Open: All Year (not Xmas)
Grades: BF Approv
01 8339990
(also fax no) Mrs Egan
Rates fr: *IR£19.00*-**IR£24.00.**
Beds: 1F 2D 2T
Baths: 4 Ensuite 1 Private
P (5) TV V

Phoning from outside the Republic?
Dial 00353 and omit the initial '0' of the area code.

... Donnybrook

...al Grid Ref: O1931

Madigans, Montrose Hotel

***Gelnfield**, 176 Stillorgan Road, Donnybrook, Dublin 4.*
Modern, comfortable house, all amenities and bus routes. Convenient city centre.
Open: All Year (not Xmas)
01 2693640 Mrs Corrigan
Rates fr: *IR£25.00*-**IR£30.00.**
Beds: 1F 1D 1T
Baths: 3 Ensuite
(3)

***Herbert Lodge**, 65 Morehampton Road, Donnybrook, Dublin 4.*
Beautiful Victorian house - superb location.
Open: All Year
Grades: BF Approv, AA 3 St
01 6603403 Fax no: 01 6688794
Mr O'Feinneadha
Rates fr: *IR£25.00*-**IR£25.00.**
Beds: 3D 3T 1S
Baths: 6 Ensuite 1 Private

Dublin Drumcondra

National Grid Ref: O1538

Maples Hotel, C.J.s,

***Parlmasilla**, 15 Iona Drive, Drumcondra, Dublin 9.*
Modern detached house, 10 minutes city centre. Convenient to airport, ferry.
Open: (Not Xmas/New Year)
01 8305724 Mrs Ryan
Rates fr: *IR£16.00*-**IR£20.00.**
Beds: 2F 1D 1T
Baths: 2 Ensuite 2 Shared
(1)

***Hollybank House**, 7 Glenarm Avenue, Drumcondra, Dublin 9.*
Modernised C17th manor-house off main airport road. Ten minutes airport.
Open: All Year (not Xmas)
01 8306032 Mrs Brennan
Rates fr: *IR£19.00*-**IR£21.00.**
Beds: 1F 1T
Baths: 1 Ensuite 1 Shared

Dublin Dun Laoghaire

National Grid Ref: O2327

The Queens Inn, Traders Wharf, Scotts, The Eagle House, Daniel's, Fitzgerald's

***Lisadell**, 212 Glenageary Road Upper, Dun Laoghaire, Co Dublin.*
Open: All Year
01 2350609
Fax no: 1 2350454
Mr Goldrick
Rates fr: *IR£20.00*-**IR£25.00.**
Beds: 1F 1D 3T 1S
Baths: 5 Ensuite 1 Private
(5)
Lisadell is family run and you are always guaranteed a warm and friendly welcome. Some written guest comments: 'The food was wonderful, the bedroom really comfy, the surroundings envious' Miss Thomson - Birmingham; 'Irish hospitality at its best' Harringtons - Georgia, USA.

***Annesgrove**, 28 Rosmeen Gardens, Dun Laoghaire, Co Dublin.*
Warm comfortable home. Well looked after. Very welcome.
Open: All Year (not Xmas)
01 2809801
Mrs D'Alton
Rates fr: *IR£18.00*-**IR£25.00.**
Beds: 2F 1D 1T
Baths: 2 Ensuite 2 Shared
(2)

***Avondale**, 3 Northumberland Avenue, Dun Laoghaire, Co Dublin.*
Open: All Year
Grades: BF Approv
01 2809628
Mrs Gorby
Rates fr: *IR£17.00*-**IR£20.00.**
Beds: 1F 2D 3T
Baths: 3 Shared
Spacious comfortable 100 year old Georgian residence in Dun Laoghaire town. Five minutes walk from Dart Station and Ferry Port. Dublin only 15 minutes by DART. Superb local amenities including scenic walks, beach, bars, restaurants and shops. Early breakfasts.

7 Claremont Villas, *Off Adelaide Road, Glenageary, Dun Laoghaire, Co Dublin,*
120-year-old Victorian house, near ferry, bus, train.
Open: All Year (not Xmas)
Grades: BF Approv, AA 2 Q
01 2805346 Mrs Harkin
Rates fr: *IR£16.50*-**IR£21.50**.
Beds: 2F 2D 1T
Baths: 4 Ensuite 1 Shared

Tara Hall, *24 Sandycove Road, Dun Laoghaire, Co Dublin.*
Beautiful Regency-style house. Near beach and James Joyce Museum.
Open: All Year
Grades: RAC Listed
01 2805120 Mr O'Feinneadha
Rates fr: *IR£17.00*-**IR£18.00**.
Beds: 1F 3D 3T
Baths: 5 Ensuite 1 Shared
(6)

Innisfree, *31 Northumberland Avenue, Dun Laoghaire, Co Dublin.*
Large Victorian house, old world elegance, select accommodation, homely, beside services.
Open: All Year
Grades: BF Approv
01 2803093 Smyth
Rates fr: *IR£15.00*-**IR£20.00**.
Beds: 3F 2D 2T
Baths: 4 Ensuite 2 Shared
(10) (7)

Rathoe, *12 Rosmeen Gardens, Dun Laoghaire, Co Dublin.*
Mature home beside DART, bus, ferry. Early breakfast.
Open: All Year (not Xmas)
Grades: BF Approv
01 2808070 Mrs Fitzgibbon
Rates fr: *IR£18.00*-**IR£23.00**.
Beds: 1F 1D 1T 1S
Baths: 2 Shared
(3)

10 Corrig Avenue, *Dun Laoghaire, Co Dublin.*
Victorian house in centre of town close to ferry and all amenities.
Open: 15th Jan - 15th Dec
01 2800997 Mrs O'Connor
Rates fr: *IR£15.00*-**IR£25.00**.
Beds: 2D 1T 1S
Baths: 3 Ensuite 1 Shared
(3)

30 Rosmeen Gardens, *Dun Laoghaire, Co Dublin.*
Quiet home in cul-de-sac, near bus, train, ferry and restaurants. Frommer recommended.
Open: May to Sept
Grades: BF Approv
01 2803360
Mrs Dunne
Rates fr: *IR£18.00*-**IR£20.00**.
Beds: 1D 2T
Baths: 1 Shared
(3)

Sandycove, *Newtownsmith, Seafront Sandycove, Dun Laoghaire, Co Dublin,*
Old worlde refurbished house overlooking Scotsmans Bay.
Open: All Year (not Xmas)
Grades: BF 3 St
01 2841600 (also fax no)
Mr Doyle
Rates fr: *IR£22.50*-**IR£28.00**.
Beds: 2D 9T 1S
Baths: 12 Ensuite
(All)

Dublin — Glasnevin

National Grid Ref: O1537

Tolca House

8 Ballymun Road, *Glasnevin Hill, Glasnevin, Dublin 9.*
Edwardian private house, convenient airport, city, ferry, friendly. Home baking.
Open: Mar to Dec
01 8376125
Mrs Lambert
Rates fr: *IR£14.00*-**IR£17.00**.
Beds: 1D 1T 1S
Baths: 1 Shared
(3)

Please respect a B&B's wishes regarding children, animals & smoking.

Dublin Inchicore

National Grid Ref: O1233

Ardagh House, *6 St Annes Road, South Circular Road, Inchicore, Dublin 8.*
House overlooking Grand Canal. 2.5km, city centre. Convenient location.
Open: All Year (not Xmas)
01 4536615 Mrs Lee
Rates fr: *IR£18.00*-**IR£16.00**.
Beds: 5F 2D 1T 2S **Baths:** 2 Private

Dublin Killiney

National Grid Ref: O2624

Eagle House, De Selby's

70 Avondale Road, *Killiney, Dun Laoghaire, Co Dublin.*
Comfortable house. Easy reach of city or County Wicklow.
Open: All Year (not Xmas)
01 2859952 Fax no: 01 0889952
Mrs McAnaney
Rates fr: *IR£15.00*-**IR£20.00**.
Beds: 1F 2D 1T
Baths: 3 Ensuite 1 Shared
(4)

Goldiwil, *Church Road, Killiney, Dun Laoghaire, Co Dublin.*
Dormer bungalow residence in beautiful gardens on one acre grounds. Private car parking. 4 minutes drive to ferry.
Open: All Year (not Xmas)
01 2852809 / 087 431822 Mrs Barry
Rates fr: *IR£18.00*-**IR£21.00**.
Beds: 1F 1D 1T
Baths: 2 Shared
(5)

Dublin Palmerstown

National Grid Ref: O0735

West County Hotel

62 Wheatfield Road, *Palmerstown, Dublin 20.*
Comfortable, quiet house just off N4. Excellent Irish breakfast.
Open: Jan to Nov **Grades:** BF Approv
01 6265279 Mrs Moorhead
Rates fr: *IR£15.00*-**IR£18.00**.
Beds: 2F 1T
Baths: 2 Shared
(3)

Dublin Raheny

National Grid Ref: O2237

The Shieling Hotel

Eden Lodge, *44 Edenmore Crescent, Raheny, Dublin 5.*
Open: All Year (not Xmas)
01 8671415 (also fax no)
Mrs Costellue
Rates fr: *IR£15.00*-**IR£19.50**.
Beds: 1F 1D 2T 1S
Baths: 2 Shared
Modern comfortable family home situated in the village of Raheny, close to airport, 10 mins Ferryport, city centre and historic villages. DART line 2 mins walk from house, city centre 10 mins

Rathmullan, *110 Bettyglen, Raheny, Dublin 5.*
Family home near Dublin, airport, ferry-port, DART, buses, golf, Point Theatre.
Open: All Year (not Xmas)
Grades: BF Approv
01 8318463 Mrs Patton
Rates fr: *IR£15.00*-**IR£20.00**.
Beds: 1D 2T **Baths:** 2 Shared
(2)

Dublin Ranelagh

National Grid Ref: O1531

Courtyard Restaurant, Madigans Pub

Sandford Lodge, *134 Sandford Road, Ranelagh, Dublin 6.*
Comfortable Victorian house, convenient to all amenities. Car park.
Open: All Year (not Xmas)
Grades: BF Approv
01 4976150 Mr Dundon
Rates fr: *IR£19.00*-**IR£22.00**.
Beds: 1F 2D 2T 1S
Baths: 2 Ensuite 1 Private 2 Shared
(8)

The lowest *double* rate per person is shown in *italics*.

Bringing children with you? Always ask for any special rates.

Dublin Rathgar

National Grid Ref: O1429

Comans Bar, Patrick's Restaurant, Ivy Court, Orwell Lodge Hotel, Carrick Hall Hotel

26 Victoria Road, *Rathgar, Dublin 6.*
Victorian terraced house in quiet suburban area. Close to public transport.
Open: All Year (not Xmas)
Grades: BF Approv
01 4923444
Mrs McCabe
Rates fr: *IR£23.00*.
Beds: 1F 1D 1T
Baths: 3 Ensuite

Garville Manor, *1 Garville Avenue, Rathgar, Dublin 6.*
In the heart of beautiful Rathgar, 10 mins from Dublin.
Open: All Year (not Xmas)
Grades: BF Approv
01 4964444
Mrs Crofton
Rates fr: *IR£20.00*-**IR£25.00.**
Beds: 1D 2T 2S
Baths: 1 Ensuite 4 Shared
(12)

Dublin Rathmines

National Grid Ref: O1430

Uppercross, *26/30 Upper Rathmines Road, Rathmines, Dublin 6.*
First class warm standard of comfort in the heart of south side Dublin.
Open: All Year
01 4975486
Rates fr: *IR£22.50*-**IR£30.00.**
Beds: 4F 4D 4T 2S
Baths: 14 Ensuite
(12)

Dublin Sandyford

National Grid Ref: O1626

Step Inn, Stepaside

Hillcrest House, *Hillcrest Road, Sandyford, Co Dublin.*
Open: All Year (not Xmas)
01 2954400 / 2956464
Mrs Anderson
Rates fr: *IR£19.00*-**IR£22.00.**
Beds: 2F 2D 2T
Baths: 4 Ensuite 1 Private 1 Shared
(6)
Modern detached house - Dublin foothills. 20 minutes city centre. Close to Leopardstown Racecourse, Irish Management Institute, Stillorgan Park & Sandyford Industrial Estate. Close by: Wicklow Walk, golf, tennis, pitch & putt, skiing, horse-riding. Convenient to good food, restaurants and pubs.

Dublin Sandymount

National Grid Ref: O1932

Sandy Mount House

8 Dromard Terrace, *Sandymount, Dublin 4.*
Period style house in village two miles from city centre.
Open: Easter to Oct
01 6683861
Mrs Bermingham
Rates fr: *IR£14.00*-**IR£16.00.**
Beds: 1F 1D 1T 1S
Baths: 1 Shared

Dublin Santry

National Grid Ref: O1740

The Swiss Cottage

132 Santry Close, *Santry, Dublin 9.*
Comfortable family home, 2 km from airport, 5 km from city centre.
Open: Feb to Dec
Grades: BF Approv
01 8424515
Mrs Levins
Rates fr: *IR£15.00*-**IR£22.00.**
Beds: 1F 1D 1T
Baths: 1 Ensuite 2 Shared
(10) (2)

Dublin — Sutton

National Grid Ref: O2539

The Marine Hotel, The Lighthouse

154 Sutton Park, *Sutton, Co Dublin.*
Spacious detached house near Bayside DART Station. 15 minutes airport.
Open: All Year (not Xmas)
Grades: BF Approv
01 8325167 Ms Sutton
Rates fr: *IR£17.00*-**IR£20.00**.
Beds: 1F 1D 1T 1S
Baths: 3 Ensuite 1 Private
P (3) TV

Windermere, *47a Howth Road, Sutton, Co Dublin.*
Luxurious accommodation. Beach - sailing - golf - scenic walks - 20 mins city.
Open: All Year (not Xmas)
Grades: BF Approv
01 8393793 Mrs Tyrell
Rates fr: *IR£17.00*-**IR£22.00**.
Beds: 5F 3D 2T
Baths: 1 Ensuite 1 Private 1 Shared
P (6) TV

Dublin — Templeogue

National Grid Ref: O1227

28 Rossmore Grove, *Templeogue, Dublin 6.*
Luxury smoke-free house in South-West of city, off N81.
Open: Feb to Dec **Grades:** BF Approv
01 4907286 Mrs McGreal
Rates fr: *IR£14.00*-**IR£21.00**.
Beds: 2D 2T **Baths:** 2 Ensuite 1 Shared
P (2) TV V

Lusk

National Grid Ref: O2154

Balrothery Inn

Ivy Bungalow, *Ballough, Lusk, Co Dublin.*
A quiet secluded country home within 15 miles from city centre.
Open: All Year **Grades:** BF Approv
01 8437031 Fax no: 01 8404011
Mrs Rigney
Rates fr: *IR£15.00*-**IR£18.00**.
Beds: 1F 2D 2T
Baths: 3 Ensuite 1 Shared
P (8) TV V

Malahide

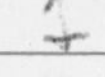

National Grid Ref: O2246

Lambay Bistro, Country Club Hotel, Sale Pepe, The Galley, Giovanni's, Smyths, Duffys, Breakers, Gibneys

Hazlegrove, *Blackwood Lane, Malahide, Co Dublin.*
Open: Mar to Sep
Grades: BF Approv
01 8462629
(also fax no) Mrs O'Leary
Rates fr: *IR£18.00*-**IR£27.00**.
Beds: 1F 1D 1T
Baths: 3 Ensuite
(2) P (10) TV
Hazelgrove, Georgian-style home on private grounds of landscaped gardens 2 km from the award winning marina village of Malahide. Offers traditional comforts, standards and hospitality. 12 minutes airport, 20 minutes ferry, nine golf clubs nearby, ethnic restaurants, shopping locally. Welcome tea on arrival.

Maywood House, *13 St Andrews Grove, Malahide, Co Dublin.*
Quiet house in Malahide. TV, tea/coffee. Beside restaurants and public transport.
Open: All Year (not Xmas)
01 8451712 (also fax no)
Ms Dagg Hanley
Rates fr: *IR£15.00.*
Beds: 1F 2D 1T
Baths: 2 Ensuite 1 Shared
P (5) TV

Carlim Lodge, *Auburn, Streanstown, Malahide, Co Dublin.*
Open: Jan to Nov
01 8452839
Mrs Dennis
Rates fr: *IR£17.50*-**IR£22.50**.
Beds: 2F 1D 1T 1S
Baths: 4 Ensuite 1 Shared
P (6) TV V
Secluded wooded setting, on private grounds. Peaceful location beside castle. Convenient for excellent restaurants, pubs, golf club, tennis, all sea-sports. Airport, ferry, bus and train. Tea/coffee facilities. Electric blankets, TV. Excellent touring base.

170 Biscayne, *Coast Road, Malahide, Co Dublin.*
Warm Irish welcome to modern home overlooking the sea.
Open: All Year (not Xmas)
01 8452668
Mrs Morris
Rates fr: *IR£15.00*-**IR£20.00**.
Beds: 1D 1T 1S
Baths: 2 Shared
(3)

Archway, *127 Seapark, Malahide, Co Dublin.*
Quiet modern detached house. Dublin airport 10 mins.
Open: Feb to Oct
01 8452080
Mrs Gardiner
Rates fr: *IR£15.00*-**IR£22.00**.
Beds: 1F 1D 1T
Baths: 1 Ensuite 1 Private 1 Shared
(2) (4)

Portmarnock

National Grid Ref: O2424

Lambay Bistro, Golf Links Pub, Country Club Hotel, Sands Hotel

Sands Hotel, *Coast Road, Portmarnock, Co Dublin.*
Open: All Year
Grades: BF 2 St
01 8460003
Rates fr: *IR£27.50*-**IR£35.00**.
Beds: 1F 5T 4S
Baths: 10 Ensuite
Beautifully situated on Port Marnock strand just 16 km from Dublin. The Sands presents friendly country comfort just outside the city's bustle. A professional friendly staff will help you make the most of your stay.

San Cristobal, *3 Balckberry Rise, Portmarnock, Co Dublin.*
Family home, friendly, comfortable. Close to beach, airport, ferry and Dublin.
Open: Feb to Oct
01 8460307
Mr & Mrs Curley
Rates fr: *IR£17.00*-**IR£20.00**.
Beds: 2D 2S
Baths: 2 Ensuite 1 Shared
(3)

All rates are subject to alteration at the owners' discretion.

Robinia, *452 Strand Road, Portmarnock, Co Dublin.*
Modern house, overlooking the Irish Sea. Wonderful location.
Open: All Year (not Xmas)
01 8462987 Mrs Creane
Rates fr: *IR£17.50*.
Beds: 3F
Baths: 3 Ensuite
(3)

29 Martello COurt, *Portmarnock, Co Dublin.*
Modern, comfortable, only five minutes from the beach and golf-course.
Open: Jan to Nov
01 8461500
Mrs Tonkin
Rates fr: *IR£15.00*-**IR£20.00**.
Beds: 1F 2D 1T
Baths: 1 Ensuite
(4)

Shankill

National Grid Ref: O2421

Silver Tassie

Abigail House, *Commons Road, Loughlinstown, Shankill, Co Dublin.*
Modern luxury accommodation close to Dunlaoire Ferryport.
Open: All Year (not Xmas)
Grades: BF 3 St
01 2824747
Mrs Reynolds
Rates fr: *IR£18.00*-**IR£20.00**.
Beds: 1F 4D 4T 2S
Baths: 11 Ensuite
(1) (11)

Always telephone to get directions to the B&B - you will save time!

Skerries

National Grid Ref: O2560

Woodview Farmhouse, *Margaretstown, Skerries, Co Dublin.*
Large comfortable farmhouse 4 km to Skerries, convenient to Dublin Airport.
Open: All Year
Grades: BF Approv RAC Listed
01 8491528 Mrs Clinton
Rates fr: *IR£13.50*-**IR£17.00.**
Beds: 2F 3D 1T
Baths: 4 Ensuite 2 Shared
(6)

Swords

National Grid Ref: O1846

The Star, Harp Bar, Coachmans Inn, Lord Mayors, Rolestown Inn

Hollytree House, *Airport Road, Nevinstown, Swords, Co Dublin.*
Open: All Year (not Xmas)
01 8406145
Fax no: 01 8900335
Mrs Collins
Rates fr: *IR£15.00*-**IR£20.00.**
Beds: 1F 1D 2T 1S
Baths: 3 Ensuite 2 Shared
(2) (8)
A large modern family-run B&B, rooms ensuite & TVs in all rooms. Located 1 mile north of Dublin Airport on the N1. Bus services to city centre. Large landscaped garden for visitors' use with ample private parking.

Oakview, *Leas Cross, Swords, Co Dublin.*
Modern rural comfortable home adjacent Dublin Airport and golf course.
Open: All Year **Grades:** BF Approv
01 8405256 (also fax no) Me Jackson
Rates fr: *IR£15.00*-**IR£15.00.**
Beds: 1D 2T (10)

Riversdale, *Balheary Road, Swords, Co Dublin.*
Six minutes Dublin Airport. Modern house in beautiful countryside.
Open: All Year (not Xmas)
01 8404802 Mrs Cavanagh
Rates fr: *IR£16.00*-**IR£25.00.**
Beds: 2F 1D 1T **Baths:** All Ensuite
(3)

Kylemore House, *Dublin Road, Swords, Co Dublin.*
Beautiful Edwardian residence. TV all rooms, private car park. Beautiful gardens.
Open: All Year (not Xmas)
01 8401605 Miss Larkin
Rates fr: *IR£20.00*-**IR£35.00.**
Beds: 2F 1D 1T **Baths:** 4 Ensuite
(6)

Glenmore House, *Airport Road, Nevinson, Swords, Co Dublin.*
Spacious country home, two acres of gardens, beside Dublin Airport.
Open: All Year **Grades:** BF Approv
01 8403610 Mrs Gammell
Rates fr: *IR£15.00*-**IR£15.00.**
Beds: 2F 1D 2T 1S
Baths: 2 Ensuite 4 Shared
(10)

County Galway

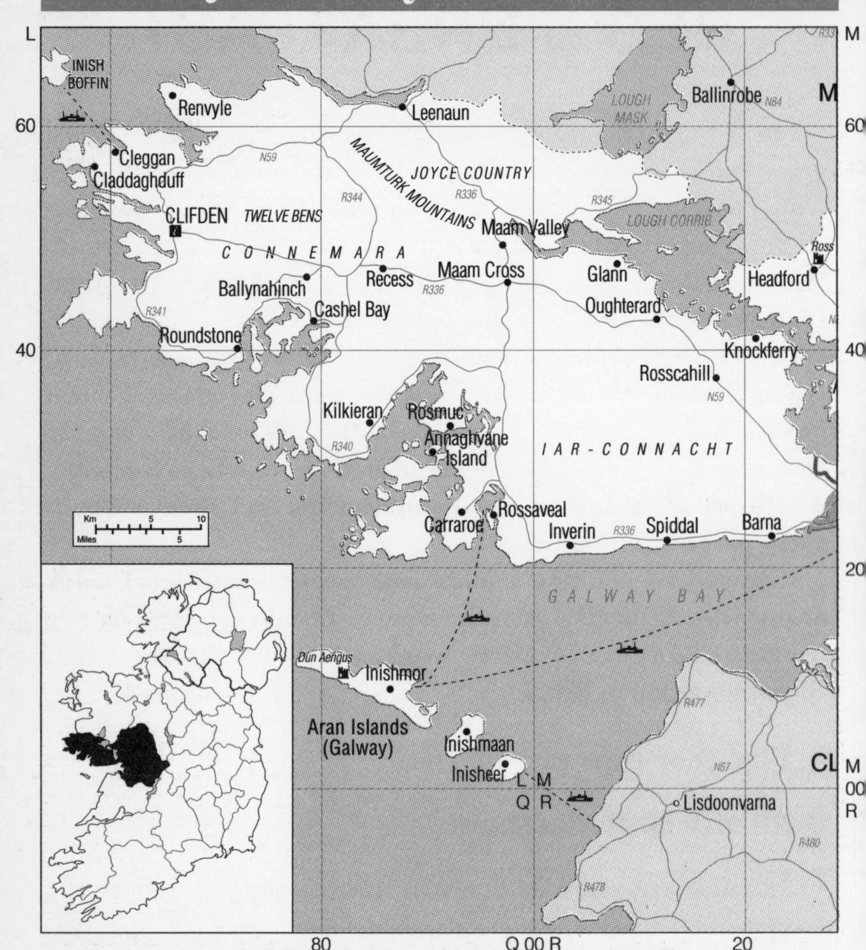

RAIL

Galway City is on the end of the main line to ***Dublin (Heuston)***, via ***Athlone***. For timetable details - **Irish Rail** on 01 8366222.

FERRIES

Boats to the ***Aran Islands*** run all the year round from ***Rossaveel*** *or* ***Galway City***

Island Ferries - 091 561767 or 091 568903

O'Brien Shipping - 091 567676

BUS

Galway *to* ***Dublin*** *(6 daily)* -
Bus Eireann on 091 562000

TOURIST INFORMATION OFFICES

Ballinasloe (Jul to Aug), 0905 42131

Market Street, **Clifden** (mid-May to mid-Sep), 095 21163

Victoria Place, **Galway City** (open all year), 091 563081

Mill Museum, **Tuam** (Jul to Aug), 093 25486

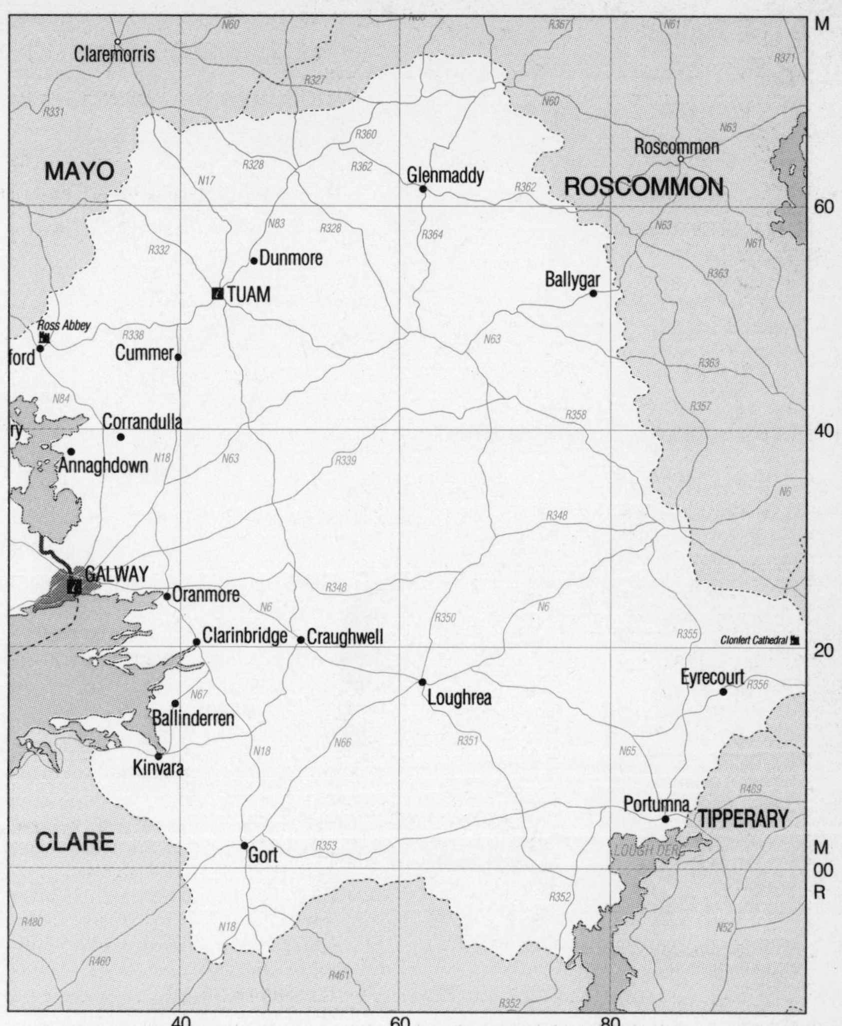

Annaghdown

National Grid Ref: M2937

Regan's

Rose Lawn, *Lisnoran, Annaghdown, Galway.*
Modern bungalow in beautiful countryside.
Open: Mar to Oct
091 791022 Mrs Lynch
Rates fr: *IR£16.00*-**IR£21.00.**
Beds: 2D 1T
Baths: 3 Ensuite
(4)

Annaghvane Island

National Grid Ref: L9030

Teach Anach Mheain, *Annaghvane Island, Lettermore, Galway.*
Modern house, beautiful countryside, view of sea and Connemara Mountains.
Open: All Year (not Xmas)
091 572348
Ms Ui Chonghaile
Rates fr: *IR£16.00*-**IR£21.00.**
Beds: 4D
Baths: 4 Ensuite
(4)

Aran Islands Inisheer

National Grid Ref: L9702

***West Village,** Inisheer, Aran Islands, Galway.*
A two-storey house. Centrally located, with views over sea.
Open: All Year
Grades: BF Approv
099 75024
Mrs Sharry
Rates fr: *IR£12.00*-**IR£13.50**.
Beds: 1F 2D 1T
Baths: 2 Shared

Aran Islands Inishmaan

National Grid Ref: L9305

Meynihans

***Ard Alainn,** West Village, Inishmaan, Aran Islands, Galway.*
Comfortable.
Open: Easter to Sept
Grades: BF Approv
099 73027
Mrs Faherty
Rates fr: *IR£10.00*-**IR£10.00**.
Beds: 3T 2S
Baths: 1 Shared

Aran Islands Inishmor

National Grid Ref: L8807

Joe Watty's, Dun Aengus Restaurant, Man of Aran

***Ard Einne,** Killeany, Inishmor, Aran Islands, Galway.*
Open: Mar to Nov
Grades: BF 2 St
099 61126
Mrs Gill
Rates fr: *IR£13.50*-**IR£25.00**.
Beds: 1F 5D 5T
Baths: 7 Ensuite 1 Private 3 Shared
(10)
'Earth has not anything to show more fair.' A few days on historical Inismor is 'a must' on your Irish holiday. Enjoy the stress-free experience in the relaxed atmosphere of spectacularly situated and high quality Ard Einne, with its sweeping panoramic views.

High season, bank holidays and special events mean low availability *anywhere.*

***Claì Ban,** Kilronan, Inishmor, Aran Islands, Galway.*
Modern dormer bungalow close to all facilities with panoramic views.
Open: All Year
Grades: BF Approv
099 61111
Mr & Mrs Hernon
Rates fr: *IR£14.00*-**IR£20.00**.
Beds: 1F 3D 2T
Baths: 4 Ensuite 2 Private
(8)

***An Crugan,** Kilronan, Inishmor, Aran Islands, Galway.*
Situated Kilronan Village, credit cards accepted, convenient all amenities.
Open: Mar to Nov
Grades: BF Approv
099 61150
Mr & Mrs McDonagh
Rates fr: *IR£14.00*-**IR£14.00**.
Beds: 1F 2D 3T
Baths: 2 Ensuite 2 Shared

***Bay View,** Kilronan, Inishmor, Aran Islands, Galway.*
Small, elegant guest house overlooking tranquil Kilronan Pier.
Open: Easter to Nov
099 61260 (also fax no)
Ms Woods
Rates fr: *IR£15.00*-**IR£15.00**.
Beds: 1F 3D 3T 1S
Baths: 2 Ensuite 2 Private
(3)

Phoning from outside the Republic?

Dial 00353 and omit the initial '0' of the area code.

Beach View House, *Oatquarter, Kilronan, Inishmor, Aran Islands, Galway.*
Family-run home. Two minutes beach. Near famous Fort Dun Aengus.
Open: May to Sep
099 61141
Mrs Conneely
Rates fr: *IR£14.00*-**IR£18.00.**
Beds: 4F 2D
Baths: 3 Shared

Atlantic House, *Manister, Inishmore, Aran Islands, Galway.*
Comfortable farmhouse in scenic surroundings.
Open: Mar to Oct
099 61185 Mrs Connolly
Rates fr: *IR£13.00*-**IR£16.00.**
Beds: 3D 2T **Baths:** 1 Shared

Ballinderren

National Grid Ref: M3915

Raftery's Restaurant

Hollyoak, *Kinvara Road, Ballinderren, Kilcolgan, Galway.*
Spacious dormer bungalow on coast road between Burren to Kilcolgan. Dunguire Castle 3 km.
Open: Mar to Nov
Grades: BF Approv
091 637165 Mrs Fawle
Rates fr: *IR£14.00*-**IR£16.00.**
Beds: 1F 2D 1S
Baths: 2 Ensuite
(6)

Ballygar

National Grid Ref: M7852

The Forest Hotel, *Ballygar, Roscommon.*
Open: All Year
Grades: BF Grade B
0903 24754
Miss Traynor
Rates fr: *IR£20.00*-**IR£20.00.**
Beds: 4D 3T 3S
Baths: 10 Ensuite
Central to all fishing and golfing spots. Home cooking with flexible meal times. All bedrooms are ensuite. Family run.

Ballynahinch

National Grid Ref: L7846

Paddy Jesty's

Hazel Farmhouse, *Ballynahinch, Recess, Galway.*
Comfortable farmhouse in peaceful surroundings amidst unspoilt beauty of Connemara.
Open: Jun to Sep
Grades: BF Approv
095 34642
Mrs Keaney
Rates fr: *IR£16.00*-**IR£20.00.**
Beds: 1F 2D 1T
Baths: 3 Ensuite 1 Shared
(12) (6)

Barna

National Grid Ref: M2222

Donnellys Bar

Silverseas, *Cappagh Road, Barna, Galway.*
Newly built modern luxury residence, on shores of Galway Bay.
Open: All Year
Grades: BF Approv, AA 3 Q
091 59075 (also fax no)
Mrs McGrath
Rates fr: *IR£15.00*-**IR£17.00.**
Beds: 3F 4D 1T
Baths: 8 Ensuite 3 Private
(12)

Carraroe

National Grid Ref: L9325

Realt na Maidne

Leannafion, *Coral Beach, Carraroe, Galway.*
Modern bungalow. Unique coral beach 0.5 km. Ideal location for touring.
Open: Mar to Oct
091 595159
Mrs McDonagh
Rates fr: *IR£16.00*-**IR£20.00.**
Beds: 2D 2T
Baths: 3 Ensuite 1 Shared

Cashel Bay

National Grid Ref: L7942

Shoreside Air, *Cashel Bay, Galway.*
Shoreside Air is a quiet tranquil house. Overlooking sea and mountains.
Open: All Year (not Xmas)
095 31141 Mrs Joyce
Rates fr: *IR£14.00*-**IR£15.00**.
Beds: 2F 1D 2T
Baths: 5 Ensuite
(10)

Glen View, *Cashel Bay, Connemara, Galway.*
Comfortable bungalow set in the heart of Connemara. Home from home.
Open: All Year (not Xmas)
Grades: BF Approv
095 31054
Mrs McDonagh
Rates fr: *IR£13.50*-**IR£16.00**.
Beds: 3D
Baths: 1 Shared

Clarinbridge

National Grid Ref: M4120

Morans Oyster Cottage, Paddy Burke's, Rafferty's Restaurant, Oyster Manor Hotel

Rock Lodge, *Stradbally, Clarinbridge, Galway.*
Open: Mar to Oct
Grades: BF Approv
091 796071 Mrs Diskin
Rates fr: *IR£14.00*-**IR£18.00**.
Beds: 1F 2D 1T
Baths: 2 Ensuite 1 Shared
(5)
Modern home in quiet location just off N18. Central to Burren, Connemara, Aran Islands. Choice of 4 excellent restaurants locally. Private walkway to seashore through wooded area feel free to have a stroll before bedtime or in the morning after breakfast.

The lowest **single** *rate is shown in* **bold.**

Please respect a B&B's wishes regarding children, animals & smoking.

Springlawn, *Stradbally North, Clarinbridge, Galway.*
Open: Mar to Nov
091 796045
Mrs McNamara
Rates fr: *IR£16.00*-**IR£21.00**.
Beds: 1F 1D 1T
Baths: 3 Ensuite
Dillard Causin Guide recommended, superbly located in the heart of oyster country, near Galway Bay, 15 mins from Galway City, ideal base for Connemara, Aran Islands, Burren, Shannon Airport. Breakfast menu. Credit cards and travel agents vouchers accepted.

Cleggan

National Grid Ref: L6057

Oliver's

Cnoc Breac, *Cleggan, Galway.*
Modern home on elevated site in peaceful location. Panoramic views.
Open: May to Sep
Grades: BF Approv
095 44688
Mrs King
Rates fr: *IR£16.00*-**IR£21.00**.
Beds: 2D 2T
Baths: 4 Ensuite
(6)

The lowest *double* rate per person is shown in *italics*.

Clifden

National Grid Ref: L6550

High Moors, O'Gradys, Mitchells, D'Arcy Inn, Alcock & Brown

Mallmore House, *Ballyconneely Road, Clifden, Galway.*
Open: Mar to Nov
Grades: BF Approv, AA 4 Q, RAC Acclaim
095 21460
Mrs Hardman
Rates fr: *IR£18.00*-**IR£30.00**.
Beds: 1F 3D 2T
Baths: 6 Ensuite
(15)
One mile from Clifden, Mallmore is a lovingly restored award winning Georgian house, with spacious well heated rooms, open fires and wonderful views, situated on the shores of Clifden Bay, in 35 acre wooded grounds. A truly unique, peaceful place.

Aisling House, *Bridge Street, Clifden, Galway.*
Comfortable tastefully decorated family-run home. Ideally located for all amenities.
Open: All Year
095 21535
Mrs Casey
Rates fr: *IR£15.00*-**IR£17.00**.
Beds: 1F 3D 1T
Baths: 5 Ensuite

Smugglers Lodge Hotel, *Clifden, Galway.*
Open: Mar to Jan
Grades: BF 2 St
095 21187
Fax no: 095 21701
Mr Prendergost
Rates fr: *IR£20.00*-**IR£20.00**.
Beds: 9D 10T 1S
Baths: 20 Ensuite
(18)
Family-run hotel overlooking the mountains. Centrally located in the town of Clifden, an ideal base for touring mountain climbing and fishing. Our restaurant provides excellent seafood and local dishes. Specials: 3 dinner & 3 B&B £95. Weekend £55, group rates, tours.

Errismore House, *Bridge Street, Clifden, Galway.*
Open: All Year (not Xmas)
095 21360 Mrs Schley
Rates fr: *IR£15.00*-**IR£20.00**.
Beds: 2D 2T
Baths: 4 Ensuite
Errismore is in the centre of Clifden, with super hill-views and only a mile from the beach. 5 miles from Connemara golf course. Good horse riding, fishing, walking all nearby.

Kille House, *Kingstown, Clifden, Galway.*
Fully restored Georgian house on the Atlantic in unspoilt Connemara.
Open: Easter to Nov
095 21849 Mrs Voormolen
Rates fr: *IR£20.00*-**IR£25.00**.
Beds: 1F 2D 2T
Baths: 3 Ensuite 1 Shared

Sky Road View, *Lower Sky Road, Clifden, Co Galway.*
Modern, comfortable family home at the edge of the Atlantic in beautiful scenic area. Ideal base for fishing, walking, sailing, golf.
Open: All Year **Grades:** BF Approv
095 21889 Mrs Mullen
Rates fr: *IR£16.00*-**IR£18.00**.
Beds: 3D 1F
Baths: 4 Ensuite 1 Private
(3)

Benbaun House, *Westport Road, Clifden, Galway.*
Modern, comfortable family home on spacious grounds. Best in Connemara.
Open: Easter to Oct
095 21462
(also fax no) Mr & Mrs Lydon
Rates fr: *IR£14.00*-**IR£18.50**.
Beds: 2F 2D 2T
Baths: 6 Ensuite
(3) (8)

Letternoosh House, *Westport Road, Clifden, Galway.*
Modern home in peaceful surroundings overlooking Streamstown Bay.
Open: All Year **Grades:** BF Approv
095 21291 Mrs Pryce
Rates fr: *IR£15.00*-**IR£14.00**.
Beds: 1F 1D 1T 1S
(7)

All details shown are as supplied by B&B owners in Autumn 1996

Barry's Hotel, *Main Street, Clifden, Galway.*
Open: Easter to Nov
095 21287 Fax no: 095 21499 Barry
Rates fr: *IR£25.00*-**IR£25.00**.
Beds: 19D 20T
Baths: 20 Ensuite

Failte, *Ardbear, Clifden, Galway.*
AA QQQ, overlooking town and bay. Breakfast award winner.
Open: Apr to Sep
Grades: AA 3 Q
095 21159 Mrs Kelly
Rates fr: *IR£14.00*-**IR£14.00**.
Beds: 2F 1D 1T 1S
Baths: 2 Ensuite 3 Shared
(15)

Cregg House, *Galway Road, Clifden, Galway.*
Modern bungalow in the heart of Connemara overlooking Roundstone Bog.
Open: Easter to Nov
Grades: BF Approv
095 21326 Mrs O'Donnell
Rates fr: *IR£16.00*-**IR£20.00**.
Beds: 2F 2D 2T
Baths: 6 Ensuite

Corrandulla

National Grid Ref: M3539

Kynes

Cregg Castle, *Corrandulla, Galway.*
C17th castle on 165 acres. Friendly and informal. Traditional music by the fire-side. Ideal for touring Clare,Connemara,Mayo,Aran Islands (four day tours). Wonderful atmosphere - stay in a castle and feel completely at home
Open: Mar to Nov
Grades: BF Approv
091 791434 Ms Broderick
Rates fr: *IR£22.00*-**IR£25.00**.
Beds: 4F 5D 1T 1S
Baths: 5 Ensuite 1 Private 2 Shared
(20)

Craughwell

National Grid Ref: M5120

Templemartin Thatched House, *Craughwell, Galway.*
Open: Apr to Oct
091 846145
Mrs Flanaghan
Rates fr: *IR£16.00*-**IR£16.00**.
Beds: 2F 1D 1T 1S
Baths: 5 Ensuite
(4) (5)
Charming thatched house on two hectares of parkland, juts off N6. Adjacent to award winning pub and restaurant, Galway City, The Burren, Connemara, Aran Islands. Arrangements made for vegetarians, touring, walking, cycling and golf. Friendly caring service ensured.

Cummer

National Grid Ref: M3945

Cummer Park House & Stables, *Cummer, Tuam, Co Galway.*
Antique furnished farmhouse.
Turf fires. Horse-riding free for guests staying three days or more.
Open: Easter to Oct
Grades: BF Approv
093 41300
Mrs Burke
Rates fr: *IR£14.50*-**IR£19.50**.
Beds: 3F 1D 1T
Baths: 3 Ensuite 2 Private
(10)

Dunmore

National Grid Ref: M5163

Piper Reilly

Little Castle House, *Little Castle, Dunmore, Tuam, Co Galway.*
Modern comfortable farmhouse.
All modern cons. Homely welcome.
Open: Easter to Oct
Grades: BF Approv
093 38236
Mr & Mrs Healy
Rates fr: *IR£16.00*-**IR£18.00**.
Beds: 2F 2D
Baths: 2 Ensuite 1 Private
(1)

Eyrecourt

National Grid Ref: M9117

Lynch's Farmhouse, *Mayour, Eyrecourt, Ballinasloe, Co Galway.*
Spacious farmhouse near River Shannon. Excellent standards of comfort, food and service.
Open: All Year (not Xmas)
0905 75156
Mrs Lynch
Rates fr: *IR£14.00*-**IR£14.00**.
Beds: 1F 1D 2T
Baths: 2 Shared

Galway

National Grid Ref: M3025

Twelve Pins, Balloon Restaurant, Anno Santo Hotel, Tysons, Spinnaker House Hotel, Galleon Grill, The Huntsman, Tigh Neuchatain, Westwood Bistro

Carraig Beag, *1 Burren View Heights, Knocknacarra Road, Galway.*
Open: All Year
Grades: BF Approv
091 521696
Mrs Lydon
Rates fr: *IR£15.00*-**IR£18.00**.
Beds: 1F 2D 2T
Baths: 5 Ensuite
(8)
Luxurious brick house, walking distance to seafront, Leisureland, tennis, golf. Ideal base for touring Connemara, Cliffs of Moher, Aran Islands, Mayo. 2 km Galway City. Rooms ensuite with TV, tea/coffee facilities. Car park. Recommended Dillard/Causin Bed & Breakfast Guide.

Padua, *Threadneedle Street, Galway.*
Traditional Irish guest house beside beach, swimming and tennis clubs.
Open: All Year (not Xmas)
Grades: BF Approv
091 529252
Mrs Staunton
Rates fr: *IR£16.00*-**IR£16.00**.
Beds: 2F 1D 1T
Baths: 4 Ensuite

Ardawn, *31 College Road, Galway.*
Open: All Year (not Xmas)
Grades: BF 4 St, AA 4 Q, Select
091 568833 Fax no: 091 563454
Mrs Guilfoyle
Rates fr: *IR£18.00*-**IR£25.00**.
Beds: 2F 4D 2T
Baths: 8 Ensuite
(7)
First class 4 star family-run guest house. Friendly atmosphere. Five minute walk from city centre. Ideal base for touring Connemara and Clare. Our extensive choice of breakfast is a speciality. Convenient to golf, horse-riding, fishing and other amenities.

Rosgal, *26 Carragh Hill, Knocknacarra, Galway.*
Modern two-storey detached house with a view of the sea and Aran Islands.
Open: Easter to Oct
Grades: BF Approv
091 523855 Mrs Kelly
Rates fr: *IR£12.00*-**IR£18.00**.
Beds: 2F 1D 1T
Baths: 1 Ensuite 1 Shared
(4)

Marian Lodge, *Knocknacarra Road, Salthill, Galway.*
Open: All Year (not Xmas)
Grades: BF Approv
091 521678 Fax no: 091 528103
Mrs Molloy
Rates fr: *IR£17.00*-**IR£20.00**.
Beds: 3F 2D 1T
Baths: 6 Ensuite
(3) (10)
Overlooking Galway Bay beside seafront. Private parking. Rooms ensuite with cable TV. Clock radios. Direct dial phones. Tea/coffee facilities. Electric blankets. Bus/Aran Island route. Fire officer approval. Beside bird sanctuary, Leisureland. Golf driving range. Hairdryer/electric iron available.

Phoning from outside the Republic?

Dial 00353 and omit the initial '0' of the area code.

***Clare Villa,** 38 Threadneedle Street, Galway.*
Open: Jan to Oct
091 522520 Mrs Connolly
Rates fr: *IR£17.00*-**IR£22.00**.
Beds: 2F 2D 2T
Baths: 6 Ensuite
Ideal base for touring Connemara, the Burren & Aran Islands or just a day's shopping in Galway's many interesting shops. Why not partake in our many excellent restaurants. Modern spacious home. Close to beach, golf, tennis. Private parking.

***3 Woodfield,** Barna Road, Galway.*
Comfortable guest house on Coast Road. Outside Galway City and Salthill. Fishing, horse-riding, golfing, swimming available locally. Gateway to Connemara.
Open: Jul to Aug
Grades: BF Approv
091 590051 Mrs Costello
Rates fr: *IR£14.00*-**IR£18.00**.
Beds: 1F 2D
Baths: 2 Ensuite 1 Private
(3)

***Knockrea Guest House,** 55 Lower Salthill, Galway.*
A refurbished 1840s home with pine floors in all rooms. Car park.
Open: All Year (not Xmas)
Grades: BF 3 St
091 521794 Storan
Rates fr: *IR£16.00*-**IR£18.00**.
Beds: 2F 2D 2T
Baths: 6 Ensuite
(4) (14)

***10 Ardnamara,** Galway.*
Modern townhouse situated close to beach, tennis, golf, Galway City.
Open: Jun to Sep
Grades: BF Approv
091 522016 Mrs O'Mahony
Rates fr: *IR£13.00*-**IR£13.00**.
Beds: 1D 1T 2S
Baths: 1 Shared
(3) (3)

The lowest **single** *rate is shown in* **bold.**

***Tysons,** Rockbarton Park Hotel, 5/7 Rockbarton, Salthill, Galway.*
Secluded, quiet, residential location, only 2 minutes walk from the shores of Galway Bay.
Open: All Year
091 522018 Fax no: 091 522286 / 527692 Mr Tyson
Rates fr: *IR£25.00*-**IR£30.00**.
Beds: 3F 2D 4T 2S
Baths: 11 Ensuite
(110)

***Ard Mhuire,** Knocknacarra Road, Galway.*
Attractive, comfortable home close to seaside and all amenities.
Open: All Year (not Xmas)
091 522344
Fax no: 091 529629
Mrs McDonagh
Rates fr: *IR£17.00*-**IR£20.00**.
Beds: 2F 2D 2T
Baths: 6 Ensuite 1 Private
(1) (8)

***Dunguaire,** 8 Lurgan Park, Murrough, Galway.*
Warm friendly family-run home, cable TV in bedrooms.
Open: All Year
Grades: BF Approv
091 757043 Mrs Cawley
Rates fr: *IR£14.00*-**IR£14.00**.
Beds: 1F 2D 1S
Baths: 2 Ensuite

***Sulbea,** 4 Lower Canal Road, Galway.*
Quiet area, overlooking river bank, adjacent to city centre.
Open: All Year (not Xmas)
091 521253 Mrs O'Sullivan
Rates fr: *IR£13.00*-**IR£14.00**.
Beds: 2D 1T 1S
Baths: 1 Shared

***Newcastle Lodge,** 28 Lower Newcastle, Galway.*
Georgian townhouse set on its own beautiful grounds. Five minutes walk city.
Open: All Year (not Xmas)
091 527888 Mrs Burke
Rates fr: *IR£15.00*-**IR£20.00**.
Beds: 2F 2D 2T
Baths: 6 Ensuite
(6)

Adare Gueat House, *9 Fr Griffin Place, Galway.*
Five minutes walking distance from Galway City with private carpark.
Open: All Year (not Xmas)
091 586421 Mr Conroy
Rates fr: *IR£16.50*-**IR£20.00**.
Beds: 2F 5D 3T **Baths:** 10 Ensuite
(1) (9)

Trieste, *12 Forster Park, Dalysfort Road, Upper Salthill, Galway.*
Established modern bungalow in quiet residential cul-de-sac, in seaside resort.
Open: Mar to Oct
091 521014 Mrs Barry
Rates fr: *IR£14.00*-**IR£16.00**.
Beds: 1F 2D 1T 1S
Baths: 3 Ensuite 2 Shared
(3)

Dunree, *57 Lower Salthill, Galway.*
Pre 1940's style house, stripped pine doors and staircase. Car park.
Open: All Year **Grades:** BF Approv
091 523196 Mrs Storan
Rates fr: *IR£14.00*-**IR£16.00**.
(3) (14)

Norman Villa, *86 Lower Salthill, Galway.*
Period residence. Antique decor, brass beds, linen sheets. Relaxed atmosphere.
Open: All Year
091 521131 (also fax no)
Mr & Mrs Keogh
Rates fr: *IR£22.00*-**IR£30.00**.
Beds: 1F 4D **Baths:** 5 Ensuite

Corrib Haven, *107 Upper Newcastle, Galway.*
New, purpose built in Galway City on route to Connemara (N59).
Open: All Year (not Xmas)
Grades: BF Approv, AA 4 Q
091 524171
(also fax no) Mrs Kelly
Rates fr: *IR£17.00*-**IR£22.00**.
Beds: 4D 4T 1T **Baths:** 9 Ensuite
(12) (6)

Many rates vary according to season - the lowest are shown here.

Salin, *Gentian Hill, Galway.*
Located in bird sanctuary beside championship golf course. Sea view.
Open: Easter to Oct
091 521676 (also fax no)
Mrs McLoughlin
Rates fr: *IR£16.00*-**IR£20.00**.
Beds: 1F 2D 1T
Baths: 4 Ensuite
(4)

Eglington Hotel, *The Promenade, Salthill, Galway.*
Comfortable budget hotel five minutes from city centre.
Open: April to October
Grades: BF 2 St
091 26400
Fax no: 091 526495
Mr Flannery
Rates fr: *IR£15.00*-**IR£15.00**.
Beds: 10F 12D 10T
Baths: 32 Ensuite

Glann

National Grid Ref: M0747

Pine Grove, *Hill of Doon Road, Glann, Oughterard, Galway.*
Secluded family home on Western Way route with lake views.
Open: Mar to Oct
Grades: BF Approv
091 552101
Mrs Maloney
Rates fr: *IR£13.00*-**IR£16.00**.
Beds: 1F 1D 2T
Baths: 3 Ensuite 1 Shared
(8) (6)

Glenmaddy

National Grid Ref: M6362

Oakland, *Glenmaddy, Oughterard, Galway.*
Fresh homegrown produce, unpolluted countryside, last remaining raised bog with unique flora/fauna.
Open: All Year
0907 59364 / 59065
Mr Raftery
Rates fr: *IR£17.50*-**IR£25.00**.
Beds: 8F 1T 1S
Baths: 10 Ensuite
(40)

Gort

National Grid Ref: M4502

O'Grady's, Tony Donnellans

Corker House, *Gort, Co Galway.*
Spacious farmhouse central for touring The Burren, Coole Park and Connemara.
Open: Apr to Oct
091 631369
Mr & Mrs Nolan
Rates fr: *IR£14.00*-**IR£19.00**.
Beds: 3F 2D 1T
Baths: 1 Ensuite 2 Shared
(6)

Headford

National Grid Ref: M2747

White Horse Inn

Hillview, *Headford, Galway.*
Modern bungalow on main N84 Road. Home cooking. Fresh farm food.
Open: Easter to Sep
093 35458 Mrs Hannon
Rates fr: *IR£14.00*-**IR£16.00**.
Beds: 1F 2D 1T
Baths: 2
(10)

Inverin

National Grid Ref: M0422

Clai-ard, *Cornarone East, Inverin, Spiddal, Galway.*
New bungalow, friendly home overlooking Galway Bay. Sandy beaches.
Open: Easter to Dec
091 593488
Mrs Folan-Burke
Rates fr: *IR£13.00*-**IR£18.00**.
Beds: 1F 2D
Baths: 2 Ensuite 1 Shared
(10)

Pay B&Bs by cash or cheque. Be prepared to pay up front for one night stays.

Kilkieran

National Grid Ref: L8431

Carna Bay Hotel

Hillside, *Kylesalia, Kilkieran, Connemara, Co Galway.*
Open: Easter to Oct
Grades: BF Approv
095 33420 Mrs Madden
Rates fr: *IR£15.00*-**IR£15.00**.
Beds: 1F 2D 1T
Baths: 2 Ensuite 1 Private
(6)
Comfortable accommodation on hillside overlooking Kilkieran Bay. A *'Cead Mile Failte'* awaits you in our peaceful picturesque surroundings situated off main road. Complimentary tea/coffee on arrival. Home cooking and baking. Ideal touring base for the Aran Islands and Clifden.

Kinvara

National Grid Ref: M3710

Pier Head Restaurant, Travellers Inn

Fortview House, *Lisheeninane, Kinvara, Galway.*
Bed and breakfast - all ensuite rooms with approved riding centre.
Open: Mar to Oct
Grades: BF Approv
091 637147
Mrs Silke
Rates fr: *IR£16.00*-**IR£21.00**.
Beds: 2F 2D 1T 1S
Baths: 6 Ensuite
(8)

Burren View, *Doorus, Kinvara, Galway.*
Beautifully situated on peninsula. Unparallelled sights. Bird-watching, nature walking. Unpolluted environment.
Open: Easter to Oct
091 637142
Mr & Mrs O'Connor
Rates fr: *IR£14.00*-**IR£14.00**.
Beds: 5F 2T 2S
Baths: 2 Ensuite 2 Private 2 Shared

***Sea Crest,** Cregboy, Doorus, Kinvara, Galway.*
Modern, with Galway Bay views and The Burren Hills.
Open: May to Sep
091 637263 / 01492 877225
Mrs Burke
Rates fr: *IR£13.50*-**IR£14.00**.
Beds: 4D 4T
Baths: 4 Ensuite

***Clareview House,** Kinvara, Galway.*
Spacious comfortable farmhouse in rural setting 3 km east of Kinvara.
Open: Apr to Oct
091 637170 Mrs McTigue
Rates fr: *IR£8.25*-**IR£19.00**.
Beds: 2D 1T
Baths: 3 Ensuite

Knockferry

National Grid Ref: M2141

***Knockferry Lodge,** Knockferry, Rosscahill, Galway.*
On Connemara shore of Lough Corrib. Excellent food and accommodation.
Open: Easter to Sep
Grades: AA 3 St
091 550122
Fax no: 091 80328
Mr & Mrs Moran
Rates fr: *IR£20.00*-**IR£6.00**.
Beds: 1F 2D 7T 2S
Baths: 10 Ensuite 2 Shared
(12)

Leenaun

National Grid Ref: L8761

***Portfinn Lodge,** Leenaun, Galway.*
Open: Easter to Oct
Grades: BF 2 St
095 42265 Fax no: 095 42315 Mr Daly
Rates fr: *IR£17.50*-**IR£34.00**.
Beds: 1F 3D 4T
Baths: 8 Ensuite
(20)
Portfinn Lodge, situated in Connemara overlooking the magnificent scenery of the Killary and Mweelrea Mountains. Our seafood restaurant is acclaimed for its locally caught produce and is Egon Ronay and Michelin guides recommended.

***Killary Lodge,** Leenaun, Galway.*
Open: Feb to Nov
Grades: AA 4 Q
095 42276 Mr Young
Rates fr: *IR£25.00*-**IR£25.00**.
Beds: 10D 7T 3S
Baths: 20 Ensuite
Probably the most spectacular setting in the country on the shore of Killary Harbour in North Connemara. Great walking/cycling. Many other activities also. Egon Ronay PAA recommended. Unique and unspoilt.

Loughrea

National Grid Ref: M6117

Kay's Restaurant, Tony's Tavern

***Villa Maria,** Bride Street, Loughrea, Co Galway.*
Modern, recently built town house, maximum heat and sound insulation.
Open: Apr to Sep
091 841864
Mrs Broderick
Rates fr: *IR£15.00*-**IR£20.00**.
Beds: 1F 1D 1T
Baths: 3 Ensuite 1 Private 1 Shared

Maam Cross

National Grid Ref: L9746

***Derryneen,** Tullaboy, Maam Cross, Galway.*
Secluded bungalow set amid scenic Connemara mountains, lakes and moorland.
Open: May to Sep
Grades: BF Approv
091 552462 Ms Lyons
Rates fr: *IR£13.50*-**IR£18.00**.
Beds: 2D 1T 1S
Baths: 1 Ensuite 1 Shared
(5)

Always telephone to get directions to the B&B - you will save time!

Maam Valley

National Grid Ref:

Keanes Country Kitchen

***Leckavrea View Farmhouse,** Maam Valley, Maam Valley, Galway.*
Lakeside house in picturesque surroundings overlooking Castle Kirk. Boats, fishing. Gillies.
Open: All Year (not Xmas)
092 48040 Mrs Gavin
Rates fr: *IR£14.00*-**IR£20.00**.
Beds: 3F 2D 1S **Baths:** 6 Ensuite

Oranmore

National Grid Ref: M3824

Oranmore Lodge, Keanes Country Kitchen

***Son Amar,** Coast Road, Oranmore, Galway.*
Open: All Year
091 794176 Mrs Leyne
Rates fr: *IR£16.00*-**IR£14.00**.
Beds: 1F 2D 1T 2S
Baths: 4 Ensuite 1 Shared
(10) (12)
Gracious Georgian home, overlooking Galway Bay and Burren Mountains. Golf, surfing and horse-riding nearby. Residents' spacious TV lounge. Smokefree home, within view of C11th Oranmore Castle - a haven of peace and quiet. Oranmore, private car hire available, at Son Amar.

***The Moorings,** Main Street, Oranmore, Galway.*
The Moorings houses a delightful nautical, fully licensed restaurant and superb accommodation.
Open: All Year
Grades: BF Approv, RAC Acclaim
091 790462 Mr & Mrs Lynch
Rates fr: *IR£20.00*-**IR£25.00**.
Beds: 1F 2D 3T

All rates are subject to alteration at the owners' discretion.

***Castle View,** Galway Coast Road, Oranmore, Galway.*
Spacious neo-Georgian home, overlooking Galway Bay and Burren mountains.
Open: All Year
091 794648
Mrs Collins
Rates fr: *IR£16.00*-**IR£21.00**.
Beds: 4F
Baths: 4 Ensuite
(10)

***Hillview,** Moneymore, Oranmore, Galway.*
Modern, comfortable bungalow in scenic area, overlooking Clare hills.
Open: Easter to Nov
Grades: BF Approv
091 794341
Mrs Regan Murphy
Rates fr: *IR£15.00*-**IR£18.00**.
Beds: 1F 1D 1T
Baths: 2 Ensuite 1 Private
(5)

Oughterard

National Grid Ref: M1143

***Lakeland Country House,** Portacarron, Oughterard, Galway.*
Open: All Year (not Xmas)
Grades: BF Approv, AA 3 Q
091 552121 / 552146
Mrs Lal Faherty
Rates fr: *IR£16.50*-**IR£19.50**.
Beds: 2F 2D 4T 1S
Baths: 8 Ensuite 1 Private
(20)
Lakeside home. Warm and welcoming. Turf fires. Electric blankets. Hair dryers. Tea trays. Breakfast choice. Private gardens to lake. Fishing/boating centre. Signposted 'Lakeland'. Off N59.

***Whitethorn House,** Portcarron, Oughterard, Galway.*
Modern bungalow in quiet countryside. Fishing, golfing, pony trekking locally.
Open: Easter to Oct
091 552586
Fax no: 091 82586
Mrs Angland
Rates fr: *IR£15.00*-**IR£18.00**.
Beds: 2D 2T
Baths: 3 Ensuite 1 Shared

Portumna

National Grid Ref: M8504

Clonwyn Hotel, O'Meara's Restaurant, Peters Restaurant, Portumna Park Hotel

Greenwood, *Lower Dominic, Portumna, Ballinasloe, Co Galway.*
Centrally heated bungalow in town, car park, garden for guests.
Open: All Year
Grades: BF Approv
0509 41273
Mrs Flanagan
Rates fr: *IR£14.00*-**IR£16.00**.
Beds: 1F 1D 1T 1S
Baths: 1 Ensuite 1 Shared
(1) (4)

Recess

National Grid Ref: L8547

Paddy Festy's

Glendalough, *Recess, Galway.*
Modern bungalow, commanding views mountains, lake in heart of Connemara.
Open: May to Sep
Grades: AA 2 Q
095 34669
Mr Joyce
Rates fr: *IR£14.50*-**IR£19.00**.
Beds: 2F 2D 2T
Baths: 2 Ensuite 2 Shared
(10)

Renvyle

National Grid Ref: L6563

Renvyle Inn, Diamonds Bar, Derryglen Restaurant

Ocean Lodge, *Tooreena, Renvyle, Letterfrack, Galway.*
Comfortable home on edge of Atlantic Ocean.
Open: Easter to Nov
095 43481
Mrs Lydon
Rates fr: *IR£15.00*-**IR£18.00**.
Beds: 1F 2D 1T
Baths: 4 Ensuite 1 Private
(4)

Fuchsia House, *Curragh, Renvyle, Connemara, Galway.*
Country house nestled between the mountains and Atlantic. Very tranquil.
Open: Easter to Nov & 20 Dec to 2 Jan
Grades: BF Approv
095 43502
Mrs Walsh
Rates fr: *IR£14.00*-**IR£19.00**.
Beds: 1F 1D 1T
Baths: 3 Ensuite
(6)

Rosmuc

National Grid Ref: L9233

Dun Manus, *Glencoh, Screebe, Rosmuc, Galway.*
Modern country home overlooking Atlantic. Friendly atmosphere, home cooking, mountain walks.
Open: Easter to Oct
Grades: BF Approv
091 574139
Mrs Conroy
Rates fr: *IR£15.00*-**IR£18.00**.
Beds: 2D 1T
Baths: 3 Ensuite
(6)

Rossaveal

National Grid Ref: L9625

An Sleoiteog

Hernan's Bungalow, *Rossaveal, Galway.*
Bungalow, five minutes for Rossaveal Harbour where boats leave for Aran Islands.
Open: Apr to Oct
091 572158 (also fax no)
Mrs Hernon
Rates fr: *IR£14.00*-**IR£20.00**.
Beds: 1F 2D 1T 1S
Baths: 1 Shared

Derrykyle, *Rossaveal, Casla, Galway.*
A haven of caring in the savage Connemara beauty.
Open: May to Oct
Grades: BF Approv
091 572412 Mrs Mullin
Rates fr: *IR£16.00*-**IR£18.00**.
Beds: 1D 1T
Baths: 2 Ensuite
(5) (7)

Rosscahill

National Grid Ref: M1838

Forest Haven, *Rosscahill, Oughterard, Galway.*
Panoramic tranquil setting 0.25 miles off N59 at Kinneveys Pub.
Open: All Year
Grades: BF Approv
091 550387
Mrs Kavanagh
Rates fr: *IR£15.00*-**IR£20.00**.
Beds: 1F 2D 1T
Baths: 4 Ensuite
(9)

Western Star House, *Rosscahill, Oughterard, Galway.*
Imposing country home with luxury accommodation. Spacious landscaped gardens.
Open: Easter to Nov
Grades: BF Approv
091 550162 Mrs Noone
Rates fr: *IR£15.00*-**IR£20.00**.
Beds: 1F 2D 3T
Baths: 6 Ensuite

Cashel Rock B&B, *Raha, Rosscahill, Galway, Co Galway.*
Modern farmhouse, quiet area 2 km off main road. Superb home cooking.
Open: Easter to Oct
Grades: BF Approv
091 550213 Mrs Walsh
Rates fr: *IR£16.00*-**IR£16.00**.
Beds: 2F 2D 1T 1S
Baths: 4 Ensuite 2 Private
(12)

Roundstone

National Grid Ref: L7240

O'Dowds, Belo, Vaughans

Heatherglen, *Roundstone, Galway.*
Overlooking Roundstone Bay. Convenient to beaches, tennis courts, golf and angling.
Open: All Year (not Xmas)
Grades: BF Approv
095 35837 Mrs Keane
Rates fr: *IR£16.00*-**IR£30.00**.
Beds: 1F 1D 2T
Baths: 4 Ensuite
(6)

Spiddal

National Grid Ref: M1222

Ceol na Mara, Bridge House Hotel, Boluisce Restaurant, Droighnean Donn

Ard Aoibhinn, *Connemara, Spiddal, Galway.*
Open: All Year **Grades:** AA 2 Q
091 553179
(also fax no) Mrs Curran
Rates fr: *IR£15.00*-**IR£15.00**.
Beds: 3F 2D 1S
Baths: 5 Ensuite
(10)
1 km west of village. Multi-recommendations. Convenient Aran Islands Ferry. Blue Flag beaches. Itineraries planned, group reductions. Wheelchair Assisted Approved, credit cards, travel agents' vouchers accepted. 50% reduction for children sharing. Seashore and bog walks.

Teach Osta Na Pairce, *Spiddal, Galway.*
Comfortable family-run hotel. Ideal base for touring Connemara and Aran.
Open: Jun to Sep
Grades: BF 2 St
091 553159 Mr Foyle
Rates fr: *IR£25.00*-**IR£30.00**.
Beds: 4F 9D 10T
Baths: 23 Ensuite
(1) (30)

Sailin, *Coill Rua, Spiddal, Galway.*
Modern bungalow overlooking Galway Bay, Aran Islands five minutes walk safe sandy beach.
Open: Easter to Oct
091 553308 Mrs McCarthaigh
Rates fr: *IR£15.00*-**IR£18.00**.
Beds: 2F 1D 1T
Baths: 4 Ensuite

Pay B&Bs by cash or cheque. Be prepared to pay up front for one night stays.

Cluain Barra, *Knock, Spiddal, Galway,*
Modern country home overlooking Galway Bay and Aran Islands.
Open: May to Nov
Grades: BF Approv
091 593140 Ms Conneely
Rates fr: *IR£14.00*-**IR£19.00**.
Beds: 3T
Baths: 2 Ensuite 1 Shared
(6)

Ard Eoinn, *Spiddal, Galway.*
Modern, comfortable home five minutes walk village. Aran Islands trips arranged.
Open: Jun to Aug
Grades: BF Approv
091 553234 Mrs Naughton
Rates fr: *IR£16.00*.
Beds: 1F 2D 3T
Baths: 5 Ensuite 1 Private
(8)

High season, bank holidays and special events mean low availability *anywhere.*

Tuam

National Grid Ref: M4351

Imperial Hotel

Kilmore House, *Kilmore, Galway Road, Tuam, Co Galway.*
Open: All Year **Grades:** BF Approv
093 28118 Mrs O'Connor
Rates fr: *IR£14.00*-**IR£16.00**.
Beds: 4F 2D 1T
Baths: 7 Ensuite
(15)
Fully registered and approved B&B on farm. All rooms ensuite and TV and Fastext. Very convenient to Knock, Connemara, Galway. Safe car parks. Extensive grounds and gardens. Registered and recommended world-wide by top tourist associations and guides.

The Imperial Hotel, *The Square, Tuam, Co Galway.*
Ideally located in the centre of the smallest city in the world, Tuam, Co Galway.
Open: All Year (not Xmas)
Grades: BF Approv
093 24188 Mr Murphy
Rates fr: *IR£25.00*-**IR£35.00**.
Beds: 2F 3D 15T 10S
Baths: 25 Ensuite

County Kerry

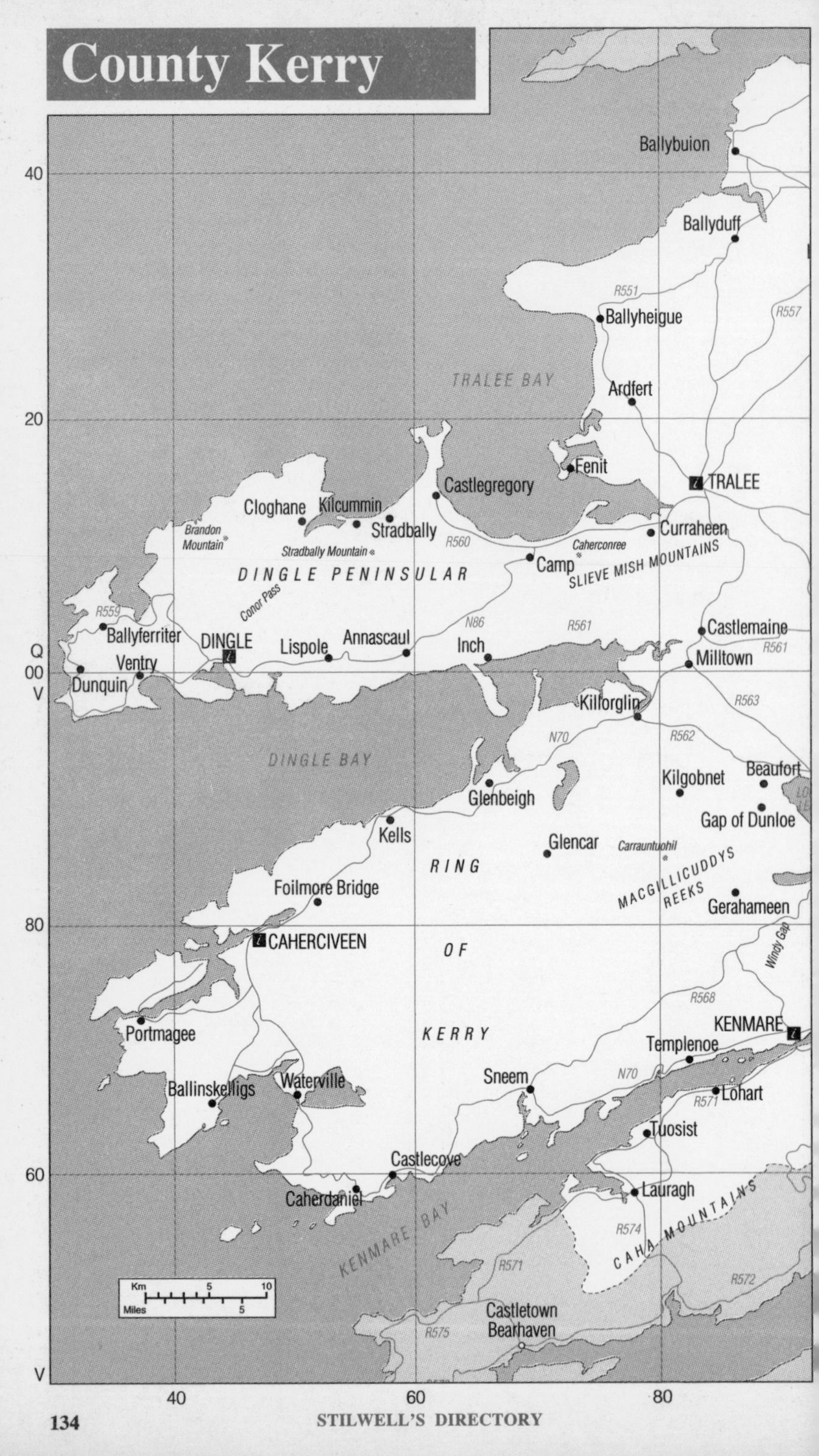

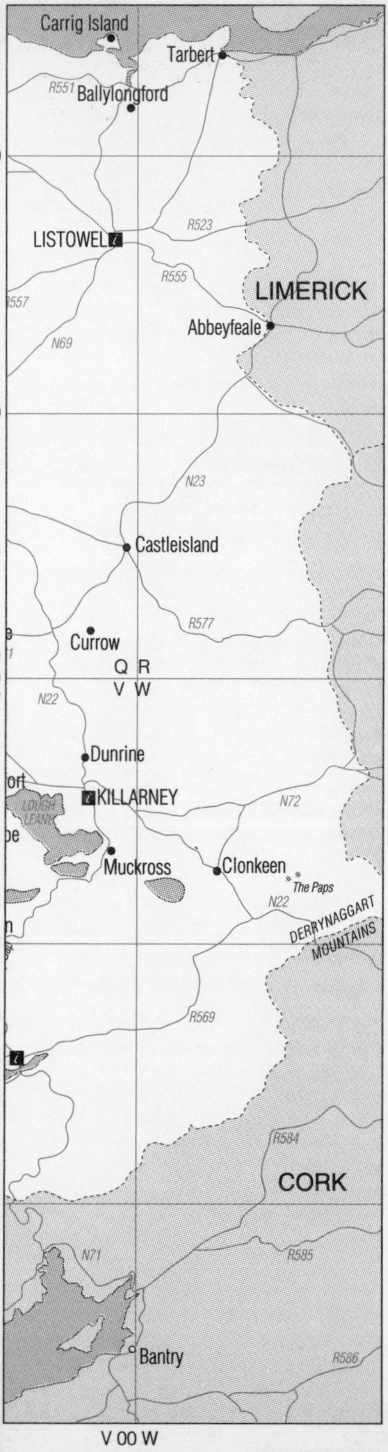

Carrig Island
Tarbert
R551 Ballylongford
LISTOWEL
R523
R555
LIMERICK
R557
Abbeyfeale
N69
N23
Castleisland
R577
Currow
Q R
V W
N22
Dunrine
KILLARNEY
LOUGH LEANE
N72
Muckross
Clonkeen
The Paps
N22
DERRYNAGGART MOUNTAINS
R569
R584
CORK
N71
R585
Bantry
R586
V 00 W

RAIL

Tralee and ***Killarney*** are at the end of a main line into ***Dublin (Heuston)***.

You can also get to ***Cork*** from ***Killarney.*** Tel **Irish Rail** on 01 8366222 for timetable details

BUS

There are services from ***Killarney*** *to* ***Tralee*** and ***Shannon Airport***, from ***Tralee*** *to* ***Cork, Dingle*** *and* ***Limerick.***

Tel **Bus Eireann** on 064 34777

TOURIST INFORMATION OFFICES

Main Street, **Caherciveen** (Jun to Sep), 066 72589

Main Street, **Dingle** (Jun to Sep), 066 51188

The Square, **Kenmare** (Apr to Oct), 064 41233

Town Hall, **Killarney** (open all year), 064 31633

Listowel (Jun to Sep), 068 22590

Ashe Memorial Hall, **Tralee** (open all year), 066 21288

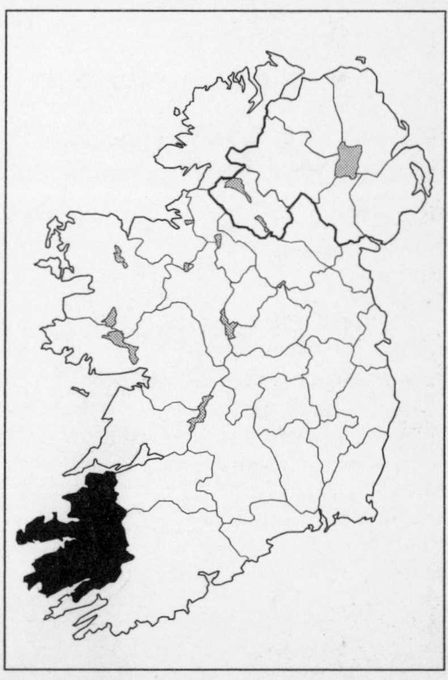

Annascaul

National Grid Ref: Q5902

Cluimin Restaurant, South Pole Bar

The Old Anchor Guest House, *Annascaul, Tralee, Co Kerry.*
Modern town house situated in Annascaul Village. All rooms ensuite.
Open: All Year (not Xmas)
Grades: BF Approv
066 57382
Miss Kennedy
Rates fr: *IR£14.50*-**IR£18.00**.
Beds: 2F 4D 4T
Baths: 8 Ensuite

Four Winds, *Annascaul, Tralee, Co Kerry.*
Modern house at top of hill, surrounded by mountain views.
Open: All Year (not Xmas)
Grades: BF Approv
066 57168
Mrs O'Connor
Rates fr: *IR£16.00*-**IR£20.00**.
Beds: 1F 3T
Baths: 4 Ensuite

Ardfert

National Grid Ref: Q7821

Ardkeel House, *Brandonwell, Ardfert, Tralee, Co Kerry.*
New house in quiet scenic location near village, beach, golf.
Open: All Year
066 34288
Mrs Higgins
Rates fr: *IR£17.00*-**IR£21.00**.
Beds: 1F 1D 1T
(7)

Banna Beach Hotel, *Banna Strand, Ardfert, Tralee, Co Kerry.*
Intimate, modern hotel located near seven miles of sandy beach.
Open: Jun to Aug
Grades: BF Approv
066 34103
Rates fr: *IR£18.00*-**IR£25.00**.
Beds: 12F
Baths: 11 Ensuite

Ballinskelligs

National Grid Ref: V4366

Island View, *Ballinskelligs, Killarney, Co Kerry.*
Modern farmhouse overlooking bay and mountains. Sandy beaches. Peaceful holidays.
Open: Easter to Nov
Grades: BF Approv
066 79128
Mrs Sugrue
Rates fr: *IR£13.50*-**IR£14.00**.
Beds: 1F 1D 1T 1S
Baths: 2 Ensuite 1 Private 1 Shared

Ballybunnion

National Grid Ref: Q8641

Costello's Bar

Greenmount Hotel, *Ballybunnion, Listowel, Co Kerry.*
Comfortable family operated hotel, overlooking beach, adjacent Ballybunnion Golf Course.
Open: Jun to Sep
Grades: BF Approv, AA 1 St
068 27147 Mr Purtill
Rates fr: *IR£15.00*-**IR£20.00**.
Beds: 3F 3D 5T 1S
Baths: 12 Ensuite
(1)

Ballyduff

National Grid Ref: Q8733

Shannon View, *Ferry Road, Ballyduff, Tralee, Co Kerry.*
Open: All Year
Grades: BF Approv
066 31324
Mr & Mrs Sowden
Rates fr: *IR£15.00*-**IR£25.00**.
Beds: 4F 1D 1T
Baths: 1 Ensuite 2 Private 1 Shared
Chef owned guest house Excellent food. Evening meals. Located between Ballybunion and Ballyheigue, close to sandy beaches, golf courses, Tralee and renowned world class golf course of Ballybunion. Game and course fishing, walking. Tralee Festival and Listowel Races. Warm welcome.

Ballyferriter

National Grid Ref: Q3503

Wine Rock, Murphy's, Tighe Tobair, Tigh Pheig

Ostan Golf Dun An Oir, *Ballyferriter, Tralee, Co Kerry.*
Overlooks the majestic Atlantic, delicious seafood dishes and traditional musical evenings, adjoining golf course.
Open: May to Oct **Grades:** BF 2 St
066 56133 Mr Slye
Rates fr: *IR£25.00*-**IR£30.00**.
Beds: 21D **Baths:** 21 Ensuite
(200)

Cois Corraigh, *Emila, Ballyferriter, Tralee, Co Kerry.*
Modern comfortable family home with view to Wine Strand.
Open: Mar to Sep **Grades:** BF Approv
066 56282 Mrs Ferris
Rates fr: *IR£16.00*-**IR£16.00**.
Beds: 1F 1D 2T 1S **Baths:** 5 Ensuite

Ballylongford

National Grid Ref: R0045

Castle View House, *Carrig Island, Ballylongford, Listowel, Co Kerry.*
Modern house on scenic island (access by bridge) facing historic Carrigafoyle Castle. **Open:** All Year (not Xmas)
Grades: BF Approv **068 43304**
Mrs Dee **Rates fr:** *IR£14.00*-**IR£18.50**.
Beds: 3D 3T **Baths:** 6 Ensuite
(8)

Ballyheigue

National Grid Ref: Q7528

White Sands

Hillcrest, *Mountway, Ballyheigue, Tralee, Co Kerry.*
Modern bungalow, large gardens. Superb views of beach and mountains. Beside golf course.
Open: Easter to October
Grades: BF Approv
066 33306 Mrs Collins
Rates fr: *IR£15.00*-**IR£18.00**.
Beds: 2F 1D **Baths:** 3 Ensuite
(2) (5)

Beaufort

National Grid Ref: V8891

Beaufort Bar, Kate Kearney's Cottage

Inisfail, *Beaufort, Killarney, Co Kerry.*
Open: Easter to Oct
Grades: BF Approv
064 44404 Mrs Kelly
Rates fr: *IR£14.00*-**IR£19.00**.
Beds: 3D 1T **Baths:** 3 Ensuite
Warm welcome awaits you at our lovely home in Beaufort Village. Gap of Dunloe 2 miles, Carrantouhill 4 miles, restaurants, pubs 200 metres, golf (Killarney 3 miles, Beaufort 2 miles), fishing, River Laune 200 metres, horse-riding close by.

Pallas Farm, *Beaufort, Killarney, Co Kerry.*
Comfortable farmhouse overlooking Killarney's lakes and mountains. Painter's and photographer's paradise.
Open: Easter to Sept **Grades:** BF 1 St
064 44294 Mrs Kissane
Rates fr: *IR£14.00*-**IR£19.00**.
Beds: 1F 1D 1T **Baths:** 2 Ensuite
(4)

Caherciveen

National Grid Ref: V4779

Shebeen Bar, Frank's Corner, O'Neills, Town House, Teach Caulann, Point Bar

Ocean View, *Renard Road, Caherciveen, Co Kerry.*
Open: All Year (not Xmas)
Grades: BF Approv
066 72261 Ms O Donoghue
Rates fr: *IR£17.00*-**IR£20.00**.
Beds: 2F 3D 1T
Baths: 6 Ensuite
(8) (6)
Luxury farmhouse overlooking Caherciveen Bay within walking distance of town. Bedrooms tastefully decorated, all with spectacular sea views, sunsets, islands, C15th castle. Peat/wood fires, horse/pony trekking on farm. Mountain-climbing, sea-sports, golf pitch/putt. Skellie Rock nearby.

Fransal House, *Foilmore Bridge, Caherciveen, Co Kerry.*
Open: All Year (not Xmas)
Grades: BF Approv
066 72997
Mr & Mrs Landers
Rates fr: *IR£14.00*-**IR£19.00**.
Beds: 1F 2D 1T
Baths: 3 Ensuite 1 Shared
(6)
Experience real Irish home hospitality in peaceful, scenic surroundings yet convenient to all amenities. Mountain view from all rooms, including Kerry Way walking route. Walking, cycling, bus, boat, fishing, horse-riding trips arranged. Complimentary tea/coffee any time. Breakfast .

Mount Rivers, *Carhan Road, Caherciveen, Co Kerry.*
Quiet, secluded, spacious Victorian house, c.1888 on two acres. Antique furnishings
Open: Easter to Sep
Grades: BF Approv
066 72509
Mrs McKenna
Rates fr: *IR£16.50*-**IR£21.00**.
Beds: 1F 4D
Baths: 5 Ensuite

The Final Furlong, *Caherciveen, Co Kerry.*
Modern farmhouse with spectacular views on 100-acre farm along River Fertha.
Open: All Year (not Xmas)
Grades: BF Approv
066 72810
Mrs O'Sullivan
Rates fr: *IR£14.00*-**IR£18.00**.
Beds: 1F 2D 2T
Baths: 4 Ensuite 1 Shared
(10)

Dun An Oir, *New Street, Caherciveen, Co Kerry.*
Comfortable two-storey house west end of Caherciveen, sea and mountain in view.
Open: Easter to Nov
066 72565
Mrs O'Neill
Rates fr: *IR£13.00*-**IR£16.00**.
Beds: 3D 1S
Baths: 1 Ensuite 1 Private
(2)

The lowest *double* rate per person is shown in *italics*.

Iveragh Heights, *Carhan Road, Caherciveen, Co Kerry.*
Picturesque view from all bedrooms, surrounded by mountains and rivers.
Open: All Year **Grades:** BF Approv
066 72545 Mrs O'Neill
Rates fr: *IR£14.00*-**IR£18.00**.
Beds: 1F 2D 1T
Baths: 4 Ensuite
(8)

Ard Na Greine, *Valentia Road, Caherciveen, Co Kerry.*
Traditional Irish house overlooking river and mountains. Beaches, golfing nearby.
Open: Easter to Oct
066 72281 Mrs Quill
Rates fr: *IR£13.50*-**IR£15.00**.
Beds: 1F 1T
Baths: 1 Shared
(1)

Caherdaniel

National Grid Ref: V5459

Scarriff Inn, Donnelly's, Blind Piper

Scarriff Inn, *Caherdaniel, Killarney, Co Kerry.*
Village inn, overlooking harbour. All rooms sea views.
Open: Mar to Oct **Grades:** BF Approv
066 75132 Mrs O'Carroll
Rates fr: *IR£18.95*-**IR£25.00**.
Beds: 2F 4D 4T
Baths: 10 Ensuite

The Old Forge, *Caherdaniel, Killarney, Co Kerry.*
Converted blacksmith's forge overlooking the sea. Home cooking.
Open: All Year **Grades:** BF Approv
066 75140 Mrs Fitzmaurice
Rates fr: *IR£16.00*-**IR£19.00**.
Beds: 5D 4T
Baths: 9 Ensuite

Bunavalla, *Caherdaniel, Killarney, Co Kerry.*
Modern dormer bungalow, situated above Derrynane Harbour.
Open: All Year **Grades:** BF Approv
066 75208 Mrs Moran
Rates fr: *IR£16.00*-**IR£20.00**.
Beds: 2F 1D 1T
Baths: 4 Ensuite

Camp

National Grid Ref: Q6909

Ashe's Bar

Barnagh Bridge Guest House, *Cappalough, Camp, Tralee, Co Kerry.*
Luxury country guest house, overlooking Tralee Bay on Dingle Peninsula.
Open: Easter to Oct
Grades: BF 3 St, AA 3 Q, Select
066 30145 Ms Williams
Rates fr: *IR£18.00*-**IR£28.00**.
Beds: 2F 2D 1T
Baths: 5 Ensuite
(10) (7)

Suan Na Mara, *Lisnagree, Camp, Tralee, Co Kerry.*
Luxurious seaside accommodation with friendly atmosphere. Rich aroma of good food.
Open: Feb to Nov **Grades:** BF Approv
066 39258 Mrs Fitzgerald
Rates fr: *IR£16.00*-**IR£21.00**.
Beds: 2F 1D
Baths: 3 Ensuite
(6)

Carragh Lake

National Grid Ref: V7293

Biaconi, Red Fox

Caran View Lodge, *Carragh Lake, Killorglin, Killarney, Co Kerry.*
Modern private house, lovely gardens, scenic surroundings. Carragh Lake nearby.
Open: Easter to Oct
Grades: BF Approv
066 69193 Mrs Clifford
Rates fr: *IR£16.00*-**IR£18.00**.
Beds: 1F 2D 1T
Baths: 2 Ensuite 2 Shared
(4) (8)

The lowest **single** *rate is shown in* **bold.**

Carrig Island

National Grid Ref: Q9848

Castle View House, *Carrig Island, Ballylongford, Listowel, Co Kerry.*
Open: All Year (not Xmas)
Grades: BF Approv
068 43304 Mrs Dee
Rates fr: *IR£14.00*-**IR£18.50**.
Beds: 3D 3T
Baths: 6 Ensuite
(8)
Modern house on scenic island (access by bridge) facing historic Carrigafoyle Castle. All rooms ensuite. Tarbert/Killimer car ferry, golf course nearby, scenic walks, angling, swimming. Evening meals available .

Castlecove

National Grid Ref: V5860

Old Forge

Birchgrove Farmhouse, *Castlecove, Kenmare, Killarney, Co Kerry.*
Beautifully situated overlooking Kenmare Bay on the beautiful Ring of Kerry. Five minutes walk to the sea. Sandy beaches. Pony riding. Hill walking, fishing.
Open: Easter to Oct
066 75106 Mrs McGillicuddy
Rates fr: *IR£13.50*-**IR£13.50**.
Beds: 2D 1T 1S
Baths: 1 Shared

Staigue Fort House, *Castlecove, Killarney, Co Kerry.*
Lovely position beneath Eagle Hill, overlooking the sea.
Open: Apr to Sep
Grades: BF Approv
066 75127 Mrs Galvin
Rates fr: *IR£15.00*-**IR£18.00**.
Beds: 2F 2D 2T
Baths: 3 Shared

Castlegregory

National Grid Ref: Q6113

Beenoskee, *Cappatigue, Connor Pass Road, Castlegregory, Tralee, Co Kerry.*
Open: All Year
066 39263 Mrs Ferriter
Rates fr: *IR£14.00*-**IR£20.00.**
Beds: 3D 1T
Baths: 3 Ensuite 1 Private
(6)
Spectacular views ocean, long sandy beaches, mountains, islands and lake. Overlooking Brandon Bay - Mountains background. 1 km west Stradbally Village. Dingle 14 km. Warm welcome and Irish hospitality. Complimentary tea/coffee and homemade cake. Breakfast menu. Fishing, golf, horseriding, archaeological sites. Traditional music. ITB Approved.

Strand View House, *Conor Pass Road, Kilcummin, Castlegregory, Tralee, Co Kerry.*
Luxury accommodation. Overlooking Brandon Bay. Water sports, fishing, horse-riding, mountain climbing.
Open: Easter to Nov
Grades: BF Approv
066 38131 Mrs Lynch
Rates fr: *IR£16.50*-**IR£25.00.**
Beds: 3D 1T
Baths: 4 Ensuite
(2) (10)

Castleisland

National Grid Ref: Q9909

Glenbrook House, *Currow, Castleisland, Co Kerry.*
Highly recommended home in country village. Ideal for touring Kerry
Open: All Year **Grades:** BF Approv
066 64488 Mrs O'Connor
Rates fr: *IR£16.00*-**IR£19.00.**
Beds: 1F 3T
Baths: 4 Ensuite

Bringing children with you? Always ask for any special rates.

Bawn Farm House, *Crag Cave Road, Castleisland, Co Kerry.*
Attractive modern house on a dairy farm with a river running through it.
Open: Mar to Nov **Grades:** BF Approv
066 42104 Ms Prendiville
Rates fr: *IR£16.00*-**IR£20.00.**
Beds: 3F 1S **Baths:** 4 Ensuite

The Gables, *Limerick Road, Dooneen, Castleisland, Co Kerry.*
Comfortable modern bungalow with panoramic view, warm welcome awaits you. **Open:** All Year
066 41060 Mrs Dillon
Rates fr: *IR£12.50*-**IR£18.00.**
Beds: 1F 2D 1T **Baths:** 1 Shared

Castlemaine

National Grid Ref: Q8303

Cosgrave's Bar, Farkins

Murphys Farmhouse, *Boolteens, Castlemaine, Killarney, Co Kerry.*
A 200-year-old farmhouse on dairy farm central for touring.
Open: All Year **Grades:** BF Approv
066 67337 Fax no: 066 67839
Ms Murphy
Rates fr: *IR£15.00*-**IR£18.00.**
Beds: 1F 5D 6T 2S **Baths:** 14 Ensuite

Tom & Ellen's Farm, *Castlemaine, Killarney, Co Kerry.*
Award-winning old-style farmhouse nestling under Sliabh Mish Mountains.
Open: May to Oct
066 67373 Mrs O'Connor
Rates fr: *IR£14.00*-**IR£19.00.**
Beds: 1F 3D 2T
Baths: 5 Ensuite 1 Shared
(6)

Caher House, *Caherfilane, Keel, Castlemaine, Killarney, Co Kerry.*
Modern bungalow overlooking Dingle Bay and mountains in quiet peaceful area.
Open: Apr to Oct **Grades:** BF Approv
066 66126 Mrs O'Sullivan
Rates fr: *IR£14.00*-**IR£15.00.**
Beds: 2F 2D 2T
Baths: 2 Ensuite 2 Shared
(6)

Cloghane

National Grid Ref: Q5011

Tigh Tomsi, O'Connors

Loch An Duin, *Ballyhoneen, Conor Pass Road, Cloghane, Tralee, Co Kerry.*
Modern bungalow in peaceful scenic area. Sheep farm. Dingle 10 km.
Open: Easter to Oct
Grades: BF Approv
066 38163 Mrs Maunsell
Rates fr: *IR£14.00*-**IR£19.00**.
Beds: 1F 1D 1T
Baths: 2 Ensuite 1 Private

O'Connor's, *Cloghane, Dingle Peninsula, Tralee, Co Kerry.*
Lovely guesthouse with majestic views located on the Dingle Way.
Open: Mar to Oct
066 38113 Mrs O'Dowd
Rates fr: *IR£15.00*-**IR£15.00**.
Beds: 2F 2T 2D
Baths: 6 Ensuite
(5)

Abhainn Mhor, *Cloghane, Tralee, Co Kerry.*
Beside village. Beaches, hill-walking, guided walks, archaeology, fishing.
Open: Easter to Sep
066 38211 Mrs Brosnan
Rates fr: *IR£16.00*-**IR£16.00**.
Beds: 1F 1D 1T 1S
Baths: 3 Ensuite 1 Private
(6)

Clonkeen

National Grid Ref: W0685

The Glen, *Islandmore, Clonkeen, Killarney, Co Kerry.*
Open: All Year
064 53067 Mrs Garner
Rates fr: *IR£15.00*-**IR£17.00**.
Beds: 2F 1T
Baths: 3 Ensuite
(3)
Traditional C18th farmhouse in quiet, unspoilt mountain setting ten minutes from Killarney on N22 Cork Road. Ideal base for mountain walking and touring Ring of Kerry, Beara and Dingle. Good local pub, fishing, horse-riding, cycling and golf, warm welcome assured.

Curraheen

National Grid Ref: Q7810

Kearne Bar

Keswick Lodge, *Curraheen, Tralee, Co Kerry.*
Country home, sea/mountain views. Ideal base for Dingle/Killarney.
Open: All Year (not Xmas)
066 28751
Perlman
Rates fr: *IR£16.00*-**IR£21.00**.
Beds: 3D 1T
Baths: 4 Ensuite
(5)

Currow

National Grid Ref: Q9704

Glenbrook House, *Currow, Fannanfore, Castleisland, Co Kerry.*
Highly recommended home in country village. Home cooking a speciality. Irish music locally.
Open: All Year
Grades: BF Approv
066 64488 Mrs O'Connor
Rates fr: *IR£16.00*-**IR£19.00**.
Beds: 1F 3T
Baths: 4 Ensuite

Dingle

National Grid Ref: Q4401

Paudie's, Longis Bar, De Barra's, Paidi O'Shea's Bar, Ventry Inn , Lord Bakers, Garvey's, Cormorant Restaurant

Doonshean View, *High Road, Garfinny, Dingle, Tralee, Co Kerry.*
Open: Easter to Oct
Grades: BF Approv
066 51032 Mrs O'Neill
Rates fr: *IR£16.00*-**IR£21.00**.
Beds: 2D 1T
Baths: 3 Ensuite
(4)
Modern dormer bungalow in tranquil location with scenic views. Private parking. Refreshments on arrival. Fire safety certificate. Local attractions include: golf, pitch & putt, angling, sailing, hill walking, cycling, horseriding, dolphin trips, Oceanworld.

***Ard Na Greine House,** Spa Road, Dingle, Tralee, Co Kerry.*
Open: All Year
Grades: AA 4 Q, Select, RAC High Acclaim
066 51113
Fax no: 066 51898
Mrs Houlihan
Rates fr: *IR£17.50*.
Beds: 1F 2D 1T
Baths: 4 Ensuite
(7) (5)
Luxury immaculate bungalow in a superb location 5 minutes walk to town centre. All rooms have bath/shower ensuite, plus satellite TV, direct dial telephone, tea/coffee making facilities, electric blankets. The breakfast menu features smoked salmon, herring, home baked breads, Irish cooked breakfast,etc.

***Duinin House,** Connor Pass Road, Dingle, Tralee, Co Kerry.*
Open: Mar to Oct
Grades: BF Approv
066 51335 (also fax no)
Mrs Neligan
Rates fr: *IR£16.00*-**IR£20.00**.
Beds: 3D 2T
Baths: 5 Ensuite
(7) (5)
Superb location with magnificent views. Overlooking Dingle Town and Harbour. Complimentary tea/coffee served in our luxurious guest conservatory. Extensive breakfast menu. Ideal base from which to explore the Dingle Peninsula. Recommended by Frommer Guide and The 300 Best B&Bs.

***Alpine House,** Mail Road, Dingle, Tralee, Co Kerry.*
Open: All Year (not Xmas)
Grades: BF 3 St, AA 3 Q, Recomm, RAC High Acclaim
066 51250 Fax no: 066 51966
Mr O'Shea
Rates fr: *IR£16.50*-**IR£17.50**.
Beds: 2F 5D 5T
Baths: 12 Ensuite
(4) (20)
Delightfully furnished bedrooms with spacious private bathrooms. Rooms with excellent views of harbour and mountains. A menu of traditional and wholesome fare served in impressive breakfast room. Dingle, famous for seafood and traditional Irish music bars. Near bus-stop.

***Moriarty's Farmhouse,** Rahanane, Dingle, Tralee, Co Kerry.*
Open: All Year
Grades: BF Approv
066 59037
(also fax no) Mrs Moriarty
Rates fr: *IR£15.00*-**IR£22.00**.
Beds: 3F 2D 1T
Baths: 6 Ensuite
Spacious family run farmhouse overlooking Ventry Harbour. Spectacular views of sea & mountains. Ideal for walkers, cyclists and those seeking peace and tranquillity. All rooms ensuite with sea ciew, tea/coffee facilities, hairdryer and radio. Irish dancing by family members.

***The Lighthouse,** Ballinaboula, Dingle, Tralee, Co Kerry.*
Spacious house with excellent accommodation overlooking Dingle Harbour.
Open: All Year (not Xmas)
Grades: BF Approv
066 51829 Mrs Murphy
Rates fr: *IR£14.00*-**IR£18.00**.
Beds: 1F 3D
Baths: 4 Ensuite

***Kirrary House,** Kirrary, Dingle, Tralee, Co Kerry.*
Open: All Year (not Xmas)
066 51606 (also fax no)
Mrs Collins
Rates fr: *IR£15.00*-**IR£18.00**.
Beds: 1D 1T 1S
Baths: 2 Ensuite 1 Shared
Family home set in a side street in the heart of Dingle Town. Own gardens. Archaeological excursions organised from house, also mountain bikes available for hire. Home baking, central heating. 3 minutes walk from bus stop. Open fire.

***Garvey's Farmhouse,** Kilvicadownig, Ventry, Dingle, Tralee, Co Kerry.*
Spacious house on dairy farm overlooking Ventry Bay in peaceful surrounings.
Open: Mar to Nov **Grades:** BF Approv
066 59914 Fax no: 066 59921
Mrs Garvey
Rates fr: *IR£14.50*-**IR£19.50**.
Beds: 2F 2D 1T
Baths: 3 Ensuite 2 Shared
(6)

Cil Bheac, *Milltown, Dingle, Tralee, Co Kerry.*
Open: Mar to Oct **Grades:** BF Approv
066 51358 Mrs McCarthy
Rates fr: *IR£16.00*-**IR£21.00**.
Beds: 2F 2D 1T
Baths: 5 Ensuite
(0) (8)
Spacious home overlooking Dingle Bay, Mount Brandon. All rooms with satelite, TV, clock radio, hair dryer, electric blankets, tea/coffee making facilities - convenient to sandy beaches and within 1 km of Dingle Town. Guest lounge balcony overlooking Dingle Bay.

Dunquin

National Grid Ref: Q3100

Kruger's Bar

Kruger's, *Ballinaraha, Dunquin, Dingle, Tralee, Co Kerry.*
Open: Mar to Oct
Grades: BF Grade A
066 56127 Mrs O'Neill
Rates fr: *IR£15.00*-**IR£15.00**.
Beds: 1F 7D 1T 1S
Baths: 9 Shared
(10) (50)
Famous and popular traditional guest house and lounge bar. Situated on the tip of the spectacular Dingle Peninsula. Ideal for touring the popular Dingle Way route and the scenic Slea Head Way route. Two lovely sandy beaches nearby. Boat trips to Blasket Islands arranged. Within walking distance of magnificent Blasket Island Museum. 'Ryan's Daughter' film sites nearby.

Slea Head Farm, *Couminole, Slea Head, Dunquin, Tralee, Co Kerry.* Most westerly farm in Europe, looking onto the Blasket Islands and the Atlantic.
Open: Apr to Oct
066 56120 Mrs Firtear
Rates fr: *IR£14.00*-**IR£15.00**.
Beds: 1F 1D 2T 1S
Baths: 3 Ensuite 1 Shared

The lowest **single** *rate is shown in* **bold.**

Dunrine

National Grid Ref: V9695

Arbutus Hotel

Homedale, *Tralee Road, Dunrine, Killarney, Co Kerry.*
Modern bungalow with expansive views. Ideal for touring South West.
Open: Easter to Nov
Grades: BF Approv
064 33855
Mrs Casey
Rates fr: *IR£15.00*-**IR£18.00**.
Beds: 1F 2D
Baths: 3 Ensuite 1 Shared
(5)

Fenit

National Grid Ref: Q7216

The Lighthouse Hotel, *Fenit, Tralee, Co Kerry.*
Family hotel in picturesque village of Fenit beside Tralee Bay.
Open: Easter to Dec
Grades: BF Approv
066 36158
Fax no: 066 36261
Mr Sullivan
Rates fr: *IR£15.00*-**IR£15.00**.
Beds: 7F 1D 5T
Baths: 13 Ensuite
(50)

Foilmore Bridge

National Grid Ref: V5282

Fransal House, *Foilmore Bridge, Caherciveen, Co Kerry.*
Open: All Year (not Xmas)
Grades: BF Approv
066 72997
Mr & Mrs Landers
Rates fr: *IR£14.00*-**IR£19.00**.
Beds: 1F 2D 1T
Baths: 3 Ensuite 1 Shared
(6)
Experience real Irish home hospitality in peaceful, scenic surroundings yet convenient to all amenities. Mountain view from all rooms, including Kerry Way Walking Route. Walking, cycling, bus, boat, fishing, horse-riding trips arranged. Complimentary tea/coffee any time.

Gap of Dunloe

National Grid Ref: V8787

Kate Kearney's Cottage

Purple Heather, *Gap of Dunloe, Killarney, Co Kerry.*
Ideally centred for all scenic routes, golf, nature walks, mountain climbing.
Open: Mar to Nov
Grades: BF Approv
064 44266 Mrs Moriarty
Rates fr: *IR£14.50*-**IR£19.50**.
Beds: 1F 2D 2T 1S
Baths: 5 Ensuite 1 Shared
(6)

Alpine Heights, *Gap of Dunloe, Killarney, Co Kerry.*
Beautifully situated at the world famous Gap of Dunloe. Ideal for hill-walking.
Open: All Year (not Xmas)
064 44284 Mrs Ferris
Rates fr: *IR£14.00*-**IR£19.00**.
Beds: 1F 2D 2D **Baths:** 2 Ensuite

Gerahameen

National Grid Ref: V8781

Hillcrest Farmhouse, *Gerahameen, Black Valley, Killarney, Co Kerry.*
Working farm directly below MacGillicuddy's Reeks, near the National Park.
Open: Mar to Oct
Grades: BF Approv
064 34702 Mrs Tangney
Rates fr: *IR£16.00*-**IR£21.00**.
Beds: 1D 4T **Baths:** 5 Ensuite

Glenbeigh

National Grid Ref: V6591

Breen's Diner, Falcon Inn, Towers Hotel, Glenbeigh Hotel

The Falcon Inn, *Glenbeigh, Killarney, Co Kerry.*
Friendly, family-run hotel with restaurant.
Open: All Year **Grades:** BF Approv
066 68215 Mr & Mrs MacDonogh
Rates fr: *IR£20.00*-**IR£22.50**.
Beds: 3F 7D 6T **Baths:** 16 Ensuite

Village House, *Glenbeigh, Killarney, Co Kerry.*
Open: All Year
Grades: BF 3 St RAC Listed
066 68128 Fax no: 066 68486
Mr J. Breen
Rates fr: *IR£18.00*-**IR£25.00**.
Beds: 2F 4D 3T
Baths: 9 Ensuite 1 Shared
Family-run guesthouse 3 Star RAC listed. Ideal for walking, sightseeing, golfing, three miles sandy beach on Kerryway and Ring of Kerry. Canoeing and orienteering.

The Fox Trot, *Mountain Stage, Glenbeigh, Killarney, Co Kerry.*
Luxury accommodation on the internationally renowned Ring of Kerry
Open: Mar to Nov
Grades: BF Approv
066 68417
Fax no: 066 68552 Mrs Fox
Rates fr: *IR£15.00*-**IR£21.00**.
Beds: 3D 1T
Baths: 4 Ensuite 1 Private
(13) (10)

Ocean Wave, *Ring of Kerry, Glenbeigh, Killarney, Co Kerry.*
Breathtaking views of Dingle Bay and Dooks golf links.
Open: Mar to Oct
Grades: BF Approv
066 68249
Fax no: 066 68412
Mrs O'Toole
Rates fr: *IR£17.50*-**IR£25.00**.
Beds: 3D 3T
(6)

Glencar

National Grid Ref: V7084

Climbers Inn

Blackstones House, *Glencar, Killarney, Co Kerry.*
Old-style farmhouse nestling in the Glencar Valley.
Open: All Year
Grades: BF Approv
066 60164 Mrs Breen
Rates fr: *IR£16.50*-**IR£21.50**.
Beds: 3F 2D 2T
Baths: 6 Ensuite 1 Private

Climbers Inn, *Glencar, Killarney, Co Kerry.*
Country inn. Post Office, shop and bar all under one roof.
Open: Mid-Mar to Oct
Grades: BF Approv
066 60101 Mr & Mrs Walsh
Rates fr: *IR£16.50*-**IR£25.00**.
Beds: 10F
Baths: 10 Ensuite
(10)

Inch

National Grid Ref: Q6501

Foley's Bar, Strand Bar

Caherbla House, *Inch, Tralee, Co Kerry.*
Modern comfortable house overlooking Dingle Bay.
Open: All Year
Grades: BF Approv
066 58120 Mrs McCarthy
Rates fr: *IR£16.00*-**IR£18.00**.
Beds: 2F 2D **Baths:** 4 Ensuite

Red CLiff House, *Inch, Tralee, Co Kerry.*
Old Georgian house, built as hunting lodge, set above sea with panoramic views.
Open: All Year (not Xmas)
066 57136 Mrs O'Leary
Rates fr: *IR£14.00*-**IR£19.00**.
Beds: 4F 1D **Baths:** 5 Ensuite

Kells

National Grid Ref: V5788

Glenville Farmhouse, *Gleesk, Kells, Co Kerry.*
Open: Apr to Sep
066 77625 Ms O'Grady
Rates fr: *IR£15.00*-**IR£20.00**.
Beds: 1F 1D 2T
Baths: 3 Ensuite 1 Private
Modern farmhouse on Ring of Kerry N70, between Glenbeigh and Cahirciveen. Panoramic view of Dingle Bay. Great fishing in Kells Bay, also safe sandy beach. Trips to Skellig arranged. Seafood and home baking. TV lounge. Private parking.

Kenmare

National Grid Ref: V9070

Wander Inn, Foley's Bar, Horseshoe Restaurant, Lime Tree, Coachman's Inn, The Shamrock, Packies

O'Donnells Of Ashgrove, *Kenmare, Co Kerry.*
Open: Easter to Oct **Grades:** BF Approv
064 41228 Mrs O'Donnell
Rates fr: *IR£15.00*-**IR£20.00**.
Beds: 1F 2D 1T
Baths: 3 Ensuite 1 Shared
(8)
Beautiful country home in peaceful setting incorporating olde worlde charm, where guests are welcomed as friends. Jacobean-style dining room. Spacious, elegant family lounge with many antiques. Recommended *Dillard/Causin Guide*. Special rates May, September, October for anglers/senior citizens. Brochure available.

Ard Na Mara, *Pier Road, Kenmare, Killarney, Co Kerry.*
Open: All Year (not Xmas)
Grades: BF Approv
064 41399 Mrs Dahm
Rates fr: *IR£15.50*-**IR£20.00**.
Beds: 2D 2T **B**
aths: 4 Ensuite
(1)
Modern house. Situated in a big garden. Front view overlooking Kenmare, mountain view to the back. Five minutes walk to town. Many good restaurants in town.

Foley's Shamrock, *Henry Street, Kenmare, Killarney, Co Kerry.*
Open: All Year
Grades: BF 3 St, AA 3 Q
064 41379
Fax no: 064 41799
Ms Foley
Rates fr: *IR£18.00*-**IR£25.00**.
Beds: 1F 4D 5T
Baths: 10 Ensuite
Foleys is situated in Kenmare, Kerry's Heritage Town. Standing on the Ring of Kerry and Beara. 10 comfortable centrally heated ensuite rooms with TV. Our chef owned restaurant and pub bistro serve Irish and international cuisine. 'One of Ireland's best' - Fodors.

Laburnum House, *Sneem Road, Kenmare, Killarney, Co Kerry.*
Comfortable home. Ring of Kerry walkers paradise. Host experienced guide.
Open: Mar to Nov **Grades:** BF Approv
064 41034 Fax no: 064 42168
Mrs Kelly-Murphy
Rates fr: *IR£16.00*-**IR£20.00.**
Beds: 2F 2D 1T **Baths:** 5 Ensuite
(3) (8)

Oakfield, *Castletown Berehaven Road, Dawros, Kenmare, Co Kerry.*
Open: May to Sept
064 41262 Mrs O'Sullivan
Rates fr: *IR£14.00*-**IR£22.00.**
Beds: 2F 1D 1T
Baths: 2 Ensuite 2 Private
Hospitality assured at Oakfield. Modern bungalow set in scenic location near waterfall and lakes on R571 Road. Home baking and seafood a speciality. Convenient for horse riding, golf and fishing. Ideal location for touring Ring of Kerry and Beara Peninsula.

Silvertrees, *Lansdowne Lodge, Kenmare, Killarney, Co Kerry.*
Elegant home set in rock garden, spacious rooms, breakfast menu.
Open: Easter to Nov
Grades: BF Approv
064 41008 Mrs Hodnett
Rates fr: *IR£16.00*-**IR£21.00.**
Beds: 2D 1T **Baths:** 3 Ensuite
(3)

Ceann Mara, *Killowen, Kenmare, Killarney, Co Kerry.*
Award-winning farmhouse 1.5 km from Kenmare on R569 overlooking Kenmare Bay. **Open:** May to Sep
064 41220 Mrs Hayes
Rates fr: *IR£16.00*-**IR£22.00.**
Beds: 1F 1D 2T
Baths: 3 Ensuite 1 Private
(4)

Avelow, *Killarney Road, Kenmare, Killarney, Co Kerry.*
Comfortable accommodation near town. Ideal touring base. Tea-making facilities. **Open:** Easter to Oct
Grades: BF Approv
064 41473 Downing & Family
Rates fr: *IR£16.00*-**IR£21.00.**
Beds: 1F 1D 2T
Baths: 4 Ensuite

O'Shea's Guest House, *14 Henry Street, Kenmare, Killarney, Co Kerry.*
Pleasing comfortable guest house in centre of town. **Open:** Easter to Oct
064 41453 Mr O'Shea
Rates fr: *IR£13.50*-**IR£13.50.**
Beds: 2F 2D 1T
Baths: 1 Ensuite 2 Shared
(10) (4)

Sea Shore, *Tubrid, Kenmare, Co Kerry.*
Blissful peace and quiet, spectacular view of Bay. Delight for nature lovers.
Open: Apr to Oct **Grades:** BF Approv
064 41270 Mrs O'Sullivan
Rates fr: *IR£16.00*-**IR£23.50.**
Beds: 2F 1D 1T **Baths:** 4 Ensuite

Kilcummin

National Grid Ref: Q5612

Strand View House, *Conor Pass Road, Kilcummin, Castlegregory, Killarney, Co Kerry.*
Luxury accommodation, overlooking Brandon Bay. **Open:** Easter to Nov
Grades: BF Approv
066 38131 Mrs Lynch
Rates fr: *IR£16.50*-**IR£25.00.**
Beds: 3D 1T **Baths:** 4 Ensuite
(2) (10)

Lynch's Farm, *Off Tralee Airport Road, Kilcummin, Castlegregory, Killarney, Co Kerry.*
Modern comfortable farmhouse. Ideal base for Ring of Kerry and Dingle.
Open: All Year **Grades:** BF Approv
064 31637 Mrs Lynch
Rates fr: *IR£13.00*-**IR£15.00.**
Beds: 1F 2D 2T 1S **Baths:** 4 Ensuite

Kilgarvan

National Grid Ref: W0173

Conaberry House, *Church Street, Kilgarvan, Killarney, Kerry.*
200-year-old modernised house. Family-run. Beautiful view of Roughty Valley and mountains. **Open:** All Year
064 85323 Mrs Coughey
Rates fr: *£13.00*-**£13.00.**
Beds: 1F 2D
Baths: 1 Ensuite 2 Private
(5)

Kilgobnet

National Grid Ref: V8191

Shanara House, *Kilgobnet, Beaufort, Killarney, Co Kerry.*
Open: may to Sept
066 61218
Mr & Mrs O'Shea
Rates fr: *IR£14.00*-**IR£19.00**.
Beds: 1F 1D 1T
Baths: 2 Ensuite
(2)
Modern bungalow. Five bedrooms - three with shower and toilet. Situated under the shadow of Carrantuohill - Ireland's highest mountain. Panoramic mountain scenery. Ideal for touring Ring of Kerry. Family-run business. Good conversation. Music a speciality. *Cead mile failte* to all our guests.

Killarney

National Grid Ref: V9690

Molly D'Arcys Pub, Paddy's, Ross Hotel, Golden Nugget, The Laune, McSweeney Arms, Murphy's Bar, Gaby's Restaurant, Flesk Restaurant, Whitegates Hotel, Kiely's Pub

Tara, *Fossa, Killarney, Co Kerry.*
Open: Feb to Nov
Grades: BF Approv, RAC Listed
064 44355 Fax no: 35364 44873
Mrs Dore O'Brien
Rates fr: *IR£14.00*-**IR£19.00**.
Beds: 1F 2D 2T
Baths: 4 Ensuite 1 Private
(2) (6)
A warm welcome to our traditional home, wonderful garden setting. RAC/Hachette Visa Guide recommended. Beside Killarney Golf Club (tee times arranged) and River Laune (salmon and trout). Off the main road N72. Information on tours. Breakfast menu, hairdryers and electric blankets.

Always telephone to get directions to the B&B - you will save time!

Brookside Gortacollopa, *Fossa, Killarney, Co Kerry.*
Open: Mar to Nov **Grades:** BF Approv
064 44187 Mr & Mrs Moriarty
Rates fr: *IR£15.00*-**IR£19.00**.
Beds: 2F 1D 2T
Baths: 4 Ensuite 1 Shared
(6)
Award-winning country home in farmland setting. 1993 and 1995 Country Rover B&B of the Year, where a home-from-home atmosphere awaits you. Complimentary tea/coffee on arrival. Extensive breakfast menu. Information and advice on local tours, etc. Pastoral view.

Sliabh Luachra, *Loretto Road, Castlelough, Killarney, Co Kerry.*
Open: April to Sept
064 32012 Mr & Mrs Kenny
Rates fr: *IR£17.00*-**IR£23.00**.
Beds: 5D 1T
Baths: 6 Ensuite
Family house standing in landscaped gardens. Award winning house 5 mins from lakes, parklands. 10-15 mins walk from town centre. Tours arranged. Family run house.

Countess House, *Countess Road, Killarney, Co Kerry.*
Luxurious house in peaceful location three minutes town/bus/rail.
Open: All Year **Grades:** AA 3 St
064 34247 Mrs Sheahan
Rates fr: *IR£16.00*-**IR£21.00**.
Beds: 1F 2D 1T **Baths:** 4 Ensuite
(8)

Direen House, *Tralee Road, Killarney, Co Kerry.*
Open: Mar to Nov
Grades: BF Approv, AA 2 Q
064 31676 Mrs Casey
Rates fr: *IR£15.00*-**IR£20.00**.
Beds: 2F 2D 1T
Baths: 5 Ensuite
(2) (6)
Comfortable bungalow offering friendly, efficient service. Ideally situated for touring Kerry, Killarney. Minutes drive from golf, lakes, National Park. Special packages - full day's coach tour (Ring of Kerry or Dingle Peninsula) with dinner at Arbutus Hotel. Low season rates, coach pick-up and drop-off from premises. Please contact Mary.

Breffni, *Cork Road, Killarney, Co Kerry.*
Open: Easter to Sep
064 31413 Mrs O'Meara
Rates fr: *IR£13.50*-**IR£15.00**.
Beds: 1F 1D 1T 1S
Baths: 2 Ensuite 4 Private 3 Shared
(8)
Our guest house has four bedrooms, two ensuite and two standard. We are just seven minutes walk from town. Free car park. If guests come by train we collect them and take them back when they leave. We also have private facilities and all modern conveniences.

Cricket View, *7 Muckross Grove, Killarney, Co Kerry.*
Modern family home. Peaceful area. Near Lake District. 1 km from town.
Open: Easter to Sep
Grades: BF Approv
064 32245 Mrs McCarthy
Rates fr: *IR£15.00*-**IR£20.00**.
Beds: 2F 1D
Baths: 1 Ensuite 2 Shared
(3)

O'Donovans Farm - Muckross Riding Stables, *Mangerton Road, Muckross, Killarney, Co Kerry.*
Open: Mar to Dec
Grades: BF Approv
064 32238
Mrs O'Donovan
Rates fr: *IR£14.00*-**IR£19.00**.
Beds: 2F 1D 3T 1S
Baths: 4 Ensuite 2 Shared
Modern farm bungalow with panoramic view of national park (oak forest with red deer). Mangerton and Toke Mountain, Killarney Lakes, Muckross House nearby. Approved riding stables on premises. 3.5 miles south of Killarney.

Green Acres, *Fossa, Killarney, CoKerry.*
Comfortable home adjacent to Killarney Golf and Fishing Club, lakes and mountains.
Open: Easter to Oct
Grades: BF Approv
064 31454 Mrs Murphy
Rates fr: *IR£14.50*-**IR£19.00**.
Beds: 2F 2D 2T 2S
Baths: 1 Ensuite 6 Private
(5) (10)

Coffey's Loch Lein Guesthouse, *Golf Course Road, Fossa, Killarney, Co Kerry.*
Open: Mar to Nov
Grades: BF 3 St, AA 3 Q
064 31260 Fax no: 064 36151
Mrs Coffey
Rates fr: *IR£16.00*-**IR£20.00**.
Beds: 7F 1D 4T
Baths: 12 Ensuite
(12)
Modern family-run guesthouse, uniquely situated by the shores of Killarney's lower lake. Ideally situated on Ring of Kerry/Dingle Roads, near Gap of Dunloe. Tours arranged. Nearby are Killarney's 18-hole championship golf courses, also available horse-riding, fishing hill-walking and cycling.

Doogary, *Lewis Road, Killarney, Co Kerry.*
Select family-run B&B. Convenient to town. Beautiful walks.
Open: May to Oct
064 32509 Mrs O'Brien
Rates fr: *IR£16.00*.
Beds: 1F 1D 1T
Baths: 3 Ensuite 1 Private
(4)

Killarney Villa, *Cork/Waterford Road (N72), Killarney, Co Kerry.*
Open: Easter to Oct
Grades: BF Approv, AA 3 Q, Recomm, RAC Acclaim
064 31878 (also fax no)
Mr & Mrs O'Sullivan
Rates fr: *IR£15.00*-**IR£16.50**.
Beds: 4D 2T
Baths: 6 Ensuite
(10) (8)
Awarded the AA Selected 3 quality marks. Set in 0.5 acres of landscaped gardens. An attractive purpose built villa with a beautifully appointed rooftop conservatory where guests can relax with complimentary tea/coffee. Ideal touring/golfing base within minutes drive from the town centre.

High season, bank holidays and special events mean low availability *anywhere*.

Slieve Bloom Manor, *Muckross Road, Killarney, Co Kerry.*
Open: All Year (not Xmas)
Grades: BF 3 St, AA 3 Q
064 34237 Clery
Rates fr: *IR£15.00*-**IR£16.00.**
Beds: 7D 3T 1S
Baths: 10 Ensuite
(10)
A luxurious family-run guesthouse, with bright spacious rooms, all ensuite with TV. Tea/coffee making facilities, hairdryers and telephone. Ideal location for touring the Kerry Region. Adjacent to national park, racecourse and all amenities. All breakfast requests catered for. Tours arranged.

Serenic View, *Coolcorcoran, Killarney, Co Kerry.*
Modern ground floor accommodation in quiet scenic area overlooking Killarney.
Open: May to Sep
Grades: BF Approv
064 33434 Ms Murphy
Rates fr: *IR£16.00*-**IR£21.00.**
Beds: 1F 2D 1T
Baths: 4 Ensuite
(6)

The Grotto, *Fossa, Killarney, Co Kerry.*
Open: Easter to Nov
064 33283 Mrs Ryan
Rates fr: *IR£16.00*-**IR£19.00.**
Beds: 3F 1D 2T
Baths: 6 Ensuite
(6)
Spacious warm home on Ring of Kerry/Dingle Road. Opposite lake and fishing club. Riding stables nearby. Ideal for walkers/climbers. Tea/coffee facilities. Breakfast menu. Tours arranged.

Muckross Lodge, *Muckross Road, Killarney, Co Kerry.*
Open: Mar to Oct
064 32660 Mrs O'Sullivan
Rates fr: *IR£17.50*-**IR£25.00.**
Beds: 1F 1D 3T
Baths: 5 Ensuite
Purpose-built dormer house situated one mile from Killarney town and adjacent to Muckross House, National Park and lakes. All bedrooms with private bathrooms, TV, tea/coffee making facilities, hairdryer and are smoke free. Traffic free walking and cycling routes nearby.

Mountain Dew, *3 Ross Road, Killarney, Co Kerry.*
Modern town house situated 3 minute walk from town centre, rail and bus. Ideal location for golf, fishing and touring. Private parking. Breakfast menu. All tours arranged.
Open: All Year
064 33892 Fax no: 064 31332
Mrs O'Carroll
Rates fr: *IR£16.00*-**IR£20.00.**
Beds: 3D 1T **Baths:** 3 Ensuite 1 Shared
(4)

Bellevue, *1 Gortroe, Killarney, Co Kerry.*
Open: Mar to Oct
064 34621 Mrs Guerin
Rates fr: *IR£16.00*-**IR£20.00.**
Beds: 3D **Baths:** 3 Ensuite
(6)
Quality B/B 1.5 km Killarney West. ITB Approved. 1.5 km Killarney Golf Club. All rooms with colour TV, Teasmade. 'Hairdryer on request'. Iron and board. Recommended.

Dromhall Heights, *Killarney, Co Kerry.*
Modern comfortable bungalow close to all amenities. Ideal touring base.
Open: Mar to Oct **Grades:** BF Approv
064 32662 Mrs McCarthy
Rates fr: *IR£16.00*-**IR£18.00.**
Beds: 1F 1D 1T
Baths: 2 Ensuite 1 Shared
(4)

Lisaden, *97 Countess Grove, Countess Road, Killarney, Co Kerry.*
Open: Mar to Oct **Grades:** BF Approv
064 32006 Mrs O'Sullivan
Rates fr: *IR£16.00*-**IR£21.00.**
Beds: 1F 1D 2T **Baths:** 4 Ensuite
(4)
Bungalow in pleasant restful area, seven minutes walk town centre. Tea/coffee and hairdryer facilities in rooms. Golf, fishing available locally. Tours arranged.

Hazel Wood, *Upper Park Road, Ballyspillane, Killarney, Co Kerry.*
Modern bungalow, quiet area, walking distance from town, private parking.
Open: May to Oct
064 34363 Mrs Kelliher
Rates fr: *IR£16.00*-**IR£18.00.**
Beds: 1F 2D 1T **Baths:** 4 Ensuite

Silver Spruce, *New Road, Killarney, Co Kerry.*
Open: All Year **Grades:** BF Approv
064 31376 Mrs Sheehan
Rates fr: *IR£15.00*-**IR£20.00**.
Beds: 1F 1D 1T 1S
Baths: 4 Ensuite
(6)
Quiet residential location. Three minutes walk to town centre, good restaurants nearby. Close to National Park for hill climbing, cycling, fishing and boat trips.

Cois Dara, *Rookery Road, Killarney, Co Kerry.*
Luxury non-smoking accommodation in a quiet area, within walking distance of town.
Open: Mar to Nov
064 35567
(also fax no) Mrs O'Brien
Rates fr: *IR£16.00*-**IR£20.00**.
Beds: 1F 2D 1S
Baths: 4 Ensuite
(10)

Foley's Town House, *23 High Street, Killarney, Co Kerry.*
Open: Easter to Nov
Grades: BF 4 St, AA 4 Q, RAC High Acclaim
064 31217 Fax no: 064 34683
Mrs Hartnett
Rates fr: *IR£35.00*-**IR£35.00**.
Beds: 4D 4T 4S
Baths: 12 Ensuite
(3) (20)
Originally an C18th coaching inn , newly refurbished, this is a 4 star, family-run, town centre located guesthouse. Luxury bedrooms designed for comfort, complete with every modern amenity. Downstairs is an award winning seafood and steak restaurant. Chef/owner Carol Hartnett supervises.

Lime Court, *Muckross Road, Killarney, Co Kerry.*
Lime Court is a purpose built luxury guest house less than 1 km from Killarney town centre.
Open: All Year (not Xmas)
Grades: BF 3 St, AA 3 St
064 34547 Fax no: 064 34121
Mr Moriarty
Rates fr: *IR£21.00*-**IR£25.00**.
Beds: 4F 8D 4T 3S
Baths: 19 Ensuite

Clonalis House, *Countess Road, Killarney, Co Kerry.*
Open: Easter to Nov
064 31043
Mrs O'Connor
Rates fr: *IR£16.50*-**IR£20.00**.
Beds: 2D 3T 2S
Baths: 6 Ensuite
(10)
Luxurious home in quiet select residential location 1km from Killarney and golf course. Ideal location for touring the beautiful South West. All tours arranged. Touring coach will colllect you at Clonalis House at no extra cost.

Tuscar Guest House, *Golf Course Road, Fossa, Killarney, Co Kerry.*
Family run guesthouse overlooking Killarney Lakes and Kerry Mountains.
Open: Mar to Oct
Grades: BF 2 St
064 31978
Ms Fitzgerald
Rates fr: *IR£13.00*-**IR£16.00**.
Beds: 4D 10T
Baths: 14 Ensuite
(14)

Killarney Town House, *31 New Street, Killarney, Co Kerry.*
Open: All Year
064 35388
Fax no: 064 35259
Mrs Hallassey
Rates fr: *IR£20.00*-**IR£25.00**.
Beds: 8D 3T
Baths: All Ensuite
(0)
Killarney Town House is ideally situated in the heart of Killarney Town centre. Rooms ensuite, satellite TV, direct dial telephone. Enjoy local amenities which include golf, fishing, Killarney's famous lakes, mountain climbing, National Park. A warm welcome awaits you.

Linn Dubh, *Aghadoe, Killarney, Co Kerry.*
Overlooking Killarney's lakes/mountains. Experience Irish hospitality in tranquil surroundings.
Open: Mar to Nov
Grades: BF Approv
064 33828 Mrs Sheehy
Rates fr: *IR£16.00*-**IR£21.00**.
Beds: 2F 2D 1T
Baths: 4 Ensuite 1 Shared
(6)

Purple Heather, *Gap of Dunloe, Killarney, Co Kerry.*
Open: Mar to Nov
Grades: BF Approv
064 44266 Mrs Moriarty
Rates fr: *IR£14.50*-**IR£19.50**.
Beds: 1F 2D 2T 1S
Baths: 5 Ensuite 1 Shared
(6)
Scenic area. All rooms with private bath/shower, toilet, electric blankets, hairdryers, tea/coffee. Has its own tennis court, pool room, free. Ideally centred for all scenic routes, golf, nature walks, mountain climbing, traditional Irish music restaurant 1 km.

Lisava, *38 Scrahan Court, Ross Road, Killarney, Co Kerry.*
Modern comfortable town house in quiet residential area - family-run.
Open: Easter to Nov
Grades: BF Approv
064 32634 Mrs Burke
Rates fr: *IR£14.00*-**IR£19.00**.
Beds: 2D 1T
Baths: 2 Ensuite 1 Shared

Kiltrasna Farm, *Lough Guitane Road, Muckross, Killarney, Co Kerry.*
Open: Mar to Nov
064 31643 Mrs Looney
Rates fr: *IR£15.00*-**IR£15.00**.
Beds: 3F 3D 2T 1S
Baths: 5 Ensuite 1 Private 1 Shared
(10)
Modern farmhouse situated in beautiful breathtaking scenic surroundings. Muckross very close.

Beaufield House, *Cork Road, Killarney, Co Kerry.*
Beautiful house, 2 km from Killarney town centre on Cork Road.
Open: All Year **Grades:** BF 3 St
064 34440 Fax no: 064 34663
Rates fr: *IR£18.00*-**IR£26.00**.
Beds: 7D 7T **Baths:** 14 Ensuite
(14)

High season, bank holidays and special events mean low availability *anywhere.*

Kylemore, *Ballydowney, Killarney, Co Kerry.*
Modern town house close to golf course and riding stables.
Open: Mar to Oct
Grades: BF Approv
064 31771
Mr Moynihan
Rates fr: *IR£14.00*-**IR£18.00**.
Beds: 4F 1D 1T
Baths: 5 Ensuite 1 Shared
(6)

Earls Court Guest House, *Woodlawn Road, Muckross, Killarney, Co Kerry.*
Architect designed, purpose built guest-house with antique furnishing. Friendly hospitality.
Open: Easter to Oct
Grades: BF 4 St, AA 5 Q, RAC High Acclaim
064 34009
Fax no: 064 34366
Mr Moynihan
Rates fr: *IR£22.00*-**IR£27.00**.
Beds: 2D 8T
Baths: 11 Ensuite

Blueridge House, *Woodlawn Road, Killarney, Co Kerry.*
Modern well furnished home walking distance to Lakes and town. Family-run.
Open: Easter to Nov
064 32221 Mrs Lynch
Rates fr: *IR£15.00*-**IR£17.00**.
Beds: 1F 1D 1T 1S
Baths: 2 Shared

Glebe Farmhouse, *Tralee Road, Killarney, Co Kerry.*
Good food, friendly atmosphere, working farm. Heritage and vintage collections.
Open: Feb to 18th Dec
064 32179 Mr & Mrs O'Connor
Rates fr: *IR£12.50*-**IR£18.00**.
Beds: 2F 2D 1T 1S
Baths: 4 Ensuite 1 Private 1 Shared
(0) (9)

The lowest *double* rate per person is shown in *italics.*

Killorglin

National Grid Ref: V7796

Nicks, Starlight, Forge, Bianconi Inn

***Carraig na Lamhna,** Killarney Road, Anglont, Killorglin, Killarney, Co Kerry.*
Friendly family home, central for touring Kerry. Overlooking McGillicuddy Reeks. **Open:** Easter to Oct
Grades: BF Approv
066 61170 Mrs Brennan
Rates fr: *IR£14.00*-**IR£16.00**.
Beds: 1F 1D 1T
Baths: 3 Private

***Bansha,** Killorglin, Killarney, Co Kerry.*
Modern luxury country house in beautiful setting in award-winning gardens.
Open: All Year
Grades: BF Approv
066 61200 Mr & Mrs O'Regan
Rates fr: *IR£14.00*-**IR£16.00**.
Beds: 1F 3D 1T **Baths:** 4 Ensuite
(6)

***Hillview Farm,** Tralee Road, Milltown, Killorglin, Killarney, Co Kerry.*
Comfortable family-run sixth generation dairy/sheep farm in scenic countryside.
Open: Easter to Nov
066 67117 Mrs Stephens
Rates fr: *IR£15.00*-**IR£19.00**.
Beds: 2F 2D 2T
Baths: 5 Ensuite 1 Private

***Park House,** Laharn, Killorglin, Killarney, Co Kerry.*
Luxurious country home, 0.5 km Killorglin, ideal touring, walking, cycling, golf.
Open: Apr to Sep **Grades:** BF Approv
066 61665 Mrs Woods
Rates fr: *IR£14.00*-**IR£18.00**.
Beds: 2D 2T **Baths:** 2 Ensuite 2 Shared
(6)

The lowest *double* rate per person is shown in *italics*.

***Ardrahan House,** Killorglin, Killarney, Co Kerry.*
Modern friendly family bungalow beside Killorglin, near mountains, seaside 10 km.
Open: Easter to Oct
Grades: BF Approv
066 62219
Mrs Griffin
Rates fr: *IR£15.00*-**IR£18.00**.
Beds: 2D 1T
Baths: 2 Ensuite 1 Shared
(0) (6)

Lauragh

National Grid Ref: V7858

Josie's, The Shebeen

***Mountain View,** Healy Pass Road, Lauragh, Kenmare, Killarney.*
Modern, comfortable bungalow, on working farm, surrounded by the Caha Mountains.
Open: All Year (not Xmas)
Grades: BF Approv
064 83143
Mrs O'Sullivan
Rates fr: *IR£15.00*-**IR£20.00**.
Beds: 2F 1D
Baths: 2 Ensuite 1 Private

***Coolounig House,** Lauragh, Kenmare, Co Kerry.*
Extended family home on working farm overlooking Kenmare Bay.
Open: Apr to Oct
064 83142
Mrs Lynch
Rates fr: *IR£12.50*-**IR£12.50**.
Beds: 1F 2D 1T
Baths: 1 Ensuite 1 Shared

***Lakeview House,** Glanmore Lake, Lauragh, Killarney, Kerry.*
Modern, comfortable house with restaurant overlooking Glanmore Lake.
Open: All Year
064 83155
Mrs Corkery
Rates fr: *IR£15.00*-**IR£15.00**.
Beds: 2F 1S
Baths: 3 Ensuite

Lispole

National Grid Ref: Q5200

Sea View House, *Banogue, Lispole, Dingle, Tralee, Co Kerry.*
Family-run B&B with beautiful views of Dingle Bay and Kerry Mountains.
Open: May to Sep **Grades:** BF Approv
066 57137 Mrs Brosnan
Rates fr: *IR£14.00*-**IR£16.00**.
Beds: 2F 1D
Baths: 1 Shared

Devane's Farmhouse, *Lisdargan, Lispole, Dingle, Tralee, Co Kerry.*
Working sheep farm with great views.
Open: Apr to Oct
Grades: BF Approv
066 51418 Mrs Devane
Rates fr: *IR£14.50*-**IR£19.50**.
Beds: 1F 4D
Baths: 3 Ensuite

Listowel

National Grid Ref: Q9933

Horse Shoe Bar, Three Mermaids Bar, O'Sullivans Bar, Fitzgeralds

Aras Mhuire, *Ballybunnion Road, Listowel, Co Kerry.*
Situated on Ballybunnion Road near Golf and beach. Credit cards accepted.
Open: All Year
Grades: BF Approv
068 21515
Mrs Costello
Rates fr: *IR£15.00*-**IR£15.00**.
Beds: 1F 2D 1T 1S
Baths: 4 Ensuite
(1) (4)

Ashgrove House, *Ballybunnion Road, Listowel, Co Kerry.*
Superb country home adjoining farmlands. Excellent accommodation near Ballybunnion Golf Course.
Open: Easter to Nov
068 21268
Mrs O'Neill
Rates fr: *IR£16.00*-**IR£20.00**.
Beds: 1F 2D 1T
Baths: 3 Ensuite 1 Private
(5) (5)

Clareville, *Tarbert Road, Listowel, Co Kerry.*
Attractive purpose-built dormer bungalow on private grounds.
Open: Easter to Oct
068 21723 Mrs Queally
Rates fr: *IR£16.00*-**IR£21.00**.
Beds: 3F 1T
Baths: 4 Ensuite

Ashford Lodge, *Tarbert Road, Listowel, Co Kerry.*
Modern, comfortable, homely bungalow, peaceful surroundings, walking distance town centre.
Open: All Year
068 21280 Mrs Mahony
Rates fr: *IR£15.00*-**IR£15.00**.
Beds: 2F 1D 1T 1S
Baths: 2 Ensuite 1 Shared
(6)

Lohart

National Grid Ref: V8266

Fern Height, *Lohart, Kenmare, Killarney, Co Kerry.*
Open: May to Sept **Grades:** BF Approv
064 84248 Mrs O'Sullivan
Rates fr: *IR£16.00*-**IR£22.00**.
Beds: 1F 2D 1T
Baths: 4 Ensuite

Milltown

National Grid Ref: Q8200

Larkin's Bar

Mangans Country Home, *Killarney Road, Milltown, Killarney, Co Kerry.*
Open: Mar to Oct **Grades:** BF Approv
066 67502 Mrs Mangan
Rates fr: *IR£14.00*-**IR£19.00**.
Beds: 1F 2D 1T
Baths: 3 Ensuite
(5)
Special low season rates. Hospitable and friendly country village. Breakfast menu. Tea/coffee making facilities. Central location on Killarney/Dingle route R563. Perfect base for touring, golfing, beaches, walking and relaxing. Shed for bicycles, caddy cars and fishing tackle.

Hillview Farm, *Tralee Road, Milltown, Killarney, Co Kerry.*
Comfortable family-run sixth generation dairy/sheep farm in scenic countryside.
Open: Easter to Nov
Grades: BF Approv
066 67117 Mrs Stephens
Rates fr: *IR£15.00*-**IR£19.00**.
Beds: 2F 2D 2T
Baths: 5 Ensuite 1 Private

Riverville, *Rathpook, Milltown, Killarney, Co Kerry.*
Family-run two-storey house in peaceful setting.
Open: May to Oct
Grades: BF Approv
066 67108 Mrs Burke
Rates fr: *IR£14.00*-**IR£15.00**.
Beds: 1F 2D 1T
Baths: 2 Ensuite 1 Shared

Muckross

National Grid Ref: V9886

Muckross Hotel

O'Donovans Farm - Muckross Riding Stables, *Mangerton Road, Muckross, Killarney, Co Kerry.*
Open: Mar to Dec
Grades: BF Approv
064 32238 Mrs O'Donovan
Rates fr: *IR£14.00*-**IR£19.00**.
Beds: 2F 1D 3T 1S
Baths: 4 Ensuite 2 Shared
Modern farm bungalow with panoramic view of national park (oak forest with red deer). Mangerton and Toke Mountain, Killarney Lakes, Muckross House nearby. Approved riding stables on premises. 3.5 miles south of Killarney.

Lios Na Manach, *Mill Road, Muckross, Killarney, Co Kerry.*
Working farmhouse, views of the Kerry Mountains.
Open: All Year
Grades: BF Approv
064 31283 Mrs O'Sullivan
Rates fr: *IR£14.00*-**IR£21.00**.
Beds: 2F 2D 2T
Baths: 2 Ensuite 1 Shared

Crab Tree Cottage, *Mangerton Road, Muckross, Killarney, Co Kerry.*
Picturesque cottage in the midst of Killarney's National Park and Lakes. Landscaped gardens.
Open: Apr to Oct
Grades: BF Approv
064 33169
Mrs Cronin
Rates fr: *IR£16.00*-**IR£14.00**.
Beds: 1D 2T 1S
Baths: 3 Ensuite 1 Private

Deerwood, *Mangerton Road, Muckross, Killarney, Co Kerry.*
Views over the Kerry Mountains, deer abound, middle of National Park.
Open: Apr to Sep
Grades: BF Approv
064 34898
Mr & Mrs Larkin
Rates fr: *IR£15.00*-**IR£18.00**.
Beds: 2F 3D
Baths: 3 Shared

Portmagee

National Grid Ref: V3773

Harbour Grove Farmhouse, *Ahadda, Portmagee, Caherciveen, Co Kerry.*
Open: Easter to Nov
066 77116
Mrs Lynch
Rates fr: *IR£15.00*-**IR£20.00**.
Beds: 2F 1D 1T 1S
Baths: 3 Ensuite 1 Shared
Dairy farm on scenic Skellig Ring, 6 km off Ring of Kerry N70. Private beach. Mature trees. Peaceful harbour location. Fishing, golf, walking, Skellig experience nearby. Portmagee, traditional fishing village, main departure point for Skellig Michael. Spacious full bathrooms ensuite.

Planning a longer stay?
Always ask for any
special rates.

Sneem

National Grid Ref: V6966

Blue Bull, Sacre Coeur, River Rain, Stone House

Hillside Haven, *Doon, Tahilla, Sneem, Kenmare, Killarney, Co Kerry.*
Bungalow with spectacular views of Kenmare Bay. Adjacent to Kerry Way walking route. **Open:** Easter to Nov
Grades: BF Approv
064 82065 Mrs Foley
Rates fr: *IR£16.00*-**IR£20.00**.
Beds: 2F 2D **Baths:** 4 Ensuite

Derry East Farmhouse, *Sneem, Kenmare, Killarney, Co Kerry.*
Working farm situated beneath the Kerry Mountains.
Open: Mar to Oct **Grades:** BF Approv
064 45193 Mrs Teahan
Rates fr: *IR£16.50*-**IR£23.50**.
Beds: 1F 1D 2T
Baths: 3 Ensuite 1 Private

Rockville House, *Sneem, Kenmare, Killarney, Co Kerry.*
Luxurious dormer bungalow in mature gardens. Scenic mountain views.
Open: Mar to Oct **Grades:** BF Approv
064 45135 Mrs Drummond
Rates fr: *IR£15.00*-**IR£20.00**.
Beds: 1F 1D 2T **Baths:** 4 Ensuite

Bell View, *Pier Road, Sneem, Kenmare, Killarney, Co Kerry.*
Modern bungalow, convenient to the pier.
Open: All Year **Grades:** BF Approv
064 45389 Mrs Drummond
Rates fr: *IR£15.00*-**IR£17.00**.
Beds: 3D 2S
Baths: 2 Ensuite 1 Private 1 Shared

Bank House, *North Square, Sneem, Kenmare, Killarney, Co Kerry.*
Old Georgian home with magnificent collection of antique crystal and china.
Open: Apr to mid-Nov
Grades: BF Approv
064 45226 Mrs Harrington
Rates fr: *IR£16.00*.
Beds: 2F 3D **Baths:** 5 Ensuite

Avonlea House, *Sportsfield Road, Sneem, Kenmare, Killarney, Co Kerry.*
Modern secluded two-storey house in its own grounds.
Open: Easter to Oct
Grades: BF Approv
064 45221 Mrs Hussey
Rates fr: *IR£16.00*-**IR£18.00**.
Beds: 1F 2D 2T
Baths: 4 Ensuite 1 Private

Tarbert

National Grid Ref: R0647

Enrights, Murphys Restaurant

Oak Haven, *Sallowglen, Tarbert, Listowel, Co Kerry.*
Attractive bungalow in quiet location on R551, near car ferry.
Open: Easter to Oct
Grades: BF Approv
068 43208 Mrs Walsh
Rates fr: *IR£14.00*-**IR£17.50**.
Beds: 1F 2D 1T **Baths:** 3 Ensuite
(6)

Templenoe

National Grid Ref: V8369

The Vestry

Rockvilla, *Templenoe, Kenmare, Killarney, Co Kerry.*
Modern house 500 yards from Templenoe Pier.
Open: Mar to Oct
Grades: BF Approv
064 41331
Mr & Mrs Fahy
Rates fr: *IR£16.00*-**IR£21.00**.
Beds: 3D 2T 1S
Baths: 5 Ensuite 1 Shared
(10)

The Oaks, *Templenoe, Kenmare, Killarney, Co Kerry.*
Modern split-level bungalow overlooking the Caha Mountains.
Open: Mar to mid-Sep
Grades: BF Approv
064 41392 Mrs Falvey
Rates fr: *IR£14.00*-**IR£19.00**.
Beds: 3D 1T
Baths: 2 Ensuite 1 Shared

Templenoe House, *Greenane, Templenoe, Kenmare, Killarney, Co Kerry.*
Old Georgian house overlooking Kenmare Bay.
Open: May to Sep **Grades:** BF Approv
064 41538 Mr & Mrs Doran
Rates fr: *IR£15.00*-**IR£20.00**.
Beds: 1F 2D 2T
Baths: 2 Ensuite 1 Shared

Tralee

National Grid Ref: Q8413

Imperial Hotel, Oyster Tavern, Larkins, Kirby's Brogue Inn, Kearne's Bar

Kilkerry, *12 Castle Demesne, Tralee, Co Kerry.*
Modern bungalow - central to all amenities. Ideal touring base.
Open: Jun to Sep **Grades:** BF Approv
066 22823 Mrs Phelan
Rates fr: *IR£12.50*-**IR£17.50**.
Beds: 1F 1D 1T 1S
Baths: 2 Ensuite 1 Shared
(3)

Carraig, *Manor East, Killarney Road, Tralee, Co Kerry.*
Open: All Year (not Xmas)
066 24840 Mrs Slye
Rates fr: *IR£14.00*-**IR£19.00**.
Beds: 1F 1D 1T
Baths: 2 Ensuite 1 Private
(4)
Luxury dormer bungalow set back from main N21/22 in mature gardens. Comfortable bedrooms with TV. Ideal touring base for South West. Attractions for all the family include Heritage Centre, restored windmill, steam railway, folk theatre, Aqua Dome, Seaworld, beaches, seafood restaurants.

Mountain View House, *Ballinorig West, Tralee, Co Kerry.*
Spacious residence, own grounds, car park. Close to all amenities.
Open: All Year (not Xmas)
Grades: BF Approv
066 22226 Mrs Curley
Rates fr: *IR£15.00*-**IR£20.00**.
Beds: 2F 2D 2T
Baths: 4 Ensuite 1 Shared
(7) (9)

Brianville, *Feint Road, Tralee, Co Kerry.*
Open: All Year
Grades: BF Approv
066 26645 Mrs Smith
Rates fr: *IR£16.00*-**IR£20.00**.
Beds: 2F 2D 1T
Baths: 5 Ensuite
(8)
Luxurious bungalow on spacious grounds. Scenic view of mountain. 18 hole golf links nearby. Seafood restaurants nearby. Hair dryers, tea and coffee facilities in bedrooms. Horse-riding, sailing closeby.

Clogherbrien House, *Clogherbrien, Tralee, Co Kerry.*
Beautiful house in scenic location, convenient to beaches and golf course.
Open: All Year (not Xmas)
Grades: BF Approv
066 28708
Ms McElligott
Rates fr: *IR£16.00*-**IR£20.00**.
Beds: 2D 2T
Baths: 4 Ensuite

Barnakyle, *Clogherbrien, Tralee, Co Kerry.*
Open: All Year (not Xmas)
Grades: BF Approv
066 25048
Mrs O'Connell
Rates fr: *IR£16.00*-**IR£22.00**.
Beds: 3D 3T
Baths: 6 Ensuite
(5) (6)
Barnakyle is a family run guest house situated 2 km from Tralee on the Ardfert/Bally Heigue R551 Road. Adjacent to excellent restaurants, Saimsa Tire, indoor water sports, horse-riding, sailing and beaches. Ideal base for golf in Tralee, Killarney, Ballybunion, Waterville, Dooks and Dingle.

Bricriu, *20 Old Golf Links Road, Oakpark, Tralee, Co Kerry.*
Bungalow in quiet area close to everything. Also self-catering.
Open: Apr to Oct
066 26374 Mrs Canning
Rates fr: *IR£14.00*-**IR£19.00**.
Beds: 2D 1T
Baths: 1 Shared

Ashlee House, *Manor West, Tralee, Co Kerry.*
New house. 15-minute walk Tralee town centre. Easy to find.
Open: All Year
066 26492
Mrs O'Loughlin
Rates fr: *IR£13.00*-**IR£17.00**.
Beds: 3F 3D 3T 1S
Baths: 10 Ensuite
(6) (10)

Keswick Lodge, *Curraheen, Tralee, Co Kerry.*
Country home, sea/mountain views. Ideal base for Dingle/Killarney.
Open: All Year (not Xmas)
066 28751 Perlman
Rates fr: *IR£16.00*-**IR£21.00**.
Beds: 3D 1T
Baths: 4 Ensuite
(5)

Tuosist

National Grid Ref: V7963

Lake House, *Cloonee, Tuosist, Kenmare, Co Kerry.*
Country house with full bar. On lakeside with boats and fly-fishing.
Open: Easter to Oct
Grades: BF 1 St
064 84205 Ms O'Shea
Rates fr: *IR£16.00*-**IR£16.00**.
Beds: 3D 2T 1S
Baths: 3 Shared

Always telephone to get directions to the B&B - you will save time!

Ventry

National Grid Ref: Q3800

Garvey's Farmhouse, *Kilvicadownig, Ventry, Dingle, Tralee, Co Kerry.*
Spacious house on dairy farm overlooking Ventry Bay in peaceful surroundings.
Open: Mar to Nov
066 59914 Mrs Garvey
Rates fr: *IR£14.50*-**IR£19.50**.
Beds: 2F 2D 1T
Baths: 3 Ensuite 2 Shared
(6)

Ceann Tra Heights, *Ventry, Dingle, Tralee, Co Kerry.*
Modern dormer bungalow overlooking Ventry Harbour.
Open: May to Sep **Grades:** BF Approv
066 59866 Mrs Carroll
Rates fr: *IR£16.00*-**IR£20.00**.
Beds: 1F 1D 2T **Baths:** 4 Ensuite

Waterville

National Grid Ref: Q5066

Butler Arms Bar, The Smuggler's Inn

Klondyke House, *New Line Road, Waterville, Killarney, Co Kerry.*
Detached residence overlooking Waterville championship golf links and Atlantic Ocean.
Open: All Year
Grades: BF Approv, AA 3 Q, RAC Acclaim
066 74119 Mrs Morris
Rates fr: *IR£8.00*-**IR£16.00**.
Beds: 1F 2D 3T 1S
Baths: 7 Ensuite
(10)

County Kildare

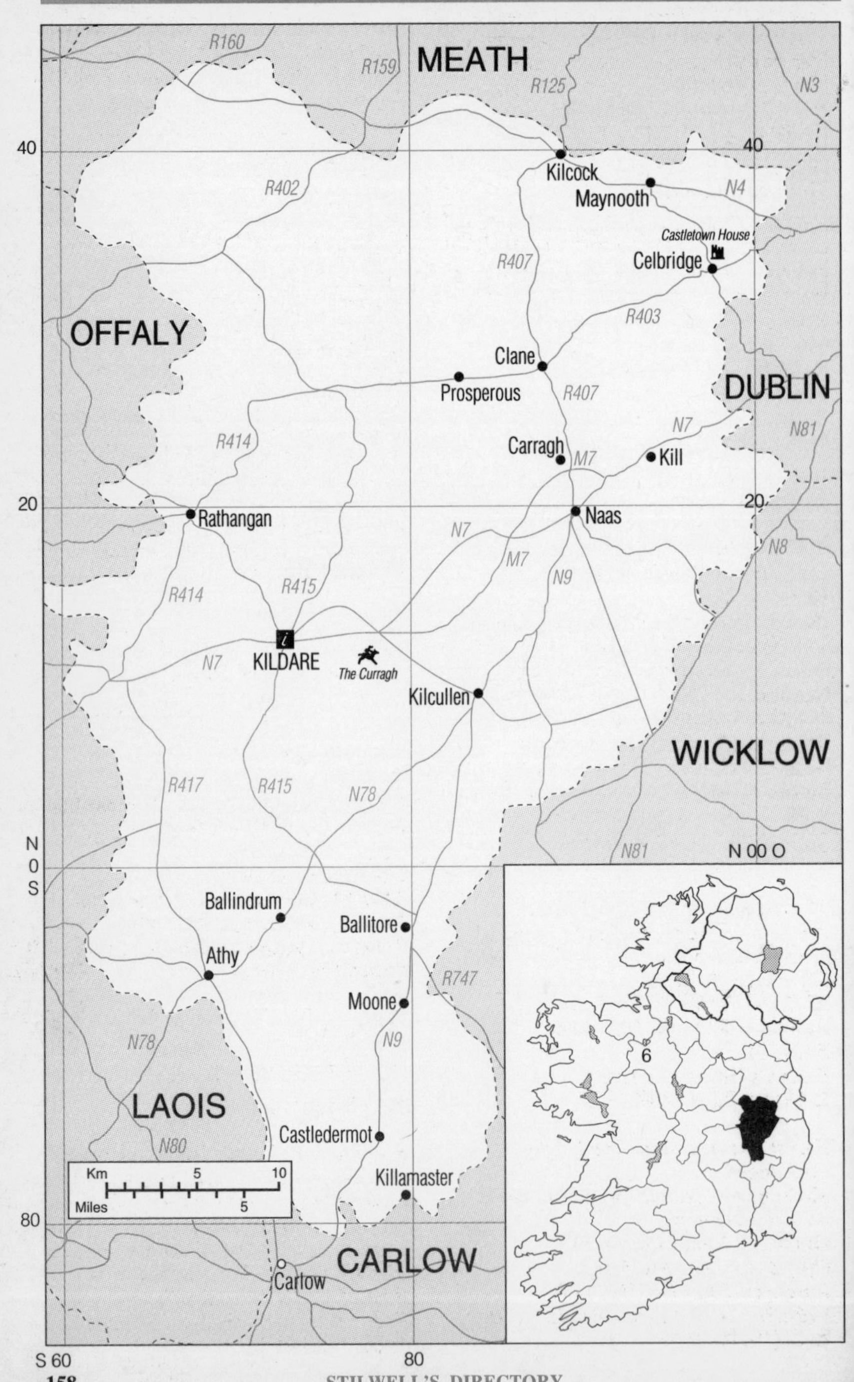

RAIL

Kildare town is well-served by the railway. Trains run into ***Dublin (Heuston)*** every half an hour. The ***Waterford, Cork, Limerick*** & ***Athlone*** lines all run through ***Kildare.***
Tel **Irish Rail** on 01 8366222 for details.

BUS

Kildare to ***Dublin*** *(every half hour)* - Tel **Bus Eireann** on 01 8366111.

TOURIST INFORMATION OFFICES

Main Square, **Kildare** (Mar to Oct), 045 522696

Athy

National Grid Ref: S6894

Leinster Arms Hotel, Castle Inn

Ardscull Farm, *Dublin Road, Athy, Co Kildare.*
Open: All Year (not Xmas)
Grades: BF Approv
0507 26188 Mr & Mrs Flood
Rates fr: *IR£16.00*-**IR£16.00**.
Beds: 1F 2D 1S
Baths: 2 Ensuite 1 Private 1 Shared
(6)
Attractive farmhouse in prestigious location on N78; 40 miles from Dublin. Bright restful rooms. Organic meat, vegetables. Delicious home baking. Tea and scones during stay. Ideal touring base for South-East. Close to Irish National Stud. Anne and Noel would like you to sample their unique Kildare hospitality.

Moate Lodge, *Athy, Co Kildare.*
A C18th Georgian house of unrivalled charm and character.
Open: All Year
0507 26137 Mr & Mrs Pelin
Rates fr: *IR£14.00*-**IR£14.00**.
Beds: 3T 1S
Baths: 1 Ensuite 2 Private
(10)

Forest Farm, *Dublin Road, Athy, Co Kildare.*
Modern comfortable farmhouse one hour from Dublin.
Open: All Year (not Xmas)
0507 31231 Mrs McManus
Rates fr: *IR£14.00*-**IR£16.00**.
Beds: 1F 1D 1T **Baths:** 2 Ensuite 1 Shared
(10)

Bray House, *Athy, Co Kildare.*
A C19th farmhouse in an extremely tranquil setting. Cead mile failte.
Open: All Year **0507 31052** Mrs Dunne
Rates fr: *IR£16.00*-**IR£16.00**.
Beds: 2F 2S **Baths:** 2 Ensuite 1 Shared

Ballindrum

National Grid Ref: S7398

Ballindrum Farm, *Ballindrum, Athy, Co Kildare.*
Open: Apr to Oct **Grades:** BF Approv
0507 26294 Mrs Gorman
Rates fr: *IR£14.00*-**IR£14.00**.
Beds: 1F 1D 2T 1S
Baths: 3 Ensuite 2 Shared
(20)
National Agri-Tourism award winner. National award of excellence. Charming farmhouse in an area of rural beauty. Homemade scones and jams served on arrival. Free farm tours. A choice of breakfast. One hour from Dublin. Brochure available on request.

Ballitore

National Grid Ref: S7996

Rathsallagh, High Cross Inn,

Griesemount, *Ballitore, Athy, Co Kildare.*
Country Georgian house. Comfortable relaxed atmosphere. Great golfing, racing, sight-seeing.
Open: Feb to Nov
0507 23158 (also fax no) Mrs Ashe
Rates fr: *IR£17.50*-**IR£25.00**.
Beds: 4D **Baths:** 1 Ensuite 2 Shared

Carragh

National Grid Ref: N8422

Manor Inn

Setanta Farmhouse, *Mondello Road, Carragh, Naas, Co Kildare.*
Modern bungalow on working farm, only 1 hour from Dublin.
Open: Easter to Oct **Grades:** AA 2 Q
045 876481 Mrs McLoughlin
Rates fr: *IR£17.00*-**IR£17.00**.
Beds: 2F 1D 2S **Baths:** 5 Ensuite
(5)

Castledermot

National Grid Ref: S7885

***Kilkea Lodge,** Castledermot, Athy, Co Kildare.*
C18th farmhouse of character. A home away from home.
Open: All Year (not Xmas)
0503 45112 (also fax no)
Mrs Greene
Rates fr: *IR£25.00*-**IR£25.00**.
Beds: 1F 2D 1T 2S
Baths: 3 Private 1 Shared
(8)

***Doyle's School House,** Main Street, Castledermot, Athy, Co Kildare.*
Converted school, furnished with family antiques.
Open: Easter to Oct
0503 44282 Doyle
Rates fr: *IR£25.00*-**IR£25.00**.
Beds: 1F 3D 3T 2S
Baths: 9 Ensuite
(20)

Celbridge

National Grid Ref: N9733

Castle Town

***Green Acres,** Dublin Road, Celbridge, Co Kildare.*
Bungalow on own grounds. Buses 67/67a 11 miles from Dublin.
01 6271163
Mrs McCabe
Rates fr: *IR£16.00*-**IR£20.00**.
Beds: 1F 3D 2T
Baths: 6 Ensuite

Clane

National Grid Ref: N8727

***The Laurels,** Dublin Road, Clane, Naas, Co Kildare.*
Delightful old two-storey house, 100 metres Clane Village, 30 minutes Dublin.
Open: All Year (not Xmas)
Grades: BF Approv
045 868274 Mrs Lynch
Rates fr: *IR£16.00*-**IR£20.00**.
Beds: 1F 1D 1T **Baths:** 3 Ensuite
(8)

Kilcock

National Grid Ref: N8839

O'Keeffe's, The Harbour

***Lios Ciuin,** Duncreevan, Kilcock, Co Kildare.*
Pleasant dormer bungalow in secluded location 30 km from Dublin air & sea ports.
Open: Jun to Sep **Grades:** BF Approv
01 6287537 Mrs Barrett
Rates fr: *IR£14.00*-**IR£19.00**.
Beds: 1F 1D 1T
Baths: 1 Ensuite 1 Shared
(4)

Kilcullen

National Grid Ref: N8309

The Priory

***Glebesouth,** Kilcullen, Curragh Camp, Co Kildare.*
Bungalow 40 minutes Dublin. 10 minutes Curragh, Punchestown, National Stud. **Open:** Easter to Oct
Grades: BF Approv
045 481486 (also fax no) Mr Aspell
Rates fr: *IR£17.50*-**IR£17.50**.
Beds: 3D 2T 1S
Baths: 4 Ensuite 1 Shared
(6)

Kildare

National Grid Ref: N7212

***Castleview Farm,** Lackaghmore, Kildare, Co Kildare.*
Modern farmhouse, exquisitely tranquil and historical surroundings, with beautiful garden. **Open:** Feb to Dec
Grades: BF Approv
045 521816 Mrs Fitzpatrick
Rates fr: *IR£14.50*-**IR£18.00**.
Beds: 1F 2D **Baths:** 1 Ensuite 1 Shared
(0) (7)

Kill

National Grid Ref: N9322

Johnstown Inn

***Oldhoce House,** Newtown, Kill, Naas, Co Kildare.*
Modern, on four acres with river, mature trees and beautiful gardens.
Open: All Year (not Xmas)
045 877022 Mr Meagher
Rates fr: *IR£18.00*-**IR£23.00**.
Beds: 3F **Baths:** 3 Ensuite
(4) (8)

Killamaster

National Grid Ref: S8080

Killamaster House, *Killamaster, Carlow.*
Luxury farm bungalow. Tea and scones on arrival. Tea-making facilities in bedrooms.
Open: Mar to Sep
0503 63654 (also fax no)
Mr & Mrs Walsh
Rates fr: *IR£15.00*-**IR£15.00**.
Beds: 3D 1T
Baths: All Ensuite

Maynooth

National Grid Ref: N9338

Leinster Arms Pub, Donatellos

Park Lodge, *201 Railpark, Maynooth, Co Kildare.*
Very clean and comfortable guest house. Beside bus and rail station. Great breakfast.
Open: All Year (not Xmas/New Year)
Grades: BF Approv
01 6286002 Mrs O'Neill
Rates fr: *IR£15.00*.
Beds: 3F 3D 1T
Baths: 4 Ensuite 1 Private
(4) (4)

Moone

National Grid Ref: S7992

Woodcourte House, *Moone, Castledermot, Athy, Co Kildare.*
Open: All Year
0507 24167 Fax no: 0507 24326
Mrs Donoghue
Rates fr: *IR£15.00*-**IR£18.00**.
Beds: 6F
Baths: 4 Ensuite 2 Shared
Modern country home, woodland setting on primary route N9. 1 hour all parts. Taxi service provided, Bus service passing almost hourly from Dublin. Golf, fishing, horse riding, bowling within ten minutes drive. Ideal base for touring counties. Guided tours.

Naas

National Grid Ref: N8919

Manor Inn

Two Mile House, *Naas, Co Kildare.*
Peaceful location. Dublin 20 miles. Convenient to airport and ferries.
Open: All Year **045 879824**
Mrs Doherty
Rates fr: *IR£17.0*-**IR£23.00**.
Beds: 3D 1T 1S
Baths: 5 Ensuite 1 Private
(6)

Setanta Farmhouse, *Mondello Road, Carragh, Naas, Co Kildare.*
Modern bungalow on working farm, only 1 hour from Dublin.
Open: Easter to Oct
Grades: AA 2 Q
045 876481 Mrs McLoughlin
Rates fr: *IR£17.00*-**IR£17.00**.
Beds: 2F 1D 2S
Baths: 5 Ensuite
(5)

Prosperous

National Grid Ref: N8327

Bowling's Pub

Hillview House, *Prosperous, Naas, Co Kildare.*
Warm friendly country home. 22.5 miles from Dublin. Large TV lounge.
Open: All Year
Grades: BF Approv
045 868252 Mr & Mrs O'Brien
Rates fr: *IR£16.00*-**IR£19.00**.
Beds: 3F 3D 3T 1S
Baths: 8 Ensuite 2 Shared

Rathangan

National Grid Ref: N6719

Grove House, *Ballinrahan, Rathangan, Kildare.*
Luxurious modern bungalow set in scenic countryside.
Open: Mar to Aug
045 524360 Fax no: 045 524785
Mrs Briody
Rates fr: *IR£16.50*-**IR£16.50**.
Baths: 3 Ensuite
(10) (6)

County Kilkenny

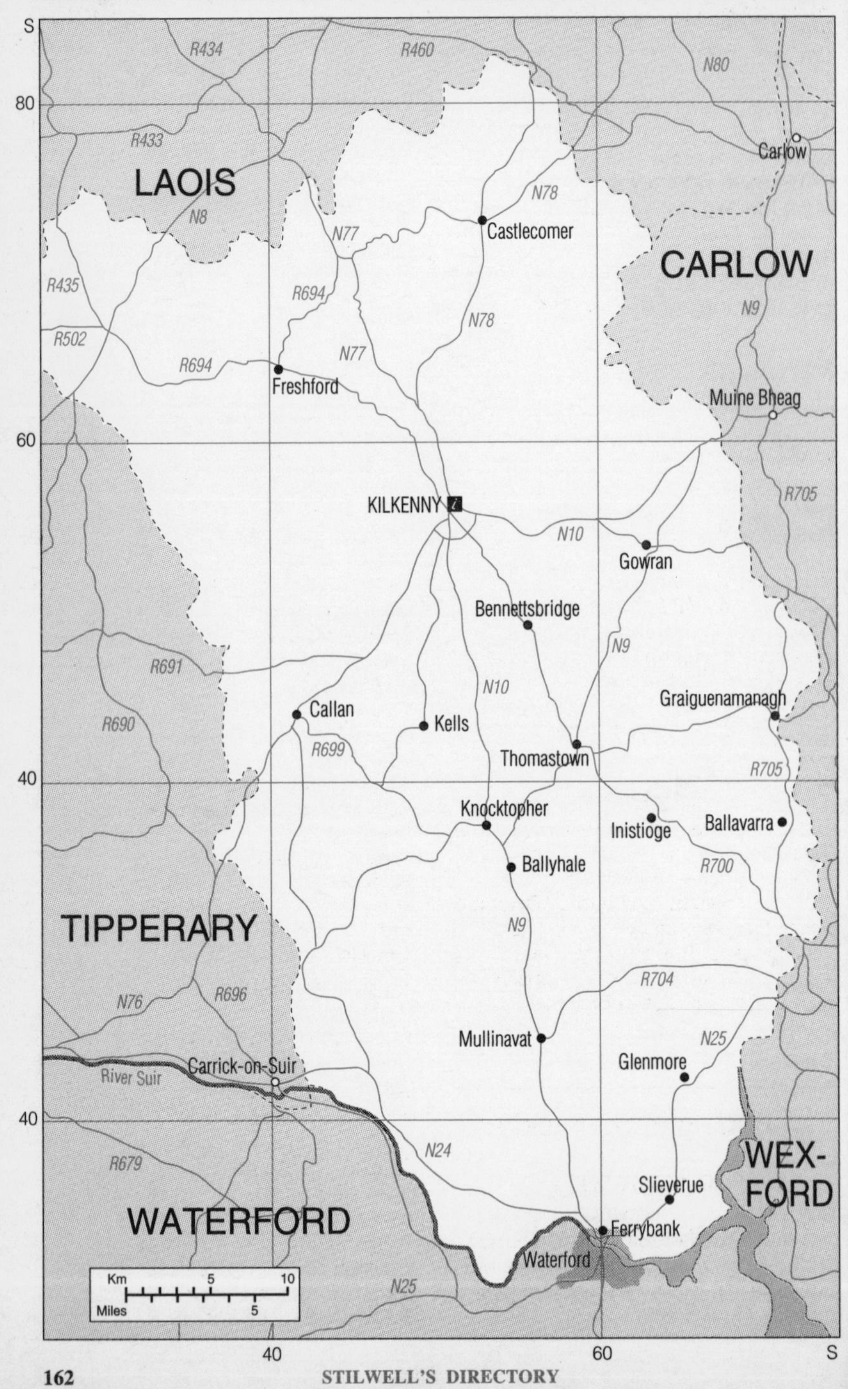

RAIL

Kilkenny town is on the ***Dublin*** *to* ***Waterford*** line (4 trains per day).

Tel **Irish Rail** on 01 8366222 for timetable details.

BUS

Kilkenny *to* ***Dublin*** *(4 per day) -*

Tel. **Bus Eireann** on 056 64933

TOURIST INFORMATION OFFICES

Rose Inn Street, **Kilkenny** (open all year), tel. 056 51500.

Ballavarra

National Grid Ref: S7137

Barleycroft, *Ballavarra, Graiguenamanagh, Kilkenny.*
Open: All Year (not Xmas)
Grades: BF Approv, RAC Acclaim
051 423668 (also fax no)
Mr & Mrs Lewis
Rates fr: *IR£15.50*-**IR£18.00.**
Beds: 3T
Baths: 3 Ensuite
(12) (4)
RAC Acclaimed home from home. Guest comfort top priority. Highly acclaimed home cooking. Private parking. Tranquil rural setting. Dramatic scenery overlooking river valley and mountains. Golf, fishing, walking, riding. Rosslare Ferryport 40 miles. Central for touring and Blue Flag beaches.

Phoning from outside the Republic?

Dial 00353 and omit the initial '0' of the area code.

Ballyhale

National Grid Ref: S5434

Debruin House, *Knockwilliam, Ballyhale, Kilkenny.*
Dormer bungalow. Rural setting mid-way Waterford/Kilkenny - 20 minutes drive to each.
Open: All Year (not Xmas)
Grades: BF Approv
056 68633
Mrs O'Gorman
Rates fr: *IR£15.00*-**IR£18.00.**
Beds: 1F 3D
Baths: 4 Ensuite

Bennettsbridge

National Grid Ref: S5549

Norely Theyr, *Barronsland, Bennettsbridge, Kilkenny.*
All you ever needed for accommodation and food. Luxurious and relaxing.
Open: All Year
Grades: BF Approv
056 27496
Mrs Cole
Rates fr: *IR£12.50*-**IR£15.00.**
Beds: 2F 2D
Baths: 1 Ensuite 1 Shared
(6)

Callan

National Grid Ref: S4143

Grangers

Castle View, *Kilkenny, Callan, Kilkenny.*
Dormer-style bungalow.
Open: All Year (not Xmas)
056 25397 Mrs Egan
Rates fr: *IR£15.00*-**IR£16.00**.
Beds: 2F 1D
Baths: 2 Ensuite 1 Shared

Castlecomer

National Grid Ref: S5373

Wandesforde House, *Moneenroe, Castlecomer, Co Kilkenny.*
Charming early C19th converted schoolhouse, great atmosphere, fabulous food.
Open: All Year (not Xmas)
Grades: BF Approv
056 42441 Mrs Fleming
Rates fr: *IR£15.00*-**IR£18.00**.
Beds: 3D 3T
Baths: 6 Ensuite
(12)

Ferrybank

National Grid Ref: S6118

Rhu Glen

Holly Lake House, *Charlestown, Ferrybank, Waterford.*
Tudor-style country home with landscaped gardens overlooking bird sanctuary.
Open: Easter to Oct
Grades: BF Approv
051 832963 Ms Heffernan
Rates fr: *IR£15.00*-**IR£18.00**.
Beds: 1F 2D
Baths: 3 Ensuite

Please respect
a B&B's wishes regarding
children, animals
& smoking.

Freshford

National Grid Ref: S4064

Langtons

Pomadora House, *Clinstown, Freshford, Kilkenny, Co Kilkenny.*
Open: All Year **Grades:** BF Approv
056 32256 Mrs Flanaghan
Rates fr: *IR£18.00*-**IR£20.00**.
Beds: 1F 1D 1T
Baths: 3 Ensuite
(6)
Country home on a small Hunter stud, in the pretty village of Freshford. Personal family service guaranteed. On road to Cashel, R693. Gardens, fishing, horse-riding, hunting in winter. Stabling for horses, dog kennels. Dinner, meals.

Castle View, *Balleen, Freshford, Kilkenny, Co Kilkenny.*
Bungalow, peaceful location, panoramic view, orthopaedic beds.
Open: All Year **Grades:** BF Approv
056 32181 Mrs Nolan
Rates fr: *IR£16.00*-**IR£18.00**.
Beds: 1F 1D 1T **Baths:** 2 Ensuite

Glenmore

National Grid Ref: S6422

The Glen, John V's Bar

Milltown House, *Milltown, Glenmore, New Ross, Co Wexford.*
Large traditional farmhouse situated in luscious green countryside.
Open: All Year **Grades:** BF Approv
051 880294 Mrs Merrigan
Rates fr: *IR£14.00*-**IR£19.00**.
Beds: 1F 2D
Baths: 3 Ensuite
(12)

Weatherstown Glenview, *Glenmore, Waterford.*
Attractive farmhouse in quiet scenic area. Signposted at first turn right for Glenmore from New Ross (N25).
Open: Easter to Nov
051 880180 Mrs Cody
Rates fr: *IR£13.50*-**IR£15.00**.
Beds: 2F 1D 1T 1S
Baths: 2 Ensuite 2 Shared
(20)

Gowran

National Grid Ref: S6253

Paddys

Whitethorns, *Flagmount, Clifden, Gowran, Kilkenny.*
Rural bungalow on two acres. Panoramic scenery. 10 minute drive from Kilkenny.
Open: Easter to Sep
Grades: BF Approv
056 26102
Mrs Kenny
Rates fr: *IR£14.00*-**IR£15.50**.
Beds: 2D 1T
Baths: 1 Ensuite 1 Shared
(6)

Graiguenamanagh

National Grid Ref: S7043

Stablecroft, *Mooneen, Graiguenamanagh, Kilkenny, Co Kilkenny.*
Stablecroft: country home with superb panoramic views - a tranquil respite.
Open: All Year (not Xmas)
Grades: RAC High Acclaim
0503 24714
Mr & Mrs Wenner
Rates fr: *IR£17.00*-**IR£20.00**.
Beds: 1F 2D 1S
Baths: 4 Ensuite
(10) (5)

Inistioge

National Grid Ref: S6337

The Motte, The Maltings

Nore Valley Villa, *Inistioge, Thomastown, Co Kilkenny.*
Georgian villa overlooking River Nore. Ideal location for fishing, walking, hill climbing
Open: Mar to Nov
Grades: BF Approv
056 58418 (also fax no)
Mr & Mrs Rothwell
Rates fr: *IR£16.00*-**IR£16.00**.
Beds: 1F 2D 2T
Baths: 3 Ensuite 2 Shared
(8)

Hillcrest, *The Rower, Inistioge, Thomastown, Co Kilkenny.*
Rosslare 50 km on R700, halfway Inistioge and New Ross. Early breakfast
Open: All Year (not Xmas)
051 423722
Fax no: 051 429722
Mrs Naddy
Rates fr: *IR£14.50*-**IR£15.50**.
Beds: 1F 1D 2T
Baths: 4 Ensuite
(6)

Ashville, *Kilmacshane, Inistioge, Thomastown, Co Kilkenny.*
Modern family home, situated in beautiful More Valley. Lovely views.
Open: Mar to Oct
Grades: BF Approv
056 58460
Mrs Naddy
Rates fr: *IR£16.00*-**IR£18.00**.
Beds: 1F 1D 1T
Baths: 3 Ensuite 1 Private
(1) (5)

Cullintra House, *The Rower, Inistioge, Thomastown, Co Kilkenny.*
C18th 'Hidden Ireland' country house serving dinner by candlelight at 9.00 pm
Open: All Year
Grades: BF Approv
051 423614
Miss Cantlon
Rates fr: *IR£20.00*-**IR£25.00**.
Beds: 7D
Baths: 3 Ensuite
(4) (12)

Grove Farm House, *Ballycocksuist, Inistioge, Thomastown, Co Kilkenny.*
200-year-old country house set in scenic countryside.
Open: Easter to Oct **056 58467**
Mrs Cassin
Rates fr: *IR£16.00*-**IR£20.00**.
Beds: 1F 2D 1T
Baths: 3 Ensuite 1 Private
(4)

Kells

National Grid Ref: S4943

Kellsgrange, *Kells, Kilkenny.*
Beautiful Georgian country house on Kings River. Kells 1 mile.
Open: All Year **Grades:** BF Approv
056 28236 Mr & Mrs Wardrop
Rates fr: *IR£16.00*-**IR£20.00**.
Beds: 3F 1D 1T
Baths: 3 Ensuite 2 Shared

Kilkenny

National Grid Ref: S5156

Langton's, Kytlers Inn, Caislean Un Chuain, Brouchmaker Inn, Newpark Hotel

Tir Na n'Og, *Greenshill (off Castlecormer Road), Kilkenny.*
Open: All Year
Grades: BF Approv
056 62345 / 65250
Fax no: 056 63491 Mrs Wogan
Rates fr: *IR£17.00*-**IR£22.00**.
Beds: 2F 1T 1D **Baths:** 4 Ensuite
(4)
Tir na n'Og is a purpose built B&B with private parking. All rooms are ensuite and have all the facilities that you would expect from any up-to-date B&B, including multi channel TV/radio, hairdryer, etc. in every room and we're within walking distance of everything this medieval city has to offer you. Travel Agent Vouchers accepted. Rates per person sharing £17.00 single £22.00

Cill Phaoin, *Greenshill, Kilkenny.*
Open: All Year (not Xmas)
Grades: BF Approv, AA 3 Q
056 22857 Mrs Hennessy
Rates fr: *IR£16.00*-**IR£21.00**.
Beds: 3D 1T
Baths: 4 Ensuite
(5)
In the heart of our medieval city experience Irish hospitality when you visit 'Cill Phaoin'. We offer luxury accommodation overlooking River Nore with private guest kitchen, TV lounge, breakfast menu. Convenient to bus, rail, golf, fishing, swimming, horse-riding. Approved by Quality Irish Homes, Town & Country Homes, AA - 3 Star, Southeast Tourism.

Bregagh House, *Dean Street, Kilkenny,*
Modern comfortable guest house opposite St Canice's Cathedral in the medieval city of Kilkenny.
Open: All Year (not Xmas)
Grades: BF 2 St
056 22315 Ms Brennan
Rates fr: *IR£17.00*-**IR£20.00**.
Beds: 4D 5T
Baths: 7 Ensuite 1 Shared
(10)

Burwood, *Waterford Road, Kilkenny.*
Modern bungalow on N10. Featured in Best Bed & Breakfasts of Ireland.
Open: Easter to Sep
Grades: BF Approv
056 62266 Mrs Flanagan
Rates fr: *IR£16.00*-**IR£20.00**.
Beds: 2D 1T
Baths: 3 Ensuite
(8)

Rodini, *Waterford Road, Kilkenny.*
Comfortable family home adjacent to city centre, hotels and castle.
Open: All Year
Grades: BF Approv
056 21822 Mrs Lawlor
Rates fr: *IR£14.00*-**IR£17.00**.
Beds: 1F 2D 1T 1S
Baths: 5 Ensuite
(6)

All rates are subject to alteration at the owners' discretion.

The lowest *double* rate per person is shown in *italics*.

Majella, *Waterford Road, Kilkenny.*
Comfortable home, walking distance Kilkenny, breakfast choice, Visa/Access accepted.
Open: All Year (not Xmas)
Grades: BF Approv
056 21129
Mrs Byrne
Rates fr: *IR£16.00*-**IR£18.00**.
Beds: 2F 1D 1T
Baths: 4 Ensuite
(4)

Kilkenny Bed and Breakfast, *Kilmore, Dean Street, Kilkenny.*
New home, convenient rail/bus, centre city, near monuments, everything.
Open: All Year
Grades: BF Approv
056 64040 / 65631
Mrs Heffernan
Rates fr: *IR£15.00*-**IR£18.00**.
Beds: 1F 4D 4T
Baths: 5 Ensuite 2 Shared

Cnoc Mhuire, *Bennetsbridge Road, Kilkenny.*
Comfortable well-heated home. Quiet area. Walking distance of town.
Open: All Year (not Xmas)
056 62161 Mrs Sheenan
Rates fr: *IR£16.00*-**IR£20.00**.
Beds: 2D 2T
Baths: 4 Ensuite
(4)

White Oaks, *Callan Road, Tennypark, Kilkenny.*
Bungalow with lounge and conservatory. Beautiful country setting beside city.
Open: Feb to Nov
Grades: BF Approv
056 63295 Mrs Brennan
Rates fr: *IR£14.00*-**IR£20.00**.
Beds: 1F 2D 1T
Baths: 3 Ensuite 1 Private
(6)

Please respect a B&B's wishes regarding children, animals & smoking.

Fennellys, *13 Parliament Street, Kilkenny.*
Fully licensed guesthouse/pub, Traditional music. Private parking. City centre.
Open: All Year (not Xmas)
Grades: BF 2 St
056 61796
Rates fr: *IR£17.50*-**IR£20.00**.
Beds: 2F 3D 3T
Baths: 6 Ensuite 6 Private 2 Shared
(7)

Glen View, *Castlecomer Road, Kilkenny.*
Warm welcome assured in our home. Walking distance medieval city, theatre, golf, activity centre.
Open: All Year (not Xmas)
Grades: BF Approv
056 62065 Mrs Dowling
Rates fr: *IR£16.00*-**IR£20.00**.
Beds: 1F 1D 1T
Baths: 3 Ensuite

Parkview House, *Parkview Drive, Kilkenny.*
Modern, centrally heated, prize garden; call & we'll pick you up!
Open: All Year (not Xmas)
056 64104
Ms Thompson
Rates fr: *IR£13.00*-**IR£17.00**.
Beds: 1F 2D 1T
Baths: 1 Ensuite 1 Shared
(8) (4)

St Marys, *25 St James Street, Kilkenny,*
Located in centre of city. Newly renovated. Rooms ensuite.
Open: All Year (not Xmas)
056 22091 Ms Hehir
Rates fr: *IR£15.00*-**IR£18.00**.
Beds: 2F 3D 1T
Baths: 2 Ensuite 2 Private 1 Shared

Churchview, *Cuffsgrange, Kilkenny.*
Luxury modern two storey house in a country village.
Open: All Year
Grades: BF Approv
056 29170
Mr & Mrs Banahan
Rates fr: *IR£14.50*-**IR£20.00**.
Beds: 2F 3D 1T
Baths: 3 Ensuite 1 Shared
(All) (6)

Hillgrove, *Bennettsbridge Road, Warrington, Kilkenny.*
Charming country home furnished with antiques. National Breakfast Award winner.
Open: Feb to Nov
056 51453 Mrs Drennan
Rates fr: *IR£16.00*-**IR£20.00**.
Beds: 1F 2D 2T
Baths: 4 Ensuite 1 Private
(5)

Mena House, *Castlecomer Road, Kilkenny.*
Neo-Tudor antique furnished home. Homemade preserves. Prize gardens. Irish welcome.
Open: All Year (not Xmas)
056 65362 Ms Molloy
Rates fr: *IR£14.00*-**IR£16.50**.
Beds: 2F 4D 3T
Baths: 7 Ensuite 2 Private 1 Shared
(9)

Lacken House, *Dublin Road, Kilkenny,*
A Victorian house with comfortable bedrooms, excellent food and service.
Open: All Year (not Xmas)
Grades: BF 3 St
056 61085 Fax no: 056 62435
Rates fr: *IR£25.00*-**IR£31.00**.
Beds: 1F 3D 5T
Baths: 9 Ensuite
(1) (30)

Laurels, *College Road (opposite Hotel Kilkenny), Kilkenny.*
Hospitable warm home. Five minutes city centre, quiet area, orthopaedic beds.
Open: All Year (not Xmas)
056 61501
(also fax no) Mrs Nolan
Rates fr: *IR£16.00*-**IR£25.00**.
Beds: 3F 1D
Baths: 4 Ensuite
(10)

Pay B&Bs by cash or cheque. Be prepared to pay up front for one night stays.

Knocktopher

National Grid Ref: S5337

Knocktopher Hall, *Knocktopher, Kilkenny.*
Large Georgian country house set in own grounds, beautiful countryside.
Open: Feb to Dec
056 68626 Mrs Prentice
Rates fr: *IR£16.00*-**IR£20.00**.
Beds: 2F 2D 1T
Baths: 5 Ensuite 2 Shared

Mullinavat

National Grid Ref: S5624

Croker's Kitchen

Tory View, *Mullinavat, Waterford.*
A 'home from home' on (N9) Dublin-Waterford Road. Tea/coffee making facilities in rooms.
Open: All Year (not Xmas)
051 885513 Mrs Prendergast
Rates fr: *IR£14.00*-**IR£18.00**.
Beds: 1F 2D 2T
Baths: 4 Ensuite 4 Private 1 Shared
(10)

Glenraha Farmhouse, *Ballinaraha, Mullinavat, Waterford.*
Spacious luxurious farmhouse bungalow situated off the N9 Road at Mullinavat.
Open: All Year (not Xmas)
051 898423 Mrs Fitzpatrick
Rates fr: *IR£14.00*-**IR£20.00**.
Beds: 1F 2D 1T
Baths: 1 Ensuite 1 Shared

Slieverue

National Grid Ref: S6314

Rhu Glew Country Club

Suncrest, *Slieverue, Waterford.*
Bungalow - rural setting. Convenient to Viking County of Waterford.
Open: Easter to Nov
Grades: BF Approv
051 832732 Mrs Wall
Rates fr: *IR£16.00*-**IR£21.00**.
Beds: 3F 1D 1T
Baths: 5 Ensuite
(7)

Thomastown

National Grid Ref: S5842

Patrick Kavanagh's, The Long Man, Bridge Brook Arms

Carrickmourne House, *New Ross Road, Thomastown, Co Kilkenny.*
Open: All Year
056 24124 Mrs Doyle
Rates fr: *IR£17.00*-**IR£20.00.**
Beds: 5F 1D 1T **Baths:** 5 Ensuite
This is a gem of a country home surrounded by beautiful country scenery, on a woody hillside above the beautiful Nore Valley. The land was selected from the Doyle family farm and trees were planted to complement the natural forest.

The lowest **single** *rate is shown in* **bold.**

Abbey House, *Jerpoint Abbey, Thomastown, Co Kilkenny.*
Open: All Year (not Xmas)
Grades: BF Approv, AA 4 Q
056 424166
Fax no: 056 424192
Mrs Blanchfield
Rates fr: *IR£16.50*-**IR£25.00.**
Beds: 5D 1T 1S
Baths: 7 Ensuite
Relax in surroundings of old world elegance of Jerpoint Abbey (c.1100). Halfway between Waterford and Kilkenny, 1 hour Rosslare. Ideal touring base.

Tower House, *Low Street, Thomastown, Co Kilkenny.*
Converted C12th tower house.
Open: All Year
056 24500 (also fax no)
Mr & Mrs Hennessy
Rates fr: *IR£17.00*-**IR£22.00.**
Beds: 4D **Baths:** 4 Ensuite
(8)

County Laois

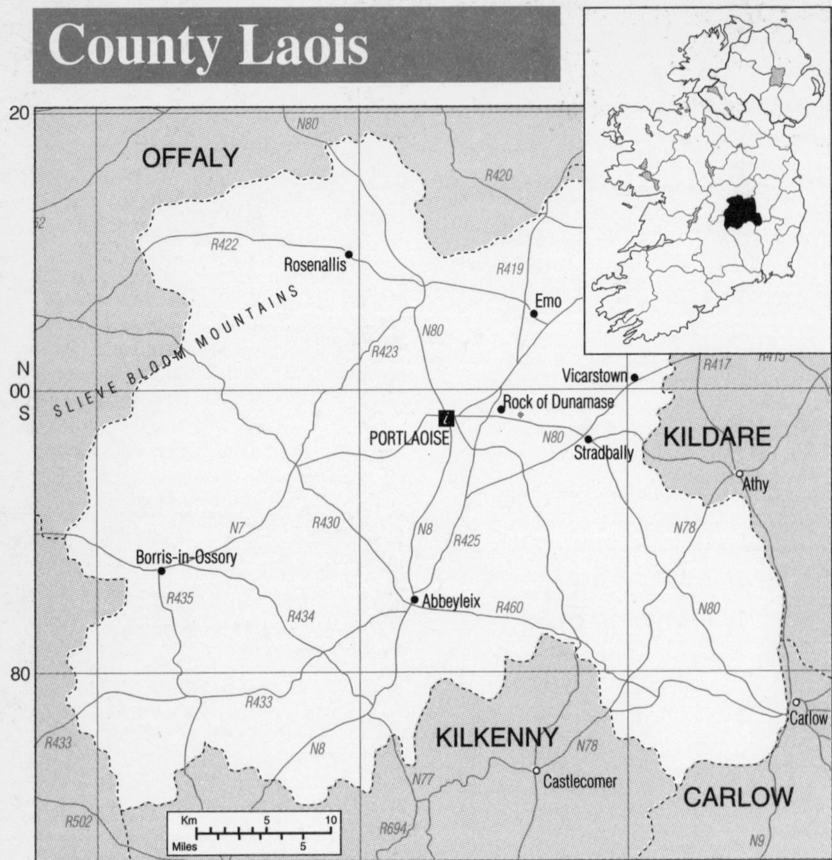

Abbeyleix

National Grid Ref: S4385

Hibernian Hotel

Norefield House, Abbeyleix, Portlaoise, Co Laois.
Open: Feb to Dec
Grades: BF Approv
0502 31059 Mrs Lawlor
Rates fr: *IR£17.50*-**IR£25.00**.
Beds: 3D 1S
Baths: 3 Ensuite
(10)
Elegance and style characterise this superb mid-C18th Georgian mansion where you can experience the joys of country living. Set on 25 acres of woodland and meadows. Golfing, fishing, tennis, pony trekking and nature walks available locally.

Borris-in-Ossory

National Grid Ref: S2487

Central House

Castletown House, *Donaghmore, Borris-in-Ossory, Portlaoise, Co Laois,*
Open: Easter to Nov
0505 46415 Fax: 0505 46788 Mrs. Phelan
Grades: BF Approv, RAC Listed
Rates fr: *IR£16.00*-**IR£16.00**.
Beds: 2F 2D 1T **Baths:** 5 Ensuite
(10)
Residence on open farm. Beautiful view of Slieve Bloom Mountains. Norman Castle remains on farm. Granstown coarse fishing lake within 4 miles. RAC listed. Recommended by Brittany Ferries, Dillard & Causin and Frommers. Complimentary tea. 5 bedrooms ensuite with colour TV.

RAIL

Portlaoise is on the main lines from ***Dublin*** *to* ***Limerick*** *and* ***Cork****.*
Tel **Irish Rail** on 01 8366222 for timetable details.

BUS

Portlaoise *to* ***Dublin*** *(6 a day).*
Tel **Bus Eireann** on 01 8366111.

TOURIST INFORMATION OFFICES

Main Street, **Portlaoise** (May to Sep), 0502 21178

Emo

National Grid Ref: N5205

Treacy's, The Heath

Morette Lodge, *Morette, Emo, Portlaoise, Co Laois.*
Modern, comfortable country home situated in centre of Laois.
Open: mid-Jan to mid-Dec
Grades: BF Approv
0502 46789 Mrs Moore
Rates fr: *IR£14.00*-**IR£19.00**.
Beds: 2F 1D **Baths:** 1 Ensuite 1 Shared

Portlaoise

National Grid Ref: S4698

Treacy's

Chez Nous, *Kilminchy, Portlaoise, Co Laois.*
Delightful luxury bungalow, tastefully decorated in interior design & antiquity.
Open: All Year (not Xmas)
Grades: RAC High Acclaim
0502 21251 Mrs Canavan
Rates fr: *IR£17.00*.
Beds: 2F 2D 1T
Baths: 2 Ensuite 1 Private
(8) (6)

Rock of Dunamase

National Grid Ref: S5298

Aspen, *Rock of Dunamase, Portlaoise, Co Laois.*
Galtee Breakfast Award winning home set in extensive landscaped gardens.
Open: Easter to Oct
0502 25405 Mr & Mrs Llewellyn
Rates fr: *IR£17.00*-**IR£20.00**.
Beds: 4D
Baths: 3 Ensuite 1 Private
(6)

Rosenallis

National Grid Ref: N3909

Clonkelly House, *Rosenallis, Portlaoise, Co Laois.*
Traditional farmhouse, friendly atmosphere, personal service, good food a priority. **Open:** Easter to Oct
Grades: BF Approv
0502 28517 Mrs Shaw
Rates fr: *IR£13.00*-**IR£15.00**.
Beds: 2F **Baths:** 2 Ensuite

Stradbally

National Grid Ref: S5796

Treacys, The Heath, Limone House

Park House, *Stradbally, Portlaoise, Co Laois.*
200-year-old farmhouse. Large garden. One hour's drive from Dublin.
Open: Easter to Oct
Grades: BF Approv
0502 25147 Mrs Cushen
Rates fr: *IR£16.00*-**IR£18.00**.
Beds: 1F 2D **Baths:** 1 Shared

The Court, *Main Street, Stradbally, Portlaoise, Co Laois.*
Modern detached town house. Family-run.
Open: Mar to Oct **Grades:** BF Approv
0502 25519 Mr & Mrs McEvoy
Rates fr: *IR£14.00*-**IR£17.00**.
Beds: 1F 2D 1T
Baths: 2 Ensuite 1 Shared
(1) (3)

Vicarstown

National Grid Ref: N6100

Vicarstown Inn, *Vicarstown, Stradbally, Portlaoise, Co Laois.*
Open: Mar to Nov **Grades:** BF Approv
0502 25189 Fax no: 0502 25652
Mrs Crean
Rates fr: *IR£16.00*-**IR£20.00**.
Beds: 2F 2T **Baths:** 2 Ensuite

County Leitrim

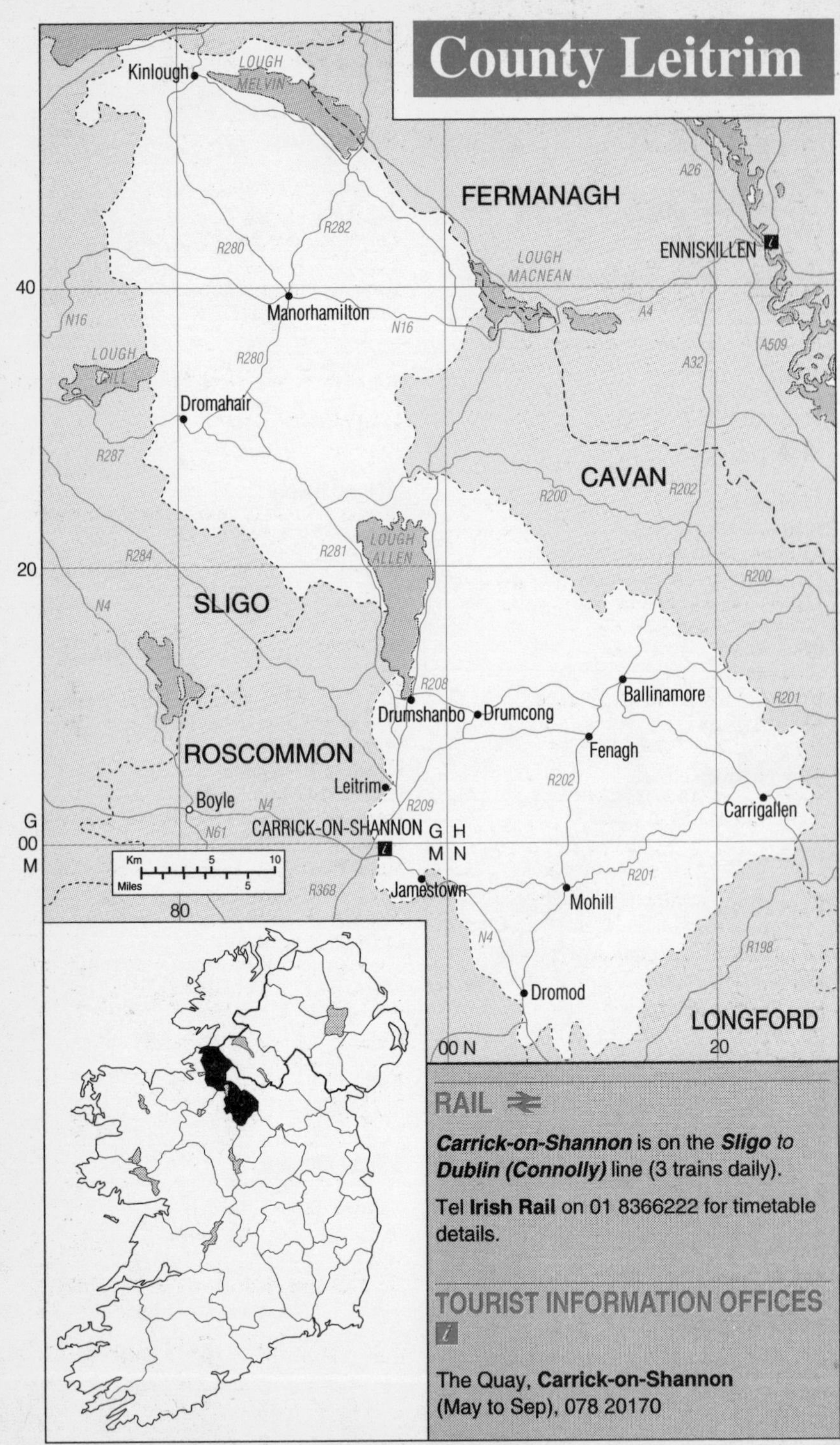

RAIL

Carrick-on-Shannon is on the ***Sligo** to* ***Dublin (Connolly)*** line (3 trains daily).

Tel **Irish Rail** on 01 8366222 for timetable details.

TOURIST INFORMATION OFFICES

The Quay, **Carrick-on-Shannon** (May to Sep), 078 20170

Ballinamore

National Grid Ref: H1211

Riversdale, *Ballinamore, Carrick-on-Shannon, Co Leitrim.*
Open: All Year (not Xmas)
Grades: BF 3 St RAC Acclaim
078 44122 Ms Thomas
Rates fr: *IR£22.00*-**IR£27.00**.
Beds: 4F 4D 1T **Baths:** 9 Ensuite
(8) (15)
Comfortable spacious residence in parkland setting alongside Shannon-Erne Waterway. Indoor heated swimming pool, squash, sauna, games room on premises. Local golf, horse-riding, stud ranch, canoeing, boat trips. Good touring centre. Brochure available. Weekly terms. Canal barge holidays.

Glenview House, *Aughoo, Ballinamore, Carrick-on-Shannon, Co Leitrim.*
Large modern farmhouse with fully licensed restaurant situated alongside Shannon/Erne Waterway.
Open: All Year (not Xmas)
Grades: BF Approv
078 44157 Fax no: 078 44814
Mrs Kennedy
Rates fr: *IR£17.00*-**IR£22.00**.
Beds: 2F 1D 3T
Baths: 4 Ensuite 2 Shared
(0)

The Commercial & Tourist Hotel, *Ballinamore, Carrick-on-Shannon, Co Leitrim.*
Open: All Year
Grades: BF 2 St, RAC Listed
078 44675
Fax no: 078 44679
Mr Walsh
Rates fr: *IR£20.00*-**IR£25.00**.
Baths: 12 Ensuite
(20)
This family-run Grade 2 hotel is located just a few hundred yards from the newly reconstructed Ballinamore/Ballyconnell Canal in the heart of the greenest and most uncluttered part of Ireland. Although a hotel since 1878 all our present rooms are new. Large comfortable rooms are all ensuite with TVs and telephone. Situated in the centre of lovely Leitrim it offers breathtaking drives and pleasant walks. Golfing, fishing, tranquillity make this paradise Ireland's best kept secret and very hard to leave.

Ardrum Lodge, *Ballinamore, Carrick-on-Shannon, Co Leitrim.*
Situated in heart of Leitrim's Lakeland 2 km from Ballinamore overlooking Shannon/Erne Waterway.
Open: Easter to Oct
078 44278 (also fax no)
Mr & Mrs Price
Rates fr: *IR£14.00*-**IR£16.00**.
Beds: 2F 3T
Baths: 4 Ensuite 2 Shared

Carrick-on-Shannon

National Grid Ref: M9499

Riverside Bar, Cryan's

Moyrane House, *Dublin Road, Carrick-on-Shannon, Co Leitrim.*
A truly Irish family home. Peaceful setting. Highly recommended.
Open: Apr to Oct
078 20325
Mrs Shortt
Rates fr: *IR£14.00*-**IR£19.00**.
Beds: 2D 3T
Baths: 3 Ensuite
(5)

Gortmor House, *Lismakeegan, Carrick-on-Shannon, Co Leitrim.*
Highly recommended accommodation in quiet scenic area. Excellent home cooking. Wine licence.
Open: Feb to Nov
Grades: BF Approv
078 20489
Mrs McMahon
Rates fr: *IR£14.00*-**IR£19.00**.
Beds: 2F 2T
Baths: 2 Ensuite 2 Shared
(10)

Please respect a B&B's wishes regarding children, animals & smoking.

Irish Grid References are for villages, towns and cities - *not* for individual houses.

***Corbally Lodge,** Dublin Road N4, Carrick-on-Shannon, Co Leitrim.*
Open: All Year (not Xmas)
Grades: BF Approv
078 20228 Mr & Mrs Rowley
Rates fr: *IR£16.00*-**IR£20.00**.
Beds: 1D 3T **Baths:** 3 Ensuite

***Aisleigh Guest House,** Dublin Road, Carrick-on-Shannon, Co Leitrim.*
We will facilitate your every requirement at our guest house.
Open: All Year (not Xmas)
Grades: BF 3 St
078 20313 Fearow
Rates fr: *IR£16.00*-**IR£18.00**.
Beds: 4F 4D 3T 11S
Baths: 11 Ensuite 11 Private
(20)

***Vila Flora,** Station Road, Carrick-on-Shannon, Co Leitrim.*
Modernised Georgian house beside River Shannon and town centre. Trips available on the Shannon.
Open: All Year (not Xmas)
078 20338 Mrs Nolan
Rates fr: *IR£14.00*-**IR£18.00**.
Beds: 2F 2D
Baths: 2 Ensuite 1 Shared
(8)

Carrigallen

National Grid Ref: H2303

Kilbracken Arms Hotel

***Cornafest House,** Carrigallen, Cavan.*
Charming country house beside lake in beautiful countryside.
Open: All Year (not Xmas)
Grades: BF Approv
049 39643 Mrs McGerty
Rates fr: *IR£14.00*-**IR£16.00**.
Beds: 2F 1D 1T
Baths: 1 Ensuite 2 Shared
(1) (10)

***Allandale,** Carrigallen, Cavan.*
Own large grounds. Private fishing with car park at lakeside. Also farm walk.
Open: Feb to Oct
Grades: BF Approv
049 39706
Mrs Murray
Rates fr: *IR£12.00*-**IR£13.00**.
Beds: 1F 1D 2T
Baths: 1 Ensuite 1 Private 1 Shared
(4) (10)

Dromahair

National Grid Ref: G8031

***The Breffni Centre,** Main Street, Dromahair, Co Leitrim.*
Modern, comfortable hotel. Family run. Situated in Yeats country.
Open: Easter to Sep
Grades: BF Approv, AA 1 St
071 64199
Mr & Mrs Patton
Rates fr: *IR£16.00*-**IR£17.00**.
Beds: 2D 7T 1S
Baths: 10 Ensuite

Dromod

National Grid Ref: N0590

***Tooman House,** Dromod, Carrick-on-Shannon, Co Leitrim.*
Open: All Year (not Xmas/New Year)
Grades: BF Approv
043 24119 (also fax no)
Mrs Herbert
Rates fr: *IR£15.00*-**IR£13.00**.
Beds: 1F 2D 1T
Baths: 2 Ensuite
A warm welcome. Family run bed and breakfast farmhouse accommodation. Ideal for touring. Four miles from N4 Sligo/Dublin Road. Home cooking, TV and tea/coffee facilities.

High season, bank holidays and special events mean low availability *anywhere.*

The lowest *double* rate per person is shown in *italics.*

Drumcong

National Grid Ref: H0209

Cryan's

Lakeview, *Drumcong, Carrick-on-Shannon, Co Leitrim.*
Relaxing, comfortable Georgian home, overlooking two lakes.
Open: All Year
078 42034 Mrs McKeown
Rates fr: *IR£14.00*-**IR£19.00**.
Beds: 2F 1T
Baths: 1 Ensuite 1 Shared
(6)

Drumshanbo

National Grid Ref: G9710

McTernans, McGourtys, McGuires, Allendale Restaurant

Forest View, *Carrick View, Drumshanbo, Carrick-on-Shannon, Co Leitrim.*
Open: Mar to Oct
078 41243 Mr & Mrs Costello
Rates fr: *IR£15.00*-**IR£19.00**.
Beds: 3F 2D 2T
Baths: 3 Ensuite 2 Shared
Tranquil, beautiful North-West lake and mountain district, beside the Shannon. Comfortable family home. Walking distance from swimming-pool and amenity area, pubs and restaurants. You'll return again and again!

Mooney's B&B, *2 Carick Road, Drumshanbo, Carrick-on-Shannon, Co Leitrim.*
Stone two-storey house, friendly, comfortable, scenic area in lovely Leitrim.
Open: All Year (not Xmas)
Grades: BF Approv
078 41013 Mrs Mooney
Rates fr: *IR£11.00*-**IR£11.00**.
Beds: 2D 1T 1S
Baths: 1 Shared

Fraoch Ban, *Corlough, Drumshanbo, Carrick-on-Shannon, Co Leitrim.*
Welcoming home overlooking Lough Allen - all rooms with spectacular views.
Open: Easter to Oct
Grades: BF Approv
078 41260
Mrs Heron
Rates fr: *IR£16.00*-**IR£21.00**.
Beds: 5T
Baths: 5 Ensuite
(8)

Fenagh

National Grid Ref: H1007

Kealadaville, *Fenagh, Ballinamore, Carrick-on-Shannon, Co Leitrim.*
Kealadaville is a two-storey modern house set in wooded area.
Open: All Year
Grades: BF Approv
078 44179
Mrs Curran
Rates fr: *IR£14.00*-**IR£14.00**.
Beds: 1D 3T
(6)

Jamestown

National Grid Ref: M9897

Mulveys

White House, *Jamestown, Carrick-on-Shannon, Co Leitrim.*
Large modern villa overlooking River Shannon. Fishing, historic village.
Open: All Year
Grades: BF Approv
078 21076
Mrs Clarke
Rates fr: *IR£14.00*-**IR£15.00**.
Beds: 2D 1T
Baths: 1 Ensuite 1 Private 1 Shared
(6)

Pay B&Bs by cash or cheque. Be prepared to pay up front for one night stays.

Kinlough

National Grid Ref: G8155

Bluerock, *Dartry Road, Kinlough, Sligo.*
Select accommodation in rural setting. Warm, friendly welcome.
Open: All Year
Grades: BF Approv
072 41610
Mr & Mrs Phelan
Rates fr: *IR£14.00*-**IR£18.00.**
Beds: 1F 5T
Baths: 3 Ensuite
(1) (6)

Leitrim

National Grid Ref: G9505

Leitrim Inn, The Canal View, McGuires

Mountain View, *Leitrim, Carrick-on-Shannon, Co Leitrim.*
Modern comfortable private bungalow in beautiful tranquil setting beside River Shannon.
Open: All Year (not Xmas)
Grades: BF Approv
078 20859
Mr & Mrs Moffatt
Rates fr: *IR£15.00*-**IR£15.00.**
Beds: 1D 2T
Baths: 3 Ensuite
(6)

Doherty's Country House, *Leitrim, Carrick-on-Shannon, Co Leitrim.*
Modern comfortable farmhouse. Lovely location. Pony trekking on-site.
Open: Jan to Oct
Grades: BF Approv
078 20853 (also fax no)
Mrs Doherty
Rates fr: *IR£16.00*-**IR£16.00.**
Beds: 2F 1D 1T
Baths: 4 Ensuite

All rates are subject to alteration at the owners' discretion.

The lowest **single** *rate is shown in* **bold.**

Manorhamilton

National Grid Ref: G8839

Milestone

Drummonds Farmhouse, *Glencar, Manorhamilton, Co Leitrim.*
Modern farmhouse in very scenic area, home-cooking. Home from home.
Open: Easter to Oct
072 55197
Mrs McGowan
Rates fr: *IR£13.00*-**IR£15.00.**
Beds: 1F 2D 1T
Baths: 1 Ensuite 1 Private 1 Shared

Mohill

National Grid Ref: N0897

O'Briens Tavern, Kellys

Glebe House, *Ballinamore Road, Mohill, Carrick-on-Shannon, Co Leitrim.*
Open: Mar to Nov
Grades: BF 3 St
078 31086 Fax no: 078 31886
Mr & Mrs Maloney
Rates fr: *IR£22.00*-**IR£26.00.**
Beds: 5F 5D 3T
Baths: 5 Ensuite 2 Private
(20)
Come! Explore this beautiful unspoilt part of Ireland ... plenty to do and see. Or simply unwind in the relaxed informality of Glebe House. Take a break with us in our lovely restored Rectory (1823). All bedrooms ensuite.

Travellers Rest, *Glebe Street, Mohill, Carrick-on-Shannon, Co Leitrim.*
Traditional Irish pub. Beautiful scenery. Numerous lakes in area with abundance of fish.
Open: All Year **Grades:** BF Approv
078 31174
Rates fr: *IR£15.00*-**IR£15.00.**
Beds: 2F 8T **Baths:** 10 Ensuite
(1)

Ballymore House, *Ballinamore Road, Mohill, Carrick-on-Shannon, Co Leitrim.*
Open: All Year
Grades: BF Approv
078 31278
Fax no: 078 31761
Mr & Mrs Barry
Rates fr: *IR£16.00*-**IR£18.00**.
Beds: 1F 2D 1T
Baths: 3 Ensuite 1 Private
(3) (5)
Charming country residence in the heart of Ireland's Lakeland District. Warm friendly atmosphere. We offer superb cuisine, excellent fishing and outdoor pursuits. Relax in style while enjoying all that Leitrim has to offer you. Well worth a visit.

Coolabawn House, *Station Raod, Mohill, Carrick-on-Shannon, Co Leitrim.*
Ideally situated, welcoming home, with beautiful gardens.
Open: Apr to Oct
078 31033 Mrs Slevin
Rates fr: *IR£16.00*-**IR£17.00**.
Beds: 1F 2D
Baths: 2 Ensuite 1 Private 1 Shared
(5)

The lowest *double* rate per person is shown in *italics*.

County Limerick

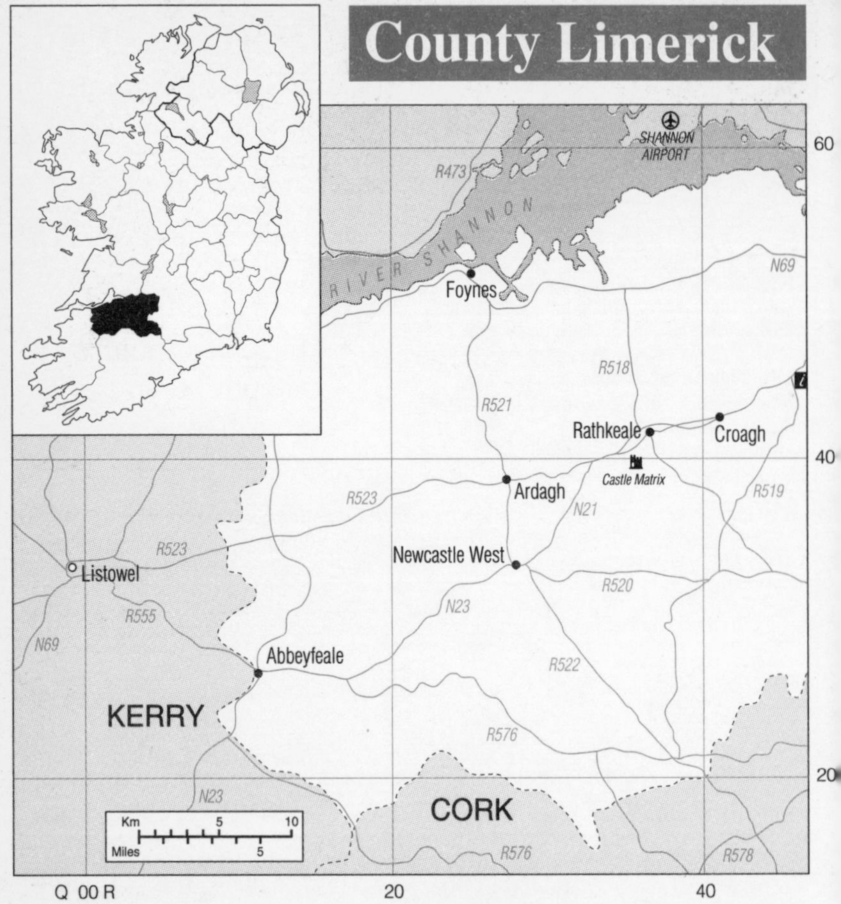

<table>
<tr>
<td>

AIRPORTS

Shannon Airport (in ***County Clare***) is 10 miles away from ***Limerick City***.

Tel 061 471444

AIR SERVICES & AIRLINES

Shannon *to* ***Heathrow -***

Aer Lingus. In Ireland tel. 061 471666; in Britain tel. 0181 899 4747.

Shannon *to* ***Manchester -***

British Airways (for **Manx Airlines**). In the Republic tel. (freefone): 1800 626747; in Northern Ireland & the UK tel. (local rate): 0345 222111

</td>
<td>

RAIL

Limerick City is well-served by railway lines. 12 trains a day run to ***Dublin***, via ***Nenagh*** and ***Portlaoise***.

Limerick is also on the ***Rosslare*** line (via ***Limerick Junction***).

Tel **Irish Rail** on 061 315555.

TOURIST INFORMATION OFFICES

Heritage Centre, **Adare** (Mar to Oct), 061 396255

Arthur's Quay, **Limerick** (open all year), 061 317939

</td>
</tr>
</table>

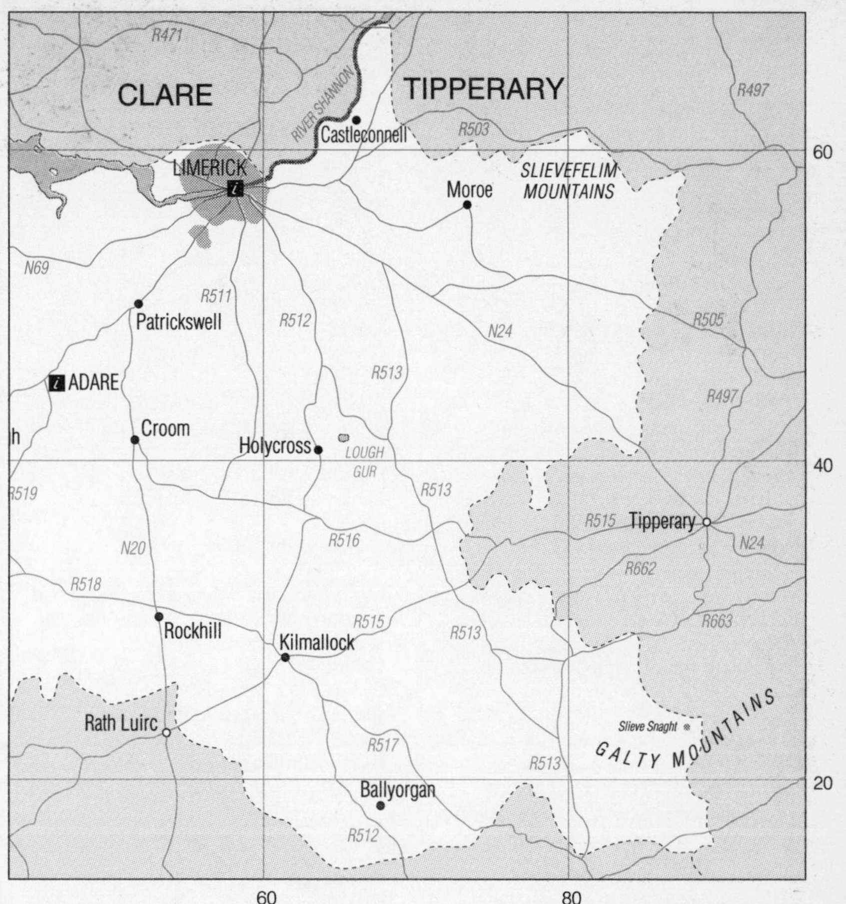

Abbeyfeale

National Grid Ref: R1126

Leens

Abbey Farm, *Abbeyfeale, Limerick.*
Modern farmhouse on outskirts of Abbeyfeale Town. Theme garden.
Open: Jun to Oct **Grades:** BF Approv
068 31282 Mr O'Rourke
Rates fr: *IR£14.00*-**IR£16.00**.
Beds: 3D 2T 1S
Baths: 2 Private 2 Shared

The lowest **single** *rate is shown in* **bold.**

Phoning from outside the Republic?
Dial 00353 and omit the initial '0' of the area code.

Leen's Hotel, *Main Street, Abbeyfeale, Limerick.*
Smally cosy family-run hotel in the heart of Abbeyfeale.
Open: All Year (not Xmas)
Grades: BF 1 St
068 31121 Mr Murphy
Rates fr: *IR£17.50*-**IR£18.00**.
Beds: 3F 4D 3T 2S
Baths: 8 Ensuite 3 Shared

Adare

National Grid Ref: R4546

Collins Bar, Arches Restaurant

Carrabawn House, *Killarney Road, Adare, Co Limerick.*
Open: All Year (not Xmas)
Grades: BF 3 St, AA 3 Q
061 396067
Fax no: 061 396925
Mr & Mrs Lohan
Rates fr: *IR£18.50*-**IR£26.00**.
Beds: 2F 3D 2T 1S
Baths: 8 Ensuite
(12)
Multi-recommended architecturally designed house, select area, dining room and sunlounge overlooking picturesque gardens. Private car park. All rooms ensuite with TV, direct dial telephone and tea/coffee making facilities. Breakfast menu. Bunratty, Shannon 30 minutes drive. 5 mins from award winning village of Adare. All major credit cards accepted. Member IHF. Le Guide du Routard Recommended. Be our guest.

Foxhollow House, *Croom Road, Adare, Co Limerick.*
Distinctive luxury home set in landscaped gardens. Peaceful countryside.
Open: All Year **Grades:** AA 4 Q
061 396776 (also fax no)
Mrs Dundon
Rates fr: *IR£17.00*-**IR£22.00**.
Beds: 1F 2D 1T
Baths: 4 Ensuite
(4) (6)

Hillcrest House, *Clonshire, Croagh, Adare, Co Limerick.*
Open: Apr to Nov
061 396534 (also fax no)
Mr & Mrs Power
Rates fr: *IR£14.50*-**IR£19.50**.
Beds: 1F 1D 2T
Baths: 3 Ensuite 1 Shared
(10)
Discover a sense of freedom and space, in surroundings where nature abounds. Set amidst beautiful tranquil pastures. Hospitable, relaxed, comfortable home. Bright, cheerful bedrooms. Traditional farming, medieval ruins, forest and hill walks. Off N21 west of Adare. Frommer Recommended.

Bringing children with you? Always ask for any special rates.

Elm House, *Mondelihy, Adare, Co Limerick.*
Open: All Year **Grades:** BF Approv
061 396306 Mrs Hedderman
Rates fr: *IR£14.50*-**IR£16.50**.
Beds: 1D 1T
Baths: 1 Ensuite 2 Private
Elegant restored 1892 Georgian home, set in tranquil garden, three minutes drive Adare Village. Shannon Airport 30 minutes. Credit cards accepted. Private car park. TV, hairdryers.

Gleneig, *Mondelihy, Adare, Co Limerick.*
Luxurious superwarm home, beautiful views from all rooms. Tea/coffee and scones on arrival.
Open: All Year
061 396077 Mrs Liston
Rates fr: *IR£16.00*-**IR£21.00**.
Beds: 1F 1D 1T
Baths: 3 Ensuite
(All)

Avona, *Kildimo Road, Adare, Co Limerick.*
Open: All Year (not Xmas)
Grades: AA 3 Q
061 396323 Mrs Harrington
Rates fr: *IR£16.00*.
Beds: 1F 2D 1T
Baths: 4 Ensuite
(5)
Enjoy warm hospitality in our home situated in Adare, one of Ireland's prettiest villages. Adjacent to church, hotels, restaurants, Heritage Centre. TV, radio, hairdryers. Tea/coffee facilities in guest lounge. Breakfast menu. Many recommendations. Shannon Airport 40 minutes.

The lowest *double* rate per person is shown in *italics*.

Ivy House, *Graigue, Adare, Co Limerick.*
Beautifully restored C18th country home. Furnished with antiques, homely atmosphere.
Open: Mar to Oct
061 396270
Mrs Hickey
Rates fr: *IR£16.00*-**IR£30.00**.
Beds: 1F 2D 1T
Baths: 3 Ensuite 1 Private
(7)

Lurriga Lodge, *Adare, Patrickswell, Limerick.*
Open: Apr to Oct
061 355411 (also fax no)
Mrs Woulfe
Rates fr: *IR£16.00*-**IR£18.00**.
Beds: 1F 2D 1T
Baths: 4 Private
(8)
Luxurious country house in secluded landscaped gardens ideally situated to start/finish tour of the South West. Shannon Airport 21 miles. Adjacent to Adare & Bunratty Castle. Ten golf courses within 20 miles. Tour advice given. Music pubs nearby.

Castleview, *Clonshire More, Croagh, Rathkeale, Adare, Co Limerick.*
Lovely, warm, highly recommended, relaxing home with award-winning gardens.
Open: All Year
061 396394 Mrs Galvin
Rates fr: *IR£16.00*-**IR£20.00**.
Beds: 1F 1D 2T
Baths: 3 Ensuite 1 Private
(4)

Ardagh

National Grid Ref: R2738

Pat Whelans

Reens Houe, *Ardagh, Newcastle West, Co Limerick.*
400-year-old comfortable farmhouse with beautiful antique furniture.
Open: May to Sep
Grades: BF Approv
069 64276 Mrs Curtin
Rates fr: *IR£18.00*-**IR£23.00**.
Beds: 2F 1D 1S
Baths: 2 Ensuite 2 Private

Ballyorgan

National Grid Ref: R6718

Lantern Lodge, *Ballyorgan, Kilfinnane, Kilmallock, Co Limerick.*
Modern comfortable farmhouse. Situated at foot Ballyhouse Hills. Home cooking a speciality.
Open: All Year (not Xmas)
Grades: BF Approv
063 91085 Mrs O'Donnell
Rates fr: *IR£16.00*-**IR£21.00**.
Beds: 1F 1T 2S
Baths: 4 Ensuite

Castleconnell

National Grid Ref: R6662

Finnegans Bar, Castle Oaks House Hotel, Worrell's Inn Bar

Loraden Lodge, *Ruan, Castleconnell, Limerick.*
Modern, unique country house adjacent to old world village.
Open: All Year (not Xmas)
061 377062 (also fax no)
Mr & Mrs Byrnes
Rates fr: *IR£16.0*-**IR£20.00**.
Beds: 1F 2D
Baths: 3 Ensuite
(6)

Edelweiss, *Stradbally, Castleconnell, Limerick.*
Cosy bungalow - family owned, nice gardens, lovely view, beside hotel.
Open: Mar to Oct
Grades: BF Approv
061 377397 Mrs Tyrrell
Rates fr: *IR£16.00*-**IR£18.00**.
Beds: 1F 1D 1T
Baths: 2 Ensuite 1 Shared
(4)

Irish Grid References are for villages, towns and cities - *not* for individual houses.

Croagh

National Grid Ref: R4142

Hillcrest House, *Clonshire, Croagh, Rathkeale, Co Limerick.*
Hospitable, relaxed, comfortable home, set amidst beautiful tranquil pastures.
Open: Apr to Oct
061 396534 Mr & Mrs Power
Rates fr: *IR£14.50*-**IR£19.50**.
Beds: 1F 1D 2T
Baths: 3 Ensuite 1 Shared
(10)

Meadowview, *Kiltannon, Croagh, Rathkeale, Co Limerick.*
Modern bungalow on a family-run dairy farm, six minutes from Adare. Spacious garden.
Open: All Year (not Xmas)
069 64820 Mrs Piggott
Rates fr: *IR£13.50*-**IR£18.00**.
Beds: 2F 1S
Baths: 1 Ensuite 1 Private 1 Shared
(3)

Duneeven, *Croagh, Rathkeale, Co Limerick.*
Old Gothic-style comfortable two storey farmhouse in peaceful rural area.
Open: May to Sep **Grades:** BF Approv
069 64049 Mrs Harnett
Rates fr: *IR£14.00*.
Beds: 1F 1D 1T 1S **Baths:** 1 Shared
(2) (4)

Croom

National Grid Ref: R5141

Ballymacamore, *Croom, Kilmallock, Co Limerick.*
Modern comfortable farmhouse in beautiful scenic area and countryside.
Open: All Year (not Xmas)
061 397497 Mrs Cronin
Rates fr: *IR£14.00*-**IR£18.00**.
Beds: 1F 2D 1T
Baths: 1 Ensuite 2 Shared

All rates are subject to alteration at the owners' discretion.

Foynes

National Grid Ref: R2552

Shannon House

Raheen House, *Foynes, Limerick.*
Detached bungalow, own grounds. In village of Foynes on N69.
Open: May to Oct
069 65236 Mrs Counihan
Rates fr: *IR£14.00*-**IR£19.00**.
Beds: 2D 1T
Baths: 2 Shared
(2)

Holycross

National Grid Ref: R6340

Reardons Bar

Bridge House, *Grange, Holycross, Bruff, Co Limerick.*
200-year-old riverside farmhouse near scenic and archaeological Lough Gur.
Open: Easter to Nov
Grades: BF Approv
061 390195
Mr & Mrs Barry
Rates fr: *IR£14.00*-**IR£19.00**.
Beds: 1F 1D 1T 2S
Baths: 2 Ensuite
(6) (10)

Kilmallock

National Grid Ref: R6028

Poachers Restaurant, The Lough Inn

Flemingstown House, *Kilmallock, Co Limerick.*
Open: Easter to Oct
063 98093
Fax no: 063 98546
Mrs Sheedy-King
Rates fr: *IR£18.00*-**IR£23.00**.
Beds: 1F 2D 2T
Baths: 5 Ensuite
(20)
C17th house (dairy farm) situated at the intersection of three counties. On R512 and 4 km form Tipperary-Killarney Road R515. National Breakfast Award Winner. Recommended in Good Hotel Guide, Karen Brown, le Guide du Routard, AA, RAC. All rooms ensuite.

Ash Hill, *Kilmallock, Co Limerick.*
A large Georgian house set in a working stud farm.
Open: All Year (not Xmas)
063 98035 Mr Johnson
Rates fr: *IR£30.00*-**IR£40.00**.
Beds: 2D 3T
Baths: 4 Ensuite

Tudorville, *Kilmallock - Charleville Road, Lower Effin, Kilmallock, Co Limerick.*
Luxurious country home in pleasant surroundings. Personal attention assured.
Open: May to Sep
Grades: BF Approv
063 81623 Mrs Murphy
Rates fr: *IR£13.50*-**IR£13.50**.
Beds: 1F 1D 1T
(5)

Hillgare, *Uregare, Kilmallock, Co Limerick.*
200-year-old farmhouse central for touring south and west.
Open: Easter to Oct
Grades: BF Approv
061 382275
Mrs Power
Rates fr: *IR£14.00*-**IR£19.00**.
Beds: 1F 2T
Baths: 2 Ensuite 1 Private

Limerick

National Grid Ref: R5857

Moll Darby's, Jury's Hotel, Freddy's, Woodfield House, Greenhills Hotel, Texas Steak Out, Patrick Punch's Pub, O'Grady's Cellar Restaurant, Sneenhills Hotel

Cloneen House, *Ennis Road, Limerick.*
Open: All Year (not Xmas)
Grades: AA 3 Q
061 454461 Ms Cusack
Rates fr: *IR£18.00*-**IR£22.00**.
Beds: 3F 1D 1T 1S
Baths: 6 Ensuite
Elegant Edwardian house, 10 mins walk from city centre, perfect base for golfing, fishing, horse riding, shopping, touring the historic and beautiful mid-west. On bus route to Shannon Airport.

Please respect
a B&B's wishes regarding
children, animals
& smoking.

Geln Eagle, *12 Vereker Gardens, Ennis Road, Limerick.*
Nearest to city centre in quiet cul-de-sac. Beside Jury's Hotel.
Open: Easter to Nov
Grades: BF Approv
061 455521 (also fax no)
Mrs O'Toole
Rates fr: *IR£16.00*-**IR£19.50**.
Beds: 2F 1T 1S
Baths: 4 Ensuite

Santoslina, *Coonagh, Ennis Road, Limerick.*
Spacious home. Next door to equestrian centre. Advice on day tours.
Open: All Year (not Xmas)
Grades: BF Approv
061 451590 Mrs Kenae
Rates fr: *IR£16.00*-**IR£20.00**.
Beds: 3F 2D 1T
Baths: 6 Ensuite
(8)

Alexandra Guest House, *O'Connell Avenue, Limerick.*
Comfortable Victorian residence on tree lined avenue five minutes city centre, bus and rail station.
Open: All Year **Grades:** BF 3 St
061 318472 Fax no: 061400433
Rates fr: *IR£20.00*-**IR£18.00**.
Beds: 7D 2T 3S
Baths: 7 Ensuite 3 Shared
(10)

Lisheen, *Coonagh, Limerick.*
Quiet rural setting off Ennis Road Roundabout. Bungalow. Comfortable, friendly.
Open: Mar to Oct **Grades:** BF Approv
061 455393 Mr & Mrs O'Shea
Rates fr: *IR£14.00*-**IR£19.00**.
Beds: 2F 1D 1T
Baths: 1 Shared
(4)

Trebor, *Ennis Road, Limerick.*
Near city centre, bus stop for airport/Bunratty at door.
Open: Feb to Nov
Grades: BF Approv
061 454632
(also fax no) Mrs McSweeney
Rates fr: *IR£13.50*-**IR£16.00**.
Beds: 2D 2T
Baths: 4 Ensuite
(6)

Annesville, *Ennis Road, Limerick.*
Modern, well heated town house, three quiet ensuite rooms. Frommer Recommended.
Open: All Year (not Xmas)
Grades: BF Approv
061 452703 Ms Beresford
Rates fr: *IR£14.00*-**IR£18.00**.
Beds: 4F
Baths: 3 Ensuite 1 Shared

Casa Maria, *16 Westfield Park, North CIrcular Road, Limerick.*
Situated in quiet cul-de-sac overlooking bird sanctuary and River Shannon.
Open: All Year (not Xmas)
Grades: BF Approv
061 453865 Mrs Frost Walsh
Rates fr: *IR£15.00*-**IR£18.00**.
Beds: 1F 1D 2T 1S
Baths: 2 Ensuite 1 Private 1 Shared

Railway Hotel, *Limerick.*
Family-run hotel, adjacent to rail and bus station.
Open: All Year (not Xmas)
Grades: BF Approv RAC 2 St
061 413653 Fax no: 061 419762
Ms Collins
Rates fr: *IR£20.00*-**IR£24.00**.
Beds: 1F 8D 7T 8S
Baths: 24 Ensuite 3 Shared
(6)

Irish Grid References are for villages, towns and cities - *not* for individual houses.

Pay B&Bs by cash or cheque. Be prepared to pay up front for one night stays.

Moyrhee, *Phares Road, Meelick, Limerick.*
Quiet bungalow off main Limerick/Shannon road. Convenient City & Bunratty.
Open: All Year (not Xmas)
061 452196
Mrs Callinan
Rates fr: *IR£16.00*-**IR£18.00**.
Beds: 4D 4T
Baths: 8 Ensuite

Clonmacken Guest House, *Clonmacken, Limerick.*
Purpose built family run guest house, with the highest standard of decor.
Open: All Year (not Xmas)
Grades: BF 3 St, AA 3 Q
061 327007
Fax no: 061 327785
Ms McDonald
Rates fr: *IR£18.00*-**IR£25.00**.
Beds: 6F 3D 1T
Baths: 10 Private
(0) (20)

Moroe

National Grid Ref: R7355

Rinnaknock, *Glenstal, Moroe, Limerick.*
Spacious bungalow, situated in scenic unspoilt rural area.
Open: Mar to Oct
Grades: BF Approv
061 386189
Mrs Walsh-Seaver
Rates fr: *IR£14.00*-**IR£18.00**.
Beds: 2D 1T
Baths: 2 Ensuite 1 Private 2 Shared
(8)

The lowest *double* rate per person is shown in *italics*.

Newcastle West

National Grid Ref: R2833

Whelan's Bar

Ballingowan House, *Gortroe, Newcastle West, Co Limerick.*
Open: All Year (not Xmas)
Grades: BF Approv
069 62341
Mrs O'Brien
Rates fr: *IR£16.00*-**IR£18.00**.
Beds: 2F 2D 1T 1S
Baths: 6 Ensuite
(6)
Luxurious pink Georgian house with distinctive features - much admired. Attractive landscaped gardens, excellent cuisine with choice of breakfast. N21 - halfway stop between Shannon and Killarney. Ten minutes drive to Adare. New 18-hole golf course nearby. One mile to Newcastle West.

Patrickswell

National Grid Ref: R5249

Lurriga Lodge, *Patrickswell, Limerick.*
Open: Apr to Oct
061 355411 (also fax no)
Mrs Woulfe
Rates fr: *IR£16.00*-**IR£18.00**.
Beds: 1F 2D 1T
Baths: 4 Private
(8)
Luxurious country house in secluded landscaped gardens ideally situated to start/finish tour of the South West. Shannon Airport 21 miles. Adjacent to Adare & Bunratty Castle. Ten golf courses within 20 miles. Tour advice given. Music pubs nearby.

Carnlea House, *Caher Road, Patrickswell, Limerick.*
Modern spacious bungalow on N20/21. Convenient for Adare, Bunratty, Shannon
Open: January to November
Grades: BF Approv
061 227576 Mrs Geary
Rates fr: *IR£14.00*-**IR£16.00**.
Beds: 1F 2D 1T 1S
Baths: 2 Ensuite 1 Shared
(1) (8)

Rathkeale

National Grid Ref: R3641

Collins Pub, Arches Restaurant

Castleview, *Clonshire More, Croagh, Rathkeale, Co Limerick.*
Lovely, warm, highly recommended, relaxing home with award-winning gardens. **Open:** All Year
061 396394 Mrs Galvin
Rates fr: *IR£16.00*-**IR£20.00**.
Beds: 1F 1D 2T
Baths: 3 Ensuite 1 Private
(4)

Rockhill

National Grid Ref: R5230

Ballyteigue House, *Rockhill, Bruree, Kilmallock, Co Limerick.*
Georgian country house set in parkland. Gracious living. Warm welcome.
Open: All Year (not Xmas)
Grades: AA 3 Q
063 90575 (also fax no) Mrs Johnson
Rates fr: *IR£20.00*-**IR£25.00**.
Beds: 1D 3T 1S
Baths: 4 Ensuite 1 Private

County Longford

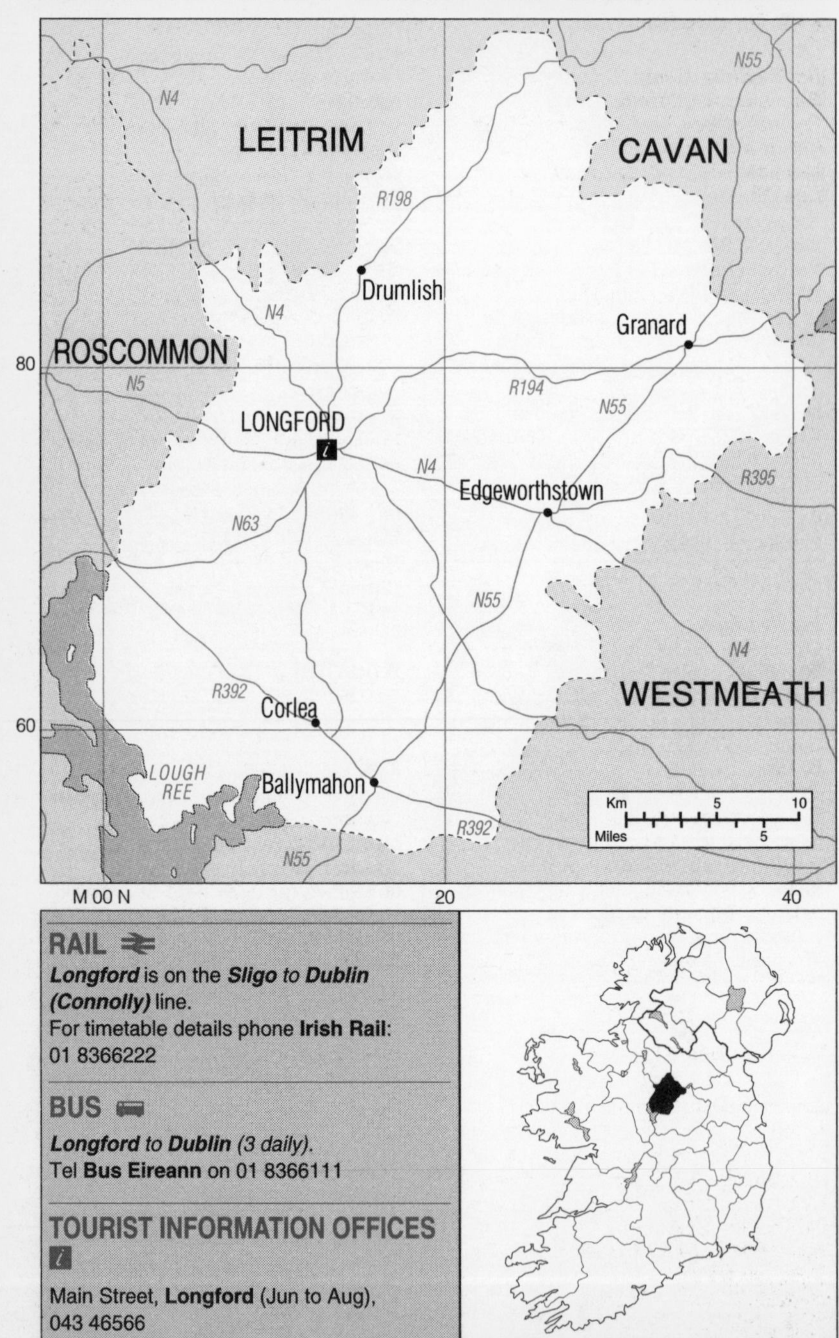

RAIL

Longford is on the ***Sligo to Dublin (Connolly)*** line.
For timetable details phone **Irish Rail**: 01 8366222

BUS

Longford *to* ***Dublin*** *(3 daily)*.
Tel **Bus Eireann** on 01 8366111

TOURIST INFORMATION OFFICES

Main Street, **Longford** (Jun to Aug), 043 46566

Ballymahon

National Grid Ref: N1517

The Roots Restaurant

***Burd's**, Ballymahon, Co Longford.*
Old-style guest house.
Open: Easter to Sep **Grades:** BF 1 St
0902 32294 Miss Burd
Rates fr: *IR£15.00*-**IR£15.00**.

Corlea

National Grid Ref: N0862

***Derrylough**, Corlea, Ballymahon, Longford.*
Comfortable farmhouse. Tranquil surroundings. Spacious gardens. Food from farm and garden.
Open: April to Sept **Grades:** BF Approv
043 22126 Mr & Mrs Gerety
Rates fr: *IR£17.00*.
Beds: 1D 1T 1S
Baths: 2 Ensuite 1 Shared

Drumlish

National Grid Ref: N1585

***Chez Nous**, Arva Road, Drumlish, Longford.*
Delightful country house with attic bedrooms, conservatory leading to beautiful gardens.
Open: All Year **Grades:** BF 3 St
043 24368 Mr & Mrs Etienne
Rates fr: *IR£14.00*-**IR£19.00**.
Beds: 2D 5T **Baths:** 7 Ensuite
(10)

Edgeworthstown

National Grid Ref: N2572

Park House Hotel

***Lackan Lodge**, Edgeworthstown, Longford.*
Modern farmhouse in peaceful surroundings on N4. Near Ardagh village.
Open: Apr to Sep **Grades:** BF Approv
043 71299 Mrs Murphy
Rates fr: *IR£14.00*-**IR£16.50**.
Beds: 1F 1D 2T
Baths: 1 Ensuite 1 Shared
(6)

Granard

National Grid Ref: N3381

Hourican's Restaurant

***St Anthonys**, Cavan Road, Granard, Longford.*
Spacious & comfortable family-run B&B on N55.
Open: All Year
Grades: BF Approv
043 86515 Mrs Sheridan
Rates fr: *IR£15.00*-**IR£15.00**.
Beds: 1F 3D 1T
Baths: 2 Ensuite
(6)

***Toberphelim House**, Granard, Longford.*
Georgian residence on 200-acre cattle and sheep farm. Dinner fee IR£14.00.
Open: Apr to Sep
Grades: AA 3 Q
043 86568 (also fax no)
Mr & Mrs Smyth
Rates fr: *IR£20.00*-**IR£25.00**.
Beds: 1F 1T
Baths: 2 Ensuite 2 Private 1 Shared

Longford

National Grid Ref: N1375

Fallons Pub

***Cumiskeys Award Winning Farmhouse**, Ennybegs, Longford.*
Splendid Tudor-style farmhouse surrounded by stone walls in quiet countryside.
Open: Mar to Oct **Grades:** BF Approv
043 23320 Fax no: 143 23516
Rates fr: *IR£16.00*-**IR£21.00**.
Beds: 1F 1D 2T
Baths: 1 Shared
(100)

***Sancian**, Dublin Road, Longford.*
Rooms ensuite with piped TVs. Situated N4 opposite golf links. Listed in Best B&B Book.
Open: All Year **Grades:** BF Approv
043 46187 Mrs O'Kane
Rates fr: *IR£15.00*-**IR£19.00**.
Beds: 2D 1T
Baths: 3 Ensuite

County Louth

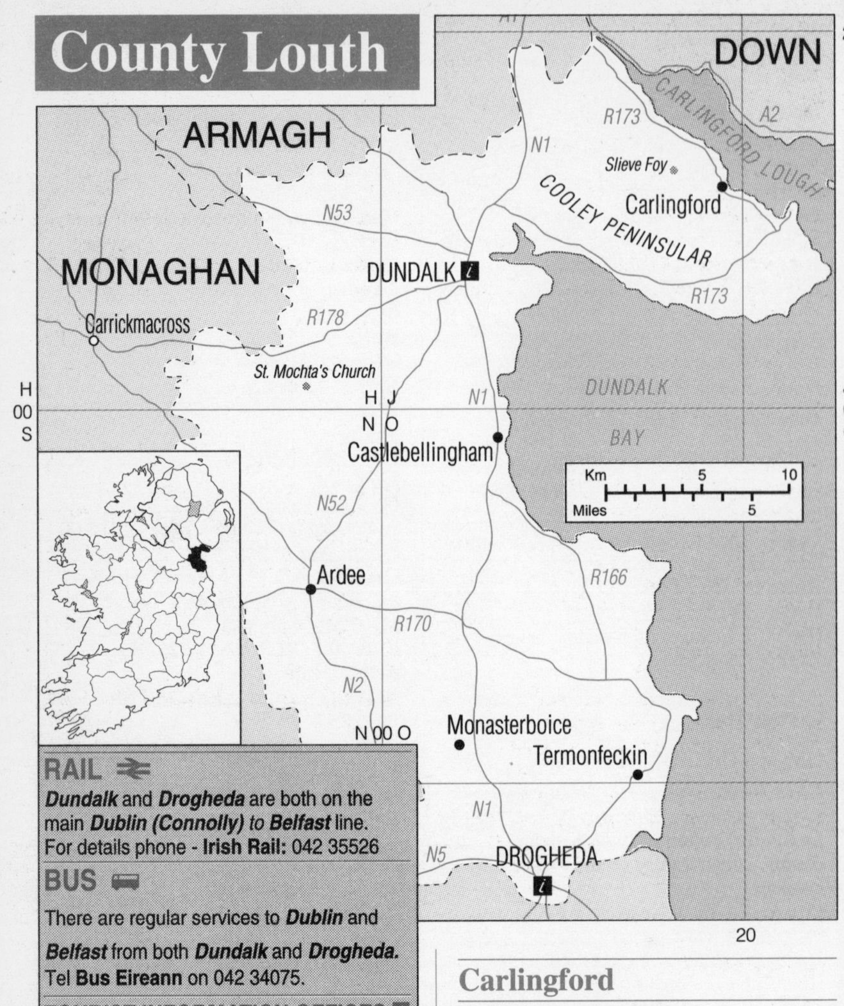

RAIL

Dundalk and ***Drogheda*** are both on the main ***Dublin (Connolly)*** *to* ***Belfast*** line. For details phone - **Irish Rail:** 042 35526

BUS

There are regular services to ***Dublin*** and ***Belfast*** from both ***Dundalk*** and ***Drogheda.*** Tel **Bus Eireann** on 042 34075.

TOURIST INFORMATION OFFICES

Jocelyn St, **Dundalk** (open all year), 042 35484

Ardee

National Grid Ref: N9690

The Gables House, *Dundalk Road, Ardee, Co Louth.*
Converted C18th school.
Open: All Year
Grades: BF Approv, AA 3 St
041 53789 Mr McQuaid
Rates fr: *IR£19.00*-**IR£23.00**.
Beds: 5F 2D 3T
Baths: 1 Ensuite 3 Private 2 Shared
(25)

Carlingford

National Grid Ref: J1811

The Village Hotel, McGees Bistro

Viewpoint Guest House, *Omeath Road, Carlingford, Dundalk, Co Louth.*
Open: All Year (not Xmas)
Grades: BF 3 St
042 73149
Fax no: 042 73733 Mr Woods
Rates fr: *IR£18.50*-**IR£26.00**.
Beds: 1F 5D 2T **Baths:** 8 Ensuite
(9)
Viewpoint motel-style guest house. All rooms ensuite. TV/teamaker every room. Private entrance to each room. Spectacular views. Highly recommended.

Shalom, *Ghan Road, Carlingford, Dundalk, Co Louth.*
Open: All Year (not Xmas)
042 73151
Mrs Woods
Rates fr: *IR£16.00*-**IR£20.00**.
Beds: 2F 3D 1T
Baths: 6 Ensuite 1 Private
(9)
Situated in this medieval town on the sea, overlooked by the Cooley and Mourne Mountains. All rooms TV and tea-making facilities. All ensuite.

Castlebellingham

National Grid Ref: O0695

Spencer House, *Spencerhill, Castlebellingham, Dundalk, Co Louth.*
Open: All Year (not Xmas)
Grades: BF Approv
042 72254
Mr & Mrs Mackin
Rates fr: *IR£18.00*-**IR£23.00**.
Beds: 4D
Baths: 4 Ensuite
(12)
Situated midway between Dublin and Belfast, Spencer House was built in 1777. Attractively furnished in period style, including 4 poster beds. The adjoining courtyard encompasses a working racing and livery yard. 4 double ensuite rooms with central heating. A warm welcome awaits you.

Drogheda

National Grid Ref: O0875

Anchorage Restaurant, Glenside Hotel, Boyne Valley Hotel, Bacchus Restaurant

Faulty Piers, *Smithstown, Drogheda, Co Louth.*
Secluded comfortable bungalow, friendly relaxing atmosphere. Home from home.
Open: Easter to Nov
Grades: BF Approv
041 29020
Mr & Mrs Dunne
Rates fr: *IR£15.00*-**IR£18.00**.
Beds: 1F 3D 1T 1S
Baths: 4 Ensuite 2 Shared
(8)

St Gobnait's, *Dublin Road, Drogheda, Co Louth.*
Rooms ensuite with TV and tea/coffee making facilities. Convenient to town, beaches, railway, bus station and New Grange. **Open:** All Year (not Xmas)
Grades: BF Approv
041 37844 Mrs Lucey
Rates fr: *IR£16.50*-**IR£20.00**.
Beds: 1F 1D 1T **Baths:** 3 Ensuite
(5)

Dundalk

National Grid Ref: J0407

Pinewoods, *Dublin Road, Dundalk, Co Louth.*
Traditional Irish welcome in modern bungalow on main Dublin/Belfast road (N1).
Open: All Year **042 21295**
Mrs Murphy **Rates fr:** *IR£17.00*-**IR£20.00**.
Beds: 1F 3D **Baths:** 4 Ensuite
(5)

Monasterboice

National Grid Ref: O0382

Monasterboice Inn

Tullyesker House, *Monasterboice, Drogheda, Co Louth.*
Large luxury country home. Four acres wooded garden grounds on N1. Extensive breakfast menu.
Open: All Year (not Xmas) **Grades:** AA 4 Q, Select, RAC High Acclaim
041 30430 / 32624 Mrs McDonnell
Rates fr: *IR£18.00*-**IR£32.00**.
Beds: 2F 3D **Baths:** 5 Ensuite
(7) (20)

Termonfeckin

National Grid Ref: O1480

Baltray Golf Club, Seapoint Golf Club, Flyns Pub, Triple House Restaurant

Highfield House, *Termonfeckin, Drogheda, Co Louth.*
Beside two links golf courses (18-hole), the Irish Sea, New Grange, Battle of the Boyne, Monasterboice.
Open: Mar to Sep **Grades:** BF Approv
041 22172 Ms McEvoy
Rates fr: *IR£16.00*.
Beds: 1F 2D **Baths:** 3 Ensuite
(10)

County Mayo

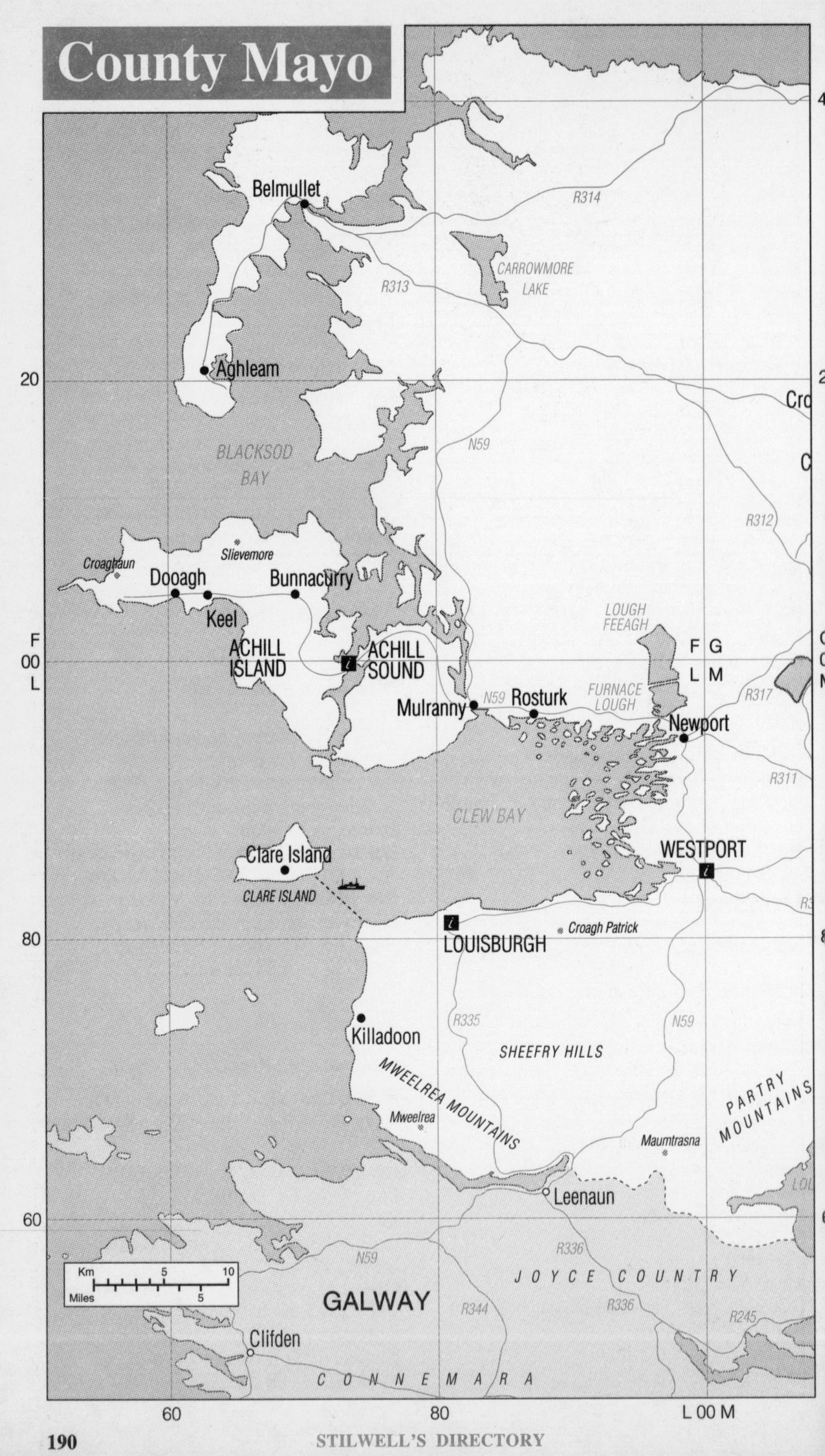

Belmullet
R314
CARROWMORE LAKE
R313
Aghleam
20
N59
BLACKSOD BAY
R312
Croaghaun
Slievemore
Dooagh
Bunnacurry
Keel
LOUGH FEEAGH
ACHILL ISLAND
ACHILL SOUND
F G
L M
F
00
L
Mulranny
N59
Rosturk
FURNACE LOUGH
R317
Newport
R311
CLEW BAY
Clare Island
CLARE ISLAND
WESTPORT
LOUISBURGH
Croagh Patrick
80
R335
N59
Killadoon
SHEEFRY HILLS
MWEELREA MOUNTAINS
PARTRY MOUNTAINS
Mweelrea
Maumtrasna
Leenaun
60
R336
N59
JOYCE COUNTRY
Km 5 10
Miles 5
GALWAY
R344
R336
R245
Clifden
CONNEMARA
60
80
L 00 M

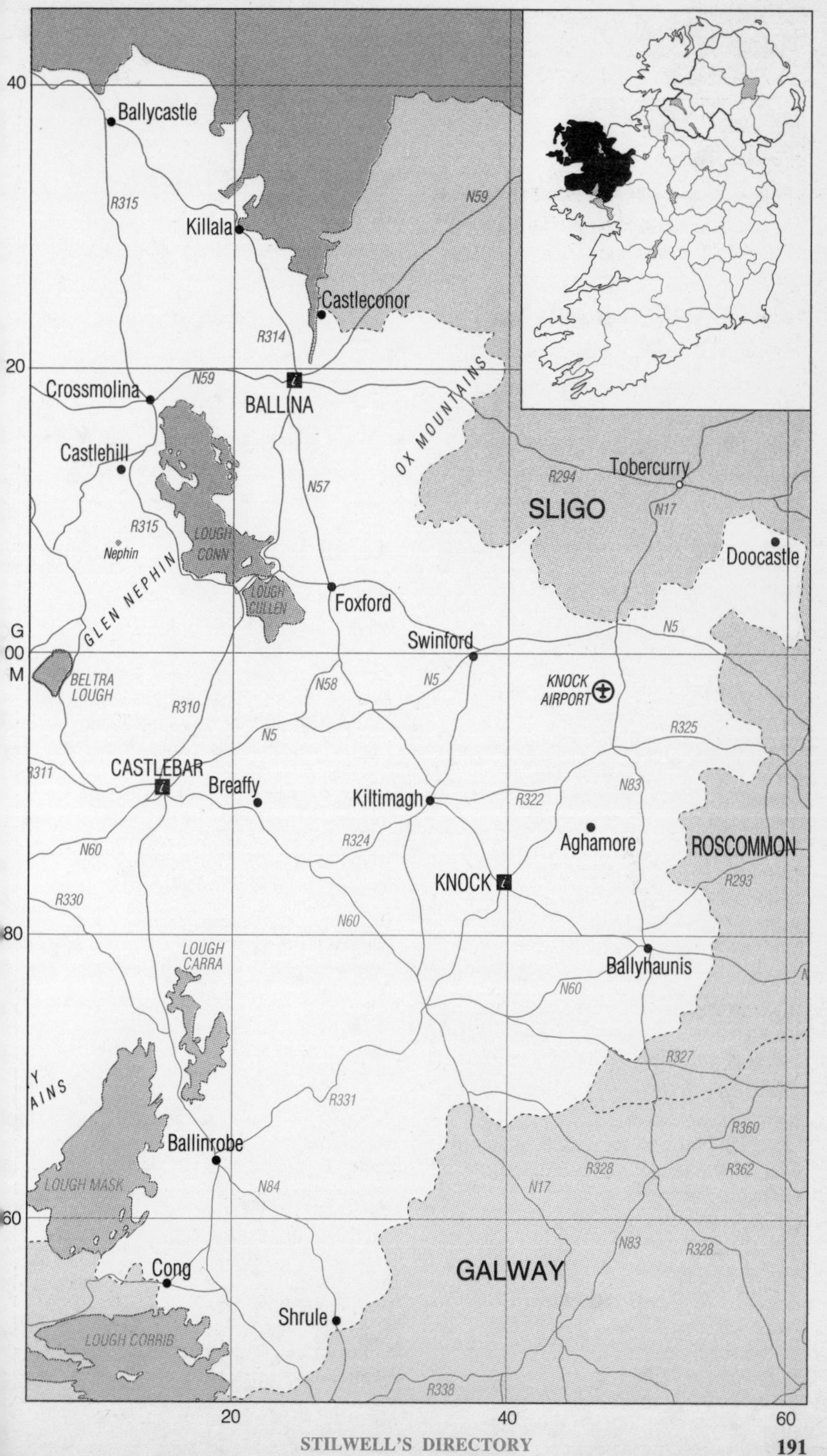
Ballycastle
R315
Killala
N59
Castleconor
R314
Crossmolina
N59
BALLINA
OX MOUNTAINS
Castlehill
N57
R294
Tobercurry
SLIGO
N17
R315
Nephin
LOUGH CONN
Doocastle
GLEN NEPHIN
LOUGH CULLEN
Foxford
N5
Swinford
BELTRA LOUGH
N58
N5
KNOCK AIRPORT
R310
N5
R325
CASTLEBAR
R311
Breaffy
Kiltimagh
R322
N83
Aghamore
N60
R324
ROSCOMMON
KNOCK
R293
R330
N60
LOUGH CARRA
Ballyhaunis
N60
R327
R331
R360
Ballinrobe
LOUGH MASK
N84
R328
N17
R362
N83
R328
Cong
GALWAY
Shrule
LOUGH CORRIB
R338
40
20
G
00
M
80
60
20
40
60

AIRPORTS

Knock Airport - 094 67222

RAIL

Ballina, Castlebar and ***Westport*** are all on lines that go to ***Dublin (Heuston)***. Tel **Irish Rail** (Westport) on 098 25253.

AIR SERVICES & AIRLINES

Knock *to* ***Glasgow, Manchester -***

British Airways (for **Manx Airlines**). In the Republic tel. (freefone): 1800 626747. In Northern Ireland & the UK tel. (local rate): 0345 222111

Knock *to* ***London (Stansted) -***

Ryanair. In the Republic tel. 01 6774422; in the UK tel: 0171 435 7101.

TOURIST INFORMATION OFFICES

Cathedral Street, **Ballina** (Apr to Sep), 096 70848

Castlebar (mid-Apr to mid-Sep), 094 21207

Knock (May to Sep), 094 88193

The Mall, **Westport** (open all year), 098 25711

Achill Island — Achill Sound

National Grid Ref: L7399

Alice's Harbour Inn

Sacre Coeur, *Achill Sound, Achill Island, Westport, Co Mayo.*
Modern comfortable bungalow ideal for touring. Scenic area, near sea.
Open: All Year (not Xmas)
098 45490
Mrs McGinty
Rates fr: *IR£13.50*-**IR£15.00**.
Beds: 2T
Baths: 1 Ensuite 2 Shared
(6)

Achill Island — Bunnacurry

National Grid Ref: F6904

The Grove, *Bunnacurry, Achill Island, Westport, Co Mayo.*
Georgian house in the middle of Achill Island, 50% reduction for children.
Open: Feb to Nov
Grades: BF Approv
098 47108
Mrs McHugh
Rates fr: *IR£14.00*-**IR£14.00**.
Beds: 4F
Baths: 1 Shared

Achill Island — Dooagh

National Grid Ref: F6005

Atlantic Hotel, Boky House

Achill West Coast House, *School Road, Dooagh, Achill Island, Westport, Co Mayo,*
Modern bungalow with panoramic views, ensuite rooms. Ideal base for cycling.
Open: Mar to Nov **Grades:** AA 2 Q
098 43317 (also fax no) Mrs McNamara
Rates fr: *IR£16.00*-**IR£20.00**.
Beds: 1F 1D 1T **Baths:** 2 Ensuite
(12) (5)

Achill Island — Keel

National Grid Ref: F6305

The Chalet, Atlantic Hotel

Achill Isle House, *Newtown, Keel, Achill Island, Westport, Co Mayo.*
Open: Mar to Nov **Grades:** BF Approv
098 43355 Mrs Mangan
Rates fr: *IR£15.00*-**IR£20.00**.
Beds: 4F 1D 1T **Baths:** 6 Ensuite
(2) (12)
Modern purpose-built B&B. Fantastic views overlooking Keel Bay area. Ideal location for painting, golf, hill-walking, sea/lake fishing, relaxing on any of the Blue Flag beaches. Choice of breakfasts. On main bus route. Packed lunches available on request.

Groigin Mor, *Pollagh, Keel, Achill Island, Westport, Co Mayo.*
Bungalow with breathtaking views overlooking the Atlantic and surrounding islands.
Open: All Year
Grades: BF Approv
098 43385
Mrs Quinn
Rates fr: *IR£15.00*-**IR£20.00**.
Beds: 2F 2T
Baths: 3 Ensuite
(6)

Aghamore

National Grid Ref: M4687

Val's

Ard Na Si, *Cartron South, Aghamore, Ballyhaunis, Co Mayo.*
Modern home in peaceful countryside. Home cooking.
Open: All Year (not Xmas)
Grades: BF Approv
0907 30920
Mrs Hunt
Rates fr: *IR£13.00*-**IR£15.00**.
Beds: 1F 1D 2T
Baths: 3 Ensuite
(8)

Aghleam

National Grid Ref: F6220

Bru Clann Lir, *Tirane, Clogher, Aghleam, Belmullet, Ballina, Co Mayo.*
Modern dormer bungalow overlooking Blacksod Bay and Atlantic. Quiet, peaceful.
Open: Easter to Oct
Grades: BF Approv
097 85741 Mrs Geraghty
Rates fr: *IR£16.00*-**IR£18.00**.
Beds: 2F 2D
Baths: 4 Ensuite
(6)

Bringing children with you? Always ask for any special rates.

Ballina

National Grid Ref: G2418

Riverboat Inn, Murphy's, The Old Bond Store, Brogans, Tullios

Brigown, *Quay Road (Coast Road), Ballina, Co Mayo.*
Open: All Year
Grades: BF Approv
096 22609
Fax no: 096 71247 Mrs Nolan
Rates fr: *IR£16.00*-**IR£18.00**.
Beds: 2F 1D 1S
Baths: 3 Ensuite 1 Shared
Experience Irish hospitality when you visit Marjorie Nolan in her Bord Failte Approved home. Rooms ensuite with colour TV, central heating, private carpark, visitors' garden, freezer facilities. Marjorie's love of cooking is experienced from the very extensive breakfast menu - from homemade pancakes to scrambled eggs with smoked salmon.

Ashley House, *Ardoughan, Ballina, Co Mayo.*
Highly recommended: peaceful country surroundings, landscaped gardens, 1 km Ballina Town.
Open: Apr to Oct
Grades: BF Approv
096 22799 Mrs Murray
Rates fr: *IR£16.00*-**IR£21.00**.
Beds: 1F 2D 1T
Baths: 4 Ensuite
(6)

Mount Falcon Castle, *Ballina, Co Mayo.*
Open: Easter to Jan
Grades: BF 1 St
096 21172
Fax no: 096 91517
Rates fr: *IR£33.00*-**IR£43.00**.
Beds: 8D 2T
Baths: 8 Ensuite 2 Private
Once described as a lady who dispenses wine and hospitality in equal measure, Constance Aldridge has run her Victorian castle with relish for over half a century. Huge log fires, quiet relaxation, walking in the surrounding woodlands or alternatively fishing on River Moy.

Belvedere House, *Foxford Road, Ballina, Co Mayo.*
Elegant Georgian stone house.
Open: All Year (not Xmas)
Grades: BF Approv
096 22004 Mrs Reilly
Rates fr: *IR£16.00*-**IR£18.00**.
Beds: 2F 3D 2T 1S
Baths: 4 Ensuite 1 Shared

Moyhaven, *Quay Road, Ballina, Co Mayo.*
Highly recommended friendly accommodation with spectacular views overlooking the salmon-famous River Moy.
Open: Easter to Sep
Grades: BF Approv
096 21715 Mrs Culkin
Rates fr: *IR£15.00*-**IR£20.00**.
Beds: 1F 1D 1T
Baths: 3 Ensuite
(3)

Greenhill, *Cathedral Close, Ballina, Co Mayo.*
Beautiful townhouse situated overlooking famous River Moy.
Open: All Year (not Xmas)
096 22767 Mrs Galvin
Rates fr: *IR£15.00*-**IR£16.00**.
Beds: 2F 2T
Baths: 2 Ensuite
(13) (4)

Riverdale, *Killanley, Castleconnor, Ballina, Co Mayo.*
Country home overlooking River Moy. Salmon and sea trout. Golf beach 4 km.
Open: All Year
096 36570
Mrs Hennigan
Rates fr: *IR£14.00*-**IR£16.00**.
Beds: 2F 1D 1T
Baths: 4 Ensuite

Hogans American House, *Station Road, Ballina, Co Mayo.*
Town centre family hotel near bus and rail stations.
Open: All Year
Grades: BF 2 St
096 21350 Mr Hogan
Rates fr: *IR£15.00*-**IR£16.00**.
Beds: 3F 4D 4T 4S
Baths: 15 Ensuite
(6)

Always telephone to get directions to the B&B - you will save time!

Moy Call, *Creggs Road, Ballina, Co Mayo.*
Modern country house, beside River Moy. Home cooking a speciality.
Open: Easter to Sep
096 22440
Mrs O'Toole
Rates fr: *IR£16.00*-**IR£19.00**.
Beds: 3F 1D
Baths: 3 Ensuite 2 Private
(5)

The Anchorage, *The Quay, Ballina, Co Mayo.*
Overlooking Moy Estuary and woods. Private gardens and parking.
Open: All Year
096 21329
Mrs Dwane
Rates fr: *IR£15.00*-**IR£18.00**.
Beds: 3D 1T
Baths: 4 Private
(4)

Riverdale, *Killanley, Castleconnor, Ballina, Co Mayo.*
Country home overlooking River Moy. Salmon and sea trout. Golf beach 4 km.
Open: All Year
096 36570
Mrs Hennigan
Rates fr: *IR£14.00*-**IR£16.00**.
Beds: 2F 1D 1T
Baths: 4 Ensuite

Whitestream House, *Foxford Road, Ballina, Co Mayo.*
Within walking distance of town and famous River Moy. Hairdryers.
Open: All Year
Grades: BF Approv, AA 3 St
096 21582
Mrs Dempsey
Rates fr: *IR£16.00*-**IR£18.00**.
Beds: 2F 3D 1T
Baths: 5 Ensuite 1 Shared
(2)

Moy House, *Station Road, Ballina, Co Mayo.*
Modern bungalow near train, bus station and famous River Moy (salmon).
Open: All Year (not Xmas)
Grades: BF Approv
096 21781
Mrs Henry
Rates fr: *IR£14.00*-**IR£16.00**.
Beds: 2F 2D 1T
Baths: 4 Ensuite 1 Private
(5)

Ballinrobe

National Grid Ref: M1964

John O'Connor's, Flannery's, Carney's, Railway Hotel.

Friars Quarter House, *Convent Road, Ballinrobe, Co Mayo.*
Open: All Year (not Xmas)
092 41154
Mr & Mrs Kavanagh
Rates fr: *IR£16.00*-**IR£18.00**.
Beds: 1F 1D 2T
Baths: 3 Ensuite 1 Shared
Elegant house in spacious gardens. Period furnishings. 0.75 km from town. Colour TV in rooms, tea-making facilities, breakfast menu. Touring base for Connemara, Ashford Castle, Knock. 18-hole championship golf course. Fishing. Recommended by the *Guide du Routard Irelande*.

Ballycastle

National Grid Ref: G1037

Doonfeeney House, Ceide House

Suantrai, *Ballycastle, Ballina, Co Mayo.*
Olde worlde style cottage incorporating every modern comfort within.
Open: Jun to Aug
Grades: BF Approv
096 43040
Mr & Mrs Chambers
Rates fr: *IR£14.00*-**IR£18.00**.
Beds: 1F 2D
Baths: 3 Ensuite
(4)

Ballyhaunis

National Grid Ref: M5079

Errit, *Carrowbehy, Ballyhaunis, Co Mayo.*
Lakeland District. Coarse and game fishing. Off N60. Knock Airport 5 miles.
Open: Apr to Sep
0907 49015 Mrs Regan
Rates fr: *IR£13.00*-**IR£15.00**.
Beds: 3D 1T
Baths: 1 Private 1 Shared
(8)

Belmullet

National Grid Ref: F2032

Western Strands Hotel, Family Fare Restaurant, Anchor Bar

Drom Caoin, *Ballinavode, Belmullet, Ballina, Co Mayo.*
Open: All Year (not Xmas)
Grades: BF Approv
097 81195
(also fax no) Mrs Maguire-Murphy
Rates fr: *IR£14.50*-**IR£19.00**.
Beds: 1F 2D 1T
Baths: 4 Ensuite
(6)
'Drom Caoin' is where guests experience true 'Irish' hospitality, with splendid sea views over Blacksod Bay and Achill Island. 'Drom Caoin' is the perfect holiday base for sea angling, links golf and quiet exploring of remote uninhabited islands, cliffs and beaches. Cycle storage and fishing tackle room.

Channel Dale, *Ballina Road, Belmullet, Ballina, Co Mayo.*
Modern farmhouse bungalow, by the sea. Panoramic views, spacious gardens.
Open: Easter to Oct
097 81377 Mrs Healy
Rates fr: *IR£14.00*.
Beds: 1F 2D 1T
Baths: 3 Ensuite 1 Private
(8)

The lowest **single** *rate is shown in* **bold.**

The lowest *double* rate per person is shown in *italics*.

***Radharc Na Mara,** Tallagh HIll, Belmullet, Ballina, Co Mayo.*
Modern house on beautiful Mullet Peninsular overlooking Blacksod Bay.
Open: All Year
097 81321 Mrs Horan
Rates fr: *IR£13.00*-**IR£16.00**.
Beds: 3D 2T 1S
Baths: 6 Ensuite
(1) (8)

Breaffy

National Grid Ref: M2089

***Hazelgrove B&B,** Breaffy, Castlebar, Co Mayo.*
Neo-Georgian house 0.5 km off N60 Claremorris Road. Peaceful location.
Open: All Year (not Xmas)
Grades: BF Approv
094 22934 Mrs Keane
Rates fr: *IR£16.00*-**IR£19.00**.
Beds: 2D 1T
Baths: 3 Ensuite 1 Shared

Castlebar

National Grid Ref: M1490

The Davitt Restaurant, Travellers Friend

***Travellers Friend Hotel & Theatre,** Old Westport Road, Castlebar, Co Mayo.*
Open: All Year (not Xmas)
Grades: BF 3 St
094 23111 Fax no: 094 21919
Rates fr: *IR£30.00*-**IR£30.00**.
Beds: 1F 7D 7T
Baths: 15 Ensuite
(10)
This luxury family-run three-star hotel offers ultimate in charm. Warm open log fires welcome you. We enjoy enviable reputation for excellent cuisine, in-house entertainment. Executive-style bedrooms ensuite, direct-dial telephone, 12-channel TV/radio, trouser-press, hairdryer. Disabled, family rooms available.

***Fort Villa House,** Moneen, Castlebar, Co Mayo.*
Lovely Georgian townhouse, own private grounds, modern comfortable and friendly.
Open: All Year (not Xmas)
Grades: BF Approv
094 21002 Mrs Flannelly
Rates fr: *IR£15.00*-**IR£20.00**.
Beds: 1F 2D 2T **Baths:** 5 Ensuite
(10) (10)

***Dun Mhuire,** 5 Quinn's Row, Westport Road, Castlebar, Co Mayo.*
Modern family-run B&B in scenic area convenient to Knock Airport. Fishing, golfing available
Open: All Year (not Xmas)
Grades: BF Approv
094 21395 Mrs Quinn
Rates fr: *IR£13.00*-**IR£18.00**.
Beds: 3D 2T **Baths:** 5 Ensuite
(4) (6)

***Devard,** Westport Road, Castlebar, Co Mayo.*
Bungalow with TV/coffee/tea in bedrooms. Fishing, boats available.
Open: Mar to Nov
094 23462 Mrs Ward
Rates fr: *IR£14.00*-**IR£19.00**.
Baths: 3 Ensuite 1 Shared

***Hazelgrove B&B,** Breaffy, Castlebar, Co Mayo.*
Neo-Georgian house 0.5 km off N60 Claremorris Road. Peaceful location.
Open: All Year (not Xmas)
Grades: BF Approv
094 22934 Mrs Keane
Rates fr: *IR£16.00*-**IR£19.00**.
Beds: 2D 1T
Baths: 3 Ensuite 1 Shared

Castleconor

National Grid Ref: G2624

***Riverdale,** Killanley, Castleconor, Ballina, Co Mayo.*
Country home overlooking River Moy. Salmon and sea trout. Golf beach 4 km.
Open: All Year
096 36570 Mrs Hennigan
Rates fr: *IR£14.00*-**IR£16.00**.
Beds: 2F 1D 1T **Baths:** 4 Ensuite

Castlehill

National Grid Ref: G1112

Hiney's Bar, Crossmolina

Kilmurray House, *Castlehill, Crossmolina, Ballina, Co Mayo.*
Large attractive two-storey farmhouse. Brochure. Farmhouse of Year award.
Open: Apr to Oct
096 31227
Mrs Moffat
Rates fr: *IR£14.00*-**IR£16.00**.
Beds: 3F 1D 1T 1S
Baths: 4 Ensuite 2 Shared

Clare Island

National Grid Ref: L6885

Bay View, *Clare Island, Westport, Co Mayo.*
Family-run hotel situated on the most scenic island off the coast of Ireland.
Open: Easter to Sep
Grades: BF Approv
098 26307
Mr O'Grady
Rates fr: *IR£20.90*-**IR£24.00**.
Beds: 4F 10D

Cong

National Grid Ref: M1555

Lydons Lodge, Danagher's Hotel, Ryans Hotel, Echoes Restaurant

Villa Pio, *Gortacurra Cross, Cong, Claremorris, Co Mayo.*
Open: All Year
Grades: BF Approv
092 46403
Mrs Holian
Rates fr: *IR£15.00*-**IR£18.50**.
Beds: 1F 1D 1T 1S
Baths: 2 Ensuite 2 Shared
(1) (5)
Situated near "Quiet Man" film locations, Ashford Castle, Cong Abbey, Ross Abbey, caves. 5 minutes walk to Moytura House (home of Oscar Wilde) and Lough Corrib boats and fishing. 40 km from Galway and Knock airports. Ideal base for touring Connemara. Bus and taxi service.

Crossmolina

National Grid Ref: G1317

Hineys

Ferngrove, *Leecarrow, Crossmolina, Ballina, Co Mayo.*
Attractive spacious modern farmhouse in quiet country surroundings 1 km from Crossmolina.
Open: Mar to Oct
Grades: BF Approv
096 31346
Mrs Hegarty
Rates fr: *IR£14.00*-**IR£19.00**.
Beds: 2F 1D 1T
Baths: 3 Ensuite 1 Private
(6)

Shalom House, *Gortnor Abbey, Crossmolina, Ballina, Co Mayo.*
Modern country house alongside Lough Conn and Moy for fishing.
Open: All Year (not Xmas)
096 31230
Mrs Cowman
Rates fr: *IR£14.00*-**IR£16.00**.
Beds: 2D 1T
Baths: 2 Ensuite 1 Private 1 Shared

Doocastle

National Grid Ref: G5808

Rossli House, *Doocastle, Tobercurry, Co Sligo.*
Beautiful country home, Irish music, golf, fishing, falconry centre.
Open: All Year
Grades: BF Approv
071 85099
Mrs Donoghue
Rates fr: *IR£14.00*-**IR£16.00**.
Beds: 1F 2D 1T 1S
Baths: 2 Private 2 Shared

Foxford

National Grid Ref: G2703

Scenic Drive, *Pontoon Road, Foxford, Ballina, Co Mayo.*
094 56614
Mr & Mrs Kilcoyne
Rates fr: *IR£14.00*.
Baths: All Ensuite

Killadoon

National Grid Ref: L7474

***Bayside,** Thallabawn, Killadoon, Louisburgh, Co Mayo.*
Modern farmhouse. Beside sea, mountains and Connemara.
Open: Easter to Dec
Grades: BF Approv
098 68613 Mrs Morrison
Rates fr: *IR£14.00*-**IR£14.00**.
Beds: 1F 2D 1T

Killala

National Grid Ref: G2030

Golden Acres Pub, Anchor Bar

***Garden Hill Farmhouse,** Killala, Co Mayo.*
Modern farmhouse in beautiful countryside worked by traditional friendly family.
Open: Mar to Sep **Grades:** BF Approv
096 32331 Mr Munnelly
Rates fr: *IR£15.00*-**IR£18.00**.
Beds: 1F 2D 3T
Baths: 6 Ensuite
(10)

***Avondale House,** Pier Road, Killala, Co Mayo.*
Dormer bungalow on seafront. Recommended in Best B&B Guide.
Open: All Year (not Xmas)
096 32229 Mr Caplice
Rates fr: *IR£13.50*-**IR£14.50**.
Beds: 1F 2D 1T
Baths: 2 Shared

Kiltimagh

National Grid Ref: M3489

Cill Aodain Hotel

***Cill Aodain,** Kiltimagh, Co Mayo.*
Old world hotel. Open fires. Great food. In quiet country town.
Open: All Year (not Xmas)
Grades: BF 2 St
094 81761
Rates fr: *IR£20.00*-**IR£22.50**.
Beds: 1F 7D 7T
Baths: 15 Ensuite
(20)

Knock

National Grid Ref: M3983

Belmont Hotel, Church Field House Hotel

***Windermere,** Churchfield, Knock, Co Mayo.*
Modern farmhouse bungalow in quiet area, within 1 km of Knock Shrine.
Open: Easter to Nov
Grades: BF Approv
094 88326
Mrs Morris
Rates fr: *IR£14.00*-**IR£17.00**.
Beds: 3D 1T
Baths: 1 Ensuite 1 Private
(6)

***Eskerville,** Claremorris, Knock, Co Mayo.*
Modern bungalow, spacious rooms, car park. Central heating. Friendly atmosphere.
Open: Easter to Oct
Grades: BF Approv
094 88413
Mr & Mrs Taaffe
Rates fr: *IR£12.00*-**IR£13.00**.
Beds: 1F 2D 1T 1S
Baths: 2 Ensuite 1 Shared
(1) (8)

Louisburgh

National Grid Ref: L8080

Durkan's, Weir Restaurant, Tavern Restaurant

***The Three Arches,** Askelane, Louisburgh, Westport, Co Mayo.*
Open: May to Sep
Grades: BF Approv
098 66484
Mrs Sammin
Rates fr: *IR£16.00*-**IR£16.00**.
Beds: 1D 2T
Baths: 2 Ensuite
(10)
Modern luxurious bungalow with panoramic view of hills and sea close to sandy beaches. Ideal touring centre for Clare Island, Achill Island, Croagh Patrick and Connemara. Ideal area for fishing and walking.

Rivervilla, *Shraugh, Louisburgh, Westport, Co Mayo.*
Open: Apr to Oct
Grades: BF Approv
098 66246
Miss O'Malley
Rates fr: *IR£14.00*-**IR£14.00**.
Beds: 2F 1D 2S
Baths: 2 Ensuite 3 Shared
(8)
Secluded riverside farmhouse in scenic area. Ideal touring centre for Mayo/Galway. Beaches, mountains, islands, riverside walks, Louisburgh 1 km. Signposted on R335 at Old Head or via Chapel Street, Louisburgh to Rivervilla signs. Travel guides' recommendations. Salmon/sea trout fishing.

Whitethorns, *Bunowen, Louisburgh, Westport, Co Mayo.*
Bungalow in scenic location off R335 opposite Roman Catholic church.
Open: Easter to Sep
098 66062 Mrs McNamara
Rates fr: *IR£16.00*-**IR£21.00**.
Beds: 1F 2D 1T
Baths: 4 Ensuite

Cuaneen House, *Carramore, Louisburgh, Westport, Co Mayo.*
Seaside award-winning farmhouse overlooking Blue Flag beach. Friendly family.
Open: Easter to Nov
098 66460 Mrs Sammon
Rates fr: *IR£14.00*-**IR£14.00**.
Beds: 1F 2D 1T 1S
Baths: 2 Ensuite 1 Private 2 Shared

Mulranny

National Grid Ref: L8296

Moynish House Bar, Campbells Bar

Breezemount B&B, *Mulranny, Westport, Co Mayo.*
Panoramic views of Clew Bay, adjoining golf links. Achill Island 15 km.
Open: All Year (not Xmas/New Year)
098 36145 Mrs Reilly
Rates fr: *IR£14.00*-**IR£19.00**.
Beds: 1F 1D 1T
Baths: 1 Ensuite
(6)

Moynish Guest House, *Mulranny, Westport, Co Mayo.*
Situated on the shores of Clew Bay.
Open: All Year (not Xmas)
Grades: BF 2 St
098 36116 Moran
Rates fr: *IR£15.50*-**IR£18.00**.
Beds: 1F 1D 3T 2S
Baths: 6 Ensuite
(8)

Newport

National Grid Ref: L9894

Black Oak Inn, Anglers Bar, Newport House, Blue Thunder, Walsh's Pub, Kelly's Kitchen Restaurant

Anchor House, *The Quay, Newport, Westport, Co Mayo.*
Quiet residential area overlooking harbour, five minutes walk from town.
Open: Mar to Sep
Grades: BF Approv
098 41178
Fax no: 094 24903
Mrs McGovern
Rates fr: *IR£14.00*-**IR£18.00**.
Beds: 4F 3D
Baths: 5 Ensuite 2 Shared

De Bille House, *Main Street, Newport, Westport, Co Mayo.*
Beautifully restored Georgian house with antique furnishings in Newport Town.
Open: Mar to Oct
Grades: BF Approv
098 41145
Fax no: 098 41777
Mrs Chambers
Rates fr: *IR£16.00*-**IR£18.00**.
Beds: 5F
Baths: 4 Ensuite 1 Private
(8)

Nephin View, *Mulrany Road, Newport, Westport, Co Mayo.*
Family-run B&B on the Western Way and near Bangor Trail.
Open: All Year (not Xmas)
Grades: BF Approv
098 41481
Mr & Mrs Mulchrone
Rates fr: *IR£14.00*-**IR£19.00**.
Beds: 1F 2D 1T 1S **Baths:** 2 Shared
(5)

Rosturk

National Grid Ref: L8796

Rosturk Woods, *Rosturk, Mallarany, Westport, Co Mayo.*
Comfortable welcoming home set in woodland. On sandy seashore of Clew Bay.
Open: All Year (not Xmas)
098 36264 (also fax no)
Mrs Stoney
Rates fr: *IR£18.00*-**IR£20.00**.
Beds: 2D 3T
Baths: 3 Ensuite 1 Shared
(0)

Shrule

National Grid Ref: M2853

Shrule Castle, *Shrule, Galway.*
Georgian house with castle in grounds and a folk life museum.
Open: All Year (not Xmas)
093 31277
Mrs Pitchford
Rates fr: *IR£14.00*-**IR£14.00**.
Beds: 3F 1S
Baths: 3 Shared
(6)

Swinford

National Grid Ref: M3799

Heather Lodge, *Main Street, Swinford, Claremorris, Co Mayo.*
This is an internationally known restaurant and B&B. Our food and accommodation is first class.
Open: All Year (not Xmas)
Grades: BF Approv, AA 2 St
094 52156
Mr Campbell
Rates fr: *IR£18.00*-**IR£20.00**.
Beds: 2F 1D 4T
Baths: 7 Ensuite

High season, bank holidays and special events mean low availability *anywhere.*

Westport

National Grid Ref: M0084

Asgard Bar, O'Malleys, Geraghty's, Ardmore House, The Towers, Grand Central Hotel, Castlecourt Hotel, Sheebeen Bar

Wilmaur, *Rosbeg, Westport, Co Mayo.*
Open: Easter to Oct
Grades: BF Approv, AA 4 Q
098 25784
Fax no: 098 26224
Mrs Printer
Rates fr: *IR£16.50*-**IR£25.00**.
Beds: 3F 1D 1T
Baths: 5 Ensuite
(10)
Spacious and luxurious guest house on the shores of Clew Bay. One mile from award winning pubs and restaurants. Perfect base for exploring Co Mayo. Blue Flag beaches, championship golf course, fishing, sailing, riding, hill walking all nearby.

Woodside, *Golf Course Road, Westport, Co Mayo.*
Modern town house built on historical site in private location.
Open: Mar to Oct
Grades: BF Approv
098 26436
Mrs Hopkins
Rates fr: *IR£16.00*-**IR£25.00**.
Beds: 1F 2D 2T
Baths: 5 Ensuite
(8) (10)

Cedar Lodge, *Kings Hill, Newport Road, N59, Westport, Co Mayo.*
Open: All Year (not Xmas)
Grades: BF Approv
098 25417
Mr & Mrs Flynn
Rates fr: *IR£14.00*-**IR£20.00**.
Beds: 2F 1D 1T
Baths: 3 Ensuite 1 Private 1 Shared
(4) (4)
Smoke-free bungalow. Award-winning mature gardens. 6 minute walk to town, near golf and tennis. Pedestrian walk to seafront. Tea on arrival. Recommended Frommer 'Best B&Bs' Guide. Car park. Vouchers accepted.

Glenderan, *Rosbeg, Westport, Co Mayo.*
Open: Mar to Oct
Grades: BF Approv
098 26585 Mr & Mrs O'Flaherty
Rates fr: *IR£14.00*-**IR£23.00**.
Beds: 1F 2D 2T
Baths: 3 Ensuite
(5)
Luxurious new house on one acre of landscaped gardens. Quiet location off main road on T39/R335 beside harbour within walking distance of pubs, restauants and shops. Bedrooms with satellite, multi-channel TV, tea/coffee facilities for guests. Hairdryers, vouchers & credit cards accepted. Conservatory.

Emania, *Sheeaune, Westport, Co Mayo,*
Impressive two-storey dwelling in own grounds - friendly, hospitable atmosphere.
Open: Jun to Sep
Grades: BF Approv
098 26459 Mrs O'Reilly
Rates fr: *IR£15.00*-**IR£16.00**.
Beds: 1F 1D 1T 1S
Baths: 2 Ensuite 2 Shared
(3) (6)

Hazlebrook, *Deerpark East, Newport Road, Westport, Co Mayo.*
Open: All Year **Grades:** BF Approv
098 26865 / 088 639043 Mrs Cafferkey
Rates fr: *IR£16.00*-**IR£25.00**.
Beds: 3F 2D 1T
Baths: 6 Ensuite
(6)
Luxurious guest house in quiet residential area. Bedrooms with TV and ensuite. Tea/coffee making facilities. Four minutes walk to town centre, ideally situated for touring West Coast. Vouchers and credit cards accepted. Bookings secured with deposit.

Lui Na Greine, *Castlebar Road, Westport, Co Mayo.*
Panoramic views sea, mountain. Spacious landscaped gardens. Private car park.
Open: Easter to Nov
Grades: BF Approv
098 25536 Mrs Doherty
Rates fr: *IR£14.00*-**IR£18.00**.
Beds: 2F 2D 2T
Baths: 4 Ensuite 2 Shared
(4) (7)

Castlecourt House, *Castlebar Street, Westport, Co Mayo.*
Modern, comfortable, lively family run house adjacent (annexe) to adjoining hotel.
Open: All Year
Grades: BF 3 St RAC 3 St
098 25444
(also fax no) Mr Corcoran
Rates fr: *IR£25.00*-**IR£35.00**.
Beds: 16T
Baths: 16 Ensuite
(10)

Riverbank House, *Rosbeg, Westport, Co Mayo.*
Peaceful country home, home baking, walking distance restaurants/pubs. T39/R335.
Open: Easter to Oct
098 25719 Mrs O'Malley
Rates fr: *IR£16.00*-**IR£19.00**.
Beds: 1F 5D 2T
Baths: 6 Ensuite 1 Private
(12)

Rath A Rosa, *Rosbeg, Westport, Co Mayo.*
One storey modern farmhouse with views of sea and mountains.
Open: Easter to Nov
098 25348
Mr & Mrs O'Brien
Rates fr: *IR£16.00*-**IR£22.00**.
Beds: 1F 2D 2T
Baths: 4 Ensuite 1 Shared
(6)

Cul Na Binne, *Leenane Road, Westport, Co Mayo.*
Family home situated at gateway to Connemara. Tea on arrival.
Open: Jun to Sep
098 25670 Mrs O'Keefe
Rates fr: *IR£13.50*.
Beds: 1F 1D 1T
Baths: 2 Ensuite 1 Private
(4)

Ceol Na Mara, *Lower Quay, Westport, Co Mayo.*
Newly constructed two storey house. Close to town and harbour.
Open: All Year (not Xmas)
098 26969 Mrs McGreal
Rates fr: *IR£17.00*-**IR£20.00**.
Beds: 4F 1D 1S
Baths: 4 Ensuite
(8)

County Meath

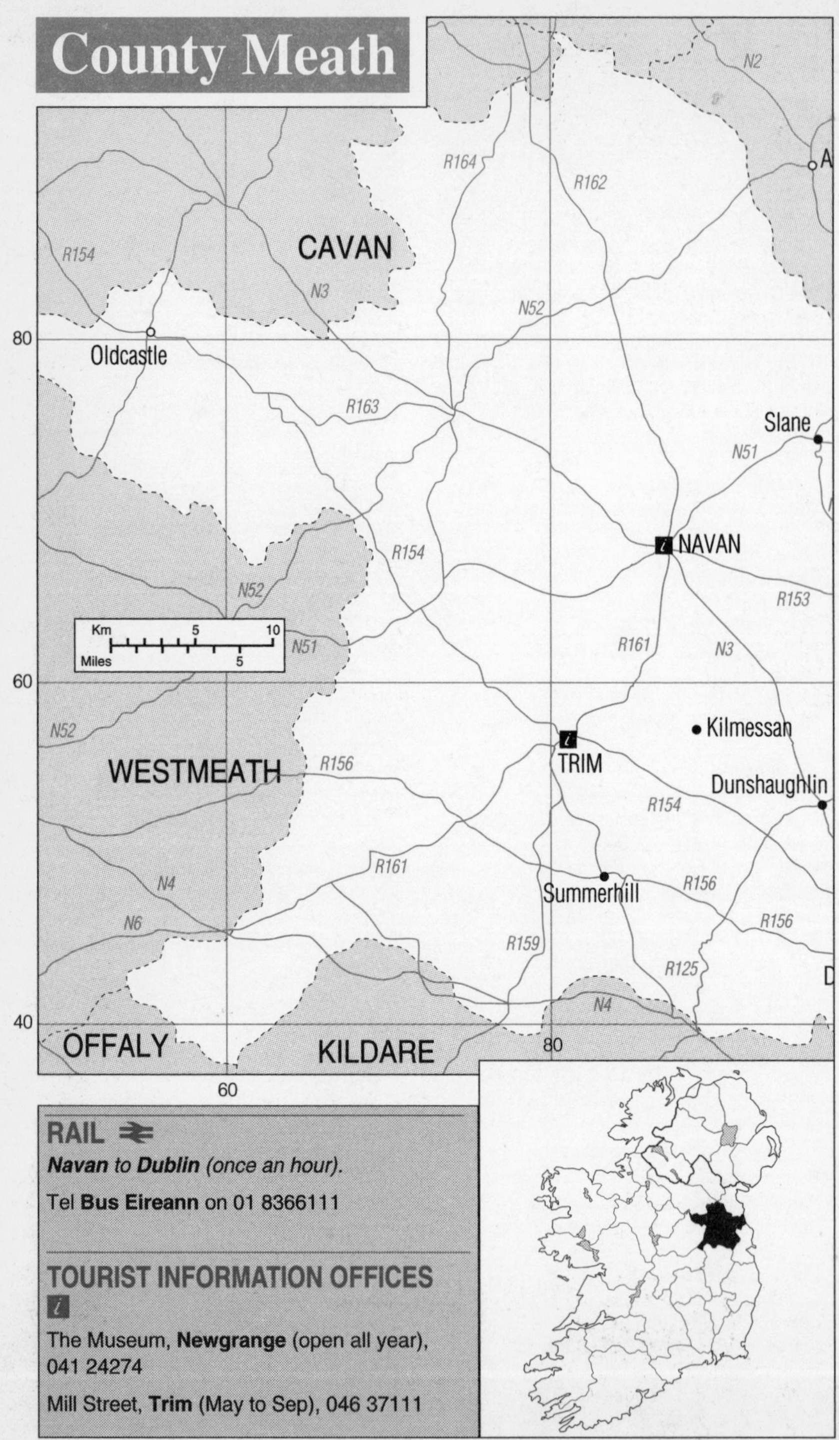

RAIL

***Navan** to **Dublin** (once an hour).*

Tel **Bus Eireann** on 01 8366111

TOURIST INFORMATION OFFICES

The Museum, **Newgrange** (open all year), 041 24274

Mill Street, **Trim** (May to Sep), 046 37111

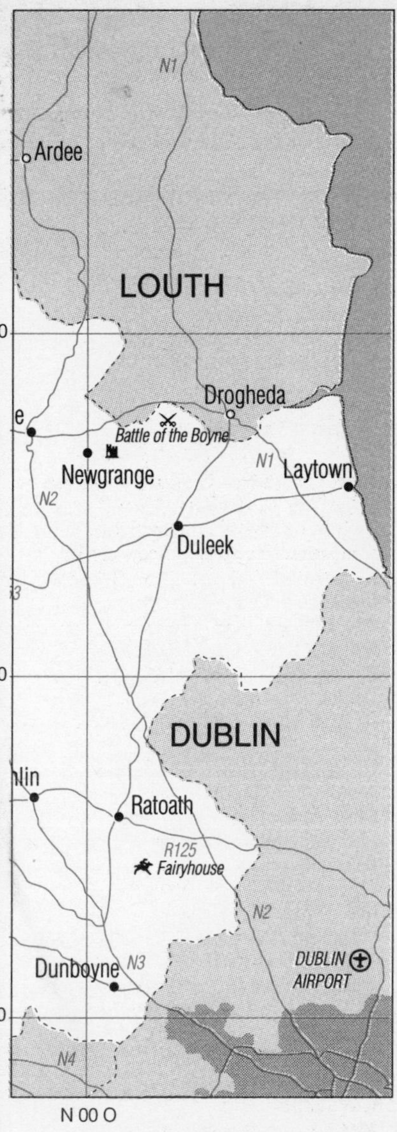

Phoning from outside the Republic?

Dial 00353 and omit the initial '0' of the area code.

Duleek

National Grid Ref: O0468

***Annesbrook,** Duleek, Drogheda, Co Louth.*
Walled garden, secluded woodland setting. Boyne Valley, Tara, Newgrange, Monasterboice.
Open: May to Sep **Grades:** BF Approv
041 23293 Fax no: 041 23024
Ms Sweetman
Rates fr: *IR£25.00*-**IR£32.00**.
Beds: 2F 1D 2T **Baths:** 5 Ensuite
(20)

Dunboyne

National Grid Ref: O0142

Cosy Corner, Country Club, Caffreys

***Cleire,** Paceland, Dunboyne, Co Meath,*
A modern country home. Situated on N3 overlooking beautiful woods and stud farm.
Open: All Year (not Xmas)
Grades: BF Approv
01 8251588 Mrs McCormick
Rates fr: *IR£14.50*-**IR£18.00**.
Beds: 1D 2T **Baths:** 3 Ensuite

Dunshaughlin

National Grid Ref: N9652

The Country Club, Caffreys

***The Old Workhouse,** Ballinlough, Dunshaughlin, Co Meath.*
Open: All Year (not Xmas)
Grades: AA 4 Q, RAC High Acclaim
01 8259251 Ms Colgan
Rates fr: *IR£20.00*-**IR£30.00**.
Beds: 2D 2T
Baths: 2 Ensuite 1 Private 1 Shared
(50)
Striking cut-stone building (c.1840) tastefully restored and furnished throughout with antiques. The atmosphere is welcoming and cooking excellent - don't miss dinner. Ideally situated for touring Boyne Valley, heritage sights and award-winning gardens. Only 17 miles from Dublin on N3.

Killeentierna House, *Powderlough, Dunshaughlin, Co Meath.*
Open: All Year (not Xmas)
01 8259722
Fax no: 01 8250673
Morris
Rates fr: *IR£17.00*-**IR£22.00**.
Beds: 4F
Baths: 4 Ensuite
(8)
Modern comfortable country home in quiet urban location. 5 km Dublin side of Dunshaughlin. N3. Convenient to Dublin Airport 30 minutes. Golf courses easily accessible. Lounge/bar and restaurant five minutes walk away.

Gaulstown House, *Dunshaughlin, Co Meath.*
Award-winning farmhouse in parkland convenient to airport, ferry ports.
Open: Easter to Oct
01 8259147
Mrs Delany
Rates fr: *IR£15.00*-**IR£20.00**.
Beds: 2F 1D 1T
Baths: 2 Ensuite 2 Private

Kilmessan

National Grid Ref: N8957

The Station House, *Kilmessan, Navan, Co Meath.*
Old railway junction incorporating signal box, platforms, ticket office, station-master's house.
Grades: BF 2 St
046 25239
Mr Slattery
Rates fr: *IR£20.00*-**IR£27.00**.
Beds: 2F 6D 2T 2S
Baths: 4 Ensuite 2 Private 6 Shared

Laytown

National Grid Ref: O1671

Tara, *Laytown, Drogheda, Co Louth.*
Comfortable guest house overlooking safe sandy beach.
Open: All Year (not Xmas)
Grades: BF Grade B
041 27239
Rates fr: *IR£13.00*-**IR£13.00**.
Beds: 2F 5D 3T 3S
Baths: 4 Ensuite 9 Shared
(20)

Navan

National Grid Ref: N8667

The Loft Restaurant, Round O, Flathouse Pub, Old Bridge Inn

Raheen, *Trim Road, Navan, Co Meath.*
Luxury bungalow, mature gardens, Navan 2 km, convenient Dublin/ferry-port/airport.
Open: All Year
Grades: BF Approv
046 23791 Mrs Burke
Rates fr: *IR£14.00*-**IR£19.00**.
Beds: 2D 1T 1S
Baths: 2 Ensuite 1 Private 1 Shared
(10) (4)

Lios Na Greine, *Athlumney, Duleek Road, Navan, Co Meath.*
Luxurious family home 1.5 km off N3 on Kentstown/Dubeck/Ashbourne/Airport R153 Road.
Open: All Year
046 28092 Mrs Callanan
Rates fr: *IR£14.00*-**IR£16.00**.
Beds: 3F 1D
Baths: 3 Ensuite

Bloomfield House, *Mooretown (R153), Navan, Co Meath.*
Modern farmhouse residence in archaeological site area, deeply seated in parkland country - convenient to Navan.
Open: All Year
046 23219 Mrs Daly
Rates fr: *IR£14.00*-**IR£19.00**.
Beds: 1F 1D 1T
Baths: 2 Ensuite 1 Private
(6)

Balreask Houe, *Navan, Co Meath.*
Open: Easter to Sep
046 21155
Mrs McCormack
Rates fr: *IR£15.00*-**IR£18.00**.
Beds: 1F 1D 1T
Baths: 2 Shared
(6)

The lowest *double* rate per person is shown in *italics*.

Bringing children with you? Always ask for any special rates.

Boyne Dale, *Slane , Donaghmore, Navan, Co Meath.*
Comfortable warm home with large garden, close to all amenities.
Open: Apr to Oct **Grades:** BF Approv
046 28015 Ms Casserly
Rates fr: *IR£16.00*-**IR£21.00**.
Beds: 2D 1T
Baths: 3 Ensuite
(6)

Newgrange

National Grid Ref: N9674

Poet's Rest, Conyngham Arms

Mattock Houe, *Balfeddock, Slane, Newgrange, Navan, Co Meath.*
Luxury bungalow in the Boyne Valley. Near Newgrange, Knowth, Dowth.
Open: All Year
041 24592 Mrs Gough
Rates fr: *IR£16.00*-**IR£21.00**.
Beds: 1F 1D 1T
Baths: 2 Ensuite 1 Private
(4)

Oldcastle

National Grid Ref: N4886

Ross House

Loughcrew House, *Oldcastle, Co Meath.*
Open: All Year (not Xmas)
049 41356 Fax no: 049 41722
Mr & Mrs Naper
Rates fr: *IR£35.00*-**IR£45.00**.
Beds: 1D 2T
Baths: 3 Private
(10)
A delightful fully modernised country house in an outstandingly beautiful location, ideally situated for rural exploration and touring, sport or relaxation. Offers easy access to countless sites of historic or archaeological interest, varied fishing, horse riding and golf. Just 1 1/4 hour drive from Dublin.

Irish Grid References are for villages, towns and cities - *not* for individual houses.

Ross Castle, *Mountnugent, Oldcastle, Kells, Co Meath.*
Open: Easter to Nov
049 40218 / 40237 Mrs Liebe-Harkort
Rates fr: *IR£18.00*-**IR£23.00**.
Beds: 3F 1D 1S
Baths: 3 Ensuite 2 Shared
(12)
Find exclusive retreat in C16th castle. The trace of ancient history combined with modern comfort. In four double rooms ensuite. Magnificent view over Lough Sheelin. Scenic background of Orvin and Sabrina's love story. Boats, tennis, horse-riding. Sauna and jacuzzi in neighbouring Ross House.

Ratoath

National Grid Ref: O0151

Ryans, Rory's

Pinehill, *Skryne Road, Ratoath, Co Meath.*
Modern comfortable home in ideal location. Situated on the edge of Boyne Valley, Newgrange, Tara, Slane.
Open: Easter to Nov
Grades: BF Approv
01 8256296 Mrs Ryan
Rates fr: *IR£16.00*-**IR£20.00**.
Beds: 1D 2T
Baths: 2 Ensuite 1 Shared
(6)

Please respect a B&B's wishes regarding children, animals & smoking.

Slane

National Grid Ref: N9674

Poet's Rest, Conyngham Arms

***Mattock Houe,** Balfeddock, Slane, Navan, Co Meath.*
Luxury bungalow in the Boyne Valley. Near Newgrange, Knowth, Dowth.
Open: All Year
041 24592
Mrs Gough
Rates fr: *IR£16.00*-**IR£21.00**.
Beds: 1F 1D 1T
Baths: 2 Ensuite 1 Private
(4)

Summerhill

National Grid Ref: N8448

***Cherryfield,** Dangan, Summerhill, Innfield, Co Meath.*
Attractive modern farmhouse set in quiet countryside on R158, all rooms ensuite, home cooking.
Open: Easter to Oct
0405 57034
Mr & Mrs Hughes
Rates fr: *IR£16.00*-**IR£21.00**.
Beds: 4F 1T
Baths: 5 Ensuite
(5)

The lowest **single** *rate is shown in* **bold.**

Trim

National Grid Ref: N8056

Haggard Inn, Wellington Court Hotel

***White Lodge,** New Road, Lackanash, Trim, Co Meath.*
Open: All Year (not Xmas)
Grades: BF Approv
046 36549 (fax no. also)
Mrs O'Loughlin
Rates fr: *IR£14.00*-**IR£18.00**.
Beds: 3F 2D 1T
Baths: 5 Ensuite 1 Shared
(9)
Modern spacious townhouse, rural setting. 500 m town centre/Norman castle - location 'Braveheart' film. Butterstream Gardens. Public telephone. TVs in bedrooms. Friendly welcome assured. Ideal for touring Newgrange, Boyne Valley. Dublin 30 minutes. Airport/ferryport 45 minutes.

***Crannmor,** Dunderry Road, Trim, Co Meath.*
Open: Apr to Sep **Grades:** BF Approv
046 31635 Mrs Finnegan
Rates fr: *IR£16.00*-**IR£21.00**.
Beds: 2F 1D 1T **Baths:** 4 Ensuite
(4)
Peaceful period house, 1.5 km from centre of medieval town. Furnished with antiques. Breakfast menu. Tea/coffee on arrival. Convenient for Dublin sea/airports, also for touring Boyne Valley. Old farm equipment displayed. Locally: golf, swimming, antique/craft shops.

County Monaghan

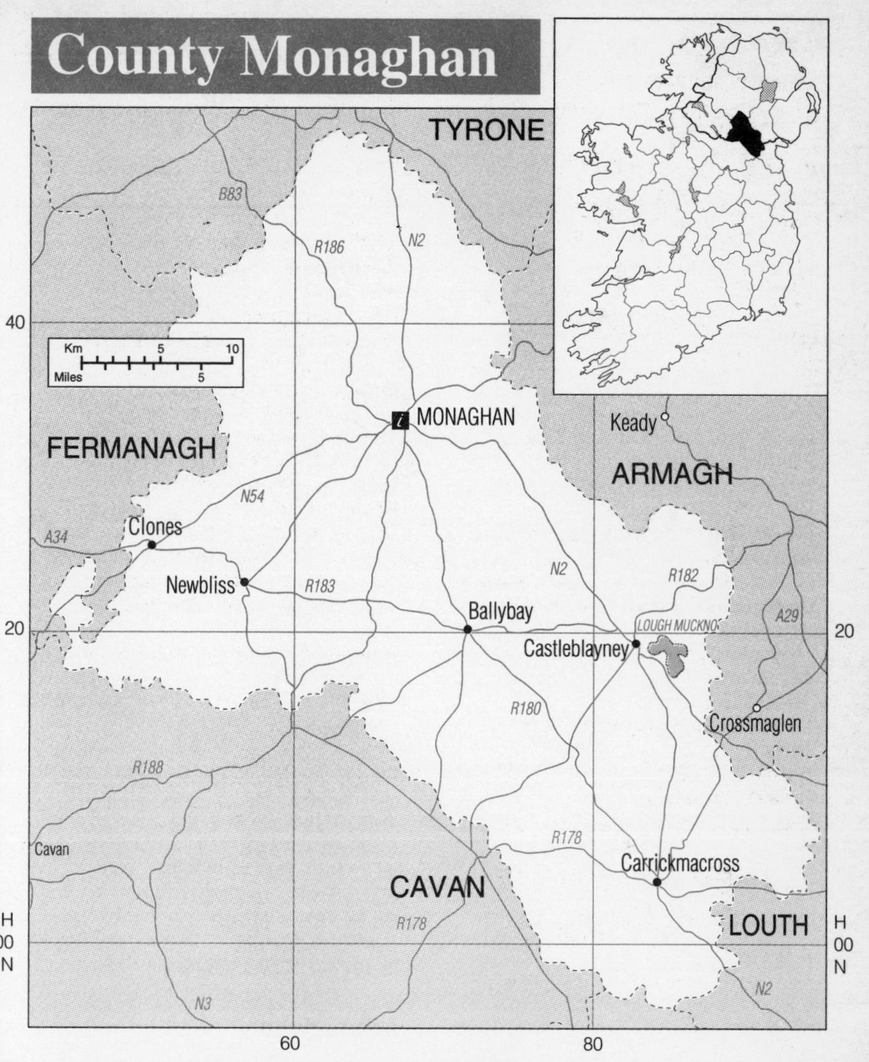

RAIL

Monaghan *to* ***Belfast*** *(7 daily).*
Monaghan *to* ***Dublin*** *(7 daily).*

Tel. Bus Eireann on 01 8366111).

TOURIST INFORMATION OFFICES

Market House, **Monaghan** (open all year), 047 81122

Ballybay

National Grid Ref: H7120

Dromore View House, *Carick Road, Ballybay, Co Monaghan.*
Anglers paradise. Lake and river fishing. Bait can be supplied.
Open: All Year (not Xmas)
042 41466 Mrs Hanley
Rates fr: *IR£14.00*-**IR£16.00**.
Beds: 6T
Baths: 3 Shared
(10)

Carrickmacross

National Grid Ref: H8403

Dun-a-Ri House, Valley Lodge

Arrandale House, *Kingscourt Road, Carrickmacross, Co Monaghan.*
Open: All Year (not Xmas)
Grades: BF Approv
042 61941 (also fax no)
Mrs McMahon
Rates fr: *IR£16.00*-**IR£18.00**.
Beds: 1S
Baths: 7 Ensuite
Arradale House, Carrickmacross, Monaghan. Unique peaceful friendly bedroom ensuite with TV and Teasmade. Lounge with video for all day use. Ideal for golfing, touring, fishing, free boats. Can accommodate large groups.

Shanmullagh House, *Shanmullagh, Carrickmacross, Co Monaghan.*
Convenient to hotel and country club. On one acre of gardens.
Open: All Year
042 63038 Mrs Flanaghan
Rates fr: *IR£15.00*-**IR£18.00**.
Beds: 1D 4T 1S
Baths: 5 Ensuite 1 Shared
(20)

Castleblayney

National Grid Ref: H8219

Glen Carn

Hillview, *Bree, Castleblayney, Co Monaghan.*
Modern dormer bungalow on edge of town. Countryside setting.
Open: Jan to mid-Dec
Grades: BF Approv
042 46217 Mrs Wilson
Rates fr: *IR£12.50*-**IR£14.00**.
Beds: 1F 1D 2T 1S
Baths: 3 Private
(8)

The lowest *double* rate per person is shown in *italics*.

Phoning from outside the Republic? Dial 00353 and omit the initial '0' of the area code.

Clones

National Grid Ref: H5023

Glynch House, *Newbliss, Clones, Monaghan.*
Open: Mar to Oct
047 54045 Fax no: 047 54321
Mrs O'Grady
Rates fr: *IR£15.00*-**IR£20.00**.
Beds: 2F 2T 1S
Baths: 1 Ensuite 1 Private 3 Shared
Listed in Important Houses of Ireland, 200-year-old Georgian house, furnished with antiques. On Clones/Newbliss Road 183. Belfast Airport 56 miles, Dublin 78 miles, Larne 74 miles. Renowned for caring for our guests.

Creighton Hotel, *Fermanagh Street, Clones, Co Monaghan.*
Family-run hotel. Golf, angling available locally. Meals served all day.
Open: All Year (not Xmas)
Grades: BF 1 St
047 51055 Ms McCarville
Rates fr: *IR£18.50*-**IR£18.50**.
Beds: 2F 3D 7T 4S
Baths: 16 Ensuite
(20)

Monaghan

National Grid Ref: H6733

Andys, Four Seasons

Willow Bridge Lodge, *Armagh Road, Monaghan.*
Premises in secluded location with panoramic views over surrounding countryside.
Open: All Year (not Xmas)
Grades: BF Approv
047 81054 (also fax no) Ms Holden
Rates fr: *IR£17.50*-**IR£20.00**.
Beds: 1F 2D 1T
Baths: 2 Ensuite 1 Private 2 Shared
(6)

No. 1, The Corran, *Cooteshill Road, Monaghan.*
New de luxe two storey house. All amenities in walking distance.
Open: All Year (not Xmas)
047 71132
Mrs McNally
Rates fr: *IR£16.00*-**IR£16.00.**
Beds: 2D 1T 1S
Baths: 3 Ensuite 1 Private

Cedars, *Clones Road, Monaghan.*
Split level bungalow overlooking Monaghan Town 1 km. Safe parking.
Open: All Year (not Xmas)
Grades: BF Approv
047 82783
Mrs McArdle
Rates fr: *IR£15.00*-**IR£18.00.**
Beds: 1F 1D 1T
Baths: 2 Ensuite 1 Shared
(8)

Newbliss

National Grid Ref: H5023

Glynch House, *Newbliss, Clones, Monaghan.*
200-year-old Georgian house, furnished with antiques. Renowned for caring for our guests.
Open: Mar to Oct
047 54045
Fax no: 047 54321
Mrs O'Grady
Rates fr: *IR£15.00*-**IR£20.00.**
Beds: 2F 2T 1S
Baths: 1 Ensuite 1 Private 3 Shared

Bringing children with you? Always ask for any special rates.

County Offaly

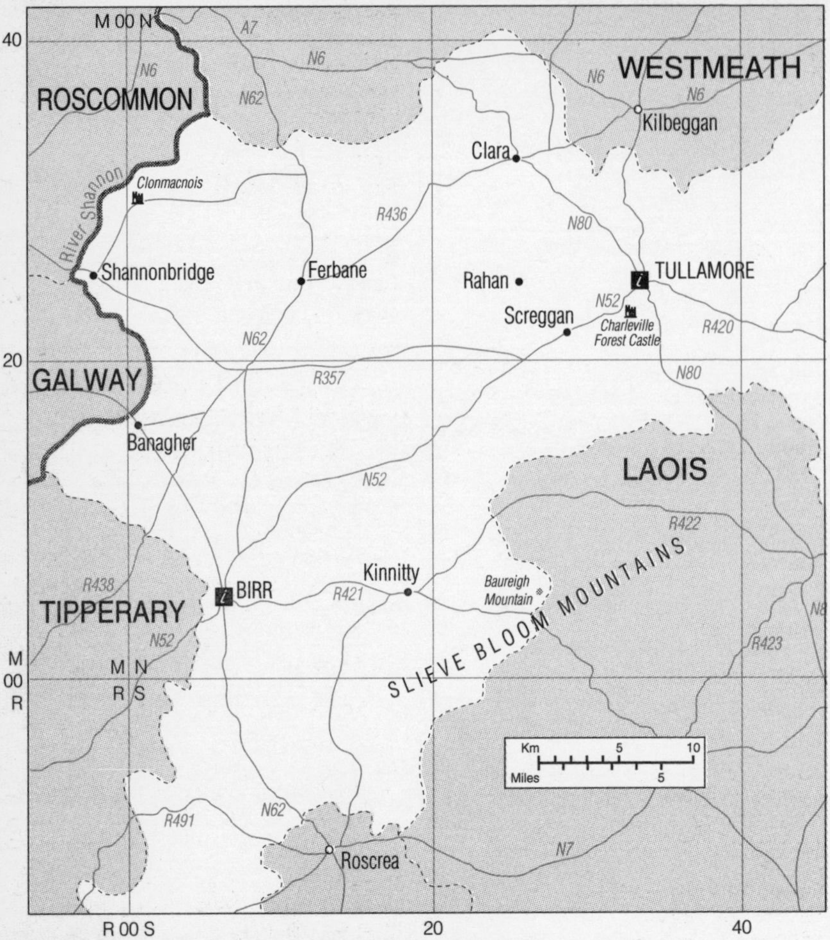

M 00 N
40
A7
N6
N6
ROSCOMMON
N62
N6
WESTMEATH
N6
Kilbeggan
Clara
River Shannon
Clonmacnois
R436
N80
Shannonbridge
Ferbane
Rahan
TULLAMORE
N52
Screggan
Charleville Forest Castle
R420
N62
20
R357
N80
GALWAY
Banagher
LAOIS
N52
R422
SLIEVE BLOOM MOUNTAINS
R438
BIRR
R421
Kinnitty
Baureigh Mountain
TIPPERARY
N52
N8
R423
M
00
R
M N
R S
Km 5 10
Miles 5
N62
R491
Roscrea
N7
R 00 S
20
40

RAIL

Tullamore is on the ***Dublin*** *to* ***Galway*** line.

For timetable details phone **Irish Rail**: 01 8366222.

TOURIST INFORMATION

Tullamore *to* ***Dublin*** (once a day).

Tel **Bus Eireann** on 01 8366111

TOURIST INFORMATION OFFICES

Rosse Row, **Birr** (mid-May to mid-Sep), 0509 20110

Clonmacnoise (Easter to Sep), 0905 74134

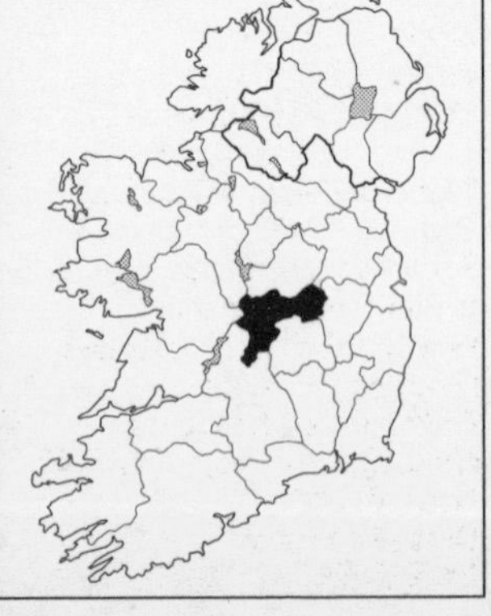

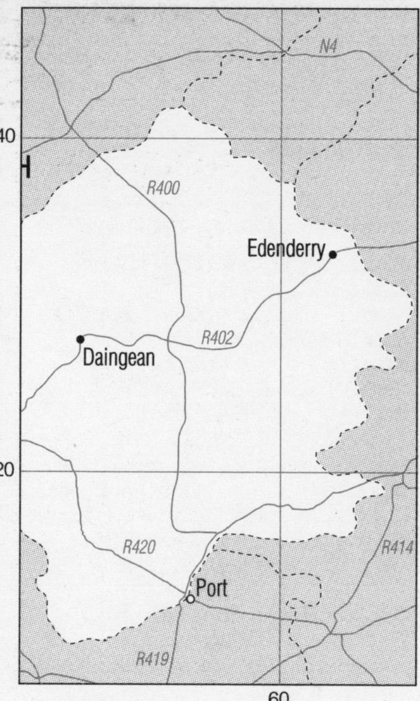

Banagher

National Grid Ref: N0015

The Vineyard

Main Street, Banagher, Birr, Co Offaly, Comfortable, modern, family-run guest house situated in town centre. Four ensuite bedrooms. Evening meals provided.
Open: All Year (not Xmas)
Grades: BF Approv
0509 51360 Mrs Hayes
Rates fr: *IR£15.00*-**IR£18.00.**
Beds: 1F 2D 1T
Baths: 4 Ensuite
(10)

The Old Forge, *West End, Banagher, Birr, Co Offaly.*
Set in the heart of Banagher, 200 m from River Shannon.
Open: All Year (not Xmas)
Grades: BF Approv
0509 51504 Mrs Duthie
Rates fr: *IR£16.00*-**IR£18.00.**
Beds: 1F 2D 1T
Baths: 4 Ensuite

Birr

National Grid Ref: N0504

Rosscrea Road, *Birr, Co Offaly.*
Modern, comfortable farmhouse on N62 set in mature gardens.
Open: All Year
0509 20591 Mrs Minnock
Rates fr: *IR£16.50*.
Beds: 3F 1D 2T **Baths:** 6 Ensuite
(8)

Clara

National Grid Ref: N2532

Bridge House

Eiscir House, *New Rd, Clara, Co Offaly.*
Open: Easter to Sep **Grades:** BF Approv
0506 31413 Mr & Mrs Baggot
Rates fr: *IR£15.00*-**IR£15.00.**
Beds: 1D 1T 1S **Baths:** 3 Ensuite
(8)
Large private house with tennis court and children's playground. Clara is situated on the N80 - the main road from the south-east to the west of Ireland. It also boasts of its famous Bog and Eskers.

Daingean

National Grid Ref: N4727

Beech Lawn House, *Clyduff, Daingean, Tullamore, Co Offaly.*
Georgian house, set in mature gardens. Home cooking our speciality.
Open: Apr to Sep **Grades:** BF Approv
0506 53099 Mrs Smyth
Rates fr: *IR£16.00*-**IR£21.00.**
Beds: 3F 1D 1T **Baths:** 5 Ensuite

Ferbane

National Grid Ref: N1124

Hineys

Daragh, *Ballyclare, Ferbane, Birr, Co Offaly.*
Modern bungalow, ensuite rooms, safe car parking, close to town.
Open: All Year (not Xmas)
Grades: BF Approv
0902 54196 Mrs Mitchell
Rates fr: *IR£14.00*-**IR£14.00.**
Beds: 1D 2T **Baths:** 1 Ensuite 2 Private

Kinnitty

National Grid Ref: N1805

High Pine Farm, *Annaghmore, Kinnitty, Birr, Co Offaly.*
Comfortable farmhouse. D/B/B, lunches and short transfers provided for walkers.
Open: May to Sep **Grades:** BF Approv
0509 37029 Mrs Lalor
Rates fr: *IR£14.00*-**IR£19.00.**
Beds: 1F 1D 1T
Baths: 1 Ensuite 1 Shared
(10)

Rahan

National Grid Ref: N2525

Canal View, *Killina, Rahan, Tullamore, Co Offaly.*
Comfortable rooms. Facilities free: sauna, steamroom, jacuzzi. Pedal, row boating. **Open:** All Year (not Xmas)
Grades: BF Approv
0506 55868 Mrs Keyes
Rates fr: *IR£16.00*-**IR£20.00.**
Beds: 3F 1D **Baths:** 4 Ensuite

Screggan

National Grid Ref: N2921

Shepherds Wood, *Screggan, Tullamore, Co Offaly.*
1930s period secluded country house designed by Michael Scott.
Open: Apr to Sep
Grades: RAC Acclaim
0506 21499
Mr & Mrs MacSweeney-Thieme
Rates fr: *IR£20.00*-**IR£27.00.**
Beds: 3D 1T
Baths: 3 Ensuite 1 Private
(12) (12)

Shannonbridge

National Grid Ref: M9725

Maisies Bar, Village Tavern

The Bungalow, *Riverview, Shannonbridge, Athlone, Co Westmeath,*
Comfortable bungalow with panoramic view of River Shannon. In village.
Open: Easter to Nov
Grades: BF Approv
0905 74180 Mrs Grennan
Rates fr: *IR£14.00*-**IR£19.00.**
Beds: 1F 1D 3T
Baths: 3 Ensuite 2 Shared

Tullamore

National Grid Ref: N3324

Nook & Cranny, The Dragon

Pine Lodge, *Ross Road, Screggan, Tullamore, Co Offaly.*
Open: Feb to Dec **Grades:** AA 4 Q
0506 51927 Mrs Krygel
Rates fr: *IR£22.00*-**IR£27.00.**
Beds: 2D 2T **Baths:** 4 Ensuite
(12) (10)
Award-winning elegant haven in a peaceful, sylvan setting for those who seek total relaxtion. Indoor pool, sauna, steam room, sunbed, massage, reflexology, acupuncture. Table tennis, croquet, bikes. Delicious breakfast menu.

Oakfield House, *Rahan Road, Tullamore, Co Offaly.*
A large family-run guest house in the heart of Ireland.
Open: All Year
0506 21385 Gibbon
Rates fr: *IR£18.00*-**IR£16.00.**
Beds: 2F 3D 2T 4S
Baths: 4 Ensuite 2 Private 3 Shared
(15)

Ballinamona Farm, *Ballinamona, Tullamore, Co Offaly.*
Farmhouse in the centre of Ireland off the N52 near Tullamore.
Open: Easter to Oct
Grades: BF Approv
0506 51162 Mr & Mrs Mealiffe
Rates fr: *IR£15.00*-**IR£17.00.**
Beds: 1F 2D 2T
Baths: 3 Ensuite 1 Shared

Shepherds Wood, *Screggan, Tullamore, Co Offaly.*
1930s period secluded country house designed by Michael Scott.
Open: Apr to Sep
Grades: RAC Acclaim
0506 21499
Mr & Mrs MacSweeney-Thieme
Rates fr: *IR£20.00*-**IR£27.00.**
Beds: 3D 1T
Baths: 3 Ensuite 1 Private
(12) (12)

County Roscommon

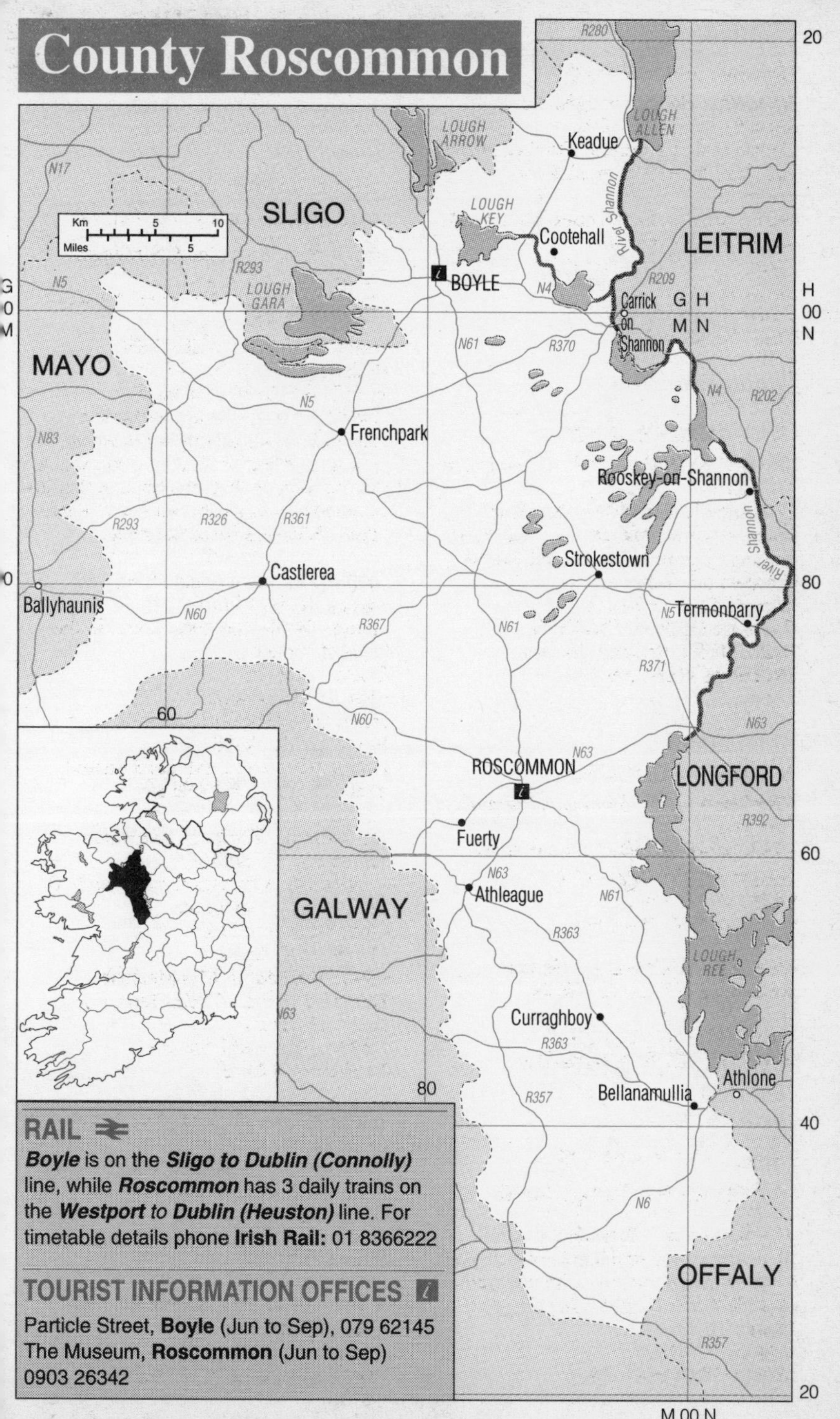

RAIL

Boyle is on the ***Sligo to Dublin (Connolly)*** line, while ***Roscommon*** has 3 daily trains on the ***Westport** to **Dublin (Heuston)*** line. For timetable details phone **Irish Rail:** 01 8366222

TOURIST INFORMATION OFFICES

Particle Street, **Boyle** (Jun to Sep), 079 62145
The Museum, **Roscommon** (Jun to Sep) 0903 26342

Athleague

National Grid Ref: M8357

Bridge House

Fort View House, *Creggs House, Athleague, Roscommon.*
Open: Easter to Oct
Grades: BF Approv
0903 63342 Mrs Galvin
Rates fr: *IR£14.00*-**IR£19.00**.
Beds: 1F 3T

Bellanamullia

National Grid Ref: M9842

The Corn Loft

Woodville, *Monksland, Bellanamullia, Athlone, Co Westmeath.*
Modern comfortable accommodation, 2 km Athlone Town and River Shannon.
Open: Easter to Oct
Grades: BF Approv
0902 94595 Mrs McCam
Rates fr: *IR£16.00*-**IR£18.0**.
Beds: 1D 2T
Baths: 3 Ensuite
(3)

Boyle

National Grid Ref: G8002

Forest Park Hotel, Maloneys Bar

Carnfree Hous, *Dublin Road, Boyle, Co Roscommon.*
Modern house, on the main N4 route. Beside Forest Park Hotel.
Open: All Year (not Xmas)
079 62516 Mrs McGowan
Rates fr: *IR£16.00*-**IR£21.00**.
Beds: 2D 2T
Baths: 4 Ensuite
(3) (6)

Abbey House, *Boyle, Co Roscommon.*
Large Georgian house adjacent Boyle Abbey in beautiful surroundings.
Open: Mar to Oct **Grades:** BF Approv
079 62385 Mr & Mrs Mitchell
Rates fr: *IR£16.00*-**IR£16.00**.
Beds: 1F 4D 1T
Baths: 5 Ensuite
(50)

Castlerea

National Grid Ref: M6779

Williamstown Road, *Castlerea, Co Roscommon.*
Country house on edge of town, in sylvan setting, unspoilt.
Open: All Year (not Xmas)
0907 20431 Mrs Ronane
Rates fr: *IR£12.50*-**IR£14.00**.
Beds: 1F 2D 2T 2S
Baths: 4 Ensuite

Cootehall

National Grid Ref: G9003

Drumharlow Lake Lodge, *Churchill, Cootehall, Boyle, Co Roscommon.*
Modern house with magnificent lake-view and lovely garden.
Open: All Year (not Xmas)
Grades: BF Approv
079 67185 Mr & Mrs Dill
Rates fr: *IR£15.00*-**IR£16.00**.
Beds: 3T **Baths:** 3 Ensuite
(3)

Curraghboy

National Grid Ref: M9248

St Ruth, *Milltown, Curraghboy, Athlone, Co Westmeath.*
Restful farmhouse, idyllic setting, 200 acres, golf, fishing, walking.
Open: All Year
0902 88090 Ms O'Brien
Rates fr: *IR£16.00*-**IR£21.00**.
Beds: 1F 2D 2T
Baths: 5 Ensuite
(10)

Frenchpark

National Grid Ref: M7291

Sheepwalk Inn

Mountview, *Portahard, Frenchpark, Castlerea, Co Roscommon.*
Comfortable family-run modern guest house with excellent views and garden.
Open: All Year (not Xmas)
0907 70016 Mrs O'Gara
Rates fr: *IR£15.00*-**IR£18.00**.
Beds: 2F 2D
Baths: 4 Ensuite
(6)

Fuerty

National Grid Ref: M8162

Golden's Bar

Lisheen House, *Castlecoote, Fuerty, Roscommon.*
River Sheil flows through farm, lakes nearby, lovely village, friendly.
Open: All Year
0903 63367
Mr & Mrs Golden
Rates fr: *IR£16.00*-**IR£20.00**.
Beds: 2D 2T
Baths: 1 Ensuite
(5)

Keadue

National Grid Ref: G9011

Leitrim Inn

Mountain View, *Leitrim, Keadue, Carrick-on-Shannon, Co Leitrim.*
Modern comfortable private bungalow in beautiful tranquil setting beside River Shannon.
Open: All Year (not Xmas)
Grades: BF Approv
078 20859
Mr & Mrs Moffatt
Rates fr: *IR£15.00*-**IR£15.00**.
Beds: 1D 2T
Baths: 3 Ensuite
(6)

Rooskey-on-Shannon

National Grid Ref: N0487

Mount Carmel Guest House, *Rooskey-on-Shannon, Carrick-on Shannon.*
1820 house, set in own private ground with well laid-out lawn by Rooskey Bridge, with lovely walks along the River Shannon.
Open: All Year
Grades: AA 2 Q, RAC Listed
078 38520
Fax no: 078 38434
Mrs Treacy
Rates fr: *IR£24.00*-**IR£20.00**.
Beds: 3T 3S
Baths: 3 Ensuite 3 Private
(10)

Roscommon

National Grid Ref: M8764

Regans

Munsboro House, *Sligo Road, Roscommon.*
Come and treat yourself at Munsboro House - a 150-acre sheep and cattle farm.
Open: Jun to Oct
Grades: BF Approv
0903 26375 Mrs Dolan
Rates fr: *IR£15.00*-**IR£15.00**.
Beds: 2D 2T
Baths: 2 Shared
(14) (20)

Strokestown

National Grid Ref: M9381

Church View House, *Strokestown, Roscommon.*
Old country house in pleasant countryside - central for touring. Historical sites nearby: Strokestown Famine Museum, House and Gardens.
Open: Apr to Oct
078 33047 Mrs Cox
Rates fr: *IR£16.00*-**IR£18.00**.
Beds: 2D 2T 1S
Baths: 2 Ensuite

Termonbarry

National Grid Ref: N0477

Shannonside House Hotel, *Termonbarry, Roscommon.*
Luxurious two-storey residence in picturesque village on banks of River Shannon.
Open: All Year (not Xmas)
Grades: BF 3 St
043 26052 Mr Keenan
Rates fr: *IR£14.50*-**IR£16.50**.
Beds: 2F 2D 3T 3S
Baths: 3 Ensuite 2 Shared

Always telephone to get directions to the B&B - you will save time!

County Sligo

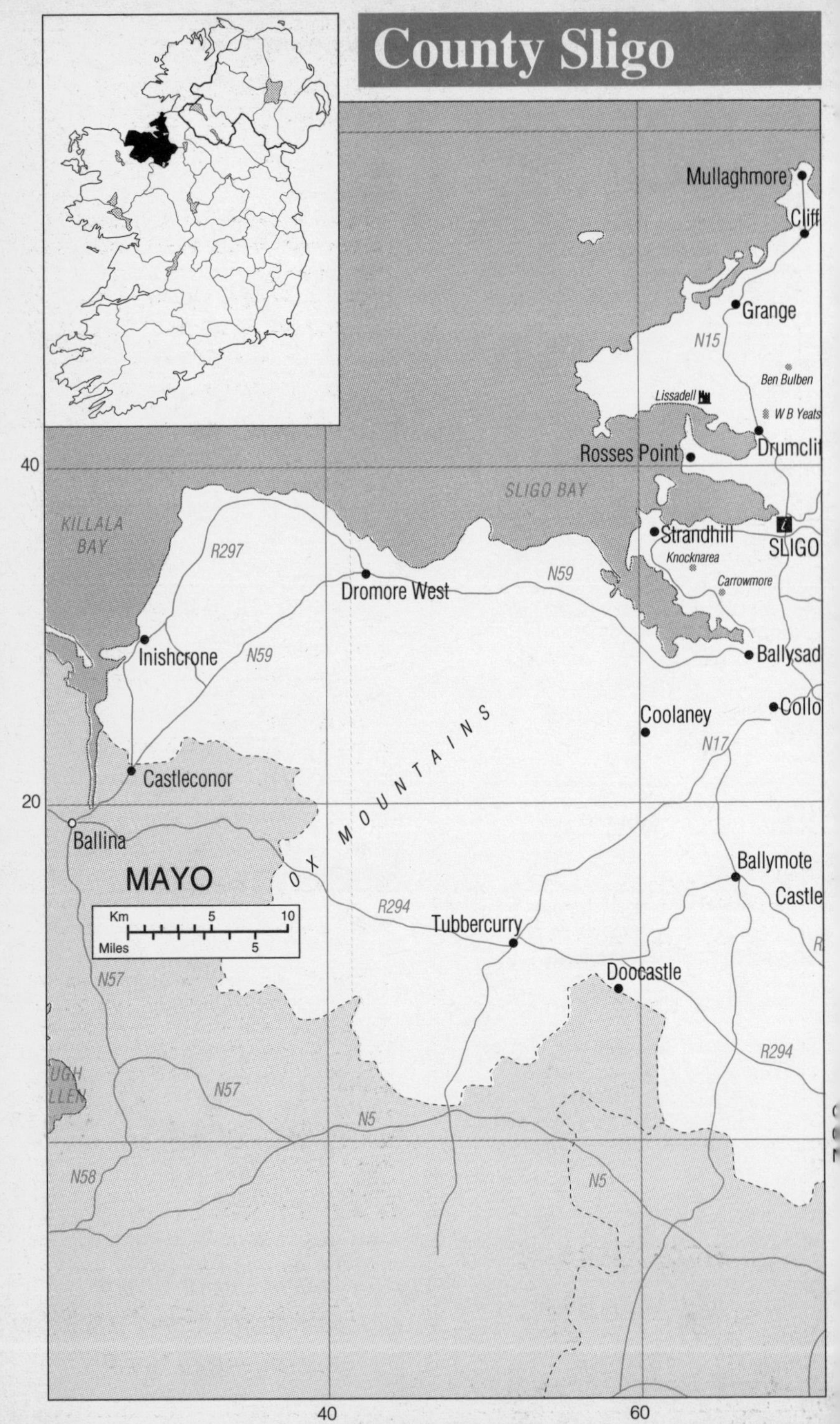

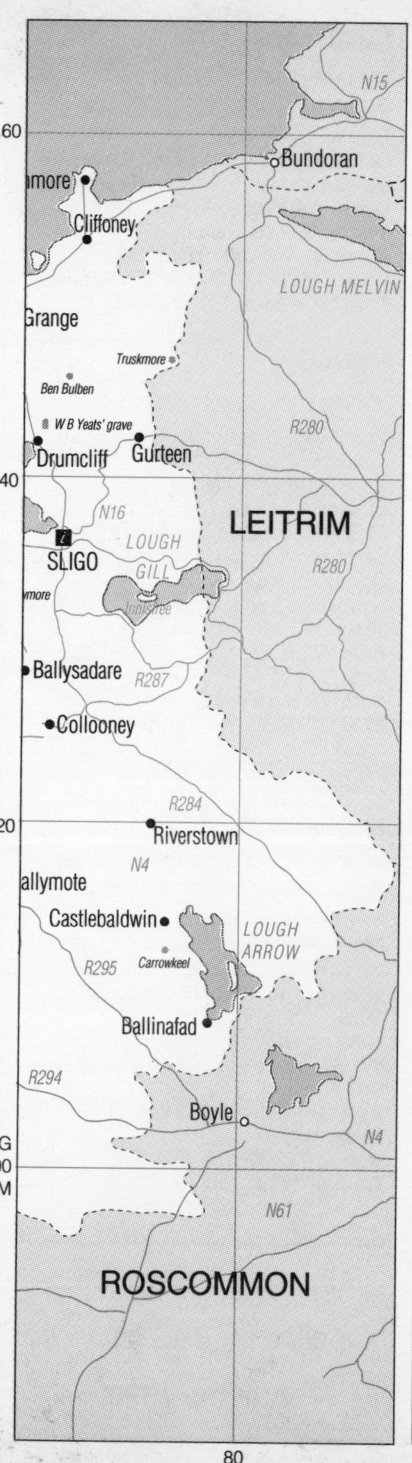

AIRPORT

The nearest international airport is **Knock** (see Co Mayo chapter)

RAIL

Sligo is on the main line to ***Dublin (Connolly)***, via ***Boyle*** and ***Carrick-on-Shannon***.

There are 3 trains daily. For timetable details phone **Irish Rail**: 01 8366222

TOURIST INFORMATION OFFICES

Temple Street, **Sligo** (open all year), 071 61201

Ballinafad

National Grid Ref: G7808

Corrig View Lodge, *Carrowkeel Drive, Ballinafad, Boyle, Co Roscommon.*
Open: Easter to Oct
079 66035 Mrs Duffy
Rates fr: *IR£14.00*-**IR£14.00**.
Beds: 1F 1D
Baths: 1 Ensuite 2 Shared

Ballymote

National Grid Ref: G6615

Stonepark Restaurant

Corran House, *Ballymote, Co Sligo.*
Select home, quiet location, beautiful gardens, golf and heritage sites close by.
Open: All Year (not Xmas)
Grades: BF Approv, AA 3 Q
071 83074
Mrs Hogge
Rates fr: *IR£14.00*-**IR£19.00**.
Beds: 3D 1T
Baths: 4 Ensuite
(5)

The lowest **single** *rate is shown in* **bold.**

Please respect

a B&B's wishes regarding

children, animals

& smoking.

Ballysadare

National Grid Ref: G6629

Thatch Pub, Glebe House

Seashore House, *Lisduff, Ballysadare, Co Sligo.*
Open: Feb to Oct
Grades: BF Approv, AA 3 Q
071 67827 (also fax no)
Mrs Campbell
Rates fr: *IR£15.00*-**IR£13.00**.
Beds: 2F 2D 1T 1S
Baths: 2 Ensuite 1 Shared
(10) (6)
Country home ideally situated for touring Yeats' country, Carromore megalithic tombs. Sample breakfast in our conservatory/dining room with panoramic views of the Ox Mountains and Knocknarea. An eye-catching area for enthusiastic bird-watchers as wildlife is freely visible in its natural habitat.

Castlebaldwin

National Grid Ref: G7513

Tower House, *Castlebaldwin, Boyle, Co Roscommon.*
Modern comfortable farmhouse, excellent view of Lough Arrow, fishing, walking.
Open: All Year (not Xmas)
079 66021 Mrs Gardiner
Rates fr: *IR£14.00*-**IR£16.00**.
Beds: 2F 1T
Baths: 2 Ensuite 1 Shared
(6)

The lowest *double* rate per person is shown in *italics*.

Castleconor

National Grid Ref: G2624

Riverdale, *Killanley, Castleconor, Ballina, Co Mayo.*
Country home overlooking River Moy. Salmon and sea trout. Golf beach 4 km.
Open: All Year
096 36570 Mrs Hennigan
Rates fr: *IR£15.00*-**IR£16.50**.
Beds: 2F 1D 1T **Baths:** 4 Ensuite

Cliffoney

National Grid Ref: G7053

Villa Rosa, *Bunduff, (N15, Donegal Road), Cliffoney P.O., Sligo.*
Chef-proprietor, Dartry Valley, Creevykeel Court Tomb, Mullaghmore/Bunduff Beach/bird sanctuary.
Open: All Year (not Xmas)
Grades: BF Approv, AA 2 Q
071 66173 Mrs McLoughlin
Rates fr: *IR£117.50*-**IR£17.50**.
Beds: 2D 2T 1S
Baths: 4 Ensuite 2 Shared
(10)

Collooney

National Grid Ref: G6727

Markree Castle, Glebe House, Kellys Roadhouse

Markree House, *Collooney, Co Sligo.*
Large luxurious country house. 62 acres sweeping parkland, river, woods.
Open: Apr to Oct
Grades: BF Approv
071 67466 Fax no: 071 69667
Mrs Murray
Rates fr: *IR£18.00*-**IR£23.00**.
Beds: 1F 2D
Baths: 3 Ensuite
(4)

All details shown are as supplied by B&B owners in Autumn 1996.

High season, bank holidays and special events mean low availability *anywhere.*

Coolaney

National Grid Ref: G6025

Mountain Inn, *Rockfield, Coolaney, Co Sligo.*
Olde worlde pub in Ox Mountains. Good food served all day. Guest accommodation.
Open: All Year (not Xmas)
Grades: BF Approv
071 67225 Mr Lipsett
Rates fr: *IR£16.00*-**IR£18.00.**
Beds: 1F 1D 2T
Baths: 1 Ensuite 2 Shared

Doocastle

National Grid Ref: G5808

Rossli House, *Doocastle, Tobercurry, Co Sligo.*
Beautiful country home, Irish music, golf, fishing, falconry centre.
Open: All Year
Grades: BF Approv
071 85099 Mrs Donoghue
Rates fr: *IR£14.00*-**IR£16.00.**
Beds: 1F 2D 1T 1S
Baths: 2 Private 2 Shared

Dromore West

National Grid Ref: G4233

Village Inn, Ocean Hotel

Dromore House, *Dromore West, Ballina, Co Mayo.*
200-year-old Georgian farmhouse on 110-acre dairy farm.
Open: May to Sep **Grades:** BF Approv
096 47018 Mr & Mrs Tully
Rates fr: *IR£16.00*-**IR£13.00.**
Beds: 1F 2D 2T
Baths: 5 Ensuite
(20)

Drumcliff

National Grid Ref: G6742

Laura's, Yeats Tavern, Dartry House

Benbulben Farm, *Barnaribbon, Drumcliff, Sligo.*
Modern farmhouse on slopes of Benbulben Mountain overlooking Yeats Country.
Open: Easter to Oct
Grades: BF Approv
071 63211 (also fax no)
Mrs Hennigan
Rates fr: *IR£15.00*-**IR£18.00.**
Beds: 2F 2D 2T
Baths: 5 Ensuite 1 Shared

Verleen, *Rathcormac, Drumcliff, Sligo.*
Comfortable home in peaceful scenic location. Ideal for visiting Yeats Country.
Open: Easter to Oct
071 43669
Mrs Hackett
Rates fr: *IR£16.00*-**IR£16.00.**
Beds: 1D 2T
Baths: 2 Ensuite 1 Private
(4)

Mountain View, *Drumcliff, Sligo.*
Modern farmhouse in the heart of Yeats country.
Open: Easter to Nov
Grades: AA 3 Q
071 63290
Mrs Murphy
Rates fr: *IR£16.00*-**IR£20.00.**
Beds: 2F 1D 2T
Baths: 3 Ensuite 2 Shared
(6)

Phoning from outside the Republic? Dial 00353 and omit the initial '0' of the area code.

***Thurmore,** Donegal Road, Tully, Drumcliff, Sligo, Co Sligo.*
Situated in Yeats country on N15. Beautiful views, restaurants, beaches, golf, tennis nearby.
Open: Easter to 30th Sept
071 43890
Mrs Feeney
Rates fr: *IR£16.50*-**IR£21.00**.
Beds: 1F 2D
Baths: 2 Ensuite 1Private
(4)

Grange

National Grid Ref: G6649

Yeats Tavern, Dartry House, Willies

***Armada Lodge,** Donegal Road, Mounttemple, Grange, Sligo.*
Open: May to Sept
071 63250 Mrs Brennan
Rates fr: *IR£16.00*-**IR£18.00**.
Beds: 2F 1D 3T
(6)
Beautiful tranquil location overlooking sea/islands/mountains off Donegal Road. Tennis court. Horseriding over miles of sandy beach and mountains. Scenic walks. Boat pier. Boat trips. Golf. Irish music pubs. Seafood restaurants. Tea/coffee facilities. Visa/Mastercard/Amex.

***Rosswick,** Grange, Sligo.*
Tranquil, welcoming, easily accessible family home, surrounded by breathtaking scenery.
Open: Easter to Oct
Grades: BF Approv
071 63516 Mrs Neary
Rates fr: *IR£14.00*-**IR£19.00**.
Beds: 1D 3T
Baths: 1 Ensuite 2 Shared
(2) (3)

Irish Grid References are for villages, towns and cities - *not* for individual houses.

The lowest *double* rate per person is shown in *italics*.

Gurteen

National Grid Ref: G6704

***San Giovanni,** Gurteen, Ballymote, Co Sligo.*
Modern farmhouse situated in peaceful surroundings. Complimentary tea on arrival. **Open:** All Year (not Xmas)
Grades: BF Approv
071 82038 Mrs O'Grady
Rates fr: *IR£14.00*-**IR£16.00**.
Beds: 1D 2T
Baths: 1 Ensuite 1 Shared
(6)

Inishcrone

National Grid Ref: G2830

Alpine Hotel, Harnetts Bar

***Gowan Brae,** Pier Road, Inishcrone, Ballina, Co Mayo.*
Georgian-style home, Enniscrone centre. Panoramic views beach and Killala Bay.
Open: Easter to Nov
096 36396 Mrs Quinn
Rates fr: *IR£16.00*-**IR£20.00**.
Beds: 3F 1D 1T **Baths:** 5 Ensuite
(10)

***Smiths Lodge,** Pier Road, Inishcrone, Ballina, Co Mayo.*
Georgian family-run town house adjacent to beach.
Open: Easter to Oct
Grades: BF Approv
096 36414 Mrs Casey
Rates fr: *IR£15.00*-**IR£18.00**.
Beds: 1F 1D 1T
Baths: 3 Ensuite
(4)

The lowest *double* rate per person is shown in *italics*.

Mullaghmore

National Grid Ref: G7057

Pier Head House, *Mullaghmore, Sligo,* Unique setting in the fishing/seaside resort village of Mullaghmore.
Open: All Year **Grades:** BF 3 St
071 66171 Mr McHugh
Rates fr: *IR£22.00*-**IR£25.00**.
Beds: 8F
Baths: 8 Ensuite

Riverstown

National Grid Ref: G7419

Ross House, *Riverstown, Boyle, Co Roscommon.*
Open: All Year (not Xmas)
071 65140 / 65787 Fax no: 071 65140
Mrs Hill-Wilkinson
Rates fr: *IR£18.00*-**IR£18.00**.
Beds: 2F 1D 1S
Baths: 2 Ensuite 2 Shared
Family residence 1.5 km from Riverstown. 15 km Sligo. Fishing on Lough Arrow & Lough Key. Boats for hire. Swimming, horse riding, golf, walking tours. Excellent home cooking. Open fires. TV.

Rosses Point

National Grid Ref: G6341

Austies

Dormer Lodge, *Rosses Point, Sligo.* Large bungalow in beautiful area close to town and beaches.
Open: Easter to Oct **Grades:** BF Approv
071 43698 Mrs Hopkins
Rates fr: *IR£14.50*-**IR£16.00**.
Beds: 1F 4D 1T
Baths: 3 Ensuite 1 Private

Phoning from outside the Republic? Dial 00353 and omit the initial '0' of the area code.

Please respect a B&B's wishes regarding children, animals & smoking.

Sligo

National Grid Ref: G6936

The Loft Restaurant, Yeats Tavern, Strand Lounge, Ocean View Hotel, The Embassy, Gullivers, Sligo Park Hotel, Blue Lagoon

Realt na Mara, *Sea Road, Sligo.*
Open: March to Oct
Grades: AA 4 Q
071 70838
Mrs Lynch
Rates fr: *IR£16.00*-**IR£21.00**.
Beds: 1F 2D 1T
Baths: 4 Ensuite 1 Private
(0) (6)

Rose Villa, *Breeogue, Knocknahur South, Sligo.*
Open: All Year (not Xmas)
Grades: BF Approv
071 68412
Mrs McCullagh
Rates fr: *IR£15.00*-**IR£19.00**.
Beds: 1F 1D 1T
Baths: 3 Ensuite
(4)
Spacious bungalow in scenic location, 3km off N4. Ideal touring centre near beaches, golf, riding centre and Carrowmore Megalithic Tombs. Nice walking area. Many recommendations.

Lissadell, *Pearse Road, Sligo.* Mature detached townhouse situated five minutes walk from town centre.
Open: All Year (not Xmas)
Grades: BF Approv
071 61937
Mrs Cadden
Rates fr: *IR£16.00*.
Beds: 2D 2T
Baths: 4 Ensuite

'Lar-Easa', *12 Kestrel Drive, Kevensfort, Strandhill Road, Sligo.*
Open: All Year
Grades: BF Approv
071 69313
Fax no: 071 68593 Mr Kilfeather
Rates fr: *IR£15.00*-**IR£20.00**.
Beds: 1F 1D 1T
Baths: 3 Ensuite
(1) (3)
Modern family run B&B set within six acres of parkland 1 km from Sligo. Two minutes drive from bus/train station. Golf, beaches, lakes, forest walks all within a radius of 9 km. We offer salmon fishery rights to Ballisodare River.

Stonecroft (off Donegal Road), *Kintogher, Sligo.*
Peaceful warm home with panoramic views of sea, mountain. N15.
Open: Mar to Nov **Grades:** BF Approv
071 45667 Mrs Conway
Rates fr: *IR£16.00*-**IR£21.00**.
Beds: 1F 2D 1T
Baths: 3 Ensuite 1 Shared
(2) (5)

Aisling, *Cairns Hill, off N4, Sligo.*
Bungalow overlooking Sligo Bay, off N4. Bord Failte, Frommer and AA approved.
Open: All Year (not Xmas)
Grades: AA 3 Q
071 60704 Mr & Mrs Faul
Rates fr: *IR£14.00*-**IR£19.00**.
Beds: 1F 2D 2T
Baths: 3 Ensuite 2 Shared
(5)

Ard Cuilinn Lodge, *Drumiskabole, Sligo.*
On two acres, spacious country home in tranquil scenic surroundings.
Open: Apr to mid-Oct
071 62925 Mrs Carroll
Rates fr: *IR£16.00*. **Beds:** 2F 1D 1T
Baths: 2 Ensuite 1 Private 1 Shared
(3) (4)

All rates are subject to alteration at the owners' discretion.

Right on the border? Look at the neighbouring county, too

Cillard, *Carrowmore, Sligo.*
Highly commended in holiday guides for good food and comfortable accommodation.
Open: Easter to Oct
071 68201 Mrs Dillon
Rates fr: *IR£16.00*-**IR£20.00**.
Beds: 1F 2T **Baths:** 3 Ensuite

Stradbrook, *Pearse Road, Cornageeha, Sligo, Co Sligo.*
Modern comfortable family-run home. Easy access to Yeats country, Donegal, etc.
Open: Easter to Oct
071 69674 Mr & Mrs Noonan
Rates fr: *IR£16.00*-**IR£21.00**.
Beds: 1F 1D 1T
Baths: 3 Ensuite
(0) (4)

Rathnashee Teesan, *Donegal Road, (Teesan) N.15, Sligo.*
Highly recommended. Select, country home. Personal attention. Early reservations essential.
Open: All Year (not Xmas)
071 43376 Mrs Haughey
Rates fr: *IR£14.00*-**IR£18.00**.
Beds: 2D 2T
Baths: 2 Ensuite 2 Shared
(7) (4)

Strandhill

National Grid Ref: G6136

Strand House, Strandhill Golf Club, Ocean View Hotel

Mardel, *Seafront, Strandhill, Sligo.*
Panoramic views Atlantic Ocean and mountains. Overlooking golf course.
Open: Easter to Oct
Grades: BF Approv
071 68295 Mrs Kelly
Rates fr: *IR£15.00*-**IR£18.00**.
Beds: 3D 2T
Baths: 4 Ensuite 1 Private

Green Park House, *Cummeen, Strandhill, Sligo, Co Sligo.*
Quiet secluded setting 3 km Sligo City, off Strandhill, Airport Road.
Open: All Year (not Xmas)
Grades: BF Approv
071 69283 Mrs Mungovan
Rates fr: *IR£15.00*-**IR£20.00**.
Beds: 2D 1T
Baths: 3 Ensuite
(4)

Tubbercurry

National Grid Ref: G5211

Killoran's Traditional Restaurant & Lounge, Cawley's Hotel, Horse Shoe Bar, May Queen, Budgies Bar

Cinraoi, *Ballymote Road, Tubbercurry, Co Sligo.*
Modern bungalow, very near 9-hole golf club. Knock Airport 17 miles.
Open: All Year (not Xmas)
071 85268 Mrs Kennedy
Rates fr: *IR£15.00*-**IR£18.00**.
Beds: 2D 2T
Baths: 2 Ensuite 2 Shared

Bringing children with you? Always ask for any special rates.

Cruckawn House, *Ballymote/Boyle Road, Tubbercurry, Co Sligo.*
Highly recommended family home, where a warm welcome awaits the visitor. Country peacefulness, situated on own grounds.
Open: All Year
Grades: BF Approv, AA 3 Q
071 85188
Mrs Walsh
Rates fr: *IR£IR16.00*-**IR£IR21.00**.
Beds: 2F 1D 2T
Baths: 5 Ensuite
(7)

Always telephone to get directions to the B&B - you will save time!

County Tipperary

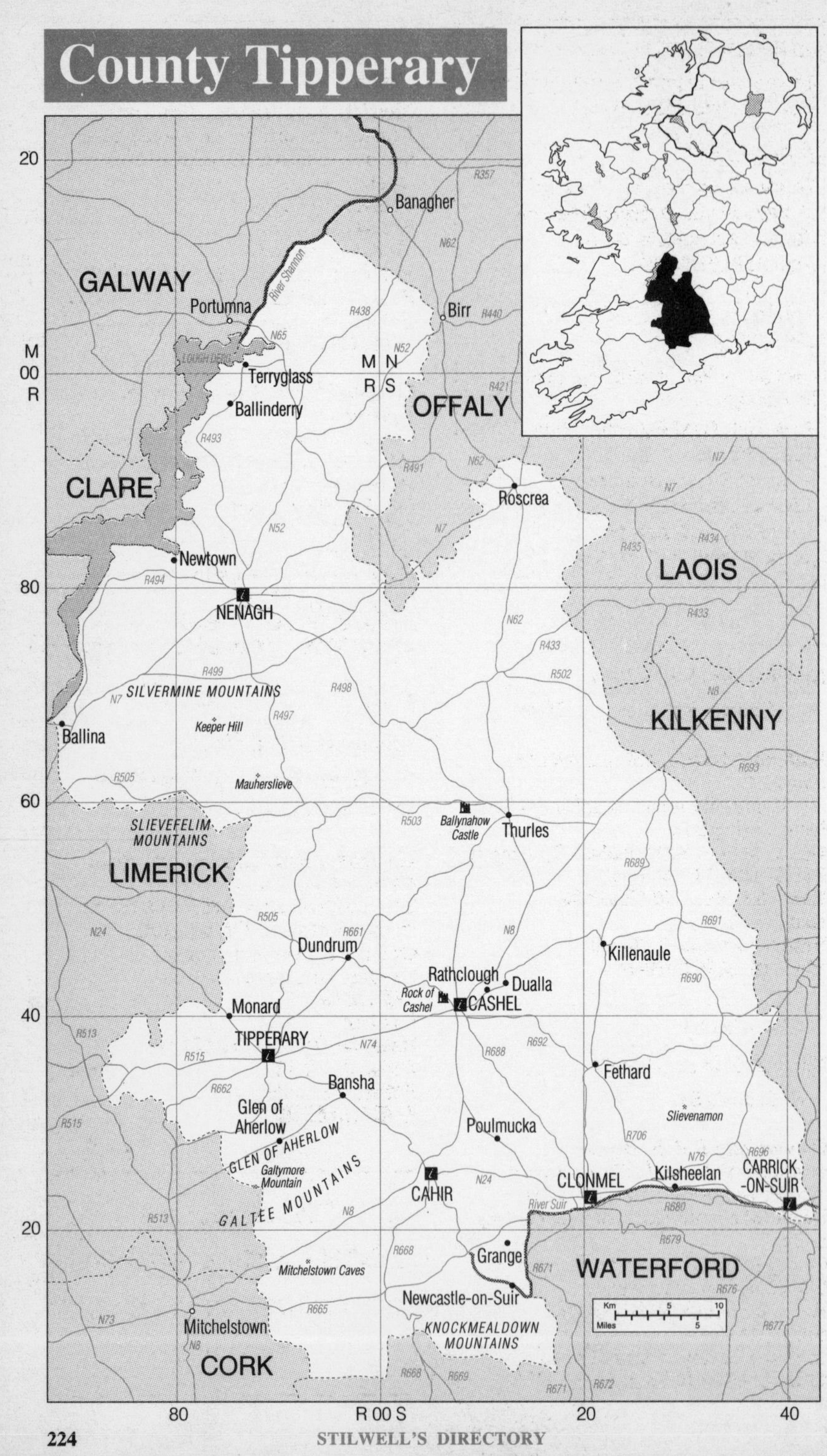

AIRPORTS

The nearest airport is **Shannon Airport** (see Co Clare chapter)

RAIL

Thurles is on the main ***Cork*** and ***Tralee*** line into ***Dublin (Heuston)***. For timetable details phone **Irish Rail:** 01 8366222

TOURIST INFORMATION OFFICES

Castle Car Park, **Cahir** (Apr to Sep), 052 41453
Town Hall, **Cashel** (May to Sep), 062 61133
Sarsfield Street, **Clonmel** (open all year), 052 22960
James Street, **Tipperary** (open all year), 062 51457

Ballina

National Grid Ref: R7073

Goosers Pub, Lakeside Hotel

Rathmore House, *Ballina, Killaloe, Limerick.*
Modern family home, near Lough Derg, ideal touring base.
Open: May to Sep **Grades:** BF Approv
061 379296 Mrs Byrnes
Rates fr: *IR£14.50*-**IR£18.00**.
Beds: 4F 2D
Baths: 4 Ensuite 2 Shared
(1) (8)

Ballinderry

National Grid Ref: R8597

Paddy's Bar

Coolnagatta B & B, *Brocka, Ballinderry, Nenagh, Co Tipperary.*
Timber and brick. Overlooking lake. Beautiful countryside. Irish set dancing nights.
Open: All Year **Grades:** BF Approv
067 22164 Mrs McGeeney
Rates fr: *IR£15.00*-**IR£15.00**.
Beds: 3D 2S
Baths: 3 Ensuite 1 Shared
(8)

Bansha

National Grid Ref: R9533

Bansha Castle, *Bansha, Tipperary.*
Beautiful historic country house set in mature grounds and gardens.
Open: All Year
Grades: BF Approv
062 54187
Mr & Mrs Russell
Rates fr: *IR£18.00*-**IR£23.00**.
Beds: 1F 2D 3T
Baths: 3 Ensuite 1 Private 2 Shared

Cooleen House, *Ardane, Bansha, Tipperary.*
Cooleen House is a modern farmhouse, at the foot of the Galtee Mountains.
Open: Jan to Nov
Grades: BF Approv
062 54392
Mrs Farrell
Rates fr: *IR£14.00*-**IR£14.00**.
Beds: 1F 2D 1T 1S
Baths: 2 Ensuite 2 Shared
(10)

Cahir

National Grid Ref: S0525

Galtee Inn, Castle Court Hotel, Cahir House Hotel

The Homestead, *Mitchelstown Road, Cahir, Co Tipperary.*
Spacious bungalow, near town centre, all rooms ensuite, TV, car-park.
Open: All Year (not Xmas)
Grades: BF Approv
052 42043
Mrs Duffy
Rates fr: *IR£16.00*-**IR£21.00**.
Beds: 1F 2D 1T
Baths: 4 Ensuite
(10)

Please respect
a B&B's wishes regarding
children, animals
& smoking.

Hollymount House, *Upper Cahir Abbey, Cahir, Co Tipperary.*
Country home in peaceful woodlands via mountain road. Walkers paradise.
Open: All Year
Grades: BF Approv
052 41580
Ms Neville
Rates fr: *IR£15.00*-**IR£18.00.**
Beds: 2F 2D 1T
Baths: 2 Ensuite 1 Private 2 Shared
(8)

Silver Acre, *Clonmel Road, Cahir, Co Tipperary.*
Modern dormer bungalow, lovely area, tourism award winner, in quiet cul-de-sac.
Open: All Year (not Xmas)
Grades: BF Approv
052 41737 Mrs O'Connor
Rates fr: *IR£15.00*-**IR£18.00.**
Beds: 3D
Baths: 3 Ensuite
(4) (6)

Carrick-on-Suir

National Grid Ref: S4021

Cedarfield Country House, *Waterford Road, Carrick-on-Suir, Co Tipperary.*
Open: All Year (not Xmas)
051 640164
Fax no: 051 641580
Mrs Eades
Rates fr: *IR£20.00*-**IR£25.00.**
Beds: 2F 2D 1T 1S
Baths: 6 Ensuite
Charming C18th country house set in rolling green countryside. Warm hospitality and good food in delightful surroundings. Excellent wine cellar. Golf, fishing, horse-riding, cycling and walking in locality. Ideal base for touring South-East.

Grand Inn, *Nine Mile House, Carrick-on-Suir, Co Tipperary.*
Former C17th Bianconi inn in scenic valley of Slievenamon (N76 Road).
Open: All Year
Grades: BF Approv, AA 2 Q
051 647035 Mrs Coady
Rates fr: *IR£14.00*-**IR£16.00.**
Beds: 2F 3D 2T 1S
Baths: 3 Ensuite 5 Private
(5)

Irish Grid References are for villages, towns and cities - *not* for individual houses.

Cashel

National Grid Ref: S0740

Hannigans, Baileys Restaurant

Copperfield House, *Cashel, Co Tipperary.*
Open: All Year **Grades:** BF Approv
062 61075 Mrs Courtney
Rates fr: *IR£14.50*-**IR£20.00.**
Beds: 2F 2D 2T
Baths: 6 Ensuite 1 Shared
(10)
Comfortable family home. Walking distance of town. Secure car park. Large garden with view of Rock of Cashel. Credit cards accepted. Tea making facilities and hairdryer in rooms. Comfortable TV lounge. Special diets catered for. Evening meals on request.

Rahard Lodge, *Dually Road, Cashel, Co Tipperary.*
Modern farmhouse overlooking historic Rock of Cashel, on prizewinning gardens. **Open:** March to Nov
062 61052 Mrs Foley
Rates fr: *IR£16.00*-**IR£20.00.**
Beds: 4F 1D 1T
Baths: 5 Ensuite 1 Shared
(12)

Bailey's, *Main Street, Cashel, Co Tipperary.*
Open: All Year (not Xmas)
Grades: BF 2 St
062 61937 Fax no: 062 62038
Rates fr: *IR£14.00*-**IR£17.50.**
Beds: 2F 4D 2T 1S
Baths: 7 Ensuite 2 Shared
(50)
'Baileys', Main St, Cashel, Tipperary. Registered 2 Star Guesthouse. Open all year (except Xmas). Historic Georgian townhouse. Car park, bounded city wall (1360). Licensed restaurant endorsed most good food guides. 8 delightful rooms.

Georgesland B & B, *Dually Road, Cashel, Co Tipperary.*
Open: Mar to Nov **Grades:** BF Approv
062 62788
(also fax no) Mr Joy
Rates fr: *IR£16.50*-**IR£22.00**.
Beds: 1F 3D 2T
Baths: 3 Ensuite 3 Shared
(10)
Modern country home set in peaceful landscaped gardens surrounded by scenic countryside. Secure parking at rear. Orthopaedic beds all rooms. 1 Km from famous Rock of Cashel and Bru Borel Heritage Centre. Ideal base for touring Kilkenny, Waterford, Cork and Limerick.

Palm Grove House, *Dualla Road, Cashel, Co Tipperary.*
Modern bungalow set in landscaped garden and scenic surroundings.
Open: May to Oct **Grades:** BF Approv
062 61739 Mrs Stapleton
Rates fr: *IR£14.50*-**IR£19.50**.
Beds: 2F 2D 1T
Baths: 3 Ensuite 1 Shared
(10)

The Chestnuts, *Dualla Road, Rathclough, Cashel, Co Tipperary.*
Open: Jan to Nov **Grades:** BF Approv
062 61469
(also fax no) Mrs O'Halloran
Rates fr: *IR£17.00*-**IR£17.00**.
Beds: 1F 3D 1T 1S
Baths: 3 Ensuite
Modern luxurious farm bungalow. Highly recommended by many travel agents. 4 km from Rock of Cashel. Frommer and Guide Du Routard Recommended. Golf, fishing, horse riding locally. Country pub within walking distance.

Dualla House, *Kilkenny Road, Dualla, Cashel, Co Tipperary.*
Elegant Georgian farmhouse in peaceful scenic countryside. Highly recommended.
Open: March to Nov
Grades: BF Approv
062 61487
(also fax no) Mrs Power
Rates fr: *IR£15.00*-**IR£20.00**.
Beds: 2F 1D 2T
Baths: 4 Ensuite 1 Private
(0) (10)

Clonmel

National Grid Ref: S2021

Tierneys Bar, Mulcahys, Hearn's Hotel

St Lomans, *The Roundabout, Cahir Road, Clonmel, Co Tipperary.*
Open: All Year (not Xmas)
Grades: BF Approv
052 22916
Mrs O'Callaghan
Rates fr: *IR£14.00*-**IR£15.00**.
Beds: 2F 1D 1T
Baths: 1 Ensuite 1 Private 1 Shared
(3)
Small family run guest house in a quiet area, located in an urban area, 15 minutes walk from town centre, prize winning gardens, complimentary tea and coffee served at night.

Edermine House, *Fethard Road, Rathronan, Clonmel, Co Tipperary.*
Spacious bungalow in rural surroundings. Close to equestrian centre.
Open: Jan to Nov
Grades: BF Approv
052 23048
Mrs Cox
Rates fr: *IR£14.00*-**IR£19.00**.
Beds: 1F 1D 2T 1S
Baths: 2 Ensuite 1 Private 2 Shared

Hill Crest, *Powerstown Road, Clonmel, Co Tipperary.*
Pleasant semi-detached house, quiet suburban area within 5 minutes walking distance town centre.
Open: All Year
052 21798
Mr & Mrs O'Reilly
Rates fr: *IR£14.00*-**IR£15.00**.
Beds: 5F 4D 1T
Baths: 2 Ensuite 1 Private
(7) (2)

Phoning from outside the Republic?
Dial 00353 and omit the initial '0' of the area code.

***Amberville,** Glenconnor Road, Clonmel, Co Tipperary.*
Spacious modern bungalow set in own attractive gardens, rural area 0.5 km from town centre.
Open: All Year (not Xmas)
Grades: BF Approv, RAC Listed
052 21470 Mrs Whelan
Rates fr: *IR£14.00*-**IR£16.00.**
Beds: 1F 1D 2T 1S
Baths: 3 Ensuite 2 Shared
(6)

Dualla

National Grid Ref: S1243

***Dualla House,** Kilkenny Road, Dualla, Cashel, Co Tipperary.*
Elegant Georgian farmhouse in peaceful scenic countryside. Highly recommended.
Open: March to Nov
Grades: BF Approv
062 61487
(also fax no) Mrs Power
Rates fr: *IR£15.00*-**IR£20.00.**
Beds: 2F 1D 2T
Baths: 4 Ensuite 1 Private
(0) (10)

Dundrum

National Grid Ref: R9745

Golden Vale

***Cappamurra House,** Dundrum, Tipperary.*
300-year-old farmhouse. Furnished accordingly. Home baking. Warm welcome. Horse riding.
Open: Apr to Nov **Grades:** BF Approv
062 71127 Mr & Mrs Grene
Rates fr: *IR£15.00*-**IR£20.00.**
Beds: 2F 1D 1T
Baths: 3 Ensuite
(10)

Glen of Aherlow

National Grid Ref: R9030

***Ballinacourty House,** Glen of Aherlow, Tipperary.*
Open: Feb to Nov
062 56230 Mr & Mrs Stanley
Rates fr: *IR£14.00*-**IR£19.00.**
Beds: 1F 2D 1T **Baths:** 3 Ensuite

Grange

National Grid Ref: S1218

Tierney's Bar

***Loughryan,** Grange, Clonmel, Co Tipperary.*
Victorian farmhouse set in nature gardens. Fishing/golf close by.
Open: Jun to Oct **Grades:** BF Approv
052 38176 Mrs Hanrahan
Rates fr: *IR£13.00*-**IR£15.00.**
Beds: 1F 1D 1T
Baths: 1 Ensuite 1 Shared
(1) (10)

Killenaule

National Grid Ref: S2246

***Ardagh House,** Main Street, Killenaule, Thurles, Co Tipperary.*
Fully licensed guest house central to golfing and historic sites.
Open: All Year (not Xmas)
Grades: BF 2 St
052 56224 Mr Cormack
Rates fr: *IR£14.00*-**IR£16.00.**
Beds: 1F 3D 2T
Baths: 6 Ensuite
(2) (5)

Kilsheelan

National Grid Ref: S2823

***Nagels Bar,** Kilsheelan, Clonmel, Co Tipperary.*
Modern bar and accommodation in scenic area, adjacent to River Suir and mountains. 35 minutes from sea.
Open: All Year
Grades: BF Approv
052 33496 Mr & Mrs Gleeson
Rates fr: *IR£15.00*-**IR£18.00.**
Beds: 3D 1T
Baths: 4 Ensuite
(20)

High season, bank holidays and special events mean low availability *anywhere.*

Monard

National Grid Ref: R8439

Chaer O'Brien

Ballyran House, *Monard, Tipperary.*
200-year-old farmhouse. Private garden. Good touring centre.
Open: Easter to 1st Oct
062 47790 Mrs Ryan
Rates fr: *IR£16.00*-**IR£18.00.**
Baths: 2 Ensuite

Nenagh

National Grid Ref: R8779

Cass Ryan's Bar, Dan Larkin's

Ashley Park House, *Nenagh, Co Tipperary.*
C18th mansion. Lakeside, wildlife sanctuary. Beautiful peaceful surroundings, boating, fishing.
Open: All Year
Grades: BF Approv
067 31474 Fax no: 067 38236
Mr & Mrs Mounsey
Rates fr: *IR£18.00*-**IR£20.00.**
Beds: 2F 4D
Baths: 2 Ensuite 1 Shared
(20)

Curraghbawn House, *Lake Drive, Newtown, Nenagh, Co Tipperary.*
Spacious period residence on Lough Derg Way. Lake boat available.
Open: All Year (not Xmas)
Grades: BF Approv
067 23226 Mrs O'Callaghan
Rates fr: *IR£14.50*-**IR£16.50.**
Beds: 3F 1T
Baths: 1 Ensuite 1 Private 1 Shared
(8)

Williamsferry House, *Fintan Lawlor Street, Nenagh, Co Tipperary.*
Built 1830. Newly refurbished. Comfortable, spacious. Ideal base for touring.
Open: All Year
Grades: BF Approv
067 31118 Mr & Mrs Devine
Rates fr: *IR£16.00*-**IR£19.00.**
Beds: 2F 2D 2T
Baths: 6 Ensuite
(10)

Newcastle-on-Suir

National Grid Ref: S1214

Kilmaneen Farmhouse, *Newcastle-on-Suir, Clonmel, Co Tipperary.*
Old farmhouse tucked beneath the mountains. Miles from nowhere! Home cooking. Rivers Suir and Tar flow through farm. Free fishing.
Open: Easter to Oct
Grades: BF Approv
052 36231 Mrs O'Donnell
Rates fr: *IR£16.00*-**IR£20.00.**
Beds: 1F 1D 1T
Baths: 3 Ensuite
(4) (5)

Newtown

National Grid Ref: R8081

Cass Ryan's Bar, Dan Larkin's

Curraghbawn House, *Lake Drive,, Newtown, Nenagh, Co Tipperary.*
Spacious period residence on Lough Derg Way. Lake boat available.
Open: All Year (not Xmas)
Grades: BF Approv
067 23226 Mrs O'Callaghan
Rates fr: *IR£14.50*-**IR£16.50.**
Beds: 3F 1T
Baths: 1 Ensuite 1 Private 1 Shared
(8)

Poulmucka

National Grid Ref: S1127

Tierneys Bar

Farrenwick, *New Inn Road, Poulmucka, Curranstown, Clonmel, Co Tipperary.*
Open: All Year (not Xmas)
Grades: BF Approv, AA 3 Q
052 35130 Fax no: 052 35377
Mr & Mrs Fahey
Rates fr: *IR£14.00*-**IR£15.00.**
Beds: 3F 1D
Baths: 3 Ensuite 1 Shared
(9)
Modern bungalow set in own attractive gardens. Golfing, fishing, hill walking, pony-trekking, horse/dog racing, heritage sites all closeby. Welcome tray on arrival. All rooms have TV, telephone. Fax/e-mail and other facilities on request. Ideal base for touring.

Rathclough

National Grid Ref: S1042

***The Chestnuts,** Dualla Road, Rathclough, Cashel, Co Tipperary.*
Open: Jan to Nov
Grades: BF Approv
062 61469 (also fax no)
Mrs O'Halloran
Rates fr: *IR£17.00*-**IR£17.00.**
Beds: 1F 3D 1T 1S
Baths: 3 Ensuite
Modern luxurious farm bungalow. Highly recommended by many travel agents. 4 km from Rock of Cashel. Frommer and Guide Du Routard Recommended. Golf, fishing, horse riding locally. Country pub within walking distance.

Roscrea

National Grid Ref: S1389

Racket Hall Hotel, Waterfront Cafe, Tower Restaurant, White House Restaurant

***Derryvale House,** Dublin Road, Roscrea, Co Tipperary.*
Open: April to Oct
Grades: BF Approv
0505 21429 Ms Powell
Rates fr: *IR£15.00*-**IR£15.00.**
Beds: 2F 1D 1T 1S
Baths: 2 Private 1 Shared
Beautiful Georgian country home in own grounds. Situated on N7 at foot of Slieve Bloom Mountains in Ely O'Carroll Heritage Country. Overlooking 18-hole golf course, fishing, canoeing, horse riding, hill walking available locally. Great breakfasts. Welcoming 'cuppa' on arrival. Hotel nearby.

***Racket Hall,** Dublin Road, Roscrea, Co Tipperary.*
Family-run hotel adjoining 18 hole golf course. Bar/restaurant/grill.
Open: All Year (not Xmas)
0505 21748 Daly
Rates fr: *IR£22.50*-**IR£25.00.**
Beds: 3D 4T 3S
Baths: 10 Ensuite

***Cregganbell,** Birr Road, Roscrea, Co Tipperary.*
Spacious bungalow, quiet location, golf, fishing, forest walks, electric blankets.
Open: All Year (not Xmas)
Grades: AA 3 Q
0505 21421 Mrs Fallon
Rates fr: *IR£14.00*-**IR£16.00.**
Beds: 2D 2T **Baths:** 3 Ensuite
(8)

Silvermines

National Grid Ref: R8471

***Sancta Maria,** Silvermines, Nenagh, Co Tipperary.*
Comfortable, family-run home in scenic village **Open:** All Year
Grades: NITB Approv
067 25281 Mrs Horan
Rates fr: *£11.00*-**£12.00.**
Beds: 1F 1D 1S **Baths:** 1 Shared
(3)

Terryglass

National Grid Ref: M8600

Paddy's Bar

***Riverrun House,** Terryglass, Nenagh, Co Tipperary.*
Open: All Year (not Xmas)
Grades: BF Approv, AA 3 Q
067 22125 Fax no: 067 22187
Mrs Sanders
Rates fr: *IR£22.50*-**IR£27.50.**
Beds: 3D 3T
Baths: 6 Ensuite
(10)
Relax in Riverrun, south facing garden, in the heart of Terryglass, a stroll away from the busy harbour on the Shannon. Tennis court, bicycles, fishing boats, warm welcome, fresh flowers, log fires. Recommended by major guides.

***Tir Na Fiuise,** Terryglass, Nenagh, Co Tipperary.*
A wonderful experience in a quiet and tranquil setting, you won't want to leave!
Open: Easter to Oct
Grades: BF Approv
067 22041 (also fax no)
Mr & Mrs Heenan
Rates fr: *IR£20.00*-**IR£20.00.**
Beds: 1F 1D 1T
Baths: 3 Ensuite
(6)

Coolnagatta B&B, *Brocka, Ballinderry, Terryglass, Nenagh, Co Tipperary.*
Timber and brick. Overlooking lake. Beautiful countryside. Irish set dancing nights.
Open: All Year
Grades: BF Approv
067 22164 Mrs McGeeney
Rates fr: *IR£15.00*-**IR£15.00**.
Beds: 3D 2S
Baths: 3 Ensuite 1 Shared
(8)

Thurles

National Grid Ref: S1258

Culin, *Templemore Road, Thurles, Co Tipperary.*
Modern spacious family home. Ground floor accommodation. Homemade food. Welcome guaranteed.
Open: Feb to Nov
0504 23237 Mrs Cavanagh
Rates fr: *IR£14.00*-**IR£16.00**.
Beds: 1F 2D 1T
Baths: 2 Ensuite 1 Private 1 Shared
(1)

Tipperary

National Grid Ref: R8935

Derby Bar

Villa Maria, *Limerick Road, Bohercrowe, Tipperary, Co Tipperary.*
Modern bungalow on Waterford to Limerick Road (N24). Family run.
Open: Jun to Sep
Grades: BF Approv
062 51557 Mrs O'Neill
Rates fr: *IR£14.50*-**IR£18.50**.
Beds: 1F 1D 1T
Baths: 1 Ensuite 1 Private 1 Shared

Purt House, *Emly Road, Bohercrowe, Tipperary, Co Tipperary.*
Modern home. Traditional Irish night arranged. Beautiful countryside, Irish welcome.
Open: All Year (not Xmas)
062 51938 Mrs Collins
Rates fr: *IR£16.00*-**s19.00**.
Beds: 2F 2D 2T
Baths: 5 Ensuite 5 Private 1 Shared
(12)

County Waterford

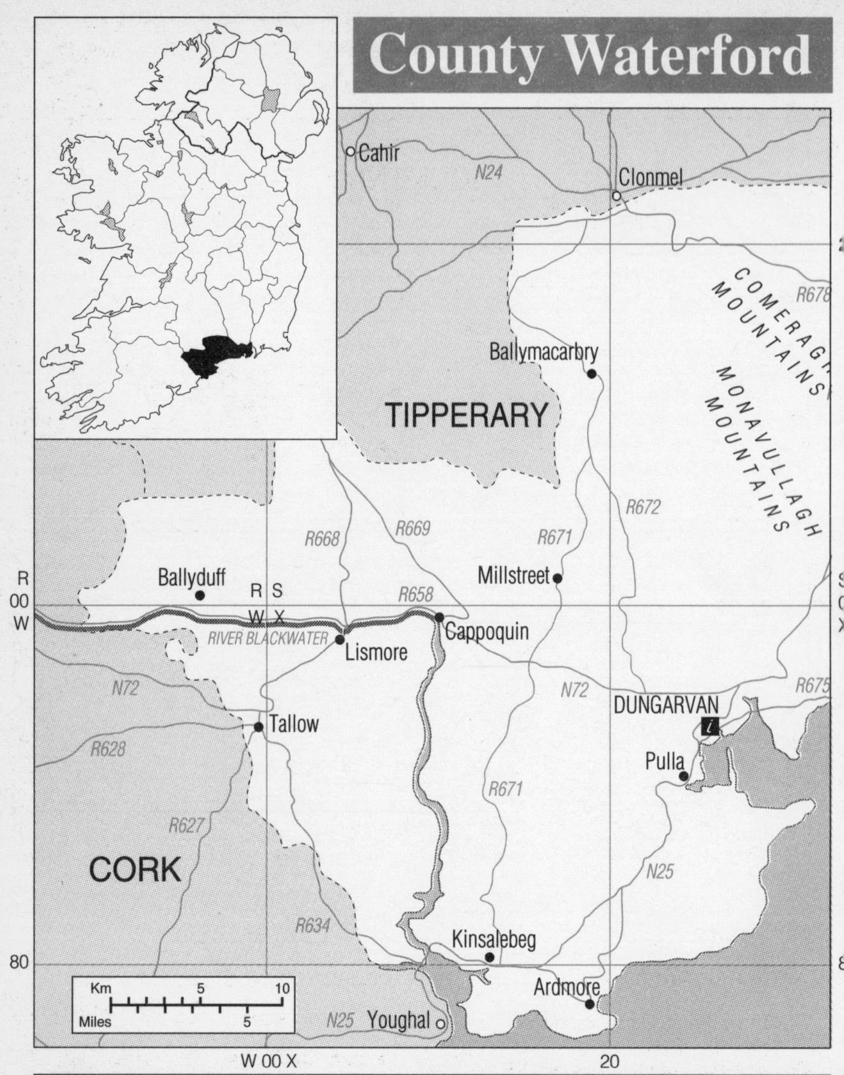

AIRPORT

The nearest international airport is at **Cork** (see Co Cork chapter).

RAIL

Waterford is on the main lines to ***Dublin (Connolly)***, ***Limerick Junction*** and ***Rosslare***.

For timetable details phone **Irish Rail:** 01 8366222

BUS

Waterford *to* ***Dublin*** *(8 daily).*
Tel **Bus Eireann** on 01 8366111

TOURIST INFORMATION OFFICES

Dungarvan (mid-Jun to Aug), 058 41741

Railway Square, **Tramore** (mid-Jun to Aug), 051 381572

41 The Quay, **Waterford** (open all year), 051 75788

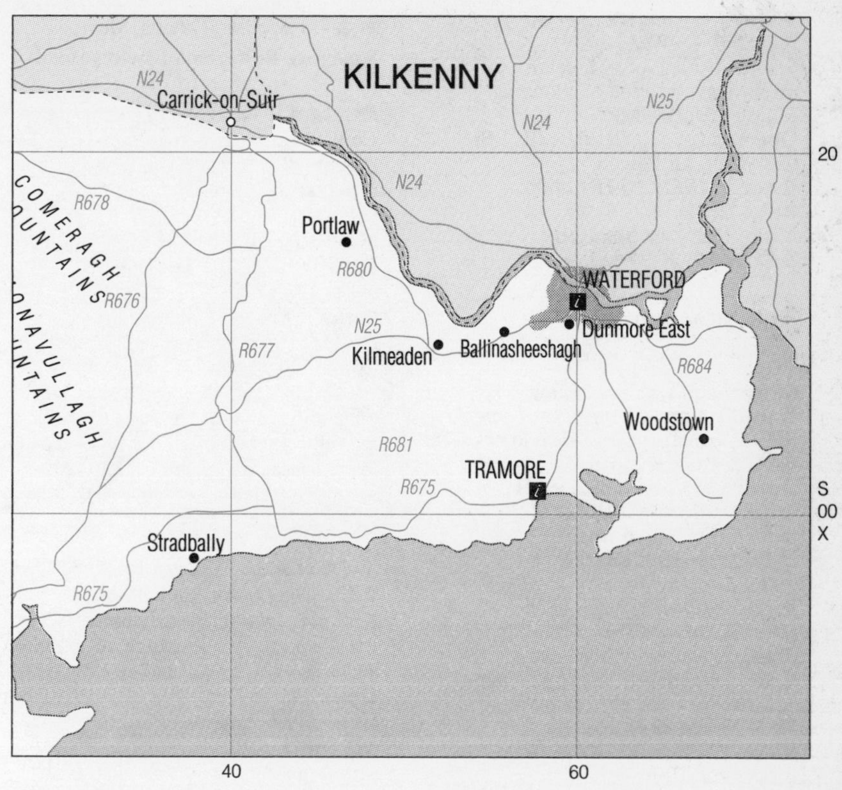

Ardmore

National Grid Ref: X1877

Newtown View, *Grange, Ardmore, Youghal, Co Cork.*
Open: Easter to Oct **Grades:** BF Approv, AA 3 Q, RAC Listed
024 94143 / 088 600799
Fax no: 024 94143 Mrs O'Connor
Rates fr: *IR£15.00*-**IR£20.00**.
Beds: 3F 2T 1S
Baths: 6 Ensuite
(8)
Come and relax at Newtown View farmhouse. A working dairy farm situated just off Rosslare/N25 between Dungarvan/Youghal. Lovely unspoilt countryside combine comfort. Award winning dishes. Cliff walks, sandy beaches, fishing and golf. All rooms ensuite. TV and tea-making facilities.

Ballinaneeshagh

National Grid Ref: S0955

Holy Cross

Brookdale House, *Carrigrue, Ballinaneeshagh, Waterford.*
Modern country home in countryside surroundings. 2 miles from city.
Open: Jan to Nov **Grades:** BF Approv
051 375618 Mrs Harrington
Rates fr: *IR£16.00*-**IR£16.00**.
Beds: 1F 2D 1T
Baths: 4 Ensuite
(0) (6)

Always telephone to get directions to the B&B - you will save time!

Ballyduff

National Grid Ref: R9600

Blackwater Lodge, *Upper Ballyduff, Ballyduff, Co Waterford.*
Salmon fishing lodge hotel in magnificent location overlooking Munster Blackwater.
Open: Jan to Sep **Grades:** BF 1 St
058 60235 Mr Powell
Rates fr: *IR£21.00*-**IR£29.00**.
Beds: 2F 3D 14T
Baths: 9 Ensuite 5 Shared
(30)

Ballymacarbry

National Grid Ref: S1912

Clonanav Farm, *Nire Valley, Ballymacarbry, Clonmel, Co Tipperary,*
Set in mountain valley, ideal location for fishing, walking and golf.
Open: Mar to Nov **052 36141**
Rates fr: *IR£24.00*-**IR£24.00**.
Beds: 2D 6T 2S **Baths:** 10 Ensuite
(15)

Bennetts Church, *Nire Valley, Ballymacarbry, Clonmel, Co Tipperary,*
Converted school in the lovely Nire Valley. **Open:** All Year (not Xmas)
052 362173 / 088 571203
Mr & Mrs Moore
Rates fr: *IR£15.00*-**IR£14.50**.
Beds: 2F 1D 1T
Baths: 2 Ensuite 2 Shared
(6)

Cappoquin

National Grid Ref: X1099

Richmond Guest House, *Cappoquin, Co Waterford.*
Open: Feb to Dec **Grades:** BF 4 St, AA 4 St, RAC High Acclaim
058 54278 Fax no: 058 54988
Mr Deevy
Rates fr: *IR£28.00*-**IR£30.00**.
Beds: 5D 4T **Baths:** 9 Ensuite
(20)
Award-winning C18th Georgian country house 0.5 miles from the picturesque town of Cappoquin. Beautifully furnished, retaining olde world charm and character. Relax in total tranquillity in front of log fires. Fully licensed restaurant using fresh local produce.

Dungarvan

National Grid Ref: X2693

Bunker Bar, Davitts, Merrys, Shamrock Restaurant, Lawlors Hotel

Rosebank, *Coast Road, Dungarvan, Co Waterford.*
Open: All Year (not Xmas)
Grades: BF Approv
058 41561
Mrs Sleator
Rates fr: *IR£14.00*-**IR£19.00**.
Beds: 1F 2D 1T
Baths: 3 Ensuite 1 Shared
(4) (8)
Comfortable home on own grounds situated in a rural area with wonderful mountain views. Refreshments on arrival. Firm beds. Electric blankets. Varied breakfast menu. Credit cards accepted. Blue flag beach and 18-hole golf 1 mile.

Ard Na Coille, *Clonmel Road R672 (off W72), Dungarvan, Co Waterford.*
Exclusive, warm, friendly home. Breathtaking views mountains, wood and sea.
Open: Mar to Dec
Grades: BF Approv
058 68145
Mrs Kennedy
Rates fr: *IR£15.00*-**IR£18.00**.
Beds: 2F 1D 1T
Baths: 1 Ensuite 2 Private 1 Shared
(1) (5)

Ballyguiry Farm, *Dungarvan, Co Waterford.*
Open: Apr to Oct
058 41194
Mrs Kiely
Rates fr: *IR£16.00*-**IR£21.00**.
Beds: 2F 2D 2T
Baths: 4 Ensuite 1 Shared
Georgian house, built 1830 situated in beautiful Brickey Valley, signposted on N25 road. Southwards of Dungarvan. Mixed farming, TV, tea making facilities, tennis court, pony swings, sand pit on farm. Heritage centres, scenic drive, golf, trekking, fishing, beaches all locally.

Abbeyhouse, *Friars Walk, Abbeyside, Dungarvan, Co Waterford.*
Open: All Year (not Xmas)
Grades: BF Approv
058 41669 Mrs Phelan
Rates fr: *IR£16.00*-**IR£20.00**.
Beds: 1F 2D 2T
Baths: 3 Ensuite 1 Private 1 Shared
Luxury bungalow by the sea with exceptionally warm welcome. Breathtaking views in tranquil surroundings. Private parking and mature gardens. Walking distance to beaches, town centre, restaurants and bars. Golfers', fishermen's and walkers' paradise. Self-catering apartment available.

Fountain Guest House, *Youghal Road, Dungarvan, Co Waterford.*
Modern purpose-built guesthouse standing on own grounds adjacent town overlooking Bay.
Open: Easter to Nov
Grades: BF 1 St
058 42280 Mr Flynn
Rates fr: *IR£13.00*-**IR£14.00**.
Beds: 6D 8T
Baths: 5 Shared
(13)

Failte House, *Youghal Road, Dungarvan, Co Waterford.*
Open: Easter to Oct
Grades: BF Approv
058 43216
Fax no: 058 44343
Mrs Spratt
Rates fr: *IR£16.00*.
Beds: 2D 2T
Baths: 4 Ensuite
(5)
Lovely townhouse, overlooking sea. Nice restful garden. Quiet location, good parking. Owners of West Waterford Golf Club, beautiful challenging course - so golfers, "Come to play, we'll make your day". Green fees IR£17-20 p.p.

The Old Rectory, *Waterford Road, Dungarvan, Co Waterford.*
Situate on 2.5 acres, cable TV, tea/coffee facilities in bedrooms.
Open: All Year (not Xmas)
058 41394 Mrs Prendergast
Rates fr: *IR£14.50*-**IR£19.50**.
Beds: 2F 2D 1T
Baths: 2 Ensuite 3 Shared

Dunmore East

National Grid Ref: S6800

Ship Restaurant, Candlelight Inn

Copper Beach, *Dock Road, Dunmore East, Waterford.*
Open: Feb to Oct **Grades:** BF Approv
051 383187 Mrs Hayes
Rates fr: *IR£16.00*-**IR£21.00**.
Beds: 1F 2D 1T
Baths: 4 Ensuite
(4)
Modern dormer bungalow overlooking harbour and sailing club. Private mature garden and car park. In centre of picturesque fishing village. Walking distance beaches, sailing, fishing, tennis, restaurants. Golf: several first class courses within 10 mile radius.

Ashgrove, *Dunmore East, Waterford.*
Country house near seaside in peaceful scenic surroundings.
Open: Mar to Oct **Grades:** BF Approv
051 383195 Mrs Battles
Rates fr: *IR£14.00*-**IR£19.00**.
Beds: 1F 2D 1T
Baths: 3 Ensuite 1 Private
(10)

Creaden View, *Dunmore East, Waterford.*
Open: Mar to Nov **Grades:** BF Approv
051 383339 (also fax no)
Mrs Martin
Rates fr: *IR£16.00*-**IR£21.00**.
Beds: 1F 3D 1T **Baths:** 5 Ensuite
(6)
Charming home in centre of village overlooking sea beside harbour & sailing club. Walking distance beaches, tennis, restaurants, bars. Golfers' paradise - 5 courses within 20 mins drive. Dunmore East Golf Club 1 km. TV in bedrooms.

Lakefield House, *Rosduff, Dunmore East, Waterford.*
Superbly situated home overlooking Belle Lake, off Waterford Dunmore Coast Road.
Open: Easter to Oct
051 382582 / 382305
Fax no: 051 382582 Mrs Carney
Rates fr: *IR£16.00*-**IR£21.00**.
Beds: 1F 2D 2T **Baths:** 5 Ensuite

Church Villa, *Dunmore East, Waterford.*
Period residence. 130-years-old. Situated in centre of village. Warm welcome.
Open: All Year (not Xmas)
Grades: BF Approv
051 383390 Mrs Butler
Rates fr: *IR£14.50*-**IR£14.50**.
Beds: 3D 2T 2S **Baths:** 5 Ensuite
(10)

Kilmeaden

National Grid Ref: S5110

Long Haul Tavern

Dawn B & B, *Kildarmody, Kilmeaden, Waterford.*
Modern bungalow on a 2.5 acre site in a partly wooded area with mature garden.
Open: All Year
Grades: BF Approv
051 384465
Mrs Fitzgerald
Rates fr: *IR£15.00*-**IR£18.00**.
Beds: 1F 1D 1T
Baths: 3 Ensuite 1 Private
(7)

Kinsalebeg

National Grid Ref: X1280

Ahernes Restaurant, The Cliff Hotel

Blackwater House, *Kinsalebeg, Youghal, Co Cork.*
Picturesque bungalow on mature garden. Panoramic view of Youghal Bay.
Open: May to Sep
024 92543 Mr & Mrs Tarrant
Rates fr: *IR£13.00*-**IR£15.00**.
Beds: 1F 1D 1T
Baths: 2 Shared
(6)

Gables, *Rath, Kinsalebeg, Youghal, Co Cork.*
Open: Easter to Oct
Grades: BF Approv
024 92739 Mrs Cliffe
Rates fr: *IR£15.00*-**IR£17.00**.
Beds: 1F 3D 1S
Baths: 1 Ensuite 1 Private 1 Shared
(7)

Lismore

National Grid Ref: X0498

Eamonn's Place, The Rafters, The Latch

Beechcroft, *Deerpark Road, Lismore, Co Waterford.*
Bungalow on own grounds, in lovely area on outskirts of heritage town close to Blackwater River.
Open: All Year (not Xmas)
058 54273 Mrs Power
Rates fr: *IR£16.00*-**IR£18.00**.
Beds: 1F 1D 2T
Baths: 3 Ensuite 1 Shared
(8)

Millstreet

National Grid Ref: S1601

The Castle, *Cappagh, Millstreet, Dungarvan, Co Waterford.*
Award-winning restored wing of a C15th castle in picturesque setting.
Open: Easter to Oct
Grades: BF Approv
058 68049 Mrs Nugent
Rates fr: *IR£18.00*-**IR£20.00**.
Beds: 2F 2D 1T
Baths: 5 Ensuite
(2)

Portlaw

National Grid Ref: S4615

The Long Haul

Digway House, *Pouldrew Bridge, Portlaw, Waterford.*
Luxury designer home, in the heart of the countryside, no noise, no traffic jams, ideal to help unwind and destress.
Open: Easter to Nov
Grades: BF Approv
051 384404 Mrs O'Keefe
Rates fr: *IR£15.00*-**IR£15.00**.
Beds: 2F 2D **Baths:** 4 Ensuite
(8)

The lowest *double* rate per person is shown in *italics*.

Pulla

National Grid Ref: X2389

Seanchai Restaurant

Seaview, *Youghal Road, Windgap, Pulla, Dungarvan, Co Waterford.*
Dormer bungalow 5 miles west of Dungarvan on N25. Best sea views in Ireland.
Open: All Year
Grades: BF Approv
058 41583
Mrs Fahey
Rates fr: *IR£16.00*-**IR£18.00**.
Beds: 5F 3T
Baths: 3 Ensuite

Stradbally

National Grid Ref: X3697

Park House, *Stradbally, Kilmacthomas, Co Waterford.*
Beautiful comfortable old farmhouse in remote woodland setting lovely gardens for guests, with bird song for background music.
Open: Easter to October
Grades: BF Approv
051 293185 (also fax no) Mrs Connor
Rates fr: *IR£16.50*-**IR£20.00**.
Beds: 5F 4D 1T
Baths: 2 Ensuite
(7) (20)

Tallow

National Grid Ref: W9993

Sunlea, *Chapel Street, Tallow, Co Waterford.*
Dormer bungalow in quiet neighbourhood, comfortable and welcoming to guests.
Open: May to Sep **Grades:** BF Approv
058 56150 Mrs Power
Rates fr: *IR£14.00*-**IR£15.00**.
Beds: 2F 1S **Baths:** 3 Ensuite
(3)

The lowest **single** *rate is shown in* **bold.**

Tramore

National Grid Ref: S5801

Tramore Golf Club, Pine Rooms, Esquire Restaurant, Sea Horse, O'Shea's Hotel

Glenorney, *Newtown, Tramore, Co Waterford.*
Open: March to end-Nov
Grades: BF Approv, AA 4 Q, RAC Acclaim
051 381056 (also fax no)
Mrs Murphy
Rates fr: *IR£17.00*-**IR£22.50**.
Beds: 2F 2D 2T
Baths: 5 Ensuite
(6)
Spaciouss, luxurious home, spectacular view of Tramore Bay. On coast road opposite Championship golf course. Extensive breakfast menu and renowned home cooking. Tastefully decorated ensuite bedrooms. Luxuriously furnished spacious residents lounge. Home from home. A pleasant experience to stay here.

Rushmere House, *Branch Road, Tramore, Co Waterford.*
Georgian house. Magnificent view of Tramore Bay. Central location.
Open: Mar to Nov
051 381041
Mrs McGivney
Rates fr: *IR£14.00*-**IR£18.50**.
Beds: 1F 3D 2T
Baths: 3 Ensuite 2 Shared
(3)

Sea Court, *Tivoli Road, Tramore, Co Waterford.*
Open: Mar to Nov
Grades: BF Approv
051 386244
Mr Moran
Rates fr: *IR£13.00*-**IR£16.00**.
Beds: 4D
Baths: 4 Ensuite
(10)
Highly recommended, modern bungalow. Rooms ensuite with multi-channel TV, tea/coffee facilities and hair-dryers in all rooms. Visa accepted. Breakfast menu. Private parking. Centrally located. Close to beach, golf, Splash World, amusements and Waterford Crystal.

Cloneen, *Love Lane, Tramore, Co Waterford.*
Open: All Year (not Xmas)
Grades: BF Approv
051 381264 Mrs Skedd
Rates fr: *IR£16.00*-**IR£20.00**.
Beds: 1F 1D 1T
Baths: 3 Ensuite
(4)
Bungalow set in landscaped gardens with private parking. Close to beaches, Splashworld, golf, horse-riding, tennis and Waterford Crystal. All rooms ensuite. Welcome tray on arrival. Access/Visa accepted. Television in bedrooms.

Ardview House, *Lower Branch Road, Tramore, Co Waterford.*
Attractive late Georgian house with excellent views of Tramore Bay.
Open: All Year (not Xmas)
051 381687 Mrs O'Connor
Rates fr: *IR£14.00*-**IR£18.00**.
Beds: 1F 4D 1T
Baths: 5 Ensuite 1 Private

Annagh B&B, *Springfield, Tramore, Co Waterford.*
Family bungalow, quiet cul-de-sac. Panoramic view. Warm welcome.
Open: May to Sep
051 381263 Ms Minchin
Rates fr: *IR£16.00*-**IR£16.00**.
Beds: 1F 1T 1D
Baths: 3 Ensuite
(8)

Waterford

National Grid Ref: S6011

Dooleys Hotel, Holy Cross Bar, Rhu Glen Country Pub, Orpens Pub, Meades Pub, Strand Inn, The Reginald , Jack Meads

Beechwood, *7 Cathedral Square, Waterford.*
Four-storey Georgian house situated in a tree-lined, pedestrianised area.
Open: Jan to Nov
051 876677 Mrs Ryan
Rates fr: *IR£13.50*-**IR£15.00**.
Beds: 1D 2T
Baths: 1 Private 1 Shared
(2) (2)

Marsuci, *Olivers Hill, Butlerstown, Waterford.*
Open: All Year (not Xmas)
Grades: AA 3 Q
051 370429 Fax no: 051 350983
Mr & Mrs Keller
Rates fr: *IR£16.00*-**IR£20.00**.
Beds: 2F 2D 1T 1S **Baths:** 6 Ensuite
(4) (10)
Set in a rural location off N25 (turn at Holy Cross Pub) this attractive stone built house stands in lovely gardens and offers comfortable, relaxing accommodation. The pleasant ensuite rooms all have telephones and tea-making facilities. Breakfast from our award-winning menu.

The Pines, *Dunmore Road, Knockboy, Waterford.*
Picturesque rural bungalow. Airport, hospital, golf, fishing, seafood restaurants locally. **Open:** All Year
051 874452 Fax no: 051 84156
Mrs O'Sullivan-Jackman
Rates fr: *IR£14.00*-**IR£19.00**.
Beds: 2F 2D 1T
Baths: 4 Ensuite 1 Shared
(8)

Sion Hill House, *Rosslare Road, Ferrybank, Waterford.*
Open: All Year (not Xmas)
Grades: BF Approv
051 851558 Fax no: 051 873900
Mr Kavanagh
Rates fr: *IR£19.50*-**IR£24.00**.
Beds: 3F 1T
Baths: 4 Ensuite
(15)
Captivating period residence. Circa 1800 on mature 4 acre secluded gardens overlooking River Suir & city centre. Spacious rooms with cable TV & tea/coffee facilities. Breakfast menu. Visa/Access/Mastercard. Ideal touring base on N25 Rosslare Road, next to Jury's Hotel.

Woodleigh, *Castle Road, Cork Road, Waterford.*
Warm Irish welcome, country setting yet close to Waterford/seaside.
Open: Easter to Sep
051 384601 Mrs O'Neill
Rates fr: *IR£16.00*-**IR£20.00**.
Beds: 1F 1D 1T
Baths: 3 Ensuite
(6)

The Coach House, *Butlerstown Castle, Butlerstown, Waterford.*
Open: All Year (not Xmas/New Year)
Grades: BF 3 St, AA 4 Q
051 384656
Fax no: 051 384751
Mr O'Keeffe
Rates fr: *IR£23.50*-**IR£29.50**.
Beds: 5D 2T
Baths: 7 Ensuite
(18)
An elegantly restored C19th home in a tranquil, romantic and historic setting (ruined C13th castle in the grounds). Evening meals available (Tuesday to Saturday) using fresh local ingredients, book by midday. Waterford Crystal five minutes, Waterford City 3.5 miles.

Abhaile, *Cork Road, Butlerstown, Waterford.*
Modern purpose built accommodation set in 3 acres, 5 minutes from Waterford Crystal factory.
Open: Easter to Oct
051 384590 Mrs O'Donnell
Rates fr: *IR£14.00*-**IR£16.00**.
Beds: 1F 2D 3T
Baths: 3 Ensuite 3 Shared
(10)

Brown's Town House, *29 South Parade, Waterford, County Waterford.*
Open: All Year (not Xmas)
Grades: BF Approv
051 870594
Fax no: 051 871923
Mr Brown
Rates fr: *IR£20.00*-**IR£25.00**.
Beds: 1F 2D 1T
Baths: 4 Ensuite
Brown's Town House is a late Victorian house of charm and character. The house is decorated in period style and has been sensitively refurbished to include C20th creature comforts.

Suncroft, *Dunmore East Road, Waterford, Waterford.*
Located midway between Waterford and Dunmore East.
Open: 1st Feb to 31st Oct
Grades: BF Approv
051 382366 Mr & Mrs Harty
Rates fr: *IR£14.00*-**IR£19.00**.
Beds: 1F 1D 1T
Baths: 2 Ensuite 1 Shared
(6)

Diamond Hill, *Slieverue, Waterford.*
Open: All Year
Grades: BF 3 St, AA 3 Q
051 832855 Fax no: 051 832254
Mr Masterson
Rates fr: *IR£18.00*-**IR£20.00**.
Beds: 1F 6D 3T
Baths: 10 Ensuite
(15)
Diamond Hill offers its guests absolute peace and tranquillity with all the comforts of a well run country home. Set in its own award-winning gardens, all bedrooms newly decorated, colour TV, D/D phones, tea/coffee. Only 2 miles Waterford City.

Villa Eildon, *Belmont Road, Rosslare Road, Ferrybank, Waterford.*
Modern dormer bungalow finished to high standard on Waterford/Rosslare Road (N25).
Open: Jun to Oct
Grades: BF Approv, AA 2 Q
051 832174 Mrs Landy
Rates fr: *IR£15.00*-**IR£23.00**.
Beds: 2D 2T
Baths: 2 Ensuite 2 Shared
(7) (6)

Loughdan, *Dublin Road, Newrath, Waterford.*
Modern house. Waterford one mile. Rooms have TV, tea/coffee.
Open: All Year (not Xmas)
051 876021 Mrs Dullaghan
Rates fr: *IR£14.50*-**IR£23.00**.
Beds: 1F 3D 2T
Baths: 5 Ensuite 1 Private 1 Shared
(2) (7)

Woodside House, *Whitfield, Cork Road (N25), Waterford.*
Architect-designed spacious bungalow with unusual glass features, set in a beautiful scenic area.
Open: All Year (not Xmas)
051 384381 Mr & Mrs Morrissey
Rates fr: *IR£15.00*-**IR£20.00**.
Beds: 1F 1D 1T
Baths: 3 Ensuite
(1) (10)

Right on the border? Look at the neighbouring county, too

County Westmeath

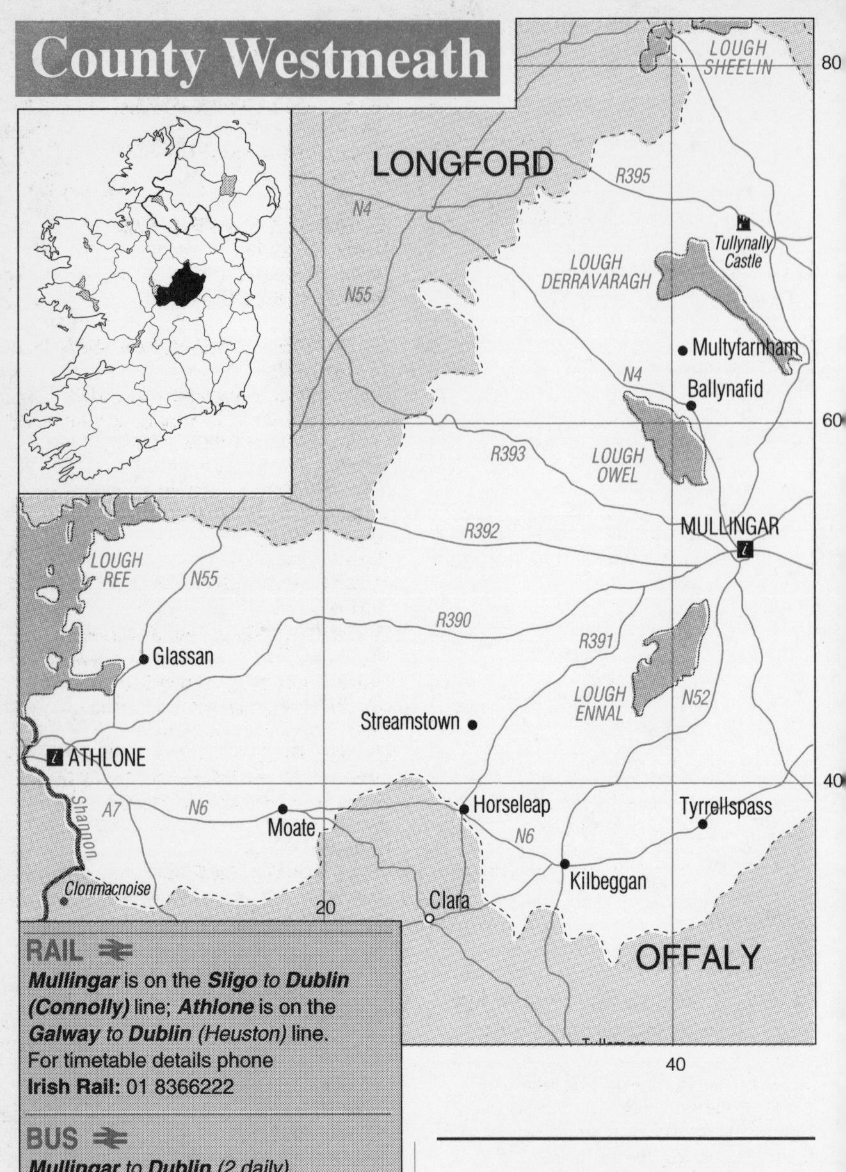

RAIL

Mullingar is on the ***Sligo*** *to* ***Dublin (Connolly)*** line; ***Athlone*** is on the ***Galway*** *to* ***Dublin*** *(Heuston)* line.
For timetable details phone
Irish Rail: 01 8366222

BUS

Mullingar *to* ***Dublin*** *(2 daily).*
Athlone *to* ***Dublin*** *(6 daily).*
Tel **Bus Eireann** on 01 8366111

TOURIST INFORMATION OFFICES

Athlone Castle, **Athlone**
(May to mid-Oct), 0902 94630
Dublin Road, **Mullingar**
(open all year), 044 48650

Irish Grid References are for villages, towns and cities - *not* for individual houses.

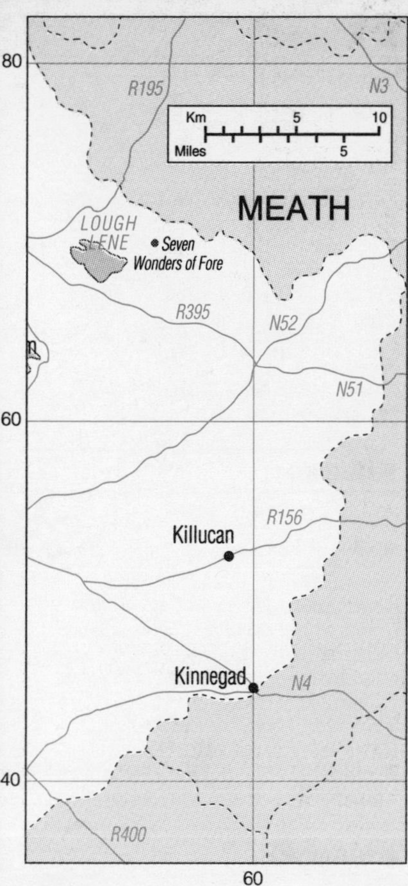

Athlone

National Grid Ref: N0441

The Corn Loft, Conlon's Bar, The Shack, Wineport Restaurant, Grogans

Woodville, *Monksland, Athlone, Co Westmeath.*
Open: Easter to Oct
Grades: BF Approv
0902 94595 Mrs McCam
Rates fr: *IR£16.00*-**IR£18.00**.
Beds: 1D 2T **Baths:** 3 Ensuite
(3)
Modern, comfortable accommodation ITB Approved, 2 km Athlone Town and River Shannon, ideally situated for sightseeing, or stopover when travelling to the West. Pub and restaurant 1 km, monastic site. Railyway Bog Tour the only one of its kind in Europe.

Bogganfin House, *Roscommon Road, Athlone, Co Westmeath.*
Tudor-style residence, private parking, rooms ensuite, TV, tea/coffee.
Open: Feb to Dec
Grades: BF Approv
0902 94255
Mrs O'Brien
Rates fr: *IR£16.00*-**IR£20.00**.
Beds: 2F 3D 1T
Baths: 5 Ensuite 1 Private

Harbour House, *Ballykeeran, Athlone, Co Westmeath.*
Luxurious quiet country home 200 metres from award winning restaurant.
Open: All Year (not Xmas)
Grades: BF Approv
0902 85063 Mrs Keegan
Rates fr: *IR£15.00*-**IR£18.00**.
Beds: 2F 2D 2T
Baths: 6 Ensuite
(8)

The Mill Bar/Corn Loft Restaurant, *Tuam Road, Athlone, Co Westmeath.*
Old mill tastefully restored to pub with fully licensed gourmet restaurant.
Open: All Year (not Xmas)
Grades: BF Approv
0902 92927 / 94753 Mr & Mrs O'Shea
Rates fr: *IR£16.00*-**IR£19.00**.
Beds: 2F 2D 2T
Baths: 6 Ensuite
(2)

Bushfield House, *Cornamaddy, Athlone, Co Westmeath.*
Luxurious country house set in landscaped gardens with exceptionally warm welcome.
Open: All Year (not Xmas)
0902 75979 Mrs King
Rates fr: *IR£16.00*-**IR£17.00**.
Beds: 3F 2D 1T
Baths: 5 Ensuite
(10)

Mount Alverna House, *Monksland, Athlone, Co Westmeath.*
Beautiful bungalow on private grounds. Five minutes drive to Athlone.
Open: Easter to Oct
0902 94016 Mrs Mulligan
Rates fr: *IR£16.00*-**IR£21.00**.
Beds: 1F 2D 1T
Baths: 4 Ensuite
(8)

Ballynafid

National Grid Ref: N4161

Danny Byrnes

Beechwood, *Ballynafid, Multyfarnham, Mullingar, Co Westmeath.*
Along N4, bungalow, beech-lined grounds, home cooking, Lough Owel nearby.
Open: Jun to Sep
044 71108 Mr & Mrs Kelly
Rates fr: *IR£12.00*-**IR£15.00**.
Beds: 1D 2T **Baths:** 1 Shared
(4)

Glassan

National Grid Ref: N0847

Glasson Village Restaurant, Grogans,The Village Inn

Benown House, *Glassan, Athlone, Co Westmeath.*
Beautiful house and gardens minutes walk from Village of the Roses.
Open: All Year
0902 85406 Mrs Byrne
Rates fr: *IR£16.00*-**IR£21.00**.
Beds: 1F 2D
Baths: 3 Ensuite 1 Shared
(6)

Horseleap

National Grid Ref: N2638

Temple, *Horseleap, Moate, Athlone, Co Westmeath.*
200-year-old country house; warm welcome, excellent cuisine.
Open: Mar to Dec
Grades: AA 4 Q, Select
0506 35118 Mr & Mrs Fagan
Rates fr: *IR£25.00*-**IR£32.50**.
Beds: 2F 2T **Baths:** 4 Ensuite

Always telephone to get directions to the B&B - you will save time!

Kilbeggan

National Grid Ref: N3335

The Black Kettle Bar, Tyrrellspass Castle

Fort House, *Dublin Road, Kilbeggan, Mullingar, Co Westmeath.*
Modern bungalow on main N6 route one mile from Kilbeggan and Loules Distillery. **Open:** Easter to Oct
0506 32316 Mr Scally
Rates fr: *IR£14.00*-**IR£17.50**.
Beds: 1F 3D 1T 1S
Baths: 3 Ensuite 3 Shared

Killucan

National Grid Ref: N5752

Harrys, Brackens

Annascanan House, *Killucan, Kinnegad, Mullingar, Co Westmeath.*
Georgian-style residence on 350 acres. 40 miles from Dublin off N4 (West).
Open: Apr to Oct
044 74130 Mrs Cooney
Rates fr: *IR£15.50*-**IR£15.50**.
Beds: 1F 1D 1T **Baths:** 3 Private

Kinnegad

National Grid Ref: N5945

Harrys Roadhouse

The Bungalow, *Mullingar Road, Kinnegad, Mullingar, Co Westmeath.*
One-of-a-kind modern bungalow, all facilities on ground floor.
Open: All Year (not Xmas)
Grades: BF Approv
044 75250 Mrs Groome
Rates fr: *IR£11.00*-**IR£11.00**.
Beds: 1F 2D 2S **Baths:** 3 Shared
(10)

Sweet Briar Lodge, *Athlone Road, Kinnegad, Mullingar, Co Westmeath.*
Beautiful modern home with private TV lounge, ensuite bedrooms, carpark.
044 75435 Mrs Kilcoyne
Rates fr: *IR£13.00*-**IR£13.00**.
Beds: 3D 1T **Baths:** 3 Ensuite 1 Private
(2) (8)

Moate

National Grid Ref: N1838

The Grand Hotel

Cooleen, *Ballymore Road, Moate, Athlone, Co Westmeath.*
Picturesque bungalow in private gardens in quiet scenic area.
Open: All Year (not Xmas)
Grades: BF Approv
0902 81044 Mrs Kelly
Rates fr: *IR£16.00*-**IR£18.00**.
Beds: 2F 2D
Baths: 3 Ensuite 1 Private
(8)

Mullingar

National Grid Ref: N4352

Danny Byrnes, Oscars

Petiswood House, *Mullingar, Co Westmeath.*
Modern two storey house. Tree-lined avenue. Mature grounds.
Open: All Year
044 48397 Mrs Farrell
Rates fr: *IR£16.00*-**IR£20.00**.
Beds: 1F 1D 1T
Baths: 3 Ensuite 1 Private

Old Dublin Road, *Mullingar, Co Westmeath.*
Farmhouse adjacent to town. Experience a working farm.
Open: All Year
Grades: BF Approv
044 41483 Mrs McCormack
Rates fr: *IR£14.00*-**IR£19.00**.
Beds: 1F 2D 1T
Baths: 2 Ensuite 1 Shared
(10)

Keadeen, *Longford Road, Irishtown, Mullingar, Co Westmeath.*
Delightful Irish guest house, quiet location, near town. Guaranteed warm welcome.
Open: All Year (not Xmas)
Grades: BF Approv
044 48440 Mrs Nolan
Rates fr: *IR£15.00*-**IR£17.00**.
Beds: 1F 1D 1T
Baths: 2 Ensuite 1 Private
(10)

Multyfarnham

National Grid Ref: N4064

The School House, *Leney, Multyfarnham, Mullingar, Co Westmeath.*
Converted school house in heart of Irish countryside.
Open: Easter to Oct
Grades: BF Approv
044 71153 Mrs Gillespie
Rates fr: *IR£15.00*-**IR£17.00**.
Beds: 1F 2D
Baths: 3 Ensuite
(8)

Streamstown

National Grid Ref: N2643

Woodlands Farm, *Streamstown, Mullingar, Co Westmeath.*
Open: Mar to Oct
Grades: AA 3 Q
044 26414 Mrs Maxwell
Rates fr: *IR£14.00*-**IR£18.00**.
Beds: 1F 2D 2T 1S
Baths: 2 Ensuite 1 Private 3 Shared
Charming old country house surrounded by ornamental trees on 120-acre farm, midway between Dublin and Galway, 4 km off N6 at Horseleap. Good angling area. Riding ponies and donkey free. Lovely atmosphere and home cooking a speciality. Frommer recommended. AA listed. Convenient to Clonmacnoise and mini golf. Six bedrooms (three ensuite, one single).

Tyrellspass

National Grid Ref: N4137

Village Inn Hotel, Tyrellspass Castle

Hillcrest, *Greevebawn, Tyrellspass, Mullingar, Co Westmeath.*
Luxury accommodation, very much a home atmosphere. Plenty to offer the tourists. **Open:** All Year (not Xmas)
Grades: BF Approv
044 23274 Mrs Maher
Rates fr: *IR£15.00*-**IR£15.00**.
Beds: 2F 1D 1T 2S
Baths: 2 Ensuite 2 Private

County Wexford

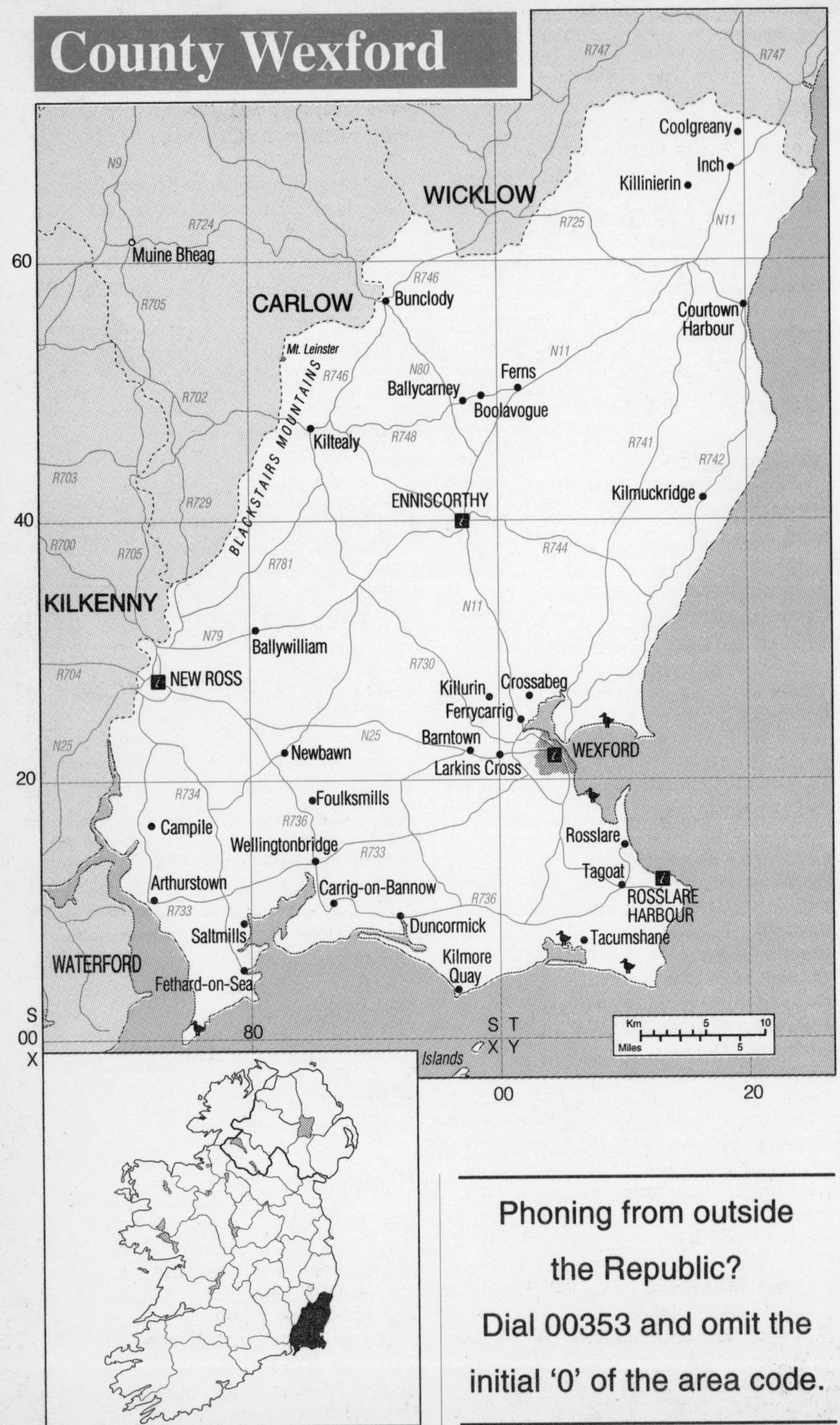

Phoning from outside the Republic?

Dial 00353 and omit the initial '0' of the area code.

RAIL

Wexford and ***Rosslare Harbour*** are on the East Coast line into ***Dublin (Connolly)***; ***Rosslare*** is also on direct lines for ***Waterford*** and ***Limerick Junction***, with connections for many other parts of the country. For timetable details phone **Irish Rail:** 01 8366222.

BUS

Rosslare Harbour *to* ***Cork*** *(4 daily), to* ***Dublin*** *(5 daily), to* ***Limerick*** *(3 daily).*
Wexford *to* ***Dublin*** *(5 daily).*
Tel **Bus Eireann** on 01 8366111

FERRIES

Rosslare Harbour *to* ***Fishguard*** *(3½ hrs).*
Stena Sealink - in Republic tel 01 2808844, in UK, 01233 647047 and 615455)
Rosslare Harbour *to* ***Pembroke*** *(4¼ hrs)*
Irish Ferries - in Republic, tel 01 661 0511, in UK, tel 051 227 3131

TOURIST INFORMATION OFFICES

Gorey (open all year), 055 21248

Enniscorthy (mid-Jun to Aug), 054 34699

Kennedy Centre, **New Ross** (mid-Jun to Aug), 051 21857

Kilrane, **Rosslare** (Jun to Sep), 053 33232

Rosslare Harbour (open all year), 053 33622

The Crescent, **Wexford** (open all year), 053 23111

Arthurstown

National Grid Ref: S7110

Kings Bay Inn, Neptune Restaurant

Glendine Country House, *Arthurstown, New Ross, Co Wexford.*
Open: All Year (not Xmas)
Grades: BF Approv
051 389258
Crosbie
Rates fr: *IR£16.00*-**IR£20.00.**
Beds: 2F 1D 1T 1S
Baths: 5 Ensuite
Glendine Georgian country house was built in 1830. It is the family home of the Crosbies, who will offer you a sincere Irish welcome in a relaxed and tranquil ambience. Our 5 spacious ensuite rooms are decorated with traditional furnishings.

High season, bank holidays and special events mean low availability *anywhere.*

The lowest *double* rate per person is shown in *italics.*

Ballycarney

National Grid Ref: S9748

Ballycarney Inn, Celtic Arms

Oakville Lodge, *Bunclody Road, Ballycarney, Enniscorthy, Co Wexford.*
Comfortable country home overlooking River Slaney with panoramic views.
Open: May to Oct
054 88626 Mrs Doyle
Rates fr: *IR£14.50*-**IR£18.00.**
Beds: 2D 1T
Baths: 2 Ensuite 14.50
(2) (15)

Ballywilliam

National Grid Ref: S8031

Ballywilliam House, *Ballywilliam, New Ross, Co Wexford.*
051 424542 Ms Fitzpatrick
Rates fr: *IR£14.00*-**IR£15.00.**
Beds: 3F 1D 1S
Baths: 2 Shared

Barntown

National Grid Ref: S9821

Old Oak Tavern, Riverside Restaurant

Carrig Crest, *Ballygoman, Barntown, Wexford.*
Modern bungalow with private car park. Lovely view of mountains and countryside.
Open: Mar to Nov
Grades: BF Approv
053 20340
Mrs Browne
Rates fr: *IR£16.50*-**IR£18.00**.
Beds: 3D 2T
Baths: 3 Ensuite 1 Shared
(4)

Boolavogue

National Grid Ref: S9949

Ballyorley House, *Boolavogue, Ferns, Enniscorthy, Co Wexford.*
Ideal place for restful rural holiday. Georgian residence set on mixed farm surrounded by wealth of wildlife. Woodland walks.
Open: All Year
Grades: RAC Listed
054 66287
Mrs Gough
Rates fr: *IR£15.50*-**IR£19.50**.
Beds: 4D 1S
Baths: 2 Ensuite 2 Shared
(4)

Bunclody

National Grid Ref: S9155

Deane's, *Main Street, Bunclody, Co Wexford.*
Open: All Year
054 77149
Ms Deane
Rates fr: *IR£16.00*-**IR£20.00**.
Beds: 2F 3D 2T 2S
Baths: 7 Ensuite 2 Shared
(20)
Old world pub with guest accommodation in town centre. Antique furniture. Secure car park at rear. Children welcome. Direct dial phones all rooms.

Irish Grid References are for villages, towns and cities - *not* for individual houses.

Campile

National Grid Ref: S7215

Park View Deer Farm, *Nr J F Kennedy Park, Campile, New Ross, Co Wexford.*
Extended, modernised traditional farmhouse, scenic garden setting. Working deer farm.
Open: May to Oct
051 388178
Mr & Mrs Barrett
Rates fr: *IR£18.00*-**IR£14.00**.
Beds: 1D 2T 1S
Baths: 3 Ensuite 1 Shared
(6)

Carrig-on-Bannow

National Grid Ref: S8610

Breen's Inn, *Carrig-on-Bannow, Wexford.*
A village inn with own tennis court and 18-hole pitch & putt.
Open: All Year
051 561101
Ms Howlin
Rates fr: *IR£16.00*-**IR£18.00**.
Beds: 1F 3D
Baths: 3 Ensuite

Coolgreany

National Grid Ref: T1969

Tomar, *Coolgreany, Gorey, Co Wexford.*
Modern bungalow in scenic area. One hour Dublin/Rosslare Port.
Open: All Year (not Xmas)
Grades: BF Approv
0402 37440
Mrs Whelan
Rates fr: *IR£16.00*-**IR£16.00**.
Beds: 1F 1D 1T
Baths: 2 Ensuite 1 Private 1 Shared
(8)

Courtown Harbour

National Grid Ref: T1956

Macamore House, *Ounavarra Road, Courtown Harbour, Gorey, Co Wexford,*
Georgian style country home overlooking woodlands, yet only 10 minutes walk to beaches.
Open: Jan to Nov
Grades: BF Approv
055 25353 Mrs Conroy
Rates fr: *IR£15.00*-**IR£18.00**.
Baths: 3 Ensuite

Duncormick

National Grid Ref: S9209

Breers, Wooden House

Ingleside Farmhouse, *Duncormick, Wexford.*
051 563154 Mrs Burrell
Open: March to Nov
Rates fr: *IR£16.00*-**IR£21.00**.
Baths: 5 Ensuite
(6)
Modern family run farmhouse on 90 acres. 20 mins from Ferry port. Early breakfast and meals on request. Horse trekking on farm & beach, beginners and experience riders welcome. Lessons available. Farm & beach walks, golf, fishing trips arranged.

Aras-Muillinn, *Ambrosetown, Duncormick, Wexford.*
New refurbished modern house comfortable surroundings and homely atmosphere.
Open: All Year
051 563145
Fax no: 051 563245
Mrs Parle
Rates fr: *IR£15.00*-**IR£15.00**.
Beds: 3F 3D 3T
Baths: 2 Ensuite 2 Private
(4)

Always telephone to get directions to the B&B - you will save time!

All details shown are as supplied by B&B owners in Autumn 1996

Ocean View, *Cullenstown Strand, Duncormick, Wexford.*
Beautifully situated seaside residence with conservatory overlooking beach. Homely welcome.
Open: Easter to Nov
Grades: BF Approv
051 561270
Mrs Browne
Rates fr: *IR£15.00*-**IR£17.00**.
Beds: 1F 4D 1T
Baths: 4 Ensuite 2 Shared
(10)

Enniscorthy

National Grid Ref: S9740

The Tavern

St Judes, *Munfin, Tommalosset, Enniscorthy, Co Wexford.*
Open: All Year
Grades: BF Approv
054 33011
Mrs Delany
Rates fr: *IR£17.00*-**IR£15.00**.
Beds: 3F 1D 1T
Baths: 4 Ensuite 1 Shared
Country house. Peaceful area. Member of Town and Country Homes. Board Failite. Travel vouchers and Visa taken. Rooms with tea making facilities. Some rooms with TV. St Judes is off the Dublin/New Ross Road N79 and 4 km from Enniscorthy Southside. 30 km from Rosslare Ferryport.

Ivella, *Rectory Road, Enniscorthy, Co Wexford.*
Charming old house, lovely view, peaceful and friendly. Home baking.
Open: All Year
054 33475
Miss Heffernan
Rates fr: *IR£14.00*-**IR£15.00**.
Beds: 3F 2D 1T
(1) (4)

Laurel Cottage, *Moneytucker, Enniscorthy, Co Wexford.*
Open: All Year
Grades: BF Approv
054 44362
Mr & Mrs Boland
Rates fr: *IR£16.00*-**IR£18.00**.
Beds: 1F 1D 1S
Baths: 2 Ensuite 1 Shared
Newly renovated and extended country cottage 9 kms from Enniscorthy on the N-79 Road to New Ross, 25 kms from Wexford. Raspberry fruit farm and vegetable garden. Leisurely activities in area. Owner qualified tour guide. Over 50s welcomed.

Don Carr House, *Bohreen Hill, Enniscorthy, Co Wexford.*
Comfortable family-run guest house. Own grounds, near town centre, parking.
Open: All Year (not Xmas)
Grades: BF Approv
054 33458
Mrs Carroll
Rates fr: *IR£13.00*-**IR£14.00**.
Beds: 2F 1D 1T
Baths: 2 Ensuite 2 Shared
(10)

9 Main Street, *Enniscorthy, Co Wexford.*
Open: All Year (not Xmas)
Grades: BF Approv
054 33522
Mrs Murphy
Rates fr: *IR£14.00*-**IR£15.00**.
Beds: 3F 2D 1S
Baths: 2 Ensuite 2 Shared
(7)
Large red brick house in town centre. Private car park. Tea and coffee making facilities plus multi channel TV in all rooms. Some rooms ensuite. Friendly pub with good atmosphere. Also beer garden.

Many rates vary according to season - the lowest are shown here.

Right on the border? Look at the neighbouring county, too

Murphy-Floods Hotel, *27 Main Street, Enniscorthy, Co Wexford.*
Overlooking market square of historic Norman town with Norman castle.
Open: All Year (not Xmas)
Grades: BF 2 St, AA 1 St
054 33413 (also fax no)
Rates fr: *IR£26.00*-**IR£28.00**.
Beds: 2F 9D 9T 1S
Baths: 17 Ensuite 4 Shared

Moyhill, *Bellefield, Enniscorthy, Co Wexford.*
Modern house, in quiet location, within one mile of Enniscorthy.
Open: All Year (not Xmas)
054 34739 Mrs Kenny
Rates fr: *IR£14.00*-**IR£15.00**.
Beds: 1F 1D 1S
Baths: 2 Ensuite 1 Shared
(4)

Vinegar Hill Country House, *Clonhaston, Enniscorthy, Co Wexford.*
Modern house. Private par 3 golf course free to residents.
Open: All Year
054 35127 Mr & Mrs McGee
Rates fr: *IR£16.00*-**IR£21.00**.
Beds: 1F 1D 1T
Baths: 3 Ensuite
(6)

Ferns

National Grid Ref: T0149

Glencarra, *Crory, Ferns, Enniscorthy, Co Wexford.*
Glencarra is situated on the N11 Dublin to Rosslare Road. It is a spacious modern home with a special welcome.
Open: Mar to Nov **Grades:** BF Approv
054 66106 Mrs Brennan
Rates fr: *IR£15.00*-**IR£16.00**.
Beds: 2D 2S
Baths: 1 Ensuite 1 Shared
(6)

Ferrycarrig

National Grid Ref: T0226

Oak Tavern, Ferrycarrig Hotel

***Tara,** Killeen, Ferrycarrig, Crossabeg, Wexford.*
Modern bungalow on N11. Close to Wexford, Rosslare Harbour, Heritage Park.
Open: All Year
053 20133 Mrs Meagher
Rates fr: *IR£16.00*-**IR£20.00**.
Beds: 2F 1D 1T
Baths: 2 Ensuite 2 Shared
(8)

***Ferry Villa,** Kitestown, Ferrycarrig, Crossabeg, Co Wexford.*
Modern red brick bungalow on quiet road.
Open: All Year (not Xmas)
Grades: BF Approv
053 20002 Mr & Mrs Noonan
Rates fr: *IR£13.00*-**IR£16.00**.
Beds: 2D 2T
Baths: 1 Shared
(10)

Fethard-on-Sea

National Grid Ref: S7905

***Naomh Seosamh,** Fethard-on-Sea, New Ross, Co Wexford.*
Situated in sunny South East in picturesque village of Fethard-on-Sea.
Open: All Year
Grades: BF 1 St
051 397129
(also fax no) Wall
Rates fr: *IR£20.00*-**IR£20.00**.
Beds: 3F 10D 2T
Baths: 15 Ensuite 1 Shared
(1) (30)

Foulksmills

National Grid Ref: S8518

***The Farmhouse,** Foulksmills, Wexford,*
Large 400-year-old farmhouse on 150 acres mixed farming.
Open: Mar to Nov **Grades:** BF Approv
051 565616 Mrs Crosbie
Rates fr: *IR£14.00*-**IR£14.00**.
Beds: 1F 4D 4T 1S
Baths: 3 Shared

Inch

National Grid Ref: T1867

***Riverside Farmhouse,** Inch, Gorey, Co Wexford.*
Gardens, tennis, pony rides, babysitting, wines, log-fire, local pub, brochure available.
Open: All Year (not Xmas)
0402 37232 Mr & Mrs Anderson-Proby
Rates fr: *IR£16.00*-**IR£16.00**.
Beds: 3F 1D 1T 1S
Baths: 5 Ensuite
(6)

Killinierin

National Grid Ref: T1566

***Woodlands House,** Killinierin, Gorey, Co Wexford.*
Open: Mar to Dec **Grades:** AA 4 Q
0402 37125 Fax no: 0402 37133
Mrs O'Sullivan
Rates fr: *IR£18.50*-**IR£25.00**.
Beds: 3F 2D 1T
Baths: 6 Ensuite
(10)
Period house, set admidst 1 acre of gardens, ideal touring base for Wicklow/Dublin. Located 3 miles north of Gorey, 1 mile off N11 near village of Killinierin. Tennis court free to guests (rackets supplied).

Killurin

National Grid Ref: S9725

Oak Tavern

***Heathfield Manor,** Killurin, Wexford.*
Georgian manor house, set in beautiful wooded riverside estate.
Open: All Year (not Xmas)
Grades: BF Approv
053 28253 Mrs Colloton
Rates fr: *IR£20.00*-**IR£25.00**.
Beds: 1F 1D 1T
Baths: 1 Ensuite 2 Private
(8)

The lowest *double* rate per person is shown in *italics*.

Kilmore Quay

National Grid Ref: S9603

Silver Fox Restaurant, Kehoes Bar, Hotel Saltees

Groveside, *Ballyharty, Kilmore Quay, Wexford.*
Open: May to Sept
053 35305 (also fax no)
Mrs Cousins
Rates fr: *IR£14.00*-**IR£16.00**.
Beds: 1F 1D 1T
Baths: 2 Ensuite 1 Shared
(10)
You are very welcome to 'Groveside' Farm Guesthouse, a spacious modern house set in quiet and peaceful surroundings with large maturing gardens. Relaxing guest TV lounge, childrens play area. Beaches nearby. Fishing, golfing, horseriding, pitch and putt, tennis arranged nearby.

Coral House, *Grange, Kilmore Quay, Wexford.*
Open: All Year
Grades: BF Approv
053 29640 Mr & Mrs Wilkinson
Rates fr: *IR£14.00*-**IR£14.00**.
Beds: 1F 4D 1T
Baths: 3 Ensuite 1 Shared
(10)
Family run guest house in 0.75 acres of lawned and flowered gardens near to the thatched village of Kilmore Quay and Saltee Islands Bird and Seal Sanctuary. Fishing, golf, horseriding, beaches are nearby. Comfort, good food are our main objectives.

Kilmuckridge

National Grid Ref: T1641

Seaview House, *Ballygarron, Kilmuckridge, Gorey, Co Wexford.*
Exclusive accommodation combining the elegance of the period with modern day comforts. The house was built in 1915.
Open: Easter to Nov
Grades: BF Approv
053 30164 / 36181 / 36163 Mrs Buttle
Rates fr: *IR£15.00*-**IR£18.00**.
Beds: 2D 1T
Baths: 3 Ensuite

Kiltealy

National Grid Ref: S8446

Granite Farm, *Wheelagower, Kiltealy, Enniscorthy, Co Wexford.*
Old-style farmhouse nestled in the foothills of the Blackstairs Mountains.
Open: Easter to Sep
054 55497 Mrs Nolan
Rates fr: *IR£15.00*-**IR£19.00**.
Beds: 1F 1D 1T
Baths: 3 Ensuite
(5)

Larkins Cross

National Grid Ref: T0001

Tara Villa, *Larkins Cross, Wexford, Co Wexford.*
Charming country villa situated close to N25.
Open: Apr to Nov
Grades: BF Approv
053 45119
Mrs Whitty
Rates fr: *IR£16.00*-**IR£25.00**.
Beds: 1F 2D 2T
Baths: 5 Ensuite

New Ross

National Grid Ref: S7227

John V's, The Quay

The Old Rectory, *New Ross, Co Wexford.*
Friendly family-run hotel, set in beautiful gardens, excellent restaurant.
Open: Feb to Dec
Grades: BF 2 St, AA 2 St
051 421719
Fax no: 051 422974
Mr Whelan
Rates fr: *IR£22.50*-**IR£32.50**.
Beds: 6D 5T 1S
Baths: 12 Ensuite
(37)

The lowest *double* rate per person is shown in *italics*.

Ossory, *Mountgarrett, New Ross, Co Wexford.*
Modern comfortable select bungalow with scenic views of Blackstairs Mountains. **Open:** All Year
Grades: BF Approv
051 422768 Mr & Mrs Neve
Rates fr: *IR£15.00*-**IR£17.00**.
Beds: 1F 2D 1T
Baths: 2 Ensuite 2 Private
(6)

Riversdale House, *Lower WIlliam Street, New Ross, Co Wexford.*
Town centre. TV, Tea and coffee in bedrooms. Private parking and gardens.
Open: Mar to Nov **Grades:** BF Approv
051 422515 Mrs Foley
Rates fr: *IR£16.00*-**IR£21.00**.
Beds: 4F **Baths:** 4 Ensuite
(10)

Venroode, *Lower South Knock, New Ross, Co Wexford.*
Venroode is set in peaceful mature gardens overlooking River Barrow.
Open: All Year
051 421446 Mrs Michels
Rates fr: *IR£14.00*-**IR£19.00**.
Beds: 1F 1D 1T
Baths: 2 Ensuite 1 Shared

Newbawn

National Grid Ref: S8222

Cedar Lodge Hotel, Horse & Hound Inn

Woodlands House, *Carrigbyrne, Newbawn, New Ross, Co Wexford.*
Open: Mar to Nov **Grades:** BF Approv, AA 3 Q, RAC High Acclaim
051 428287 (also fax no)
Mrs Halpin
Rates fr: *IR£16.00*-**IR£16.00**.
Beds: 1F 2D 1T 1S
Baths: 4 Ensuite 1 Private
(5) (6)
Situated on N25 Rosslare/Waterford Road close to Cedar Lodge Hotel, luxurious bungalow. Private parking, ensuite bedrooms with TV, tea/coffee facilities, early breakfast. Rosslare ferry 30 minutes. Ideal base to tour Wexford, Waterford, Kilkenny. Excellent restaurants locally. Access, Visa, Mastercard, Amex.

Rosslare

National Grid Ref: T1015

Cullens, Coopers Inn, Oyster Restaurant, Lobster Pot

Cill Dara House, *Ford-of-Lyng, Rosslare, Wexford.*
Tastefully restored old farmhouse. Quiet area (R740) off main N11 Road. 10 minutes to ferry, and many fine beaches.
Open: Easter to Nov
Grades: BF Approv
053 32459 Mr & Mrs Stack
Rates fr: *IR£16.00*-**IR£20.00**.
Beds: 2F 1T 1S **Baths:** 4 Ensuite
(10)

Rosslare Harbour

National Grid Ref: T1312

Cullens, Hotel Rosslare, Devereux Hotel, Tuskar Hotel, Kilrane Inn

Ballygillane House, *Cawdor Street, Rosslare Harbour, 6 Wexford,*
Open: Easter to Sept
053 33899 Mr & Mrs Drennan
Rates fr: *IR£15.00*-**IR£15.00**.
Beds: 2F 1T **Baths:** 3 Ensuite
(5) (10)
Ballygillane House, secluded off road half acre site. Don & Nuala Drennan. Quiet comfortable home in village centre within minutes of ferries. Early breakfast served. Five minutes walking distance to beach, restaurants and bars. Satellite TV and tea/coffee all rooms. Golf fifteen minutes.

Oldcourt House, *Rosslare Harbour, Wexford.*
Open: All Year
053 33895 Mrs McDonald
Rates fr: *IR£16.00*-**IR£20.00**.
Beds: 1F 4D 1T
Baths: 6 Ensuite 1 Private
(10)
Modern house situated in centre of Rosslare Harbour Village, overlooking Rosslare Bay. Many scenic views. Only 5 minutes walk from ferry/train terminal. Many leisure activities available locally. Ideal base for golfing at Rosslare or St Helens golf clubs.

***Kilrane House,** Kilrane, Rosslare Harbour, Wexford.*
Open: All Year (not Xmas)
Grades: BF Approv, AA 3 Q
053 33135
Fax no: 053 33739
Mrs Whitehead
Rates fr: *IR£16.00*-**IR£21.00**.
Beds: 2F 2D 2T
Baths: 6 Ensuite
(8)
A lovely 1830 house with immense character & charm. Recently refurbished offering attractive bedrooms. Highly recommended by many travel guides. Ornate, gracious guest lounge. Opposite delightful old pub/restaurant. 3 minute's drive from Rosslare Harbour. Close to many fine beaches.

***Glenville,** St Patricks Road, Rosslare Harbour, Wexford.*
Modern detached bungalow in seaside setting.
Open: All Year (not Xmas)
Grades: BF Approv
053 33142 Mrs Barry
Rates fr: *IR£15.00*-**IR£15.00**.
Beds: 1D 1T 1S
Baths: 2 Ensuite 1 Private
(5)

***Hotel Rosslare,** Rosslare Harbour, Wexford.*
Open: All Year (not Xmas)
Grades: BF 3 St
053 33110
Fax no: 053 33386
Rates fr: *IR£25.00*-**IR£30.00**.
Beds: 6F 10D 7T
Baths: 23 Ensuite 3 Shared
Rosslare Harbour's oldest hotel. Home of the famous award winning 'Portholes Bar'. Overlooking Rosslare Bay and ferryport. Excellent restaurant and bar food. Fish a speciality. Part owners of St. Helens Bay 18-hole Championship Golf Course - welcome!

All details shown are as supplied by B&B owners in Autumn 1996.

***Glenville,** St Patricks Road, Rosslare Harbour, Wexford.*
Modern detached bungalow in seaside setting.
Open: All Year (not Xmas)
Grades: BF Approv
053 33142 Mrs Barry
Rates fr: *IR£15.00*-**IR£15.00**.
Beds: 1D 1T 1S
Baths: 2 Ensuite 1 Private
(5)

***Elmwood,** Rosslare Harbour, Wexford.*
Highly recommended home, in peaceful location, two minutes from ferry.
Open: Mar to Oct **Grades:** BF Approv RAC Acclaim
053 33321 Mrs Duggan
Rates fr: *IR£16.00*-**IR£21.00**.
Beds: 1F 1D 1T
Baths: 3 Ensuite

***Cloverlawn,** Kilrane, Rosslare Harbour, Wexford.*
Highly recommended comfortable home 1 km from Rosslare Ferryport. Vouchers accepted.
Open: All Year (not Xmas)
Grades: BF Approv
053 33413 Mrs Lonergan
Rates fr: *IR£14.00*-**IR£19.00**.
Beds: 1F 1D 1T 1S
Baths: 2 Ensuite 2 Shared
(6)

***O'Leary's Farm,** Killilane, Kilrane, Rosslare Harbour, Wexford.*
Overlooking St Helens beach. Comfortable old farmhouse. Convenient for ferries.
Open: All Year (not Xmas)
053 33134 Mrs O'Leary
Rates fr: *IR£14.00*-**IR£16.00**.
Beds: 2F 4D 2T 2S
Baths: 7 Ensuite 2 Shared
(3)

***Moonfleet,** Cowdar Road, Rosslare Harbour, Wexford, Co Wexford.*
Peaceful location. Ferry port three minutes drive. Pubs and restaurants close by.
Open: All Year (not Xmas)
053 33791 Mrs Keilthy
Rates fr: *IR£15.00*-**IR£15.00**.
Beds: 1F 1D 1T
Baths: 2 Ensuite 1 Private
(7) (6)

The lowest *double* rate per person is shown in *italics*.

Tuskar House, *St Martins Road, Rosslare Harbour, Wexford.*
Family-run hotel overlooking Rosslare Harbour offering panoramic views.
Open: All Year **Grades:** BF 3 St
053 33363
(also fax no) Roche
Rates fr: *IR£26.00*-**IR£32.00**.
Beds: 3F 27D
Baths: 30 Private
(120)

Saltmills

National Grid Ref: S7908

Grove Farm, *St Kearns, Saltmills, Fethard-on-Sea, New Ross, Co Wexford,*
A modern, yet old styled, comfortable farmhouse ideally situated overlooking Bannow Bay.
Open: Mar to Oct **Grades:** BF Approv
051 562304 Mrs Power
Rates fr: *IR£13.50*.
Beds: 1D 1T 1S
Baths: 2 Ensuite

Tacumshane

National Grid Ref: T0707

Lobster Pot

Furziestown House, *Tacumshane, Rosslare Harbour, Wexford.*
Small comfortable farmhouse in peaceful rural/coastal area.
Open: Easter to Nov
Grades: BF Approv
053 31376 Mrs Pim
Rates fr: *IR£17.00*-**IR£17.00**.
Beds: 1D 1T 1S **Baths:** 3 Ensuite
(3)

Always telephone to get directions to the B&B - you will save time!

Tagoat

National Grid Ref: T1011

Churchtown House, *Tagoat, Rosslare, Wexford.*
Open: Mar to Nov **Grades:** BF 4 St, AA 5 Q, Prem Select
053 32555 Mrs Cody
Rates fr: *IR£21.50*-**IR£29.50**.
Beds: 1F 5D 5T **Baths:** 11 Ensuite
(11) (12)
Churchtown is a charming period house circa 1703, set in 8.5 acres. Traditional country house hospitality, log fires, wine licence, freshly prepared fish, farm and local produce in elegant surroundings. 3 miles from Rosslare Ferryport. Half mile from N25 at Tagoat on R736.

Wellingtonbridge

National Grid Ref: S8513

River Valley, *Ballylannon, Wellingtonbridge, Wexford.*
Modern farmhouse, situated short distance from Rosslare, with many beaches, good touring situation.
Open: Mar to Oct **Grades:** BF Approv
051 561354 Mrs Breen Murphy
Rates fr: *IR£16.00*-**IR£20.00**.
Beds: 1F 2D **Baths:** 3 Ensuite

Wexford

National Grid Ref: T0421

Tim's Tavern, The Granary, Oak Tavern, Farmers Kitchen

Farmer's Kitchen Hotel, *Rosslare Road, Drinagh, Wexford.*
Open: All Year (not Xmas Day or Good Fri) **Grades:** BF 2 St
053 45816 / 43295 Fax no: 053 45827
Mr Osborne
Rates fr: *IR£24.00*-**IR£24.00**.
Beds: 6F 3D 1T 1S
Baths: 11 Ensuite
(50)
Small friendly hotel with the well-known Farmer's Kitchen Restaurant and two lounge bars serving food daily from 12.30 - 10.00 p.m. Close to Rosslare Ferry and Wexford Town, golf courses, horse-riding, walking, fishing, beaches all available locally.

Kilderry, *St Johns Road, Wexford.*
Open: All Year
053 23848 (also fax no)
Mrs Wallace
Rates fr: *IR£16.00*-**IR£20.00**.
Beds: 2F 1T
Baths: 2 Ensuite 1 Private

Downtown Wexford. Rosslare ferries 15 minutes. Convenient to golf, beaches, Heritage Park, horse-riding. Tea and coffee facilities, hairdryer and clock radio in bedrooms. Access and Visa accepted. TV lounge.

Townparks House, *Coolcotts, Wexford.*
Purpose-built Georgian house in quiet residential area.
Open: All Year (not Xmas)
053 45191 Mrs Doocey
Rates fr: *IR£16.00*-**IR£20.00**.
Beds: 3F 1D 1T
Baths: 4 Ensuite, 1 Private

Sequoia, *Newtown Road, Wexford.*
Open: All Year (not Xmas)
Grades: BF Approv
053 45919 Mrs Corish
Rates fr: *IR£17.00*-**IR£20.00**.
Beds: 2F 1D
Baths: 3 Ensuite
(4)
Sequoia is a large bungalow on 0.75 acre of manicured gardens. Tastefully decorated throughout. Ideal location for touring. 5 minutes from rail station and town centre. 15 minutes from Rosslare Harbour.

Auburn House, *2 Auburn Terrace, Redmond Road, Wexford.*
C19th brick townhouse tastefully renovated for B&B by its owners David and Mary O'Brien.
Open: All Year (not Xmas)
Grades: BF Approv, AA 3 Q
053 23605 Mr & Mrs O'Brien
Rates fr: *IR£17.00*-**IR£18.00**.
Beds: 2F 2D 1T
Baths: 4 Ensuite 1 Private

The lowest *double* rate per person is shown in *italics*.

McMenamin's Town House, *3 Auburn Terrace, Wexford.*
Open: All Year (not Xmas)
Grades: BF Approv, AA 4 Q
053 46442
Mr & Mrs McMenamin
Rates fr: *IR£19.50*-**IR£22.50**.
Beds: 1F 2T 2D
Baths: 5 Ensuite
(10)
Lovely Victorian town house. Beautifully furnished. Centrally located with lock up parking. Close to shops and restaurants. Awarded one of 100 best places to stay in Ireland.

Faythe Guest House, *Swanview, The Faythe, Wexford.*
Wexford's oldest guesthouse, set in a quiet part of the old town.
Open: All Year (not Xmas)
Grades: BF 2 St, AA 2 Q
053 22249
Mr Lynch
Rates fr: *IR£16.00*-**IR£18.00**.
Beds: 1F 6D 2T 1S
Baths: 10 Ensuite
(7) (30)

St George, *George Street, Wexford.*
Open: All Year (not Xmas)
Grades: BF 2 St
053 43474
Fax no: 053 24814
Mr Doyle
Rates fr: *IR£17.00*-**IR£20.00**.
Beds: 2F 7D 1T
Baths: 10 Ensuite
(3) (10)
A family-run guesthouse in the centre of Wexford Town, close to shops, churches, restaurants and all other amenities while a brief drive will take you to miles of sandy beaches, angling, golf, tennis and horse-riding.

Rathaspeck Manor, *Rathaspeck, Wexford.*
Restored C17th Georgian house . All rooms ensuite. Colour TV, tea/coffee making facilities.
Open: 1st May to 7th Nov
Grades: AA 3 Q
053 42661
Mrs Cuddihy
Rates fr: *IR£18.00*.
Beds: 1F 1D 3T
Baths: 6 Ensuite

Newtown Heights, *Newtown Road, Wexford.*
Open: All Year **Grades:** BF Approv, AA 3 Q, Recomm
053 41414 Mr & Mrs O'Brien
Rates fr: *IR£16.00*-**IR£16.00**.
Beds: 1F 2D 1T 2S
Baths: 3 Ensuite 1 Shared
(8)
Comfortable modern home with friendly hosts and overlooking Slaney Valley. Beautiful scenery. Electric blankets. Hairdryers all rooms. Safe car park. Early breakfast. 15 minutes Rosslare Ferryport. Near many beaches, golf, angling, horseriding, and adjacent to National Heritage Park. Visa accepted.

Always telephone to get directions to the B&B - you will save time!

Glenfarne, *5 Richmond Terrace, Spawell Road, Wexford.*
Georgian house. Spacious rooms. Five minutes to town centre.
Open: All Year (not Xmas)
Grades: BF Approv
053 45290 Mrs O'Flaherty
Rates fr: *IR£16.00*-**IR£21.00**.
Beds: 1F 1D 1T **Baths:** 3 Ensuite
(2) (5)

Clonard House, *Clonard Great, Wexford.*
Award-winning Georgian farmhouse. Egon Ronay Recommended. 10 minutes to Rosslare Ferry. Four-poster beds.
Open: Easter to Nov
Grades: AA 4 Q, Select
053 43141 (also fax no)
Mrs Hayes
Rates fr: *IR£20.00*-**IR£24.00**.
Beds: 4F 4D 1T
Baths: 9 Ensuite
(12)

County Wicklow

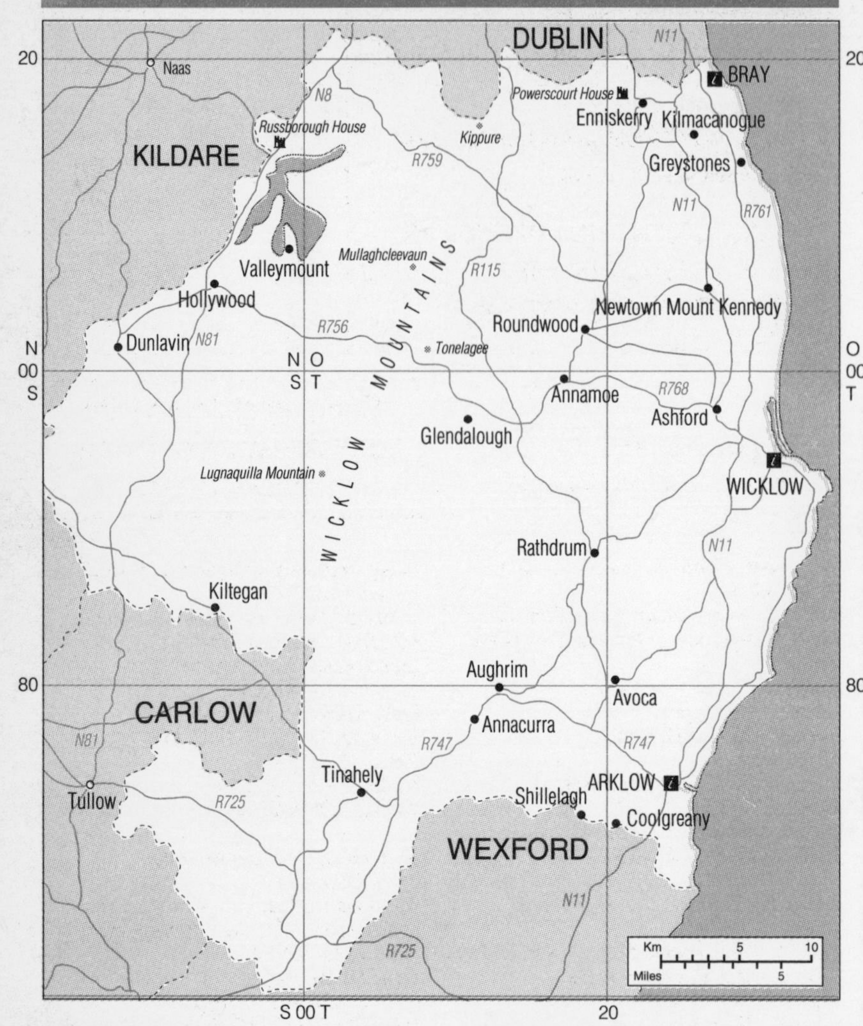

Annacurra

National Grid Ref: T1078

Annacurra Inn, *Annacurra, Aughrim, Arklow, Co Wicklow.*
Situated in a small village. Golf, fishing beaches nearby.
Open: All Year (not Xmas)
Grades: BF Approv **0402 36430**
Mr/Mrs Grove
Ratesfr:*IR£14.00***IR£16.00.**
Beds: 1F 2D 1T **Baths:** 2 Ensuite 2 Shared

Annamoe

National Grid Ref: T1799

Lyhams, Laragh Inn

Carmels, *Annamoe, Co Wicklow.*
Select home in the heart of the Wicklow Mountains.
Open: Mar to Oct
Grades: AA 3 Q, RAC Acclaim
0404 45297 Mrs Hawkins
Rates fr: *IR£16.00*-**IR£25.00.**
Beds: 1F 1D 2T
Baths: 4 Ensuite

RAIL

Wicklow and ***Arlow*** are on the East Coast line from ***Rosslare*** *to* ***Dublin (Connolly)****.*

For timetable details phone **Irish Rail:** 01 8366222.

BUS

Arklow *to* ***Dublin*** *&* ***Wicklow*** *to* ***Dublin*** *(4 daily).*

Tel **Bus Eireann** on 01 8366111

TOURIST INFORMATION OFFICES

Arklow (open all year), 0402 32484

Fitzwilliam Street, **Wicklow** (open all year), 0404 69117

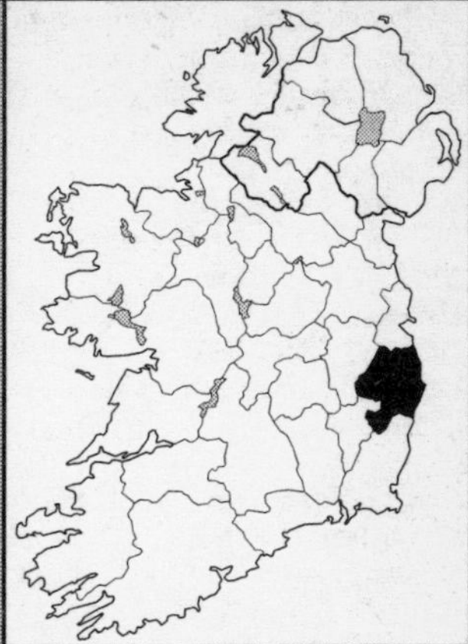

Arklow

National Grid Ref: T2473

Arklow Bay Hotel, Bridge Hotel, Kitty's

Vale View, *Coolgreany Road, Arklow, Co Wicklow.*
Edwardian house with period furnishings. Honeymoon suites with four poster beds.
Open: All Year (not Xmas)
Grades: BF Approv
0402 32622 (also fax no)
Mrs Crotty
Rates fr: *IR£16.00*-**IR£22.00.**
Beds: 3F 2D 1T
Baths: 4 Ensuite 2 Shared
(6)

Lakevilla, *Seaview Ave, Ferrybank, Arklow, Co Wicklow.*
Quiet location beside beach, resort and town amenities. Visa, Access.
Open: Easter to Sep
Grades: BF Approv
0402 32734
Mrs Dennehy
Rates fr: *IR£14.00*-**IR£14.00.**
Beds: 1F 1D 1T
Baths: 3 Shared
(4)

The lowest **single** *rate is shown in* **bold.**

Bringing children with you? Always ask for any special rates.

Snug Harbour, *Abbeylands, Arklow, Co Wicklow.*
Located in town overlooking sea and golf links. Modern home.
Open: easter to December
Grades: BF Approv
0402 32059 Mrs English
Rates fr: *IR£14.50*-**IR£14.00.**
Beds: 1F 3D 1T
Baths: 2 Ensuite 2 Shared
(5)

Rathmore, *Coolroe, Arklow, Co Wicklow.*
Spacious Dormer bungalow on quiet country road. Excellent touring base.
Open: Mar to Oct
Grades: BF Approv
0402 37438 Mrs Kelleher
Rates fr: *IR£15.50*-**IR£21.50.**
Beds: 1F 1D 1T **Baths:** 3 Ensuite

Ros Maolan, *Sea Road, Arklow, Co Wicklow.*
Modern detached family house in quiet area on outskirts of Arklow.
Open: Easter to Oct
0402 31297 Mrs Heaney
Rates fr: *IR£13.50.*
Beds: 1F 2D 1S
Baths: 2 Ensuite 1 Shared
(3)

Plattenstown House, *Coolgreaney Road, Arklow, Co Wicklow.*
Country residence built 1853. Tranquil setting near seaside and forests.
Open: Mar to Oct
Grades: BF Approv
0402 32582 (also fax no)
Mr & Mrs McDowell
Rates fr: *IR£20.00*-**IR£25.00.**
Beds: 2D 2T
Baths: 3 Ensuite 1 Private

Bridge Hotel, *Arklow, Co Wicklow.*
Family-run hotel beside river and seaside, near beautiful Wicklow Hills.
Open: All Year (not Xmas)
Grades: BF 1 St
0402 31655 / 31666
Mr Hoey
Rates fr: *IR£22.00*-**IR£25.00.**
Beds: 8D 2S
Baths: 5 Ensuite 4 Shared

Dunguaire, *Coolgreany Road, Arklow, Co Wicklow.*
Spacious modern split level bungalow, panoramic views, large garden/patio.
Open: Easter to Sep
0402 32774 Mrs Fennell
Rates fr: *IR£14.00*-**IR£16.00.**
Beds: 2D 1T
Baths: 1 Ensuite 1 Private 1 Shared
(5)

Ashford

National Grid Ref: T2797

Ashford House, Chester Beaty's

Bartragh, *Dublin Road, Ashford, Wicklow.*
Open: All Year (not Xmas)
Grades: BF Approv
0404 40442
Mrs Long
Rates fr: *IR£16.00*-**IR£21.00.**
Beds: 2D 2T
Baths: 4 Ensuite
(4)
Modern comfortable bungalow on the Dublin Road (N11) at Ashford village. Close to pubs and restaurants. Ideal base for touring the Wicklow Mountains and gardens or Dublin city. 30 minutes from Dun Laoghaire ferryport. Access, Visa, Amex accepted.

Ballylusk Farm, *Ashford, Wicklow.*
Old farmhouse in beautiful Wicklow Mountains. Near N11.
Open: Apr to Nov
0404 40141 Mrs Kelly
Rates fr: *IR£16.00.*
Beds: 2F 2D **Baths:** 4 Ensuite
(4)

Ballyknocken House, *Glenealy, Ashford, Wicklow.*
Victorian farmhouse in scenic countryside beside forest walks. Wine licence.
Open: Easter to Nov
0404 44614 Fax no: 0404 44627
Mrs Byrne
Rates fr: *IR£16.00*-**IR£21.00.**
Beds: 2D 4T 2S **Baths:** 8 Ensuite
(3) (10)

Aughrim

National Grid Ref: T1279

Lawless's Hotel

Lawless's Hotel, *Aughrim, Co Wicklow.*
C18th village inn, traditionally furnished. Great bar and restaurant.
Open: All Year (not Xmas)
Grades: BF Approv
0402 36146 Mr & Mrs O'Toole
Rates fr: *IR£28.50*-**IR£38.00.**
Beds: 5F 5D
Baths: 8 Ensuite 2 Private

Avoca

National Grid Ref: T2080

Wooden Bridge Hotel, Meeting of the Waters

Koliba, *Beech Road, Avoca, Arklow, Co Wicklow.*
Open: All Year **Grades:** BF Approv
0402 32737 Mrs Gilroy
Rates fr: *IR£17.00*-**IR£22.00.**
Beds: 1F 2D
Baths: 3 Ensuite
(0) (6)
'Koliba' country home, overlooking Arklow Bay/Avoca. (Home to BBC's 'Ballykissangel') Dublin, Rosslare ports 1 hour. 3 km off N11. Dublin side Arklow. Ideal base for touring Wicklow and south-east. Arklow 4 km. Avoca 3 km.

Keppels Farmhouse, *Ballanagh, Avoca, Arklow, Co Wicklow.*
Exceptionally comfortable home beside 'Ballykissangel'. Wonderful food. Spectacular scenic countryside
Open: Easter to Oct
Grades: BF Approv
0402 35168 Mrs Keppel
Rates fr: *IR£17.00*-**IR£28.00**.
Beds: 1F 2D 2T
Baths: 5 Ensuite
(6) (8)

Ashdene, *Knockanree Lower, Avoca, Arklow, Co Wicklow.*
Highly recommended, ITB Approved. Touring centre - convenient to Dublin/Rosslare
Open: Mar to Nov
Grades: BF Approv, AA 2 Q
0402 35327 (also fax no)
Mrs Burns
Rates fr: *IR£17.00*-**IR£15.00**.
Beds: 2D 2T 1S
Baths: 4 Ensuite 1 Private
(5)

The Old Coach House, *Avoca, Arklow, Co Wicklow.*
Restored Georgian coach-house. Wonderful views of Avoca River and valley. Location of 'Ballykissangel'.
Open: All Year (not Xmas)
Grades: BF Approv, AA 3 Q
0402 35408
Fax no: 0402 35720
Mr & Mrs Dempsey
Rates fr: *IR£20.00*-**IR£27.00**.
Beds: 2F 2D 2T
Baths: 6 Ensuite
(8)

Bray

National Grid Ref: O2718

Coast Guard

Rathlin, *Killarney Road, Bray, Co Wicklow.*
Large Victorian residence close to Dart, car ferry bus, Dublin 20 km.
Open: Mar to Nov
Grades: BF Approv
01 2862655 Mrs Smith
Rates fr: *IR£16.00*-**IR£25.00**.
Beds: 2F 2T
Baths: 2 Ensuite 2 Shared

Bayswell House, *Strand Road, Bray, Co Wicklow.*
Victorian three storey house. Family run. On the seafront.
Open: May to Sep
01 2863984 Mrs Gallagher
Rates fr: *IR£14.00*-**IR£15.00**.
Beds: 2F 2D 1T 1S
Baths: 2 Shared
(8)

Ulysses Guest House, *Centre Esplanade, Bray, Co Wicklow.*
High quality guest house with beautiful view of Bray seafront.
Open: All Year (not Xmas)
Grades: BF 1 St
01 2863860
(also fax no) Mr Jones
Rates fr: *IR£17.50*-**IR£17.50**.
Beds: 2F 5D 1T 2S
Baths: 8 Ensuite
(8)

Sans Souci, *Meath Road, Bray, Co Wicklow.*
Secluded Victorian residence beside sea and mountains. Dart to Dublin.
Open: Mar to Nov
01 2828629 Mr MacDonald
Rates fr: *IR£14.00*-**IR£18.00**.
Beds: 2F 2D 1S
Baths: 3 Ensuite 1 Private 2 Shared
(7)

Coolgreaney

National Grid Ref: T1969

Ballykilty House, *Coolgreaney, Arklow, Co Wicklow.*
Homely old-world farmhouse, mature gardens. Log fires. Early breakfasts for ferries.
Open: Easter to Oct
Grades: BF Approv
0402 37111 Mrs Nuzum
Rates fr: *IR£17.00*-**IR£23.00**.
Beds: 1F 2D 2T
Baths: 5 Ensuite
(5) (7)

Always telephone to get directions to the B&B - you will save time!

Dunlavin

National Grid Ref: N8701

Tynte House, *Dunlavin, Co Wicklow.*
Period farmhouse in picturesque village. Antique furnishings throughout. Beautiful countryside.
Open: All Year (not Xmas)
Grades: AA 3 Q
045 401561
Mrs Lawler
Rates fr: *IR£16.00*-**IR£21.00**.
Beds: 2F 4D
Baths: 6 Ensuite
(15)

Enniskerry

National Grid Ref: O2217

Johnny Fox's, Enniscree Lodge, Palmers, Stepping Stones, Poppies

Cherbury, *Monastery, Enniskerry, Co Wicklow.*
Large bungalow. Ideal base for touring Wicklow. Beside Powerscourt Gardens.
Open: All Year
Grades: BF Approv
01 2828679
Mrs Lynch
Rates fr: *IR£16.00*-**IR£22.50**.
Beds: 1D 2T
Baths: 3 Ensuite
(6)

Summerhill House Hotel, *Enniskerry, Co Wicklow.*
Period country house hotel.
Open: All Year (not Xmas)
Grades: BF Approv
01 2867928
Mrs Sweeney
Rates fr: *IR£27.50*-**IR£27.50**.
Beds: 3F 5D 2T 3S

Corner House, *Enniskerry, Co Wicklow.*
Lovely 200-year-old house in Enniskerry.
Open: All Year (not Xmas)
Grades: BF Approv
01 2860149
Mrs Cummins
Rates fr: *IR£15.00*-**IR£22.00**.
Beds: 2D 3T
Baths: 1 Ensuite 1 Shared

Cregg House, *Glencree Road, Enniskerry, Co Wicklow.*
Modern country house overlooking the mountains.
Open: Mar to Oct **Grades:** BF Approv
01 2863557 Mrs Clarke
Rates fr: *IR£14.50*-**IR£20.00**.
Beds: 2D 2T 1S
Baths: 2 Shared

Glendalough

National Grid Ref: T1196

Mitchell's, Wicklow Heather, Lyhams of Laragh, Laragh Inn

Derrybawn House, *Glendalough, Bray, Co Wicklow.*
C18th manor house on 95 acres wood/parkland. Very comfortable.
Open: All Year (not Xmas)
0404 45134 Fax no: 0404 54109
Mr & Mrs Vambeck
Rates fr: *IR£25.00*-**IR£32.50**.
Beds: 4D 2T
Baths: 6 Ensuite
(12) (10)

Carmels, *Glendalough, Annamoe, Co Wicklow.*
Select home in the heart of the Wicklow Mountains.
Open: Mar to Oct
Grades: AA 3 Q, RAC Acclaim
0404 45297 Mrs Hawkins
Rates fr: *IR£16.00*-**IR£25.00**.
Beds: 1F 1D 2T
Baths: 4 Ensuite

Larragh Trekking Centre, *Laragh East, Glendalough, Bray, Co Wicklow.*
Set in the Glendalough National Parkland.
Open: All Year **Grades:** AA 4 Q
0404 45282 Mrs McCallon
Rates fr: *IR£20.00*-**IR£30.00**.
Beds: 1F 3D 2T **Baths:** 6 Ensuite
(10)

The lowest *double* rate per person is shown in *italics*.

Doire Coille, *Cullentragh, Glendalough, Bray, Co Wicklow.*
Friendly, working farm - great views.
Open: Easter to Oct
Grades: BF Approv
0404 45131 Mrs Byrne
Rates fr: *IR£15.00*-**IR£20.00**.
Beds: 3D 1T
Baths: 3 Ensuite 1 Private

Greystones

National Grid Ref: O2912

Coopers, Beach House

Glandore, *St Vincents Road, Greystones, Co Wicklow.*
Charming olde-world house in mature gardens in tranquil tree-lined estate.
Open: All Year
Grades: BF Approv
01 2874364 (also fax no)
Mrs Hall
Rates fr: *IR£15.00*-**IR£20.00**.
Beds: 2F 2D
Baths: 2 Ensuite 1 Shared

Thornvale, *Kidpedder, Greystones, Co Wicklow.*
Modern detached dormer bungalow on 1.5 acres in the heart of the golfing, garden and gourmet capital of Ireland.
Grades: BF Approv
01 2810410
Ms Hogan
Rates fr: *IR£16.00*-**IR£16.00**.
Beds: 2F 1D 1S
Baths: 3 Ensuite 1 Private 1 Shared
(8)

Hollywood

National Grid Ref: N9405

Heathers, *Poulaphouca, Hollywood, Blessington, Co Wicklow.*
Dormer bungalow beside Poulaphouca Lakes, National Stud, and Japanese gardens.
Open: All Year
Grades: BF Approv
045 864554
Mrs Curley
Rates fr: *IR£14.00*-**IR£19.00**.
Beds: 2D 1T
Baths: 1 Ensuite 1 Shared
(6)

Kilmacanogue

National Grid Ref: O2614

Wicklow Arms

Glencormac Inn, *Kilmacanogue, Co Wicklow.*
Central location on N11. Rural setting with views of hills.
Open: All Year
01 2862996 Mr Kiernan
Rates fr: *IR£17.00*-**IR£17.00**.
Beds: 4D
Baths: 4 Ensuite
(4)

Kiltegan

National Grid Ref: S9384

Beechlawn, *Kiltegan, Co Wicklow.*
Converted Georgian rectory. Secluded garden. Beside village, mountains. Personal attention.
Open: Easter to Oct
0508 73171 Mrs Jackson
Rates fr: *IR£15.00*-**IR£20.00**.
Beds: 1F 2D 2S
Baths: 2 Shared
(6)

Newtown Mount Kennedy

National Grid Ref: O2606

Butterfly Hill Farm, *Kilmullen, Newtown Mount Kennedy, Greystones, Co Wicklow.*
Country cooking, cottage style house. Beautiful scenery. Convenient location.
Open: Mar to Nov
Grades: BF Approv
01 2819218 Mrs Roberts
Rates fr: *IR£IR17.00*-**IR£IR20.00**.
Beds: 1F 1D 2T
Baths: 2 Ensuite 1 Shared
(4)

Please respect
a B&B's wishes regarding
children, animals
& smoking.

Rathdrum

National Grid Ref: T1888

Woolpack, Cartoon Inn, Meetings of the Waters

St Bridgets, *Corballis, Rathdrum, Wicklow.*
Countryside location, adjacent to Avondale. Glendalough. Travel agency vouchers accepted.
Open: All Year (not Xmas)
0404 46477 Mrs Scott
Rates fr: *IR£14.00*-**IR£18.00**.
Beds: 2F 1T
Baths: 2 Shared

The Hawthorns, *Corballis, Rathdrum, Wicklow.*
Modern bungalow in large garden. 0.5 km from village, walkers paradise.
Open: All Year (not Xmas)
0404 46217 / 46683
Fax no: 0404 46217 Mrs Sheehan
Rates fr: *IR£14.00*-**IR£20.00**.
Beds: 1D 2T
Baths: 1 Ensuite 2 Shared
(10)

Minmore House, *Cunniamstown, Beg, Rathdrum, Wicklow.*
Modern bungalow on top of hill, wonderful view of mountains.
Open: All Year
Grades: BF Approv
0404 46629 Mrs Browne
Rates fr: *IR£13.00*-**IR£13.00**.
Beds: 1T 2S
Baths: 1 Ensuite 1 Shared

Roundwood

National Grid Ref: O1802

Coach House

Ballinacor House, *Roundwood, Bray, Co Wicklow.*
Modern working farm.
Open: May to Aug
Grades: BF Approv
01 2818168 Mrs Malone
Rates fr: *IR£13.00*-**IR£13.00**.
Beds: 2D 1T 1S
Baths: 1 Shared

Irish Grid References are for villages, towns and cities - *not* for individual houses.

Shillelagh

National Grid Ref: S9868

Park Lodge Farmhouse, *Clonegal, Shillelagh, Arklow, Co Wicklow.*
A warm Irish welcome to our charming Georgian family-run farmhouse.
Open: Easter to Nov
Grades: BF Approv
055 29140
Mrs Osbourne
Rates fr: *IR£16.00*-**IR£20.00**.
Beds: 2F 1D 2T
Baths: 2 Ensuite 2 Shared

Tinahely

National Grid Ref: T0372

Murphy's

Murphys Hotel, *Tinahely, Arklow, Co Wicklow.*
Family-run hotel in the centre of the town.
Open: All Year
Grades: BF Approv
0402 38109 Mr Fergus
Rates fr: *IR£20.00*-**IR£22.00**.
Beds: 4D 2T
Baths: 6 Ensuite

Phoning from outside the Republic?

Dial 00353 and omit the initial '0' of the area code.

Wicklow

National Grid Ref: T3194

Blainroe Hotel, Old Court Inn

Lissadell House, *Ashdown Lane, Wicklow.*
Open: Mar to Nov
Grades: BF Approv, AA 3 Q, Recomm
0404 67458 Mrs Klane
Rates fr: *IR£15.00*-**IR£21.00**.
Beds: 1F 2D 1T
Baths: 2 Ensuite 2 Shared
(10)
Lissadell House, one mile from Wicklow Town, Wicklow/Wexford route, first turn off Marlton Road (L29A) signposted. Two miles off Dublin/Wexford Road (N11). Exit at Beehive Pub, junction for Marlton Road (L29A) (R751). First turn left - see signpost.

Greenfields, *Blainroe, Wicklow.*
A guest house haven for golf enthusiasts.
Open: All Year (not Xmas)
0404 68309 Mr Moloney
Rates fr: *IR£17.00*-**IR£20.00**.
Beds: 2F 2D 1T **Baths:** 5 Ensuite
(1) (10)

Rospark, *Dunbur, Wicklow.*
Comfortable family run dormer bungalow in own grounds. 2 km golf and beach.
Open: Easter to Oct
Grades: BF Approv
0404 69615
Mrs Naughton
Rates fr: *IR£16.00*.
Beds: 3F 1D 1T
Baths: 2 Ensuite

Silver Sands, *Dunbar Road, Wicklow.*
Dormer bungalow overlooking Wicklow Bay and golf course.
Open: All Year
0404 68243
Mrs Doyle
Rates fr: *IR£14.50*-**IR£20.00**.
Beds: 1F 2D 2T
Baths: 3 Ensuite 2 Shared
(6)

The lowest *double* rate per person is shown in *italics*.

Location Index

The cities, towns, villages and hamlets listed in this index all have entries in **STILWELL'S DIRECTORY** under their respective regional heading. If there is no listing for the place you wish to stay in, the section map for that particular region will show you somewhere else to stay close by.